JONES & BARTLETT LEARNING INFORMATION SYSTEMS SECURITY & ASSURANCE SERIES

Security Policies and Implementation Issues

ROB JOHNSON WITH MIKE MERKOW

JONES & BARTLETT
LEARNING

World Headquarters
Jones & Bartlett Learning
40 Tall Pine Drive
Sudbury, MA 01776
978-443-5000
info@jblearning.com
www.jblearning.com

Jones & Bartlett Learning Canada
6339 Ormindale Way
Mississauga, Ontario L5V 1J2
Canada

Jones & Bartlett Learning
International
Barb House, Barb Mews
London W6 7PA
United Kingdom

Jones & Bartlett Learning books and products are available through most bookstores and online booksellers. To contact Jones & Bartlett Learning directly, call 800-832-0034, fax 978-443-8000, or visit our website, www.jblearning.com.

Substantial discounts on bulk quantities of Jones & Bartlett Learning publications are available to corporations, professional associations, and other qualified organizations. For details and specific discount information, contact the special sales department at Jones & Bartlett Learning via the above contact information or send an email to specialsales@jblearning.com.

Production Credits
Chief Executive Officer: Ty Field
President: James Homer
SVP, Chief Operating Officer: Don Jones, Jr.
SVP, Chief Technology Officer: Dean Fossella
SVP, Chief Marketing Officer: Alison M. Pendergast
SVP, Chief Financial Officer: Ruth Siporin
SVP, Business Development: Christopher Will
VP, Design and Production: Anne Spencer
VP, Manufacturing and Inventory Control: Therese Connell
Editorial Management: High Stakes Writing, LLC, Editor and Publisher: Lawrence J. Goodrich
Reprints and Special Projects Manager: Susan Schultz
Associate Production Editor: Tina Chen
Director of Marketing: Alisha Weisman
Associate Marketing Manager: Meagan Norlund
Cover Design: Anne Spencer
Composition: Sara Arand
Cover Image: © Handy Widiyanto/ShutterStock, Inc.
Chapter Opener Image: © Rodolfo Clix/Dreamstime.com
Printing and Binding: Malloy, Inc.
Cover Printing: Malloy, Inc.

ISBN: 978-0-7637-9132-2

6048
Printed in the United States of America
14 13 12 11   10 9 8 7 6 5 4 3

Contents

Contents

CHAPTER 9   User Domain Policies   204

CHAPTER 14 **IT Security Policy Enforcement   348**

To my wife Lin and my children,
who have blessed me with gifts that words cannot express

Preface

Purpose of This Book

This book is part of the Information Systems Security & Assurance Series from Jones & Bartlett Learning (*www.jblearning.com*). Designed for courses and curriculums in IT Security, Cybersecurity, Information Assurance, and Information Systems Security, this series features a comprehensive, consistent treatment of the most current thinking and trends in this critical subject area. These titles deliver fundamental information-security principles packed with real-world applications and examples. Authored by Certified Information Systems Security Professionals (CISSPs), they deliver comprehensive information on all aspects of information security. Reviewed word for word by leading technical experts in the field, these books are not just current, but forward-thinking—putting you in the position to solve the cybersecurity challenges not just of today, but of tomorrow, as well.

Implementing IT security policies and related frameworks for an organization can seem like an overwhelming task, given the vast number of issues and considerations. *Security Policies and Implementation Issues* demystifies this topic, taking you through a logical sequence of discussions about major concepts and issues related to security policy implementation.

It is a unique book that offers a comprehensive, end-to-end view of information security policies and frameworks from the raw organizational mechanics of building to the psychology of implementation. This book presents an effective balance between technical knowledge and soft skills, both of which are necessary for understanding the business context and psychology of motivating people and leaders. It also introduces you to many different concepts of information security in clear, simple terms such as governance, regulator mandates, business drivers, legal considerations, and much more. If you need to understand how information risk is controlled, or are responsible for oversight of those that do, you will find this book helpful.

Part 1 of this book focuses on why private and public sector organizations need an information technology (IT) security framework consisting of documented policies, standards, procedures, and guidelines. As businesses, organizations, and governments change the way they operate and organize their overall information systems security strategy, one of the most critical security controls is documented IT security policies.

Part 2 defines the major elements of an IT security policy framework. Many organizations, under recent compliance laws, must now define, document, and implement information security policies, standards, procedures, and guidelines. Many organizations and businesses conduct a risk assessment to determine their current risk exposure within their IT infrastructure. Once these security gaps and threats are identified, design and implementation of more stringent information security policies are put in place. This can provide an excellent starting point for the creation of an IT security policy framework.

Policies are only as effective as the individuals who create them and enforce them within an organization. Part 3 of this book presents how to successfully implement and enforce policies within an organization. Emerging techniques and automation of policy enforcement are also examined.

This book is a valuable resource for students, security officers, auditors, and risk leaders who want to understand what a successful implementation of security policies and frameworks looks like.

Learning Features

The writing style of this book is practical and conversational. Each chapter begins with a statement of learning objectives. Step-by-step examples of information security concepts and procedures are presented throughout the text. Illustrations are used both to clarify the material and to vary the presentation. The text is sprinkled with Notes, Tips, FYIs, Warnings, and sidebars to alert the reader to additional helpful information related to the subject under discussion. Chapter Assessments appear at the end of each chapter, with solutions provided in the back of the book.

Chapter summaries are included in the text to provide a rapid review or preview of the material and to help students understand the relative importance of the concepts presented.

Audience

The material is suitable for undergraduate or graduate computer science majors or information science majors, students at a two-year technical college or community college who have a basic technical background, or readers who have a basic understanding of IT security and want to expand their knowledge.

Acknowledgments

I would like to thank Jones & Bartlett Learning for the opportunity to write this book and be a part of the Information Systems Security & Assurance Series project. I offer my deep appreciation to Kim Lindros, who did an excellent job coordinating this book despite many challenges. Her guidance, patience, and support were instrumental to its success. A special thank-you goes to Mike Chapple, whose experience and debate on risk topics was helpful. His thought-provoking challenges were much appreciated. Thanks also to Mark Merkow and Darril Gibson for contributing chapters to this book.

I would also like to thank the staff and volunteers at ISACA, who dedicate themselves to providing global thought leadership to help define best practices for information audit, security, and risk management. Special thanks to Joann Skiba and Robert Bergquist, who helped facilitate access to ISACA IP material.

Special thanks goes to John Pironti, IP Architects, LLC, who is a true professional in the field in every sense of the word. His willingness to share his deep experiences at all hours of the night was very helpful.

My gratitude to Gary Dickhart, SAP, who passed on lessons to me over the years on driving for high-quality results and never forgetting about compassionate management. His lessons on teamwork and motivation are insightful.

Additional thanks to a myriad of friends and supporters at E&Y and KPMG who offered suggestions and insights. The caliber of these professionals is amazing, and the experiences they shared extremely valuable.

—*Rob Johnson*

Thank you to my family, who always support me when I need them the most, and thanks to my colleagues at PayPal Inc., who define excellence in putting information security to work!

—*Mark Merkow*

About the Author

ROB JOHNSON has over 20 years of experience in information risk, IT audit, privacy, and security management. He has a diverse background that includes hands-on operational experience, as well as providing strategic risk assessment and support to leadership and board-level audiences. He is currently an Executive Management Consultant with Aegis USA, an end-to-end total solution provider focused on identity and access management (IAM). Aegis USA is a privately owned technology company based in Colorado, delivering client solutions for information audit, security, and enterprise risk management.

Johnson has held senior roles in large global companies, large domestic banks, and as product architect for an international software company. Several of the key risk-related roles he has held include Head of Information and Operations Risk Management for ING U.S. Financial Services CITS, First Vice President and IT Audit Director for WAMU, Vice President/CISO for Security Services at First Bank Systems, and Product Manager and Architect for SAP/ERP solutions at Bindview.

Johnson lives in the Seattle with his wife and children. He holds a BS in interdisciplinary studies from the University of Houston with a concentration in computer science and mathematics. He is a Certified Information Systems Auditor (CISA), Certified Information Security Manager (CISM), Certified Information Systems Security Professional (CISSP), and Certified in the Governance of Enterprise IT (CGEIT). Rob has served on several international education and standards committees. He is also a member of the Information Systems Audit and Control Association COBIT 5 Task Force.

PART ONE

The Need for IT Security Policy Frameworks

Information Systems Security Policy Management

FOR AN ORGANIZATION TO WORK WELL it requires business processes that are reliable, keep costs low, and obey the law. Most organizations use policies and procedures to tell employees what the business wants to achieve and how to perform tasks to get there. This way each result is similar to the last.

In a perfect world, policies and procedures would always produce the perfect product. This requires employees to follow policies and procedures at all times. However, we do not live in a perfect world. Neither policies nor procedures are always perfect nor do employees always follow them. Anyone who has cashed a check at a bank understands what a basic procedure looks like. A check-cashing procedure includes checking the person's identification and the account balance. The bank's policy states that if a teller follows the check-cashing procedure, and the account has sufficient funds, the teller may give the cash to the account holder. If this procedure and policy are not followed, the bank could lose money.

It is equally important to create and enforce policies to make sure an organization's information is protected. Organizations of all types, including business and government, should implement such policies. There is no cookie-cutter approach—each will have its own way of implementing and enforcing policies. One of the challenges organizations face is the cost of keeping pace with ever-changing technology. This includes the need to update policies at the same time the organization updates technology. Failure to do so could create weaknesses in the system. These weaknesses could make business processes and information vulnerable to loss or theft.

In creating information system **security policies**, or simply called "security policies" or "ISS policies," many factors drive policy requirements. These requirements include organization size, processes, type of information, and laws and regulations. Once an organization creates policies, it will face both technical and human challenges implementing them. The keys to implementing policies are employee acceptance and management enforcement. A policy is worth little or nothing if no one follows it.

Chapter 1 Topics

This chapter covers the following topics and concepts:

- What information systems security is
- How information assurance plays an important role in securing information
- What governance is
- Why governance is important
- What information systems security policies are and how they differ from standards and procedures
- Where policies fit within an organization's structure to effectively reduce risk
- Why security policies are important to business operations, and how business changes affect policies
- When information systems security policies are needed
- Why enforcing, and winning acceptance for, security policies is challenging

Chapter 1 Goals

When you complete this chapter, you will be able to:

- Compare and contrast information systems security and information assurance
- Describe information systems security policies and their importance in organizations
- Describe governance and its importance in maintaining compliance with laws
- Explain what policies are and how they fit into an organization

What Is Information Systems Security?

A good definition of **information systems security (ISS)** is the act of protecting information and the systems that store and process it. This protection is against risks that would lead to unauthorized access, use, disclosure, disruption, modification, or destruction of information. It's not just the information inside a computer you need to protect. Information needs to be protected in any form. Some examples include print, magnetic media, and portable media. In fact, well-structured security policies ensure protection of information in any location and in any form. Many organizations come up with effective ways of protecting buildings, people, and other physical resources. Those are the typical and obvious areas of business concern. You will see that organizations put stronger security in areas where perceived threats to resources or employees is higher. For example, the vault of a bank will be more secure than the bank's public lobby.

Sometimes these same organizations fail to properly protect the information they process. Some do not consider information important to their operations. Some believe that security measures designed to protect buildings and people will protect information. Some just do not want to spend more money. However, protecting information is vital to business operations.

Information Systems Security Management Life Cycle

Generally, in any process of some importance, you would use some type of life cycle process to reduce errors and make sure all requirements are considered. It is no different for implementing security measures. Information security controls and processes use common approaches that simplify the build, and reduce mistakes. A typical life cycle process breaks up tasks into smaller, more manageable phases.

The Information Systems Audit and Control Association (ISACA) developed a widely accepted international best practices framework. This framework, called Control Objectives for Information and related Technology (COBIT), is much more than a life cycle. At its core are four domains that collectively represent a conceptual **information systems security life cycle**:

> **NOTE**
>
> You will learn about security policy frameworks in detail in Chapter 6.

- Plan and Organize
- Acquire and Implement
- Deliver and Support
- Monitor and Control

The life cycle process can use these simple domains, or phases, to build policies or controls. Each phase builds on the other. A failure in one phase can lead to a weakness or vulnerability downstream. For the purposes of discussion, you will learn about the four domains from a high level life cycle view. The COBIT framework goes into great depth to further break down these domains into detailed tasks and processes. Many organizations look at the richness of a framework like COBIT to tailor a life cycle management approach that makes sense for their business.

Figure 1-1 depicts one simplified example of an ISS management life cycle.

FIGURE 1-1

A simplified ISS management life cycle.

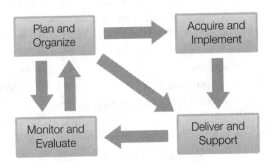

Plan and Organize

The COBIT Plan and Organize domain includes basic details of an organization's requirements and goals. This domain answers the questions "What do you want to do?" and "How do you want to get there?" The information in this phase is still high level. You review how you are going to manage your IT investment such as contracts, **service level agreements (SLAs)**, and new policy ideas. An SLA is a stated commitment to provide a specific service level. For example, a SLA could state how often a supplier will provide the service or how quickly the firm will respond. For managed services, the SLA often covers system availability and acceptable performance measures. It's also important to look at where or how the system will operate to determine the SLA. SLAs are important to ensure that all parties know their obligations. There are different types of service levels that apply to contracts versus what you need to deal with day to day. The Deliver and Support domain helps you define and manage day-to-day SLAs. In the Plan and Organize domain, you are primarily concerned with the type of equipment and services you are acquiring and how to hold a supplier accountable for those deliveries.

 NOTE

Notice in Figure 1-1 that the Plan and Organize domain touches all the other domains. This is because you will determine how the project will be managed in the Plan and Organize domain. This means you need to initially decide and then adjust management and staff throughout the project.

It makes no sense to sign a contract for a supplier who cannot meet the basic business requirements. This is why SLAs are part of the contracts between an organization and a provider. The organization creates a description, or design, of the system. The more accurate the system description, the more thorough the security controls. The role of a security professional is to look at these designs for weakness in which the systems and information are at risk.

For example, assume a business signs a contract with a telecommunications service provider. The service provider supplies voice and data transmissions. The business could also enter into a contract with a managed service provider. This provider may provide and manage the equipment. The contracts would also outline the suppliers' commitment in terms of an SLA.

Acquire and Implement

The COBIT Acquire and Implement domain addresses schedules and deliverables. The basic build occurs within this phase. The "build" is where the security control is built, and policies and supporting documents written. The build is based on the requirement created in the Plan and Organize phase. The more detailed the requirements, the more easily the build will go. The more details included in the Plan and Organize phase, the easier the Acquire and Implement phase will be. The SLA becomes an important consideration of the build because it determines the type of solutions that will be selected.

By the end of the Acquire and Implement phase, you have acquired and implemented your equipment. You have controls built into the systems. You have policies, procedures, and guidelines written. You have teams trained.

Deliver and Support

In the COBIT Deliver and Support domain, the staff tunes the environment to minimize threats. This could mean adjusting controls, policies, procedures, contracts, and SLAs. It is here you analyze data from the prior phase and compare it to day-to-day operations. You also perform internal and external penetration testing and, based upon the results of those tests, make critical adjustments in areas such as perimeter defense, remote access, and backup procedures. You review contracts and SLAs for validity and modify them as needed.

This phase requires regular meetings and good communications with your vendor. You must quickly identify any issues with the vendor's ability to meet SLAs. Typically, the vendor provides its record on meeting SLAs. You compare the vendor's report to your organization's internal reports. If you rely heavily on the vendor, you should meet monthly to compare records and recap incidents during the month.

In this phase, the day-to-day operation is managed and supported. You manage problems, configurations, physical security, and more. If you planned correctly and implemented the right solution, your organization sees value.

Monitor and Evaluate

After evaluating the ISS management life cycle, you see that ISS focuses on specific types of controls at specific points within the system. Testing and monitoring of controls occur and the results analyzed for effectiveness. The oversight of the COBIT Monitor and Evaluate domain looks at the big picture. Are your controls and supporting policies and procedures keeping pace with changes in technology and in your environment? This phase looks at specific business requirements and strategic direction, and determines if the system still meets these objectives.

Internal and external audits occur during the evaluation phase. Audits also take place through all testing in this and prior phases to ensure requirements are being met. This may include penetration testing by a third-party trusted agent. The testing performed during this phase must be comprehensive enough to encompass the entire ISS environment. The level of additional security testing will depend on business requirements and complexity. For example, if your requirements include regulatory compliance, include appropriate control tests. You should also evaluate the incident response process.

What Is Information Assurance?

Too often you will hear the terms "information systems security" and "information assurance" interchangeably. They are not the same thing. **Information assurance (IA)** grew from information systems security. The high-level difference is that ISS focuses on protecting information regardless of form or process, whereas IA focuses on protecting information during process and use. You can see some these differences as you examine the security tenets, also known as "the five pillars of the IA model":

- **Confidentiality**—Generally accepted as ISS and IA tenets
- **Integrity**—Generally accepted as ISS and IA tenets
- **Availability**—Generally accepted as ISS and IA tenets
- **Authentication**—Generally accepted as an IA tenet
- **Nonrepudiation**—Generally accepted as an IA tenet

This is not to suggest that authentication and nonrepudiation are not information security concerns. The goals are similar. It's the approach and focus that are different. IA imposes controls on the entire system regardless of the format or media. In other words, IA ensures data is protected while being processed, stored, and transmitted. This ensures the confidentiality, integrity, availability, and nonrepudiation of the data.

Confidentiality

Confidentiality refers to information dissemination. This means you allow only authorized individuals to see or possess the information. Every user typically needs access to an organization's intranet. That does not mean, however, that every user needs access to all information.

For example, only human resources (HR) personnel need access to employee information. Similarly, only accounting personnel require access to all accounting data. Consider employee pay data. This type of information could span the two business areas. Installed controls ensure that only specific HR or accounting staff members access the pay data. This concept is **need to know**, the idea that individuals should have access only to information required to do their jobs.

Figure 1-2 depicts the confidentiality tenet. The figure represents three users—two are regular users; one is a privileged user. User A and User B have limited access rights to data. User A can only read data stored in the product list, whereas User B can read and update all data in the database. The privileged user has elevated database administration privileges; however, even he might not have access to all data.

> **NOTE**
>
> Another consideration of confidentiality is how to protect data in the event of a breach or unauthorized access. One way to resolve this issue is to use encryption. We can encrypt data while it's at rest on the hard drive or when it is being transmitted. You will learn about encryption in Chapter 2 and in other chapters throughout this book.

Integrity

Integrity ensures that information has not been improperly changed. In other words, the data owner must approve any change to the data or approve the process by which the data changes. There are several ways to ensure that data is protected. Many operating systems allow permissions on data files and directories to provide restricted access. These containers typically reside on a server that requires users to log on and authenticate to gain approved access. This ensures that only users who have the data owner's permission can change the information. Encryption also ensures integrity as well as confidentiality. Encryption protects data from being viewed or changed by unauthorized users. Only users with the proper key can change or view encrypted data.

FIGURE 1-2

A confidentiality tenet.

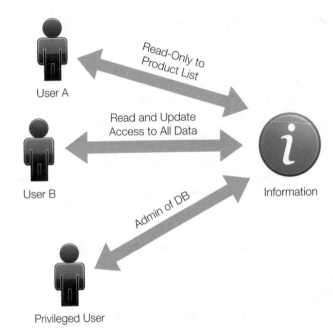

FIGURE 1-3

An integrity tenet.

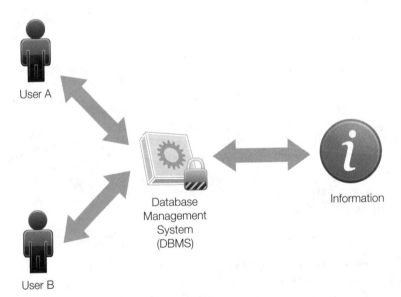

Figure 1-3 depicts the integrity tenet. There are two users, a Database Management System (DBMS) and the data. The DBMS rules prevent unauthorized changes to data. User A can change data. User B can only retrieve data.

Authentication

Authentication is the ability to verify the identity of a user or device. You probably see authentication in use every day. For example, you might use an online e-mail system such as Google Gmail or Yahoo! Mail. What protects your e-mail is your user ID and password, which you selected when you signed up for the service. This user ID and password is your authentication approach to accessing your e-mail service.

It's not just humans who need their identities verified. Computers often exchange information or process transactions on our behalf. While you are asleep, a computer system may by printing your payroll check. Many of these functions are sensitive. As a security professional, you should ensure that only these authorized processes are accessing this sensitive information. This means these computers and automated processes need to be authenticated. Just like an individual, their identity is verified before being granted access to data. For example, services running in Microsoft Windows Server could have an ID assigned. Network devices can exchange information at a network protocol level to verify identity.

There is a lot involved in maintaining good authentication processes, such as forcing users to change their passwords periodically and forcing rules on how complicated passwords should be. These housekeeping tasks are becoming easier and automated. One of the more critical keys to success is having credentials that are hard to forge or guess. A good example is a strong password known only to the user. Additionally, these credentials must not be transmitted in the clear over the network. Sending passwords over the network in plain text, for example, can be observed with network sniffers. In a typical business environment, if these two goals are accomplished as well as many of the housekeeping items previously discussed, you begin to have reasonable assurance you know who is accessing your computer systems.

Availability

Availability ensures information is available to authorized users and devices. Conversely, availability also means preventing denial of service (DoS) attacks.

Initially, the information owner must determine availability requirements. The owner must determine who needs access to the data and when. Is it critical that data be available 24/7 or is 9 to 5 adequate? Does it need to be available to remote or only local users? The raw business requirements would then be translated into technical and SLA requirements such as 24/7/365 and uptime 99.9 percent.

Once those types of requirements are determined, you can develop and implement system availability measures. The servers where the information resides must be operational. Associated with the servers is all the network equipment that provides interconnectivity and remote access. Proper configuration of these devices will allow access to the information when needed.

Nonrepudiation

The concept of **nonrepudiation** is that an individual cannot deny or dispute they were part of a transaction. It's a simple concept but hard to achieve in the digital world where the other party is not in front of you. This is a concept where technology helps provide this assurance.

Authentication, for example, helps establish identity. When you tie strong authentication to a transaction or message, you know who submitted it. Some businesses implement biometric scanners as an authentication control. Others use a key management tool in which users receive a token that generates a code that allows access to the system. These types of authentication tools are hard to forge. These tools provide some confidence you know who sent a message or started the transaction.

However, that is not nonrepudiation. You still don't know if the message or transaction was tampered with during transmission. Other tools come into play for that. You can encrypt the data or use digital signatures to ensure what was transmitted is the same as what was received. Key management and digital signature technology are beyond the scope of this chapter. What's important to know is that once the message or transaction is sent, it cannot be tampered with in transit. As a security professional, you must protect the transmission of data.

You're almost there but haven't achieved nonrepudiation quite yet. Information can also be tampered with at point of delivery. If the data was protected during transmission, there most likely is a corresponding technology on the delivery side. If the data was encrypted, you must decrypt it. If you use digital signatures, you must verify those signatures. Essentially, you need to apply technology to ensure that "what was sent" is the same as "what was received."

Congratulations, you now have nonrepudiation! You know the party that sent it. You know the information was not tampered with along the way. You know that what you received represents the original piece of information. No one can dispute what was sent or who sent it.

What Is Governance?

Governance is both a concept and specific actions an organization takes to ensure compliance with its policies, processes, standards, and guidelines. The goal is to meet business requirements. However, the focus of governance is ensuring everyone is following established rules. What is assumed in governance is that these business objectives were well understood and baked into the rules. Thus, by following the rules, you achieve these business goals. Good governance should include a good understanding of the business, so when enforcement of a rule doesn't make sense, adjustments to the governance process can take place.

Governance in the real sense is much more than a concept. An organization puts formal processes in place and committees to act as gateways. These are tangible acts that collectively define the governance structure of an organization. For example, an organization could require any IT project costing more than $100,000 to be presented to a review committee before the money is spent. This committee would review the basic objectives, design, and technology to be used. This committee would act as a project governance committee to ensure the project follows the rules and aligns to organization's priorities.

Governance includes a series of oversight processes and committees. Collectively, governance ensures accountability, monitors activity, and records what is going on. What is also implied is that the governance structure will take action when the rules are ignored or not properly applied.

Why Is Governance Important?

Good governance provides assurance and confidence that rules are being followed. Who needs that assurance? First, senior management needs to know that its business objectives are being met. If the rules are being followed, there is some assurance the value promised to the business is being delivered. Also, senior management needs to know that the investment the organization has made is being properly managed. Second, regulators look at the governance structure for assurance that risks to shareholders, customers, and the public are being properly managed.

It's not unusual to perform compliance testing of governance processes. Compliance testing provides consistent, comparable insights into the governance process. By making this process consistent and repeatable, organizations can compare improvement over time. Administrators can refine the process over time, making it more effective. This leads to a better understanding of risk and allows you to deploy measures to close vulnerabilities. It also allows you to reduce the impact to the organization in the event of a breach.

For example, the importance of governance is evident in a configuration management process. By controlling system configuration, previously mitigated vulnerabilities remain in check. This results in greater uptime rates. Governance is important to the daily operation of an organization and should not be viewed as a "once a year" occurrence. By integrating the annual cost of governance into the annual budget, the continual benefits governance provides are not viewed as an unexpected expense.

What Are Information Systems Security Policies?

You can think of a policy as a business requirement on actions or processes performed by an organization. An example is the requirement to provide a receipt when returning an item to a retail store. That may be a simple example of a policy, but essentially, it places a control on the return process. In the same manner, ISS policies requires placement of controls in processes specific to the information system. ISS policies discuss the types of controls needed but not how to build the controls. For example, a security policy may state that some data can be accessed only from the office. The selected technology and how the security control would be built to prevent remote access, for example, would not appear in the policy.

FIGURE 1-4

Internal versus
external documents.

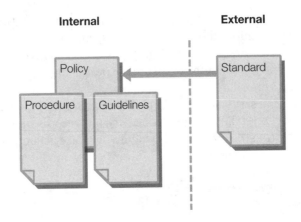

ISS policies should cover every threat to the system. They should include protecting
people and information. The policies must also set rules for users, define consequences
of violations, and minimize risk to the organization. Therefore, any process that involves
one of those business requirements should be supported by a policy. Other documents
in the **policy framework** provide additional support. There are typically four different types
of documents in a framework:

- **Policy**—A document that states how the organization is to perform and conduct
  business functions and transactions with a desired outcome
- **Standard**—An established and proven norm or method, which can be a procedural
  standard or a technical standard implemented organization-wide
- **Procedure**—A written statement describing the steps required to implement a process
- **Guideline**—A parameter within which a policy, standard, or procedure is suggested
  but optional

Many people refer to all these documents as "security policies." But they aren't necessarily.
Figure 1-4 depicts the relationship of these four types of documents. The figure shows
that procedures and guidelines support policies. In addition, the figure indicates that
standards influence policies. The four documents fall into two groups: internal and
external. Standards are external documents. The other three are internal documents.

A **standard** can be a process or a method for implementing
a solution. This involves technology, hardware, or software
that has a proven record of performance. This can be a procedural or implementation standard or a technical deployment
standard implemented company-wide. For the purposes of ISS,
a standard is the set of criteria by which an information system
must operate. Standards exert external influence on the creation
of policies. An organization can have internal standards. Often
these standards are tailored to the organization based on some
external best practice.

> **NOTE**
>
> Standards become the measuring
> stick by which an organization
> is evaluated for compliance. The
> Federal Information Processing
> Standards (FIPS) publications
> are examples of standards. You
> can view FIPS publications online
> at *http://itl.nist.gov/fipspubs/*.

A **policy** is a document that states how the organization is to perform. It describes how to conduct business functions and transactions with a desired outcome. It sets the stage for secure control of information. It is the "who does what to whom and when" document. It should reflect what leadership commitments are to protecting information.

A proc─ ─ ─
required
support p
accompli
a more er

A **guid
standard,
It is a poli
help busin

How Polici

Now that y
standards.
Standards
requiremer
standards.
accreditatic

Standard
industry de
stick by whi
adjust stand
standard.

...es

...lines

...nce between policies and ...compliant to a standard. ...determine a minimum ...d-upon practices produce ...or certification and

...nizations that represent the ...become the measuring ...non for a company to ...em internally as a company

How Policies and Procedures Differ

In a similar manner, you can contrast the difference between policies and procedures. As a reminder, policies are requirements placed on processes. Procedures are the technical steps taken to achieve those policy goals. Procedures can contain step-by-step instructions on the performance of a task. They can also identify how to respond to an incident.

Within a policy framework, there could exist a policy stating the requirement for disaster recovery planning. A separate procedural document would call out specific tasks to provide recovery services. In other words, procedures are the how-to document.

Where Do Information Systems Security Policies Fit Within an Organization?

Most business areas have some policies that guide their operations. These are usually departments such as HR, production, or sales. However, one of the most misunderstood areas in the application of policies is information systems security. With technology ingrained into today's society, protecting information is everyone's concern. As you discovered about information systems security, there is more to consider than just the wires and computers.

Organizations rely as much on information systems as they do on human resources. In a production facility, computers control most manufacturing devices. In a nuclear power plant, electrical generation and contamination containment rely on controlling systems to ensure the flow of power keeps the lights on safely. In a legal office, an aide researches thousands of documents and case law through a remote vast online database. These are just a few examples of the impact information systems have on a daily basis. As you can see, technology continues to become a greater part of our daily lives.

Figure 1-5 shows the seven domains of a typical IT infrastructure. Each domain provides unique policy requirements. Within each domain, ISS policies are vital to maintaining a secure work environment that protects the information resources critical to their individual requirements. You will learn about the seven domains in depth and associated policy issues and challenges in Chapter 4.

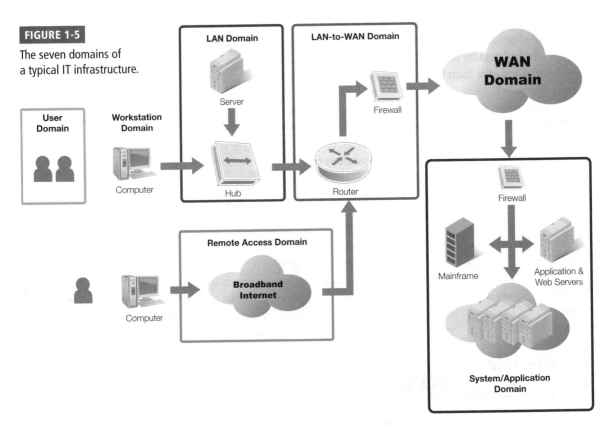

FIGURE 1-5

The seven domains of a typical IT infrastructure.

Why Information Systems Security Policies Are Important

ISS policies ensure the consistent protection of information flowing through the entire system. Information is not always static and often changes at its processed. The information must be protected throughout the process at all times. To an extent, physical security policies and procedures will protect data. However, that is not always the case. What about a disgruntled employee with elevated access privileges? How do you protect resources from someone with this kind of authorized access? Physical security has limits and should be viewed as one of several layers of control.

The following are reasons for using and enforcing security policies:

- **Protecting systems from the insider threat**—The "insider threat" refers to users with authorized access. These are privileged users who would have the ability and access to wreak havoc on the system. The insider threat is probably the most significant threat to any information system. Policies help monitor authorized user activity.

- **Protecting information at rest and in transit**—Data is generally in one of two states—**data at rest**, such as on a backup tape, or **data in transit**, such as when traveling across a network. Essentially, policies help to protect data all the time.

- **Controlling change to IT infrastructure**—Change is good. Managing change is better. This reduces the risk of vulnerabilities being introduced to the system.

Security polices strengthen an organization's ability to protect its information resources at all times while providing secure access to employees when they need it. Policies allow for control of the system, changes to the system, and reduction of much of the risk to the system.

Policies That Support Operational Success

Key to determining if a business will implement any policy is cost. Is there a cost involved? It takes time to identify risks to an information system, determine mitigation strategies, and implement those strategies.

By using policies to support that risk assessment, you can reduce the cost by providing controls and procedures to manage the risk. This also allows for change in a controlled manner. A good policy includes support for incident handling. Containing an incident can help reduce an exposure time to the organization. Identification of the reason for the incident can begin immediately and attackers potentially determined. A solution is more forthcoming, allowing the resource to be made available in a shorter amount of time. As most business folks will tell you, "Time is money."

By controlling costs and focusing on the most important risks, an organization can eliminate waste and support operational success. The key risks to the organization are reduced over time through continuous improvement achieved in part by having a good post-incident handling process.

Challenges of Running a Business Without Policies

When an organization lacks policies, its operations become less predictable. Individuals will operate based on what they think is a good idea at the time. Imagine a rowing team without direction. Everyone has an oar and tries to arrive at a destination and avoid obstacles along the way. Even if you managed to arrive, think of the waste of going in circles as one side of the boat rows faster and with more urgency than the other. This assumes you can get the team to row at the same time. It's no different with polices. Policies allow an organization to row in the same direction applying the same rules, priorities, and business goals across the teams.

Here are a few challenges you can expect without policies:

- **Higher costs**—Due to wasted efforts and a lot of rework
- **Customer dissatisfaction**—Unable to produce quality because individuals make their own judgment as to what is right or good
- **Lack of regulatory compliance**—Individuals decide when and how to follow legal mandates

Let's look at an accounting example. What would happen if the accounting or payroll information system were compromised or not available? Employees might not be paid. If the company had a policy that addressed outages for accounting, the system could be recovered in time to make payroll. Alternately, the company could have a policy that addresses a manual procedure in the event the system was unavailable. The lack of security policies and resulting lack of methodical ways to manage risks allow vulnerabilities to these system to go undetected.

Dangers of Not Implementing Policies

If security policies are to ensure information is properly protected, failing to implement policies leaves information vulnerable. The information may be vulnerable to an attack or mishandling. Some employers say "Our employees are the smartest in their fields." Or "We've been operating like that for years without a single problem (knock on wood)." These are also responses to the question, "Why implement policies?"

The dangers of not implementing policies are unexpected and undesirable outcomes. In the event of an ISS incident, employees will not know what to do, how to react, or whom to notify. This will lead to general confusion. As they're trying to figure out the answers to those questions, an attacker may be copying more information from the system.

Without configuration management control, modifications to systems once secure will render them non-secure. Managers will be unable to control changes to the information systems, which will lead to increased vulnerabilities to the systems.

Dangers of Implementing the Wrong Policies

Similar to not implementing policies is implementing the wrong policies. You should create policies to address the proper processes, or detrimental consequences can occur.

For example, consider a policy that states all employees should be granted administrator privileges to a system. Under this policy, the basic tenets of information assurance cannot be guaranteed. Users will have access to all information, which is probably not intended, nor is it a best security practice. As security policy is often a family of policies, be sure they do not conflict with each other.

When Do You Need Information Systems Security Policies?

"Timing is everything." This is most likely the No.1 tenet used by comedians. The same applies to the timeliness of policies. Why implement a policy on milking cows when your business model raises chickens? The possibility exists that your farm will expand operations one day, but there is no reason to write policies until that expansion occurs.

There will be times when the need for an ISS policy is evident. Security policies need to ensure that new technology is not introduced without a supporting set of policies in place. If your company has not implemented mobile computing, for example, there is no reason to write policies governing that process. However, once you decide to roll out a mobile computing implementation, you need policies in place. Another consideration is that you may have a process that occurs daily and all the involved employees are aware of that process. However, this process is undocumented even though employees know all the steps. The key employee for this process is retiring next month. This is the perfect opportunity to formalize a written procedure.

Business Process Reengineering (BPR)

Business processes are constantly under scrutiny for improvement. As that business process life cycle is accomplished, the process is improved and changed. However, the associated policies must also be changed and updated. Typically, the associated policies and procedures recognized during the life cycle are operational in nature. Policies that support operations, like security policies, are not always considered. Not updating those policies and procedures leaves a window of opportunity for error or disaster.

The process change could be dramatic enough to introduce new security vulnerabilities. If the equipment operating within the process completely changes, old security vulnerabilities reappear. Therefore, it is imperative to ensure that when reengineering any business process you also review security. This will ensure that **business process reengineering (BPR)** includes ISS concerns, and those policies and procedures are updated as needed.

Figure 1-6 shows the four phases of BPR. Phase 1 is the planning phase. Phase 2 sees the creation or modification of the process baseline. Research and benchmarking happen in Phase 3. Phase 4 develops the future process; it is during this phase that new policies are written or current ones updated.

Continuous Improvement

You can view **continuous improvement** as finding a better way or as a lesson learned. As employees find new ways to improve a system or process, you need to have a way to capture their ideas. The concept of continuous improvement applies to all aspects of ISS and IA. For example, when looking at availability issues, you may come across an authentication weakness. Regardless of how the weakness or risk was found, you need to capture the information, assess the importance, and apply an improvement. Sometimes this means changing policy. When policy goals cannot be achieved, enforcement becomes impossible and the overall security policy framework is weakened.

The driver for "finding a better way" should not be a system crash or breach. In those cases, you may have to deal with lessons learned from the incident. Think of continuous improvement as a suggestion box. Employees identify needed changes and write a suggestion. The suggestion is either accepted or rejected. If accepted, it enters the formal reengineering process.

Problem Related

Even with a sound policy framework, issues will occur. Depending on the criticality of the issue, policy implementation or change can occur at any time in the process. Policy changes brought about in this manner help avoid future incidents. In a perfect environment, policies fall into place before incidents occur. However, most organizations do not operate in a perfect environment. Once an event not covered by a policy occurs, an event analysis takes place and a recommendation is drafted. For events that are noncritical in nature, policy drafting comes about in concert with the remediation process. If it is more critical in nature, remediation should occur prior to writing the policy.

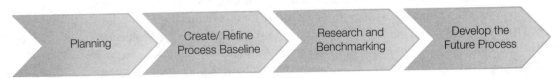

Planning   Create/ Refine Process Baseline   Research and Benchmarking   Develop the Future Process

FIGURE 1-6

Basic business process reengineering.

Why Enforcing and Winning Acceptance for Policies Is Challenging

There are many barriers to policy acceptance and enforcement. Without acceptance and enforcement of policies, employees could operate in a laissez-faire state. This runs counter to common business goals. Within an organization, there must be support at all levels, from the top to the bottom. Employees must have a stake in ISS. They must understand how those policies and procedures affect them and their business area. If they have a stake in creating or approving policies, they will be more likely to accept those policies. The following is a list of policy acceptance challenges:

> **NOTE**
>
> The biggest hindrance to implementation of policies is the human factor.

- **Organizational support at all levels**—Without cohesive support from all levels of the organization, acceptance and enforcement will fail.

- **Employees must have a stake**—There must be something to motivate employees to buy in to the process. This could be some kind of award for participating, or disciplinary action if they don't.

- **Policy awareness and understanding**—Employees must know a policy exists and understand what it means. Crafting the document to make this easy can be very challenging.

Enforcement of policies can be just as difficult as policy acceptance. There are several reasons why enforcement is challenging. The language in which policies are written can be vague enough to be unenforceable. Infractions are not reported, which is often a key contributor to the lack of enforcement. Other business areas in the organization, such as HR or the legal department, might not be part of the enforcement process. This can give employees license to either disregard the policies or perform actions contrary to them. The following list recaps policy enforcement challenges:

- Poorly written policies
- Not reporting infractions
- Key departments and management not involved in enforcement

CHAPTER SUMMARY

In this chapter, we defined foundational ISS concepts and key terms. We examined the key tenets of ISS management to ensure confidentiality, integrity, availability, authentication, and nonrepudiation. Additionally, we determined that information systems security (ISS) and information assurance (IA) are two separate but similar concepts. Associated with IA and ISS is governance. Governance ensures we are following the rules, such as policies, regulations, standards, and procedures.

We discovered several situations when security policies are to be considered. Opportunities include:

- New business processes
- Changes in current business processes
- Business process reengineering (BPR)
- Incident occurrence

We examined where policies fit within an organization to meet operational and governance requirements. These include all seven domains, across the business spectrum. ISS policies are important for several reasons. A primary reason is controlling authorized access to information. Another reason is to control change to systems. Finally, we looked at policy acceptance and enforcement, and factors that make those processes difficult. Employee support is required at all levels for policy buy-in and enforcement. Enforcement also hinges on effective policy writing.

KEY CONCEPTS AND TERMS

Authentication	Guideline	Policy
Availability	Information assurance	Policy framework
Business process reengineering (BPR)	Information systems security (ISS)	Procedure
Confidentiality	Information systems security management life cycle	Security policies
Continuous improvement		Service level agreement (SLA)
Data at rest	Integrity	Standard
Data in transit	Need to know	
Governance	Nonrepudiation	

CHAPTER 1 ASSESSMENT

1. John works in the accounting department but travels to other company locations. He must present the past quarter's figures to the chief executive officer (CEO) in the morning. He forgot to update the PowerPoint presentation on his desktop computer at the main office. What is at issue here?

   A. Unauthorized access to the system
   B. Integrity of the data
   C. Availability of the data
   D. Nonrepudiation of the data
   E. Unauthorized use of the system

2. Governance is the practice of ensuring an entity is in conformance to policies, regulations, _____ , and procedures.

3. COBIT is a widely accepted international best practices policy framework.

   A. True
   B. False

4. Which of the following are generally accepted as IA tenets but not ISS tenets? (Select two.)

   A. Confidentiality
   B. Integrity
   C. Availability
   D. Authentication
   E. Nonrepudiation

5. Greg has developed a document on how to operate and back up the new financial sections storage area network. In it, he lists the steps required for powering up and down the system as well as configuring the backup tape unit. Greg has written a _____ .

6. When should a wireless security policy be initially written?

   A. When the industry publishes new wireless standards
   B. When a vendor presents wireless solutions to the business
   C. When the next generation of wireless technology is launched
   D. After a company decides to implement wireless and before it is installed

7. A toy company is developing the next generation of children's reading aids. They already produced a comparable product, but the new one will not be available on shelves for another two years. What process would drive policies related to the new product's information systems security?

   A. Continuous improvement
   B. Business process reengineering
   C. Encryption
   D. Information systems security management life cycle
   E. Software development life cycle

8. Implementation and enforcement of policies is a challenge. The biggest hindrance to implementation of policies is the _____ factor.

9. Information systems security policies should support business operations. These policies focus on providing consistent protection of information in the system. This happens by controlling multiple aspects of the information system that directly or indirectly affect normal operations at some point. While there are many different benefits to supporting operations, some are more prevalent than others. Which of the following are aspects of ISS policies that extend to support business operations?

   A. Controlling change to the IT infrastructure
   B. Protecting data at rest and in transit
   C. Protecting systems from the insider threat
   D. B and C only
   E. All the above

10. Ted is an administrator in the server backup area. He is reviewing the contract for the offsite storage facility for validity. This contract includes topics such as the amount of storage space required, the pickup and delivery of media, response times during an outage, and security of media within the facility. This contract is an example of information security.

   A. True
   B. False

Business Drivers for Information Security Policies

MOST ORGANIZATIONS TODAY rely on computers to conduct business. Whether in the public or private sector, the threat of information being stolen or unauthorized access is a major concern. When you reduce these types of risks to information assets, you reduce risks to the business as well. Security policies let your organization set rules to reduce risks to information assets. Management has a direct interest and role to play in ensuring these rules are followed.

You can't eliminate all business risks. In some cases, a good policy can reduce the likelihood of risk occurring or reduce its impact. The business must find a way to balance a number of competing drivers. Some of these drivers include:

- **Cost**—Keep costs low.
- **Customer Satisfaction**—Keep customer satisfaction high.
- **Compliance**—Meet regulatory obligations.

Security policies define how to protect and handle information. These security policies should be brief and concise. They should define in simple terms the business requirements. Aligning security policies with business objectives makes policies easier to understand and more likely to be followed.

This chapter provides an overview of concepts that can reduce business risk. Although the term "business" is used, the concepts apply equally to both public and private organizations. When we use the term "risk" in this chapter, we refer only to the risk to information assets. It is impossible to discuss all potential business drivers to reduce risk for every organization. This chapter focuses on key risk areas.

Chapter 2 Topics

This chapter covers the following topics and concepts:

- What a business driver is and why business drivers are important
- What it means to maintain compliance
- What business risk exposure is
- What business liability is
- What operational consistency is and why it is important

Chapter 2 Goals

When you complete this chapter, you will be able to:

- Describe basic business risks
- Explain the difference between business risk exposure and business liability
- Describe some techniques the business uses to reduce risk
- Explain the important issues related to operational consistency
- Describe the relationship between business risks and security policies

Why Are Business Drivers Important?

Computer systems continue to evolve and become more complex. This makes it hard for the business to understand the technology that supports it. Yet a security **breach** can have a significant impact on the bottom line. The following are two examples of why organizations need good security policies:

The retailer TJX has over 2,000 stores in the United States and Puerto Rico. The company computers were breached in 2003 and 2006. Credit card information was stolen from more than 45 million customers. The company estimated losses as high as $139 million.

The health care provider BlueCross BlueShield of Tennessee in 2009 had a theft of hard drives. It reported 57 hard drives stolen. The company had to notify 220,000 members that their personal information might have been compromised. BlueCross reported spending more than $7 million. Customers were offered free credit monitoring for two years.

> **NOTE**
> "The business" refers to the operations of either a public or private sector organization.

> **NOTE**
> A breach is a confirmed event that compromises the confidentiality, integrity, or availability of information.

Both these cases resulted from a security policy failure. In the TJX case, it was reported that hackers breaching the store's Wired Equivalent Privacy (WEP) wireless network started the attack. This weak security link should have been prohibited by strong security policies and detected by good monitoring practices. In the case of BlueCross BlueShield, it was reported the drives were taken from a closet at a call center. The security policy should have required stronger physical controls over hard drive storage. It isn't possible to know if the policies failed to recognize the risks or if the security controls were inadequate. In both cases, implementing and enforcing good security policies should have prevented these types of breaches.

Organizations are increasingly concerned with how information risks are managed and reduced. Security policies are not considered solely a technology issue anymore. Organizations also expect security policies to reflect how they want information handled. An organization's security policies, taken collectively, show its commitment to protect information. Good security policies keep the business healthy. Some of the basic concerns with implementing such a policy include:

- **Cost**—Cost of implementing and maintaining controls
- **Impact**—Impact to customers
- **Regulatory**—Ability to legally defend

WARNING

Developing policy statements on legal and regulatory issues is highly sensitive work. Be sure to have your legal department review draft policy wording. Also find out how the department wants working copies of policies labeled.

Policies are only effective if they are enforced. Managers dislike surprises. Finding out later that security policies are too costly or that they negatively impact customers is not acceptable. To avoid this, management needs to take part in implementing security policies. Even in the best of situations data can be stolen. By having good security policies, the organization is better positioned to defend its actions to the public and in the courts. For example, an e-mail security policy that warns employees that their messages may be monitored can help defend against a lawsuit for violation of privacy.

Maintaining Compliance

The term "compliance" refers to how well an individual or business adheres to a set of rules. **Security policy compliance** means adhering to security policies. It is difficult to know whether an organization complies with every security policy. To state that an organization is compliant, you must be able to validate that the requirements within security policies have been applied to security controls and information. This is difficult, because even a small business with hundreds of employees could have tens of thousands of files. These files travel between servers, desktops, laptops, backup media, universal serial bus (USB) drives, and more. The issue becomes more complex in large organizations with thousands of employees and millions of files. The difficulty is compounded as technology is upgraded each year. Businesses are concerned with not only files that employees can access but also with files exposed to vendors and suppliers.

Compliance Requires Proper Security Controls

The key to security policy is being able to measure compliance against a set of controls. Security controls define "how" you protect the information. The security policies should also define "why" you set the goal. This effectively bridges business requirements with security controls. The security policies also define "what" type of protection will be achieved. The security policies do not define how to achieve these goals. That is left to the software logic within the security control, which depends on the technology.

Table 2-1 provides a conceptual example of a high-level security policy and control statement. A trader could bypass the security control in a number of ways. This is a real-world challenge. You would apply much more detail to both the security policy and control. The security control would be far more detailed regarding firewall rules. Often, the "why" part of a policy is difficult to establish. This is an important concept. The trader might be more inclined to comply with security policies if he or she understands the business need.

> ▶ **TIP**
>
> Make your security policies relevant to business needs. They stand a better chance of being followed.

To know whether an organization is complying with security policies, you must measure the level of compliance. The level of compliance can change depending on what exactly is measured. Consider the example in Table 2-1. You could perform a simple measurement of compliance by verifying that firewall rules exist. However, simple measurements can be less accurate or misleading. For example, assume four firewalls allow the traders access to the Internet. You check each firewall and find that three contain the proper firewall rule described in Table 2-1. At first glance, a simple

TABLE 2-1 An example of security policy and control components.

POLICY OR CONTROL	ANSWERS	ISSUE
Security policy	Why	Securities and Exchange Commission (SEC) under rule 17A-4 requires stock traders' conversations with clients to be recorded and retained. In this case the purpose is to ensure a detailed record of transactions with the client. Establishing a record allows regulators to audit for compliance to disclosure rules.
Security policy	What	To ensure compliance, all traders should only communicate with clients through company telephones or the company's e-mail system.
Security control	How	Using the firewall, stop all traffic for traders to the Internet except for Web browsing and company e-mail.

TABLE 2-2   Control measurement benefits.

CONTROL MEASUREMENT CONSIDERATION	BENEFIT TO THE BUSINESS
Determine which security controls to measure.	Defines the scope of the compliance being measured
Verify these controls are working.	Defines the effectiveness of the controls being measured
Express compliance in terms of adherence to policy, not controls.	Defines what business goals are to be achieved
Express compliance in terms of potential impact to the business.	Defines the impact to the business if the goals are not achieved

measurement indicates the business is 75 percent compliant with this policy. On further inspection, you discover that the fourth firewall does not follow the required rule. This firewall represents 70 percent of the traders' Internet traffic. This new fact could mean the business is only 30 percent compliant.

A more accurate measurement gives the business more confidence to understand its risks. This clarity of thought on risk often leads to a consensus on a solution. Even when no solution is available, this strong understanding of risk can help an organization prepare if an incident occurs.

Table 2-2 illustrates what can be achieved with good policy compliance measurements.

Security Controls Must Include Information Security Policies

Security controls are the means of enforcing security policies that reflect the organization's business requirements. These controls ensure the confidentiality, integrity, and availability of the information. These controls can be used to protect physical resources, including worker safety. They are also the means to measure security compliance. You should build security controls based on the security policies. If you know the security controls work, you know you are complying with security policies.

 TIP

Reducing the frequency of security policy changes makes policies easier to enforce. It's also easier to train employees.

Security policies do not contain security controls. However, a security control may have to change if the related security policy changes. By treating them separately, you can change the control to meet the security policy. This is an advantage as technology evolves. For example, suppose you have six separate IDs and passwords to access six different systems. Let's assume technology is introduced to allow all six systems to recognize one ID and password. Much of the security policy on password controls may not change: You still know to keep your password a secret and how to select a complex password. When security policies are well established and understood by employees, they are more easily enforced. When policies change too frequently, they become confusing.

A number of classifications can be applied to security controls. The three most common are:

- **Physical control**—As the name implies, this refers to some physical device that prevents or deters access. A locked door, a camera, an electric fence, and a security guard are all examples of physical controls.

- **Administrative control**—Also known as a "procedural control," relies on a human to take some action. A few examples of a procedural control could be providing security awareness training or having a manager check an employee's work.

- **Technical control**—Refers to software that creates a logical control. Passwords and antiviral software are examples of technical controls. Dedicated hardware, such as a firewall, would be considered a technical control because it contains the necessary software to create the logical control.

Security controls also follow three unique design types—preventive, detective, and corrective, as shown in Figure 2-1.

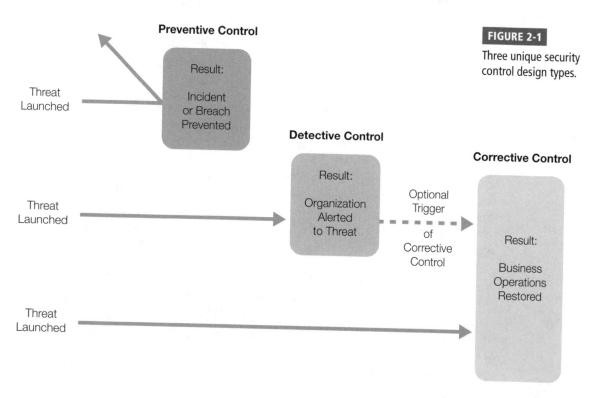

FIGURE 2-1

Three unique security control design types.

Preventive Security Controls

A **preventive control** stops incidents or breaches immediately. As the name implies, it's designed to prevent an incident from occurring. A firewall ideally would stop a hacker from getting inside the organization's network. This kind of control is an automated control.

An **automated control** has logic in software to decide what action to take. With an automated control, no human decisions are needed to prevent an incident from occurring. The human decisions occurred when designing the security control.

Detective Security Control

A **detective control** does not prevent incidents or breaches immediately. Just as a burglar alarm might call the police, a security control alerts an organization that an incident might have occurred. When you review a credit card statement, your review is a detective control. You review the statement for unauthorized charges. The process of reviewing the statement did not prevent the unauthorized charge from occurring. The review, however, triggers corrective action if needed.

 NOTE

If human action is required, the control is considered manual. If no human action is required, the control is automated.

A detective control is considered a **manual control**. A manual control relies on a human to decide what action to take. Still, manual controls can have automated components. For example, a system administrator could automatically receive a cell phone text when the number of invalid logon attempts reaches some threshold on a server. The administrator still needs to take some manual action.

Corrective Security Control

A **corrective control** does not prevent incidents or breaches immediately. A corrective security control limits the impact to the business by correcting the vulnerability. How quickly the business can restore its operations determines the effectiveness of the control.

For example, backing up files to enable data restoration after a system crash is a corrective security control. A corrective control is either automated or manual. For instance, you may automatically mirror (create exact copies of) files and then restore them in the event of hard drive failure. This is an automated control. If a human is required to decide when to restore the backup, that is a manual control.

Relationship Between Security Controls and Information Security Policy

Security policies and security controls have a mutual relationship. Security policies rely on security controls to enforce their rules. A security control is based on security policy goals. Without security controls, you could not enforce security policies. Without security policies, you could not systematically put controls in place that protect business information adequately. You rely on both to prevent a breach or restore operations after a breach. Figure 2-2 illustrates these key relationships.

FIGURE 2-2

Key relationships
of security policies.

It's possible to have too many security controls and policies too complicated to follow. A security control is not effective when it cannot distinguish between good and bad behavior. Security policies are not effective when they're too confusing to follow. If the policy is not clear, you cannot build reliable security controls. If a policy is too long, it is simply hard to understand. It also becomes a challenge to train employees.

The most important relationship between controls and policy is the business requirement. A common error is to overlook the business context. Knowing the context helps you keep competing priorities in balance. Equally important, when an incident occurs, you can better understand the impact if you know the business context.

Mitigating Risk Exposure

How can information security policies help? Well-defined security policies balance business requirements and limit behavior. The policy reflects how the business wants to manage its risks. The importance placed on such issues as customer privacy and protecting company secrets directly influences employee behavior.

Security policies must drive a culture that mitigates risk exposure. Policies are more than simple business requirements that translate into security controls. Policies, and how they are enforced, reflect the business perception of risk. Policies can reduce business risks by setting the tone at the top and promoting a risk-aware culture.

 NOTE

"Tone at the top" refers to a company's leaders making sure every employee knows the priorities. In this case, it means senior management's stated commitment to security policies. Beyond words, the actions taken by senior managers to implement and enforce policies build trust with the public and with regulators.

Educate Employees and Drive Security Awareness

Security is ultimately a function of people, processes, and technology working well together. A well-educated employee goes a long way toward reducing risk. Policies cannot define every risk. Unlike automated security controls that only look for specific risks, an aware employee can detect unusual activity. This ability to detect and deal with the unexpected makes employees extremely valuable in reducing business risk.

NOTE

If policies are optional, employees might treat them as simply guidelines. If you never enforce a policy, employees might perceive it as irrelevant or unimportant.

A good **security awareness program** makes employees aware of the behaviors expected of them. All security awareness programs have two enforcement components, the carrot and the stick. The carrot aims to educate the employee about the importance of security policies. You can use rewards to motivate compliance. The stick reminds the employees of the consequences of not following policy. Unfortunately, you need both components to implement a successful security policy program.

You can implement a security awareness program in many ways. Here are some generally accepted principles:

- **Repeat**—Most employees do not deal with risk daily so they need to be reminded.
- **Onboard**—New employees should be told of their responsibilities immediately.
- **Support**—Leaders should provide visible support.
- **Relevance**—Rules that show awareness of the business context are more likely to be followed.
- **Measure**—Competency should be measured.

TIP

Refresh your security awareness training program at least annually. Retrain employees after revising the program. It is important to connect with your audience. Just like a commercial, you are selling a message. Use whatever approach works. Humor works well.

Security awareness is about good communication. It's not about memorizing policy word for word. You need to focus on key concepts and teach employees when to ask for help. An employee should know what to do when encountering something suspicious or unexpected. Be sure to point out resources such as intranet sites within the organization. Most important, a security awareness program should teach an employee where to go for help. New employees especially need to know they are not alone in dealing with unexpected issues.

Leaders need to provide visible support for the program. Training takes time away from employees' regular work. Leaders need to walk the talk. They themselves need to take the training and reinforce the message with their teams. How leaders reward when policies are consistently followed or react when they are not sends a strong message. The daily message sent by leaders determines the risk culture of an organization.

A security awareness program gains credibility when the business sees a reduction of risk. Each employee plays a role in the business process. Multiple benefits come with a security awareness program that emphasizes the business risk, including:

- **Value**—Policies relevant to business are more likely to be followed by the business.
- **Culture**—Well-understood and enforced security policies promote a broad risk culture.
- **Resiliency**—Policies provide a basis for dealing with the unexpected.

Competence is difficult to measure. At a minimum, most programs track names of those who attended classes. However, simply taking roll is not a good way to measure competency. Many awareness programs have short quizzes to test key areas of knowledge. The challenge is that an employee may need to apply the knowledge long after the class ends. Often the best measure is noting real-world problems that occurred by not following policy. That way you can go back and continuously improve the training.

Prevent Loss of Intellectual Property

Legal-definitions.com, an online law dictionary, defines **intellectual property (IP)** as "any product of human intellect that is unique and un-obvious with some value in the marketplace. Intellectual property laws cover ideas, inventions, literary creations, unique names, business models, industrial processes, computer program code, and more."[1] In business, IP is a term you apply broadly to any company information that is thought to bring an advantage. For example, you need to protect secrets in order to protect the advantage over competitors. IP comes in many forms, and can be electronic or physical. Security policies should state how to protect that information regardless of format.

Protecting IP through security policies starts with human resources (HR) policies. These HR policies establish a code of conduct. They should give employees clear direction as to what the organization owns with respect to IP. HR policies also specify what employees may own prior to employment. Employment agreements may even attempt to enforce the confidentiality of IP after an employee leaves the organization or for work performed during the employee's spare time. These HR policies and employment agreements may or may not be enforceable depending on current law and location. Nonetheless, when building security policies, you should take a close look at HR policy. You want to be sure there are no conflicts.

Labeling Data and Data Classification

Once an organization clearly defines its IP, the security policies should define how to label or classify the information. There is a difference between labeling and classifying data. In both cases, a label identifies the level of protection needed. A **label** is typically a mark or comment placed inside the document itself; for instance, putting a "confidential" label in the footer of a document. When you classify a file (also known as **data classification**), a label may or may not be applied. When data classification is applied, the sensitive file is placed in a secured location.

IP can be difficult to label or classify and even harder to inventory. IP material comes in many forms. Consider a simple document labeled as sensitive IP. Portions of the document may be cut and pasted to create new material. How much of that new material should be considered IP? Although difficult, the generally accepted approach is to label what you can. Restrict access based on the label. Treat any new document containing any portion of the original IP with the same limits you placed on the original material.

One of the most important deliverables of security policies is the labeling and data classification approach. The approach selected will drive the cost of handling data. An employee needs to know how to handle both kinds of information—labeled and classified. Security policies instruct an employee on the proper handling depending on the business requirements. The combination of the following is a widely accepted practice to help prevent loss of IP:

- Label and classify IP data.
- Restrict access.
- Filter e-mail and other communication tools for IP data.
- Educate employees on handling IP material.

Protect Digital Assets

Digital assets are any digital content an organization owns or has acquired the right to use. *PC Magazine* defines digital assets as "Any digital material owned by an enterprise or individual including text, graphics, audio, video and animations. A digital asset is owned by an organization if it was created on the computer by its employees or if it was custom developed for and purchased by the organization. Images scanned into the computer are

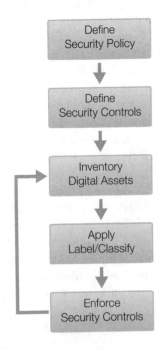

FIGURE 2-3

Key components in protecting digital assets.

Define Security Policy → Define Security Controls → Inventory Digital Assets → Apply Label/Classify → Enforce Security Controls

also a digital asset if the original work was owned by the company."[2] The term "digital assets" is often inaccurately applied to all computer-related resources. For the purposes of this chapter, we will use the strict definition.

You can protect digital assets with a good inventory. Only at the moment you identify a specific digital asset and apply a label or data classification do you know where the data is. The challenge is keeping track of the information as it is moved, changed, created, and deleted. A good inventory of digital assets allows you to design security controls where the data resides. Security policies define what an asset is. They also define what label or classification should be applied. You can see these key relationships needed to protect information in Figure 2-3.

The ability to protect information starts with well-defined security policies. The definition of digital assets is so broad it is difficult to create a complete inventory. Many organizations rely on tools that scan servers, desktops, and laptops. They try to inventory sensitive information based on patterns such as Social Security numbers (SSNs). When they see a pattern match, they can determine the level of security control to apply.

To protect digital assets, you need to know where your data is. You need good tools to inventory information and networks. You will need to refresh this inventory often. Finally, you need to be able to label or classify data quickly. The sooner data is labeled or classified the sooner it is protected. The ability to inventory digital assets is a major policy implementation issue.

Once data is inventoried, it's fairly straightforward to apply a label or classify the data. But you need to be sure the security policies clearly define the handling for each label and data class.

> **WARNING**
>
> Creating an accurate inventory is a major problem given the speed at which data files are created, deleted, moved, and changed. Not knowing where your highly sensitive data is at any point in time is a major risk. Mobile devices such as USB drives and smartphones that can receive e-mail compound the problem. And how do you protect information when it leaves your network? An organization should prioritize the inventory of assets starting with the most sensitive.

technical TIP

Whenever possible, you should put inventory tools that automatically classify data into log mode. In "log mode," the security control records only what it would have done but does not take the action. Then, by reviewing the logs with management, you can assess the impact of classifying data in that way. It is not unusual for automated tools to over-classify, locking the business out of key systems. For example, let's assume you highly restrict access to customers' date of birth. Potentially, the logs would show that the customer care desk could not access the data to verify customer identity when they call in for help. You can avoid upset users by rehearsing log use before applying preventive controls. In this example, no actual customers or business functions were affected. The security control could then be adjusted to include access for the customer care desk. Log mode is a good way to gain business support for implementing more restrictive security controls.

Secure Privacy of Data

We all value a degree of privacy when it comes to highly personal information. What comes to mind first? Perhaps you think about your bank or medical records. Yet this information and more can be stored in digital files in computers anywhere in the world. Our personal information might be found with an offshore vendor, say in India, who was processing a mortgage loan application for us on a home in Ohio. Regardless of where your personal data travels, securing and protecting this information is both a trust and legal obligation. This book focuses on United States privacy obligations. However, all modern countries throughout the world have some form of privacy laws.

The concept of protecting our privacy starts with data that identifies us as a unique individual. In 2007, the Office of Management and Budget (OMB) defined **personally identifiable information (PII)** as:

> **NOTE**
>
> Many states have laws that also define PII. These states define how the data should be handled to protect privacy. Not all of these laws define privacy and PII data the same way. One state may consider your home address a **public record** while another state considers it PII data to be protected.

> Information which can be used to distinguish or trace an individual's identity, such as their name, social security number, biometric records, etc. alone, or when combined with other personal or identifying information which is linked or linkable to a specific individual, such as date and place of birth, mother's maiden name, etc.[3]

Security policies need to define PII data by business type and location. A bank, for example, follows different federal regulations than a local check-cashing service or medical clinic. The state in which you operate could have different requirements than a neighboring state. Widely accepted practices help businesses navigate the maze of privacy regulations. For example, most states consider the combination of a person's name and SSN as PII. With identity theft, a major concern for both businesses and consumers, you should be careful of any combination of information that could be used to open or access an account. Depending on the business, these types of data have a good chance of falling within the PII definition.

> **NOTE**
>
> The chief privacy officer provides direction on how to handle legal requirements regarding PII data, including how to report incidents.

Because organizations must follow many different privacy regulations, some organizations have established a **chief privacy officer (CPO)** position. This is the most senior leader responsible for managing an organization's risks. The CPO is responsible for keeping up with privacy laws. The CPO also needs to understand how the laws impact business. Due to the nature of the work, many CPOs are lawyers. Although they are generally not technology people, they work closely with technology teams to create strong security policies.

You should consider the following guidelines when developing policy to secure PII data:

- **Examine**—Understand local state and federal requirements.
- **Collaborate**—Work closely with CPO.
- **Align**—Coordinate privacy policies with data classification policies.
- **Educate**—Conduct awareness training on handling of PII data.
- **Retain**—Ensure proper controls around data retention and destruction.
- **Limit**—Collect only the data from an individual you need to provide the service or product.
- **Disclose**—Fully disclose to the individual what data is being collected and how it will be used.
- **Encrypt**—Consider using encryption when storing or transmitting PII data.

Full Disclosure and Data Encryption

Privacy regulations involve two important principles. "Full disclosure" gives the consumer an understanding of what and how the data is collected and used. "Data encryption" provides a standard for handling consumer information.

> **NOTE**
>
> Some regulations allow companies to sell customer data if the individual gives permission through an "opt-in" process. Other states allow for the sale of information but require that the consumer be given a choice through an "opt-out" process.

The first principle—**full disclosure**—is the idea that an individual should know what information is being collected. They should also be told how that information is being used. Many of us use the Internet as a quick-and-easy way to buy products and services. It seems just as quickly our e-mail inbox fills with offers from other companies. Did the online service collect and sell your information? Did the company fully disclose how that data was to be used? These are the issues that a privacy policy needs to address.

The second principle—**data encryption**—recognizes that even with the best efforts data can fall into the wrong hands. This happens when data is stolen, lost, or accidentally accessed. Encrypted data can only be read when the user has the correct decryption key. Assume you have a backup tape containing individual names and SSN numbers. Now assume this tape is lost. The data on the tape could not be viewed without the key. This provides an additional layer of security.

Encryption is a preventive security control. But encrypting data and managing encryption keys can be complicated and expensive. Although expensive, it's often a lot less expensive than having to notify millions of customers that their personal information has been lost or stolen. Beyond loss of trust, companies may face legal penalties.

Encryption is considered an effective practice. Encrypting data when transmitting over the Internet is commonplace today. Encrypting data at rest on a server's hard drive or mass storage array is far more complicated if multiple technologies are involved. Sometimes, encrypting data at rest is not technically possible.

technical TIP

Payment Card Industry Data Security Standard (PCI DSS) mandates the use of encryption for transmitting and storing credit card information. Companies and vendors have created materials to support these PCI requirements. Even if your organization does not process credit cards, this material could provide helpful guidance on encryption for protecting PII data. The Cisco PCI Solution for Healthcare Design and Implementation Guide, for example, outlines a conceptual model for protecting data including encryption components. The Guide is located at *http://cisco.com/en/US/docs/solutions/Verticals/PCI_Healthcare/PCI_Healthcare_DIG.html*.

Lower Risk Exposure

Well-defined and enforced security policies lead to well-defined controls. These controls in turn protect the information. So how do you achieve lower risk exposure? The concept of exposure relies on a calculation that estimates the losses to the business in the event the risk is realized. First you need a scale that allows you to measure risk against predicted business losses. Over time, you invest in people, processes, and technology to lower that risk to an acceptable level. That acceptable level is sometimes called your "risk appetite."

What a risk appetite tells you is how much loss an organization is willing to accept in the normal course of business. These calculations are made in many different businesses and industries. Credit card companies estimate losses from fraud and invest in countermeasures. As the fraud rises, so does the spending to stop it and lower the risk exposure. You calculate the loss if these events occur and invest in programs to lower the risk exposure. For example, most banks today have changed their security policies to require much more rigorous screening of calls to the customer service desk. It's not unusual for a customer to be asked more detailed questions than just their name, account number, and SSN. A customer could be asked current balances, last transactions, and other details in an attempt to reduce risks of fraud.

There is no easy way to calculate risk to the business in the event of a security breach. Ideally, you should calculate risk exposure in terms of total potential losses in financial terms. Given that security breaches could also result in reputation damage, it is hard to calculate that in financial terms.

Some organizations take an easier approach. They calculate risk exposure in terms of security policy compliance. This approach takes a leap of faith that if you comply with good security policies, you are adequately controlling the risk. This approach lets you lower risk exposure to the business by measuring and improving policy compliance over time.

Regardless of approach, it is ultimately the potential negative impact to the business that is being measured and lowered.

Minimizing Liability of the Organization

A "business liability" emerges when an organization cannot meet its obligation or duty. Business liability is a subset of an organization's overall risk exposure. An obligation can be either a legal or a promised commitment.

If a business fails to follow the law, it has violated its "legal obligation." This liability leaves the organization open to potential fines or limits how it conducts business. In rare cases, an organization can be found to have engaged in criminal conduct. Its officers could then face criminal charges.

A business not living up to promised commitments loses the trust of customers. When a business fails to deliver the product or service it promised, the liability is lost business. Customers post complaints on the Internet, creating the potential for lawsuits and more business loss.

The role of security policies is to reduce these liability risks. When hackers breach a company's security, for example, you often have both trust and regulatory issues to deal with. Each event has potential liabilities. Reviewing past events to predict future situations will help you gauge overall risk exposure and specific business liabilities. Policies must define the proper handling of each of these types of events.

Separation Between Employer and Employee

An employer is not responsible for every potential employee action. Yet an employer may need to deal with the liability created by an employee. It's not just about lost business. An employee may violate a person's privacy by mishandling information. An employee may violate discrimination laws by collecting sensitive information not needed to conduct business. There could be a host of penalties placed against the organization.

Policies make clear to an employee what acceptable behavior is. Policies also provide a degree of separation from employees who fail to follow rules. A business can point to its policies as a statement of what should have occurred. The ability to defend the organization's position to the public and regulators is an important byproduct of security policies.

However, just having security policies will not create this separation. The business is obligated to take steps to implement and enforce the policy. Some of these reasonable steps include:

- **Policy**—Have clear security policies on the handling of customer information.
- **Enforce**—Express strong disapproval when policy is not followed.
- **Respond**—Quickly respond to incidents to minimize the impact to customers.
- **Analyze**—Understand what happened.
- **Educate**—Improve employee training.

These steps will minimize losses and show a commitment to customers. When challenged by the public or regulators, this will also help separate the employer's actions from a rogue employee.

 TIP

Be sure to work with in-house legal counsel on policy strategies to lay the foundation for defending the organization in the event of an incident.

Acceptable Use Policies

Acceptable use policies (AUPs) are formal written policies describing employee behavior when using company computer and network systems. Most AUPs outline what is acceptable and unacceptable behavior. They also need to outline the disciplinary process when an employee violates policy. Because the disciplinary process could lead to termination, the policy must be clear and concise. Many companies require the employee to sign the AUP to acknowledge receipt of the rules. Both the legal and HR departments always approve final draft policies.

The AUP is an important tool to create a legal separation between the employer and employee. Little tolerance exists for employees who create unnecessary liability for the organization. For example, using company computers to harass or threaten others, or view obscene materials, could result in termination.

Confidentiality Agreement and Non-Disclosure Agreement

A **confidentiality agreement (CA)**, also known as a **non-disclosure agreement (NDA)**, is a binding legal contract between two parties. It is a promise not to disclose to any third party information covered by the agreement. The agreement needs to clearly define the information covered. This reduces problems that may arise between the two parties or any other party asked to resolve legal disputes.

> **NOTE**
>
> CAs and NDAs tend to be one-sided. One party discloses information and the other party promises confidentiality. However, the agreement can also be mutual, under which both parties promise to keep each other's information confidential.

These types of employment agreements are often made at the time of hire. They outline what information should not be disclosed outside the company. These agreements could bind the employee from disclosing company information after employment terminates.

The CA or NDA is often used to explore business opportunities before buying a product or service. Let's say a company wants to hire a consultant to redesign a major computer application. Both parties would sign a CA. The company could then disclose its problems and the consultant would have more precise information to base an estimate. The CA would bind both parties even if the company decided not to hire the consultant.

Security policies typically include guidance when a CA or NDA should be required. Most security policies require such agreements to be in place before any data can be exchanged. This includes requiring such agreements to cover employees and non-employees, such as temporary or contract workers. A CA or NDA is a tool to reduce risk to business by ensuring that all individuals handling company data know their responsibility. This is especially important for non-employees who may not go through the company's normal security awareness training.

Business Liability Insurance Policies

Business liability insurance lowers the financial loss to the business in the event of an incident. Even when a business has well-defined security policies problems can still occur. Business liability insurance will pay for losses within the limits of the policy.

Business liability insurance can be issued to both organizations and individuals. For example, a computer engineer performing consulting services could obtain professional liability insurance. Such a policy would cover any successful claims that the engineer was negligent or made errors. The same type of coverage would apply to large companies facing claims that their product or services were negligent or in error.

An important benefit of this insurance coverage is the payment of legal fees. Even when a company is found innocent, the legal costs can be substantial. These policies do have limits, conditions, and requirements that the policyholder must meet. These policies also have exclusions. They do not protect a company that has committed illegal acts. Overall these policies are another tool to further reduce the risk.

Implementing Policies to Drive Operational Consistency

Operational consistency means an organization's processes are repeatable and sustainable. The business goal is to have these processes execute each time with the same consistency and quality. This reliability allows the business to continuously improve quality. Processes evolve over time and the more repeatable a process can be, the more likely risks can be detected and removed.

You can implement security policies the same way. This ensures that the same consistency and quality is applied to protection of information. This consistency of execution also means that when a weakness or new risk is identified, the same solution can mostly likely be applied to a host of processes. This is how policies help drive operational consistency.

Forcing Repeatable Business Processes Across the Entire Organization

Operational efficiency means lower costs to the business. By applying this principle across the enterprise, greater quality results can be achieved at a lower cost. For organizations with multiple divisions, developing processes once and repeating them saves time and resources. This approach also allows the organization to develop centers of excellence. These centers are typically small teams with very deep knowledge of a subject area.

An "enterprise view" allows senior leaders to understand how risk affects the entire organization. Although individual process failures may seem insignificant, collectively they may indicate a systemic problem.

This is particularly important when it comes to security policies. Leadership needs a high level of certainty that there is operational consistency in how information is protected. Leadership is often asked by regulators to attest to security controls. For example, the chief information officer (CIO) under the Sarbanes-Oxley (SOX) Act is required to describe IT security controls goals. Many CIOs point to their company's enforced security policies.

Policies Are Key to Repeatable Behavior

To achieve this repeatable behavior, you must measure both consistency and quality. Additionally, you will need to measure whether the implemented policy is achieving the desired results. It is not surprising to find processes that run for years while providing no real value. A typical example might be a report that was specially designed for an executive who has since left the company. The new executive continues to receive the report. He or she may even occasionally review it out of curiosity. But the executive never leverages its content for any real purpose. This report might be highly repeatable and sustainable but does not provide the desired results.

Security policies drive operational consistency by enforcing how information is handled the same way within business processes. Policies also force close oversight and measurement of the processes. Security policies often outline oversight requirements. They explain which measurements should be captured and how often reporting is required. The following oversight phases are typically found when trying to achieve operational consistency:

 TIP

Be sure to interview the individuals who perform the process. They will have insights beyond the measurements.

- **Monitor**—Monitor process execution.
- **Measure**—Measure consistency and quality.
- **Review**—Periodically review to ensure desired results are achieved.
- **Track**—Track defects, errors, and incidents.
- **Improve**—Improve quality continuously.

Policies Help Prevent Operational Deviation

Operational deviations are inevitable. Policies tend to cover broad topic areas and cannot foresee every possible situation. Technology is always evolving. What works on one set of technologies may not work on another. Product offerings or differences in customer demands may vary by business unit. There may be many reasons why a business may want to deviate from policy.

Operational deviation from policy in itself may not be a problem when there is a solid business reason. However, as the number of exceptions grows, the policy's credibility is potentially reduced. Security policies are put in place to reduce risk. Deviating from those policies could increase the risk and prevent meeting legal obligations.

To balance these interests, most organizations have an exception process. This is also called a "waiver process." Typically you submit a waiver request to a centrally managed team that reviews and approves the deviation. The waiver process examines the business rationale and tries to determine if the exception is necessary or not. When implementing a waiver process the following should be considered:

- **Independence**—Be independent of the business unit seeking approval.
- **Impact**—Examine the risk to the entire organization.
- **Benefits**—Understand the business benefits.
- **Mitigation**—Identify security controls outside policy.
- **Approvals**—Residual risk should be formally accepted by management.

Residual risk is the risk that remains after security controls have been applied. When the business cannot comply with policy, the residual risk needs to be measured and compensating controls considered. A compensating control can reduce the same risk identified by policy but in a different way as outlined in policy. Ideally you want to implement compensating controls that reduce the same amount of risks identified in policy. If not, at least reduce some of the risk. For example, when you cannot implement a preventive control as required by policy, consider using a detective control. These compensating controls may be outside policy but may be able to reduce some or all of the risk. Any remaining risk would then have to be properly approved. Proper approval includes vetting residual risk with those leaders who would be held accountable in the event the risk is realized. For example, if the application could not meet security policy requirements on protecting PII data, the CPO needs to approve the exception. Ultimately, if PII data is lost or stolen because of the policy exception, the CPO may have to explain to regulators why the exception was permitted.

CHAPTER SUMMARY

We manage risk every day of our lives. We choose when to go bed, when to wake up, what foods to eat, what route to drive our cars, and much more. Each decision has risk and rewards attached. This is no different in the business world. Many decisions face us daily. We often operate with incomplete information. We are faced with critical deadlines that could be more easily met by sharing information outside policy guidelines. As you gain experience, these decisions become more instinctive.

Businesses strive to maximize profit and reduce risks by producing consistent and reliable products or services. In part a business manages risk by clearly defining its requirements in the form of security policies. It designs security controls to enforce those requirements. The business will educate its employees through security awareness programs on evolving threats and expected behavior. Risk can be further reduced through legally binding agreements and liability insurance. Regardless of the methods used to reduce risk, the goal is to create value to the customer through secure, repeatable, and sustainable processes. It all starts by implementing and enforcing well-defined security policies.

KEY CONCEPTS AND TERMS

Acceptable use policies (AUPs)
Automated control
Breach
Chief privacy officer (CPO)
Confidentiality agreement (CA)
Corrective control
Data classification
Data encryption

Detective control
Digital assets
Full disclosure
Intellectual property (IP)
Label
Manual control
Non-disclosure agreement (NDA)

Operational deviation
Personally identifiable information (PII)
Preventive control
Public record
Residual risk
Security awareness program
Security policy compliance

CHAPTER 2 ASSESSMENT

1. What is policy compliance?

  A. The effort to follow an organization's policy
  B. When customers read a Web site policy statement
  C. Adherence to an organization's policy
  D. Failure to follow to an organization's policy

2. What is an automated control?

  A. A control that stops behavior immediately and does not rely on human decisions
  B. A control that does not stop behavior immediately and relies on human decisions
  C. A control that does not stop behavior immediately but automates notification of incident
  D. A control that stops behavior immediately and relies on human decisions

3. Which of the following is not a business driver?

  A. Ability to acquire the newest technology
  B. Cost of maintaining controls
  C. Ability to legally defend
  D. Customer satisfaction

4. A firewall is generally considered an example of a _____ control.

5. What is an information security policy?

  A. A policy that defines acceptable behavior of a customer
  B. A policy that defines what hardware to purchase
  C. A policy that defines how to protect information in any form
  D. A policy that defines the type of uniforms guards should wear

6. Which of the following is not a type of security control?

  A. Preventative
  B. Correlative
  C. Detective
  D. Corrective

7. Security awareness programs have two enforcement components: the _____ and the _____.

  A. Carrot, rewards
  B. Leaders, managers
  C. Board of directors, HR
  D. Carrot, stick

8. Most security policies require that a label be applied when a document is classified.

   A. True
   B. False

9. What are the benefits to having a security awareness program emphasize the business risk?

   A. Risk becomes more relevant to employees
   B. Security policies are more likely to be followed
   C. Provides employees a foundation to deal with unexpected risk
   D. All of the above

10. Within which of the following do security policies need to define PII legal requirements?

    A. The context of the business and location
    B. The limits set by the business to maximize profit
    C. What is acceptable by the shareholders
    D. Moral obligation to the greater good

11. Information used to open or access a bank account is generally considered PII data.

    A. True
    B. False

12. Which of the following is not a benefit of having an acceptable use policy?

    A. Outlines disciplinary action for improper behavior
    B. Prevents employees from misusing the Internet
    C. Reduces business liability
    D. Defines proper behavior while using the Internet

13. Lower risk exposure can be perceived only through actual measurement.

    A. True
    B. False

14. Which of the following do you need to measure to achieve operational consistency?

    A. Consistency
    B. Quality
    C. Results
    D. All of the above

15. Well-defined and properly implemented security policies help the business in which of the following ways?

    A. Maximize profit
    B. Reduce risk
    C. Produce consistent and reliable products
    D. All of the above

ENDNOTES

1. "Intellectual Property Law Definition." *(Legal-definitions.com,* n.d.). *http://www.legal-definitions.com/IP/intellectual-property-law.htm* (accessed March 5, 2010).

2. "Definition of: digital asset." *(Pcmag.com,* 2010). *http://www.pcmag.com/encyclopedia_term/0,2542,t=digital+asset&i=41283,00.asp* (accessed March 5, 2010).

3. "Safeguarding Against and Responding to the Breach of Personally Identifiable Information." (Whitehouse.gov, Office of Management and Budget memorandum, May 22, 2007). *http://www.whitehouse.gov/omb/memoranda/fy2007/m07-16.pdf* (accessed March 6, 2010).

U.S. Compliance Laws and Information Security Policy Requirements

W E HAVE SEEN MANY BENEFITS from the Internet. It allows us to talk to people around the world to exchange ideas and information. It allows us to buy products and services without leaving home. It has increased competition and made products, once rare, now affordable. It's not just the technology of the Internet that has changed our lives. The introduction of technology in companies gives employees unprecedented access to information and greatly improves the quality of products we use. Many factories use automation, and we see computerized safety equipment in ordinary products like car emission systems. In offices around the world, it is common to see desktops with an array of applications that give instant access to knowledge that would have been difficult or impossible to gain previously. Beyond access to knowledge, the applications allow us to collaborate and create new bodies of knowledge. Many of us create products not with hammer and nails but with email, spreadsheets, personal databases, and word processing software.

The result is that information and technology drive a significant part of our economy. Some estimate that U.S. online retail sales in 2009 rose to $141 billion.[1] Beyond direct sales, the Internet affects the general economy. For example, interactive advertising was responsible for $300 billion of economic activity in the United States in 2008, according to a study released in June 2009 by the Interactive Advertising Bureau (IAB).[2] The Federal Trade Commission (FTC) published an article in November 1999 that summarized the Internet economy figures as "the largest industry in our country."[3] The Internet has certainly grown since then, but regardless of the number you use, the broad impact of technology on the economy is immense.

No government can sit on the sidelines with so much at stake. Federal and state governments establish laws that define how to control, handle, share, and process sensitive information that this new economy relies on. Much of that information is about you! It's personal data about your finances, health, buying habits, and more. To these laws are added "regulations," typically written by civil servants to implement the authority of the law. "Regulators" are the individuals who help enforce these rules. Industries also try to "self-regulate," which means they create standards their members must follow. Failure to follow regulations or industry standards can result in fines or limits placed on the ability to operate. Gross violations of regulations can be seen as violation of criminal law. These violations can result in the arrest of officers of the company and possible jail time.

In this chapter, we discuss major government laws and their compliance requirements. When we refer to regulations in this chapter, we mean those that relate to U.S. laws. We see how these requirements will influence security policies. We examine major drivers for the regulations and the importance of protecting personal privacy. We show how to make compliant polices, standards, procedures, and guidelines. The chapter also examines industry standards that drive security policies. Any one of these laws or standards could take up the pages of an entire book. For our purposes, we focus on high-level principles that drive security policies and controls.

Chapter 3 Topics

This chapter covers the following topics and concepts:

- What U.S. compliance laws are and why they are important
- Who is protected by these laws
- How security policies are influenced by the laws
- What approaches are used to make security policies, standards, procedures, and guidelines comply with regulations
- What industry leading practices are
- Why industry standards are important

Chapter 3 Goals

When you complete this chapter, you will be able to:

- Compare and contrast different U.S. compliance laws
- Describe regulations and their importance in organizations
- Describe government drivers to implement regulations and their importance in maintaining compliance with laws
- Explain approaches to align policies with regulations
- Explain leading practices and how they fit into the industry

U.S. Compliance Laws

Tremendous economic benefits flow from private markets. These benefits often rely on the use of technology. There is no single way of looking at government's role in regulating or intervening in these markets. However, government is concerned with consumer protection, promoting a stable economy, and maintaining a reliable source of tax revenue. All three of these drivers are linked. If people feel safe using the Internet to buy goods and services, a stable economy emerges. When you have a stable sector of the economy, government has a reliable source of tax revenue. This is not to imply that any one of these drivers is the primary goal of government regulation. However, government regulations do exist, and the question is what to regulate and how much.

When you implement security policies, remember that there are pressures and tradeoffs. For example, you may have to place restrictive controls on data to comply with a regulation that limits how your business operates. As you balance competing interests, you must talk to business leaders to understand their priorities and issues. Security policies reflect how the business wishes to balance competing interests.

Shareholders of a company are investors who expect to make money. Maximizing profit and maintaining a healthy stock price is a business concern. The government focuses more on fairness, health, and safety issues. Both business and government goals face risks from the limitations and vulnerabilities of technology. The role of well-defined security policies is to be clear and concise on how these goals and vulnerabilities will be addressed. Figure 3-1 illustrates these competing interests—shareholder value, technology vulnerabilities and limitations, and regulations.

FIGURE 3-1

Pressures on security policies.

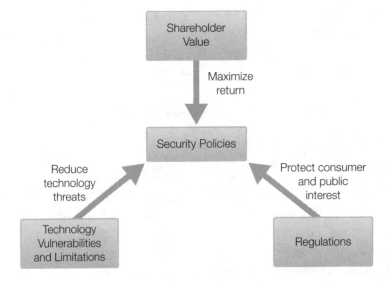

Government agencies that regulate information handling exist at the federal and state levels. These agencies sometimes have competing interests. As a result, laws often overlap requirements but are written from different perspectives. A federal banking regulation, for example, might define **data privacy** differently than a state law does. Competing regulatory agencies may have different missions and use different enforcement tools. Compliance can be difficult and costly with conflicting language and different interpretations. For example, a large U.S.-based bank needs to comply with hundreds of regulations.

Staying compliant means incurring the cost to keep up with changes in many laws, continually documenting evidence of compliance, and dealing with onsite visits of regulators. Staying compliant with regulations can be a distraction for businesses and the technology teams that support them. Yet they are very important. Therefore, some companies have staff whose job is to deal with regulatory compliance full time.

What Are They?

What are the major concerns of U.S. regulations? How do you manage competing interests in security policies? As much as these regulations might differ, there are also common concepts. If you can master these concepts, you can learn how to recognize these principles in regulations. This gives you the basic tool needed to keep your security policies compliant.

The best approach to regulatory compliance is common sense. Rather than building rules into security policies for each regulation, you should build in the key control concepts found in many regulations. By mapping these key control concepts to specific security policies, you can quickly demonstrate compliance across a broad set of regulations.

In this chapter, it's not practical to discuss all key concepts for information security in every U.S. regulation. Instead, you will learn about several major regulations. These regulations deal with consumer rights and personal privacy. These laws protect consumers from potential scams and ensure the privacy of personal information. **Consumer rights** in e-commerce broadly deal with creating rules on how to handle a consumer's transaction and other information. **Personal privacy** in e-commerce broadly deals with how to handle personal information and what it is used for. Table 3-1 identifies key concepts found in many regulations that influence what will appear in your security policies.

Federal Information Security Management Act (FISMA)

The Federal Information Security Management Act (FISMA) is a good example of government self-regulation. The federal government is unique in that it can identify the standards it wants to follow and passes laws requiring the standards to be followed. FISMA was put into law in 2002.

TABLE 3-1 Key concepts contained in U.S. compliance laws affecting information security policies.

CONCEPT	OBJECTIVE
Full disclosure	The concept that individuals should know what information about them is being collected. They should be told how that information is being used.
Limited use of personal data	The concept that only the data needed for the transaction should be collected. Basically, do not collect more information than you need to provide the product or service.
Opt-in/opt-out	The practice of asking permission on how personal information can be used beyond its original purpose. For example, a real estate company asking permission of someone who sold their home if their information can be shared with a moving company.
Data privacy	Expectations on how personal information should be protected and limits placed on how the data should be shared.
Informed consent	The concept the person is of legal age, capable, has the needed facts, and without undue pressure can make an informed judgment.
Public interest	The concept that an organization has an obligation to the general public beyond its self-interest. Although a vague term, it's not unusual for regulators to look at the impact an organization has on the industry or the economy in general.

> **NOTE**
>
> The difference between opting in and opting out generally refers to clicking a box on a Web page. In an **opt-in** process, unless the consumer clicks the "Yes" box, no additional service is offered. In an **opt-out** process, the consumer is automatically enrolled in a service unless he or she clicks the "No" box or de-selects the "Yes" box.

FISMA requires government agencies to adopt a common set of information security standards. Some parts of the government go beyond these standards, such as the military. For many government agencies, FISMA creates mandatory requirements to ensure the integrity, confidentiality, and availability of data. If your organization processes data for the government, you may be required to follow these same standards. FISMA also requires that agencies send annual reviews to the Office of Management and Budget (OMB).

The National Institute of Standards and Technology (NIST) is responsible for developing FISMA-mandated information security standards and procedures. Each agency is then responsible for adopting them as part of their agency's information security policies. NIST standards, processes, and guidelines are available at *http://csrc.nist.gov/publications/PubsSPs.html*.

NIST publications outline a complete set of security standards and processes. To be compliant, your policies must include key security control requirements. Some of these key requirements include:

- **Inventory**—The NIST standards require an inventory of hardware, software, and information. The inventory identifies the type of information handled, how data passes to the systems, and special attention to national security systems.

- **Categorize by risk level**—The NIST standards outline an approach to classify risk. They outline how to map risk level to computer systems and information. The risk drives what security is to be applied.

- **Security controls**—The NIST standards outline which controls should be applied and when. They outline how these controls are documented and approved. It is a risk-based approach giving some flexibility to the agency to tailor controls to meet its operational needs.

- **Risk assessment**—The NIST standards define and outline the process to conduct risk assessments. **Risk assessments** are an essential part of a risk-based security approach. The risk assessment results drive the type of security controls to be applied.

- **System security plan**—The NIST standards require a formal security plan for major systems and for the system or application owner. The security plan serves as a road map. It is updated to keep current with threats and is an important part of a certification and accreditation process.

- **Certification and accreditation**—This process occurs after the system is documented, controls tested, and risk assessment completed. It is required before going live with a major system. Once a system is certified and accredited, responsibility shifts to the owner to operate the system. This process is also referred to as the "security certification" process.

- **Continuous monitoring**—All certified and accredited systems must be continuously monitored. Monitoring includes looking at new threats, changes to the system, and how well the controls are working. Sometimes a system has so many changes that it must be re-certified.

Health Insurance Portability and Accountability Act (HIPAA)

The Health Insurance Portability and Accountability Act (HIPAA) became law in 1996. The law protects a person's privacy. If you handle someone's health records, you must adhere to HIPAA. This includes doctor's offices, hospitals, clinics, and insurance companies. The law recognizes that digital data exchange of health records, such as between insurance companies and doctor's offices, is a necessity. The law wants to make sure that patient privacy is maintained.

FYI

The U.S. Department of Health and Human Services has several publications on
HIPAA privacy and security standards at *http://www.cms.hhs.gov/HIPAAGenInfo/04
_PrivacyandSecurityStandards.asp.*

The HIPAA law defines someone's health record as protected health information
(PHI). The term PHI refers to both digital and physical paper copies of health records.
Electronic PHI (EPHI) refers to just the electronic form of PHI records. HIPAA establishes
privacy rules that outline how EPHI can be collected, processed, and disclosed. There are
significant penalties for violating these rules. Given the sensitive nature of one's personal
health records, this regulation is usually taken very seriously and affects:

- **Health care providers**—Doctors, hospitals, clinics, and others
- **Health plans**—Those that pay the cost for the medical care such
  as insurance companies
- **Health care clearinghouses**—Those that process and facilitate billing

To be HIPAA-compliant, the following key control requirements must be in your
security policies:

- **Administrative safeguards**—Refers to the formal security policies and
  procedures that map to HIPAA security standards. It also refers to the
  governance of the security policies and their implementation
- **Physical safeguards**—Refers to the physical security of computer systems
  and the physical health records
- **Technical safeguards**—Refers to the controls that use technology to protect
  information assets. The law also requires risk assessment and risk-based
  management approach to information security

Gramm-Leach-Bliley Act (GLBA)

The Gramm-Leach-Bliley Act (GLBA) became law in 1999. The law is not focused
on technology. In fact, the reason for the law was to repeal past laws so that banks,
investment companies, and other financial services companies could merge. Prior
to GLBA, banks, for example, were restricted on the types of products they could offer.
However, under what is known as Section 501(b), the law outlines information security
requirements for the privacy of customer information.

The law is enforced through regulators who are members of the Federal Financial
Institutions Examination Council (FFIEC). The FFIEC publishes booklets of what type
of computer security policies and controls must be in place to be compliant with GLBA.
These booklets define availability, integrity, confidentiality, accountability, and assurance
as key objectives.

GLBA applies to any financial institution defined as "any institution the business of which is engaging in financial activities as described in section 4(k) of the Bank Holding Company Act (12 U.S.C. § 1843(k))." This is broadly defined to mean any organization that lends, exchanges, transfers, invests, or safeguards money or securities. It applies to many types of businesses, such as banks, mortgage companies, brokerage houses, universities that offer financial aid, credit and financial advisors, medical providers that offer payment plans, auto dealers, relocation services, or even a local supermarket that sells money orders.

The FFIEC booklets are publicly available through the council's Web site. The following Web site introduces the 501(b) rules: *http://www.ffiec.gov/ffiecinfobase/booklets/information_security/00_introduction.htm*.

To be GLBA-compliant, your security policies must include the following key components:

- **Governance**—Requires a strong governance structure in place. This includes formal reporting to the board of directors. Most boards receive formal GLBA reporting through the audit committee. The head of information security usually writes this report each quarter.
- **Information security risk assessment**—Requires a well-defined **information security risk assessment** to identify threats, potential attacks, and impacts to the organization
- **Information security strategy**—Requires a formal security plan to reach compliance
- **Security controls implementation**—Requires a process to properly design and install security controls that meet the security plan objectives
- **Security monitoring**—Requires continuous monitoring of security controls. This is to ensure that the design meets the objectives. This is event-based monitoring and includes incident response.
- **Security monitoring and updating**—Requires monitoring of trends, incidents, and business strategies, and appropriate updates to the security plan

Sarbanes-Oxley (SOX) Act

The Sarbanes-Oxley (SOX) Act became law in 2002. The law was enacted in reaction to a series of accusations of corporate fraud. Some companies were accused of "cooking the accounting books" or making illegal loans to their top executives. Companies such as Enron and WorldCom became symbols of corporate greed and corruption. Enron filed for bankruptcy in 2001 amid accusations of cooking the books to inflate its stock price. WorldCom filed for bankruptcy in 2002 amid accusations of illegal loans to its chief executive officer (CEO), as well as billions in accounting fraud to inflate the stock price. These two highly visible corporate fraud cases shook shareholder and public confidence. SOX was enacted to restore confidence in the markets.

 NOTE

SOX sets up strict rules on accounting methods and requires new corporate governance measures to be taken by publicly traded companies. SOX does not apply to privately held companies.

3

U.S. Compliance Laws and Security Policy

SOX goes well beyond information security policies. It also describes how a company should report earnings, valuations, corporate responsibilities, and executive compensation. The act is intended to improve the financial accuracy and public disclosure to investors. In fact, some argue the act goes too far and is too costly. This chapter focuses on those portions that affect security policies known as SOX 404.

The basic idea behind SOX 404 is to require security policies and controls that provide confidence in the accuracy of financial statements. In other words, security policies must ensure the integrity of the financial data. Independent testing of these controls is required. Additionally, top executives are required to sign off quarterly that these controls meet SOX 404 requirements or explain why they did not.

The act created the Public Company Accounting Oversight Board (PCAOB). The PCAOB sets accounting and auditing standards. The Securities and Exchange Commission (SEC) is responsible for enforcing SOX. The challenge for information security is that SOX 404 sets broad IT objectives. It does not define how to comply. Rather than developing new information security and control standards, the PCAOB and SEC have endorsed using industry best practice frameworks. The following are endorsed frameworks that companies commonly use to meet SOX 404 requirements. These frameworks are widely used by external auditors as well to certify SOX compliance:

- **Committee of Sponsoring Organizations (COSO)**—As it relates to security policies, this organization creates rules for implementing internal controls and governance structures.
- **Control Objectives for Information and related Technology (COBIT)**—Created by the Information Systems Audit and Control Association (ISACA). This framework is an internationally recognized best practice. The framework contains four domains and defines 34 core IT processes. Chapter 1 addressed the four domains of COBIT.

COBIT in many ways is one-stop shopping for SOX security policies and controls. The 34 processes define a rich range of activities: strategic planning, governance, life cycle, implementation, production support, and monitoring. The framework fits in and supports the COSO framework. The COBIT framework allows COSO to focus on the business side while COBIT focuses on the IT side. By leveraging both, you are able to bridge control requirements, technology issues, business risk, and shareholder concerns. The reason the framework is so popular among regulators, auditors, and IT risk professionals is that if you implement the COBIT framework, you are most likely SOX 404-compliant.

FYI

ISACA has a number of publications publicly available through its Web site. You can find an executive summary of COBIT 4.1 at *http://www.isaca.org/ContentManagement/ ContentDisplay.cfm?ContentID=50254.*

Family Educational Rights and Privacy Act (FERPA)

The Family Educational Rights and Privacy Act (FERPA) was put into law in 1974. This law applies to educational institutions such as college and universities. Any educational institution must protect the privacy of its student records and must provide students access to their own records. This gives students a way to correct errors and control disclosure of their records.

The Family Policy Compliance Office of the U.S. Department of Education enforces the act. The law broadly defines education records as any information related to the educational process that can uniquely identify the student. This has been widely interpreted as any student information from financial means to class lists to grades. The student records can be in any form from handwritten notes to digital files. There are exclusions such as law enforcement or campus security records. For the purpose of this discussion, the important point is that this broad set of student records (in any form) must be protected.

To be FERPA-compliant, security policies must contain the following key elements:

- **Awareness**—The school must post its FERPA security policies and provide awareness of them.
- **Permission**—Generally, schools must have recorded permission to share the student's education records.
- **Directory information**—The school can make directory information (such as name, address, telephone number and date of birth) about the student publicly available but must provide the student with a chance to opt out of such public disclosure.
- **Exclusions**—The school can share information without permission for legitimate education evaluation reasons as well as for health and safety reasons.

Security policies must ensure records are kept when student permissions are not obtained under the exclusions. In addition, policies must ensure that opt-in and opt-out records are properly maintained for historical purposes to record student permissions.

Children's Internet Protection Act (CIPA)

The Children's Internet Protection Act (CIPA) was put into law in 2000. The law tells schools and libraries that receive federal funding that they must block pornographic and explicit sexual material on their computers. The law attempts to limit children's exposure to such material.

> **FYI**
>
> The American Library Association and the American Civil Liberties Union brought a lawsuit that challenged CIPA. The lawsuit claimed that CIPA violated free speech rights of adults. It also claimed it would have unintended consequences such as preventing minors from getting information about topics such as breast cancer. The U.S. Supreme Court heard the case of *United States v. American Library Assn., Inc.* (02-361) 539 U.S. 194 in 2003. The court upheld the law. Today only schools and libraries that receive E-Rate funding for Internet access must comply with CIPA. A school or library can choose not to accept the E-Rate funding and would then not have to comply with CIPA.

The Federal Communications Commission (FCC) establishes the rules that schools and libraries must follow. The CIPA regulation was challenged in a lawsuit. The Supreme Court heard the lawsuit. The basis of the challenge is that restricting access to information is unconstitutional. Additionally, there were questions about whether the technology would end up blocking sites not originally intended by the law. The result of the court challenge was mixed. The court held that the CIPA law was constitutional. However, the courts do require schools and libraries to unblock sites when requested by an adult. The FCC has several publications on CIPA available at *http://www.fcc.gov/cgb/consumerfacts/cipa.html*.

Here are key CIPA components that must be adopted in your security policies:

- **Awareness**—The school or library must post its CIPA security policies and provide awareness of them.
- **Internet filters**—Best efforts must be made to keep the **Internet filters** current so that only the targeted material intended by CIPA is blocked.
- **Unblocking**—There must be a process to allow the filter to be unblocked or disabled for adults who request access to blocked sites.

Why Did They Come About?

These laws recognize the power of information. The more personal the data, the more powerful the information. The power comes from the impact that personal information has in our lives. It affects what type job we can get, the car we can buy, and the home we can afford. It also determines the quality of medical care we receive. The misuse and abuse of this information is equally powerful and can make our lives miserable. Identity theft is a major problem. It can take years of effort to restore a credit rating. We've all heard stories of millions of credit cards stolen each year. While slow to react, the government does respond to these headlines and public pressure.

Many of these laws have come about to protect our personal privacy and to limit how companies can use the information. When millions of citizens' personal data is lost or stolen, many questions are raised. The public expects government to protect us. In 2010, a study quoted the FTC as saying that identity theft was on the rise, with an increase of 22 percent over the prior year. The study also reported that the cost to the consumer was more than $50 billion.[4] We know the cost to business is also high. As a result, a number of regulations in recent years have come about to prevent such breaches. These regulations also hold an organization accountable when they occur.

Whom Do the Laws Protect?

Is an individual's privacy the government's sole concern? No, it is not. As discussed in the SOX section in this chapter, there are broader implications than personal privacy. Three major groups receive protection from these laws:

- **Individual**—A number of laws focus on protecting an individual's private information.
- **Shareholder**—A number of laws are designed to provide confidence in the markets. When investors feel that a company's financials and risks are properly managed, the investors feel they can make informed judgments. This promotes a healthy economy.
- **Public interest**—The idea that an organization has an obligation to the general public beyond their self-interest. Although a vague term, regulators often look at the impact a company has on the industry group or the economy in general.

Let's be clear. The world is not perfect, and the goals of regulations are not always achieved. In fact, sometimes regulations get in the way of doing the right thing. Regardless of the value you place on regulations, you shouldn't treat them as abstract concepts. Regulations do affect security policies. They limit how business can collect, store, and process information. Security policies are looked to as a way to enforce these limitations.

It's an accepted concept that when everyone has to follow the same rules, the playing field is level. Without regulation, companies feel the pressure to take shortcuts to maintain competitive advantage. Regulations remove some of this pressure because everyone must comply. This allows organizations to meet their obligations to the public and economy. In other words, doing the "right thing" is not a matter of cost or advantages, it's part of the business culture and the law.

Which Laws Require Proper Security Controls Including Policies?

Policies document how the organization is to perform and conduct business. As you learned in earlier chapters, you cannot design effective security controls without good security policies. Then, by definition, all laws that seek to protect or control data must have good security controls and policies.

Regardless of the information being protected, a security control needs to be designed and implemented to enforce the control. If a law requires any type of information protection, the law indirectly requires proper security controls. This includes physical security controls to protect information in physical form such as paper reports.

> **NOTE**
> Every regulatory requirement on the handling of data should map to one or more security policies.

Which Laws Require Proper Security Controls for Handling Privacy Data?

The heading for this section poses a bit of trick question—the answer is most laws. This chapter discusses HIPAA, GLBA, and FERPA, which call out specific security controls for handling privacy data. You also have to look at the standards these laws leverage. For example, NIST standards require protection of personal privacy. In the case of FISMA, it does not emphasize privacy as much as HIPAA. However, FISMA does require security controls to protect privacy.

A good rule of thumb is whenever your organization handles personal information, be sure your security policies and controls protect privacy. Whether at a state or federal level, if you are not currently obligated to do so, there's a good chance at some point you will be. Over time, it's far less expensive and easier to implement core privacy principles, such as those in Table 3-1, and then to implement specific controls to keep pace with each changing law. One can also argue it's simply the right thing to do.

The only conflict comes when an organization wants to use the information beyond the scope of these core principles. At that point, management should determine if using the information violates current law. If not, then a determination can be made to either change the core principles or make an exception. This pushback from business to use information beyond the core principles is healthy. It results in a candid conversation with the business about current regulations and the values the organization wants to embrace. The approach results in better understanding of the law, awareness of core organizational values, and a stronger foundation of controls.

TIP

An organization's privacy or compliance officer is a good source for determining what should be in security policies to meet regulation requirements.

Aligning Security Policies and Controls with Regulations

You have reviewed six major laws at a high level and their affects on security policies and controls. Depending on your organization, you may have hundreds of laws to deal with. So how do you cope? There are many factors you must consider to ensure your security policies and controls align with regulations, such as the following:

- **Inventory**—Make sure you have a solid inventory of hardware, software, and information. You need know to where the information is collected, stored, and processed.

- **Business requirements**—Your business is ultimately accountable to regulators. Ensure the business understands the data handling requirements of each regulation. Map how the business handles data to the security policy. For example, is the customer presented with an opt-in or opt-out check box? Even these simple choices may have regulatory implications.

- **Security policies**—Security policies need to reflect these business requirements. It's equally important to establish a core set of principles, such as those in Table 3-1. These core principles allow you to educate the business and address a significant number of regulations.

- **Security framework**—The selection of a security framework allows you to show regulators that you are using best practices. Use widely accepted standards, procedures, and guidelines. Ideally, you want all instructions on how to handle data to be a policy, standard, or procedure. If you cannot apply a standard in certain cases, you can make the instructions a guideline. If you can apply the instructions most of the time, make it a standard or procedure. Even if sometimes the instructions cannot be applied you can always document the exception.

- **Security control mapping**—When you build security controls, be sure to map them to the related policy or policies. Policies also map to regulations. **Security control mappings** are important to demonstrate coverage of regulatory requirements. It shows the importance of each security control.

- **Monitoring and testing**—Your organization must monitor and test any security control related to regulatory compliance. You should try to monitor and test all security controls. If you cannot, prioritize the controls starting with the most important ones.

- **Evidence**—At some point you will be required to provide regulators with **evidence.** Regulators want to see a well-thought-out approach to compliance. The security policies, framework, and control mapping is a good start. The mapping demonstrates a thorough understanding and intent to comply. Your monitoring and testing efforts also provide evidence that things are working as planned.

You learned earlier in the chapter that COSO and COBIT are widely accepted frameworks. Other frameworks are equally important. A good source is publications from the International Organization for Standardization (ISO), which is covered in Chapter 11. Another important framework is the Information Technology and Infrastructure Library (ITIL). ITIL is a set of practices and predefined procedures for managing specific IT services such as change management. You will learn about ITIL later in this chapter.

Let's look at how these frameworks help you build security policies and controls. Make sure you understand the security requirements for each regulation and your business. Also be sure your organization understands the data handling requirements of the regulation. Then you can start building or updating security policies, standards, controls, and procedures. The following is one approach:

1. Document the concepts and principles you will adopt.
2. Apply them to security policies and standards.
3. Develop security controls and procedures.

The typical approach involves moving from conceptual principles to implementing specific controls. Figure 3-2 illustrates this point using COSO, COBIT, and ITIL. In this example, COSO provides the necessary governance structure. Although COBIT defines policies and controls requirements, you can then define your procedures using ITIL predefined libraries.

FIGURE 3-2

Security policies
and controls mapping
to frameworks.

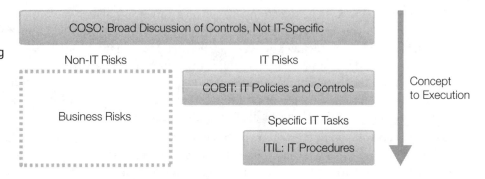

The ability to map to existing standards and frameworks is powerful. This approach leverages years of experience across industries. It also provides confidence to regulators and auditors that you are properly managing risks. Even if you fail to catch a risk, there's a strong likelihood that the framework will mitigate the risk through other means. It also reduces implementation time and produces high-quality policies, procedures, and security controls.

The approach is straightforward. The ability to quickly implement is not. The challenge is not in the approach but in volume. As mentioned, you might have hundreds of regulations to follow. Add to that hundreds of end user applications, thousands of users, and millions of files. You might have an untold number of controls. Suddenly the volume can get overwhelming. That's why it's important not to take shortcuts with the key considerations listed above.

Industry Leading Practices and Self-Regulation

You learned how news stories and public pressure drive government regulations. They also drive many industries to more self-regulation. The hope is to demonstrate to the government and the public that these industries are aware of the problem and are taking action. An industry prefers to self-regulate for two key reasons, cost and flexibility. There's a perception that regulations increase cost because they can be restrictive and require lots of compliance evidence to be collected. Additionally, regulations can require specific solutions to a problem. Retaining the flexibility to select from an array of solutions and apply new technology is one reason given to avoid regulations. The counter argument is that, without laws, industries won't fully address problems.

Regardless of your viewpoint on the merits of regulation, the result is that industries create standards over time that may become best practices. The term "best practices" is commonly understood. However, it can be confusing when trying to understand industry standards. The term "best practices" is overused and difficult to quantify. What does "best" compare with? Is a simple solution best because it costs the least? Or is a solution better because it is more reliable? Another term with more precision is "leading practice," which is easier to quantify. If most members of an industry adopt a method, it's considered to be "leading." It might be the best solution, but that's not always the case.

Regulated companies look to leading practices as one way to shield themselves from regulators. If regulators have confidence in a leading practice by virtue of adopting it, a company should be confident it is complying with the law. You may not always be able to apply the best solution, but it's important to be able to tell a regulator that you do conform to industry norms.

> **NOTE**
>
> Most information security professionals belong to associations or regional groups. There are also online communities. These communities share solutions and publish survey results. It's important to take advantage of this knowledge to understand if you are using leading practices.

Some Important Industry Standards

Payment Card Industry Data Security Standard (PCI DSS)

Payment Card Industry Data Security Standard (PCI DSS) is a worldwide information security standard that describes how to protect credit card information. If you accept Visa, MasterCard, or American Express, you are required to follow PCI DSS. These card companies formed the Payment Card Industry Security Standards Council to create the standard. The PCI DSS standard was released in 2006. The standard applies to every organization that stores, processes, or exchanges cardholder information.

The standard requires an organization to have specific PCI DSS security policies and controls in place. The organization must also have these controls validated. If you are small merchant, you can perform a Self-Assessment Questionnaire (SAQ). Large-volume merchants must obtain their validation through a Qualified Security Assessor (QSA). Failing to validate, or failing the validation, can result in fines from the credit card companies. In extreme cases of noncompliance, you may be prevented from handling credit cards. Taking credit cards away could put you out of business.

The PCI DSS is an information security framework, so it contains a lot of technical requirements. Two in particular have been a challenge for organizations to implement: network segmentation and encryption. PCI DSS strongly encourages isolating credit card systems at a network layer. For many open network designs and shared systems, this is a challenge. If you cannot segment the systems that contain cardholder data, PCI DSS requires that all systems on that segment must comply with PCI DSS. This means if you have 20 systems on a segment and one processes credit card information, all 20 systems should comply with PCI DSS standards. This could be expensive. The second major challenge is encrypting data at rest. As discussed in previous chapters, encrypting data in transit is common over the Internet and public networks. Encrypting data at rest, however, can be technically challenging and at times not feasible.

> **TIP**
>
> The PCI DSS materials are free and publicly available through the PCI Security Standard Council Web site at *https://www.pcisecuritystandards.org/*.

There are six control objectives within the PCI DSS standard. To be compliant, you need to include these control objectives in your security policies and controls. These control objectives are:

- **Build and maintain a secure network**—Refers to having specific firewall, system password, and other security network layer controls.
- **Protect cardholder data**—Specifies how cardholder data is stored and protected. Also sets rules on the encryption of the data.
- **Maintain a vulnerability management program**—Specifies how to maintain secure systems and applications. Including the required use of antivirus software.
- **Implement strong access control measures**—Refers to restricting access to cardholder data on a need-to-know basis. It requires physical controls in place and individual unique IDs when accessing cardholder data.
- **Regularly monitor and test networks**—Requires monitoring access to cardholder. Also requires periodic penetration testing of the network.
- **Maintain an information security policy**—Requires that security policies reflect the PCI DSS requirements. Requires these policies are kept current and an awareness program is implemented.

Statement on Auditing Standard 70 (SAS 70)

The American Institute of Certified Public Accountants (AICPA) created **Statement on Auditing Standard 70 (SAS 70)**. It is a widely accepted auditing standard. A SAS 70 audit examines an organization's control environment. This usually includes an audit of the information security controls. A SAS 70 allows an independent auditor (called a "service auditor") to review an organization's control environment. The service auditor then issues an independent opinion in a cover letter. The actual audit report and opinion is provided to the organization being examined.

 NOTE

The AICPA has free publications on SAS 70 available at *http://www.aicpa.org/*.

The popularity of SAS 70 comes from the use of the opinion letters. Anyone trying to buy services from a vendor should ensure the data is protected. Organizations often request a SAS 70 opinion letter from a vendor to help build that confidence. Vendors often promote how well they passed a SAS 70 audit as way of selling their service.

There is a mutual benefit in having a SAS 70 audit performed. To the customer, it provides some assurance that their vendor's control environment has been audited. The benefit to the vendor is they can say there's been independent opinion that the customer's data is protected. Another reason SAS 70 is popular is the cost structure. You can spread the cost of a SAS 70 audit across many customers. However, many companies don't charge their customers at all. Those companies consider the cost of a SAS 70 audit as a marketing expense or the cost of doing business.

The opinion of the auditor depends in part on the scope of the SAS 70 review. When requesting a SAS 70 opinion, be sure to ask for the scope of the examination. This helps you understand the context of the opinion. For example, if you are concerned whether a vendor can recover its system in case of an outage, be sure to ask if backup and recovery were included in the SAS 70 review. Generally, SAS 70 examinations are broad. But they can be narrowly scoped. If you accept a vendor's SAS 70 audit results, be sure you know what you are placing reliance on.

Does a SAS 70 truly test if controls provide adequate safeguards to protect data? That depends in part on the type of SAS 70 audit performed. There are two types of SAS 70 audits:

- **Type I**—This is basically a design review of the controls. The auditor's opinion would note if the controls are designed well. The audit also looks at documented policies and procedures. The opinion states if the policies, controls, and procedures would meet the control objective stated. In other words, if you did what you said, you should get the results you expected.

- **Type II**—Includes everything in Type I. In addition, the controls are actually tested to see if those controls are properly installed and working effectively.

Information Technology Infrastructure Library (ITIL)

The **Information Technology Infrastructure Library (ITIL)** is a series of books that describe IT practices and procedures. The collection of books originally came from a United Kingdom government initiative. The first version was published in 1989 as ITIL v1.0. The next version was published in 2001 as ITIL v2.0. The current version as of this writing is ITIL v3.0, which was published in 2007.

ITIL has evolved over time from over 30 booklets on different topics to a unified IT service management (ITSM) approach. ITIL v3 focuses on the entire service life cycle. It outlines goals, activities, tasks, inputs, and outputs.

The ITL official Web site states "ITIL provides a cohesive set of best practices, drawn from the public and private sectors internationally."[5] The concept behind ITSM is to use ITIL to optimize the IT infrastructure, lower costs, and improve quality.

ITIL is not free and can be expensive to buy the entire library. You can purchase just the ITIL books of specific interest. The official Web site has some free material at *http://www.itil-officialsite.com/home/home.asp*.

3

U.S. Compliance Laws and Security Policy

ITIL v3 has five core books called volumes. The following outlines each of the five volumes:

- **Service Strategy**—Relates to how to define the governance and portfolio of services. This includes aligning to the business and IT finance requirements

- **Service Design**—Relates to the actual design of the service and controls. Here is where you take into account all the business and technology concerns. For example, risk management, capacity management, availability, information security, and compliance are among the elements considered.

- **Service Transition**—Relates to the transition of services into production. For example, validation testing, release management, and change management are among the elements considered.

- **Service Operation**—Relates to ongoing support of the service. For example, incident and problem management, and access management, are among the elements considered.

- **Continual Service Improvement**—Relates to continuous improvement of the service. For example measuring, reporting, and managing service level agreements (SLAs) are among the elements considered.

CHAPTER SUMMARY

You learned in this chapter how important it is to conform to U.S. compliance laws. It is important for an organization to build trust with its customers, shareholders, and the public. You also learned the importance of compliance to the broad economy and how it serves the public interest. The chapter examined a number of major compliance regulations. From these examples, it is easy to see the reason why many regulations have come about. Sometimes regulations result from public pressure when something goes wrong. The chapter examined these pressures and motivations of both the government and the industry. We discussed how the industry tries to self-regulate to avoid government regulation to keep costs down and retain flexibility.

The chapter also examined how security policies, controls, and procedures need to align with regulations. We discussed how to create this alignment. We also examined how to show evidence of compliance to a regulator. We discussed the challenges to comply with regulation and industry standards. We talked about the challenges facing an organization that is required to follow hundreds of regulations. Finally, a key lesson in this chapter is not to chase laws by building specific security policies and controls tailored to each new regulation. You should base policies on key concepts that address a broad range of regulatory concerns such as consumer protection and privacy.

KEY CONCEPTS AND TERMS

Consumer rights	Internet filters	Risk assessment
Data privacy	Opt-in	Security control mapping
Evidence	Opt-out	Shareholder
Information security risk assessment	Payment Card Industry Data Security Standard (PCI DSS)	Statement on Auditing Standard 70 (SAS 70)
Information Technology and Infrastructure Library (ITIL)	Personal privacy	

3

U.S. Compliance Laws and Security Policy

CHAPTER 3 ASSESSMENT

1. When creating laws and regulations, the government's sole concern is the privacy of the individual.
   A. True
   B. False

2. Which of the following are pressures on creating security policies?
   A. Shareholder value
   B. Regulations
   C. Technology vulnerabilities and limitations
   D. B and C only
   E. All of the above

3. Which of the following laws require proper security controls for handling privacy data?
   A. HIPAA
   B. GLBA
   C. FERPA
   D. B and C Only
   E. All of the above

4. Which of the following are control objectives for PCI DSS?
   A. Maintain an information security policy
   B. Protect cardholder data
   C. Alert when credit cards are illegally used
   D. A and B only
   E. None of the above

5. A SAS 70 audit is popular because it allows a service auditor to review an organization's _____ and issue an independent opinion.

6. Health care providers are those that process and facilitate billing.
   A. True
   B. False

7. The law that attempts to limit children's exposure to sexually explicit material is _____.

8. It's easier to quantify leading practices than best practices.
   A. True
   B. False

9. You should always write new security policies each time a new regulation is issued.
   A. True
   B. False

10. What should you ask for to gain confidence that a vendor's security controls are adequate?
    A. A SAS 70 Type I audit
    B. A SAS 70 Type II audit
    C. A list of all internal audits
    D. All of the above

11. Why is it important to map regulatory requirements to policies and controls?
    A. To demonstrate compliance to regulators
    B. To ensure regulatory requirements are covered
    C. To demonstrate the importance of a security control
    D. All of the above

ENDNOTES

1. "E-Commerce Market Size and Trends." (MachroTech.com, 2009). *http://www.machrotech.com/services/ecommerce-marketsize-statistics.asp* (accessed March 22, 2010).

2. "Ad-Supported Internet Contributes $300 Billion to U.S. Economy, Has Created 3.1 Million U.S. Jobs, Confirms Groundbreaking Study." (IAB, June 10, 2009). *http://www.iab.net/about_the_iab/recent_press_releases/press_release_archive/press_release/pr-061009-value* (accessed March 22, 2010).

3. Swindle, Orson. "A Common Sense Approach To High Tech." Federal Trade Commission, FTC.gov, June 25, 2007). *http://www.ftc.gov/speeches/swindle/sandiego.shtm* (accessed March 22, 2010).

4. Finklea, Kristin M. "Identity Theft: Trends and Issues." (Federation of American Scientists, FAS.org, January 5, 2010). *http://www.fas.org/sgp/crs/misc/R40599.pdf* (accessed March 24, 2010).

5. ITIL. *http://www.itil-officialsite.com/home/home.asp* (accessed March 22, 2010).

Business Challenges Within the Seven Domains of IT Responsibility

SMALL AND MEDIUM-SIZE ORGANIZATIONS can have millions of transactions occurring every day between customers, employees, and suppliers. Today, many systems are automated. They generate their own transactions in the form of online product queries, searches, inventory checks, authorization checks, and log entries. Tracking of product, pricing, invoicing, service calls, e-mail, instant messages, support tickets, and order processing all require data. One touch of a keyboard generates potentially hundreds of transactions in today's complex business environment. All of this information needs to be protected. Whether the data is stored "at rest" on a hard drive or "in transit" over the network, regardless of form or method of access, threats to the information must be considered.

Like most technology problems that are enormous in size, scope, and complexity, the best approach to finding a solution is to break down the problem into manageable pieces. You can apply the same concept to solving complex information security needs for your organization. One approach is to follow the data as it is collected, transmitted, processed, and stored. In this way, you can then determine what access requirements exist and address various threats. For example, the threats to information are different when a user accesses data over the Internet versus computers processing information in a secure data center.

In this chapter, we divide the IT environment into seven logical domains. Each domain represents a logical part of the technology infrastructure. We follow the data through these seven domains to understand the business challenges collecting, processing, and storing information. We also consider the business, technical, and security policy challenges that affect organizations.

Chapter 4 Topics

This chapter covers the following topics and concepts:

- What the seven domains of a typical IT infrastructure are
- How security policies mitigate risk within the seven domains

Chapter 4 Goals

When you complete this chapter, you will be able to:

- Identify the seven domains of typical IT infrastructure
- Identify the risks and concerns involved with the various domains
- Describe the top business risks within each of the seven domains
- Understand how security policies map to business requirements
- Understand the role security policies play in mitigating business risks within the domains

The Seven Domains of a Typical IT Infrastructure

Examining risk from a data perspective means to follow data through an end-to-end process. As you move through your technology infrastructure, you'll find similar risk and policies issues. You can group common risks and related policy issues into **domains**. These domains share similarities but are distinctive enough to allow logical separation into more manageable secure areas.

In this section of the chapter, you will learn the definition of these domains. This section examines the attributes of each domain so you can gain a better understanding of the issues. Later in the chapter, you will examine the business issues and policy challenges of these problems, along with risk mitigation techniques.

Figure 4-1 illustrates seven typical domains of an IT infrastructure, which include:

- **User**—This domain refers to any user accessing information. This includes customers, employees, consultants, contractors, or any other third party. These users are "end users."
- **Workstation**—This domain refers to any computing device used by end users. Most times this means a desktop or laptop that is the main computer for the end user. For the purposes of this chapter, a workstation means any device used to access information, such as a desktop computer or a smartphone.

- **LAN**—This domain refers to the organization's local area network (LAN) infrastructure. A LAN connects two or more computers within a small area. The small area could be a home, office, or group of buildings.
- **WAN**—A wide area network (WAN) covers a large geographical area. The Internet is an example of a WAN. A private WAN can be built for a specific company to link offices across the country or globally.
- **LAN-to-WAN**—This domain refers to the technical infrastructure that connects the organization's LAN to a WAN. This allows end users to access the Internet. Likewise, end users can use a WAN to access a LAN, such as through virtual private networking. Communications flow in both directions in the LAN-to-WAN Domain.
- **Remote Access**—This domain refers to the technologies that control how end users connect to an organization's LAN. A typical example of remote access is someone connecting to the office network from a home computer.
- **System/Application**—This domain refers to the technologies needed to collect, process, and store information. The System/Application Domain includes hardware and software.

However you decide to logically segment your infrastructure, it's important to appreciate the complexity of the infrastructure and how data is treated. You can map business requirements by examining each of these logical segments. These requirements provide constraints upon end users and ultimately determine how security controls are designed.

Let's examine each of the seven domains to better understand how data is treated and how many common constraints are placed on them by the business.

User Domain

The **User Domain** refers to any end user accessing information in any form. This includes how end users handle physical information such as reports. Control of physical information starts well before someone ever touches a keyboard. It must start with end user awareness of policies and on-the-job training. As good as an awareness program is, formal education programs are no substitute for the experience gained from on-the-job training. "Onboarding" refers to new employee training. Even if your organization doesn't have a formal on-the-job training program, something as simple as giving someone a "buddy" to show him or her how the area operates often achieves many of the same goals.

There are several key policies that an end user must be familiar with before accessing company information. Some of the more important policies you should include in an awareness training program include:

> ⚠️ **WARNING**
>
> What end users see within their department and how coworkers treat data can significantly influence an employee's behavior beyond any formal awareness training. Regardless of training, if coworkers and management treat policies as unimportant, a new employee might treat policies as unimportant as well.

4

Business Challenges Within the Seven Domains

FIGURE 4-1

The seven domains of
a typical IT infrastructure.

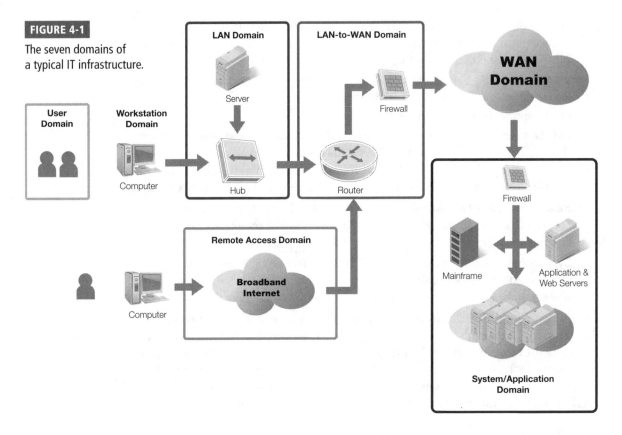

- **Acceptable use policy**—An acceptable use policy (AUP) establishes a broad set of rules for acceptable conduct when a user accesses information. For example, this policy may set rules on what type of Web site browsing is permitted or if personal e-mails over the Internet are allowed.

- **E-mail policy**—An **e-mail policy** discusses what's acceptable when using the company e-mail system. The policy is much more specific than the broad statements found in an AUP policy.

- **Privacy policy**—A **privacy policy** addresses the importance the organization places on protecting privacy. It also discusses the regulatory landscape and government mandates. This policy often covers physical security and the importance of "locking up" sensitive information.

- **System access policy**—A **system access policy** includes rules of conduct for system access. This policy covers end user credentials like IDs and passwords. The policy may also be specific to the business or application.

Authentication is one of the most important components of the User Domain. You must determine an authentication method that makes sense for your organization. Your authentication method must also meet business requirements. At a minimum, an ID and password is most often used. However, many systems require additional levels of controls to authorize access. Biometric authentication, such as a fingerprint scan, may be appropriate to authenticate on a large wire transfer. Often, simple authentication approaches are more efficient to achieving business goals than highly secure systems. Asking for a fingerprint scan to authenticate to a Web site to order flowers from home, for example, isn't realistic. The key lesson is that authentication has to make sense in the business context in which it is used.

Another key component is authorization. Authorization is especially important in large complex organizations with thousands of employees and hundreds of systems. The authorization method must clearly define who should have access to what. One popular method is role based access control (RBAC). In this method, instead of granting access to individuals, you assign permissions to a role. Then you assign one or more individuals to that role.

The huge advantage of RBAC is speed of deployment and clarity of access rights. Let's assume you hire an accountant named Nikkee and you grant her access to 12 systems, many spreadsheets, e-mail folders, and more. If you had to grant that access to her individual ID, it could take you days or even weeks. Given the complexity of a system, you may need to grant hundreds of permissions. The volume of permissions means there is a good chance of an error by missing something or granting too many rights. Now let's assume you hire a second accountant named Vickee. You would have to start the process over again to grant her rights to the systems, spreadsheets, and so on. What's even more time consuming is if one of these individuals leaves, you have to go through a similar process to remove her access.

Instead, let's assume you previously set up a role called "Accountant" and granted all necessary permissions to this role. Creating a new account would take the same time as creating a single user without RBAC. But creating a role is a onetime event. When you hire Nikkee and Vickee, you can connect their IDs to the Accountant role, quickly giving them access to the systems, spreadsheets, and e-mail folders they need to perform their jobs. Now let's say Vickee is promoted. You can quickly remove her ID from the Accountant role and place her ID in a Senior Accountant role. You reduced deployment time for these individuals from days or weeks to hours or minutes. By listing the people connected to the roles and the permissions within the roles, you can clearly see who has access to what business resources. This clarity of access helps an organization control access to its critical processes, manage its risk, and prove to regulators that it manages customer data properly. Figure 4-2 illustrates the RBAC concept.

Workstation Domain

The **Workstation Domain** includes any computing devices used by end users. Usually, the term "workstation" refers to a desktop or laptop computer. However, a workstation can be any end user device that accesses information. Control on your handheld device, like a smartphone, would fall within this domain.

4

Business Challenges Within the Seven Domains

> **NOTE**
>
> For the purposes of this chapter, the term "workstation" refers to an end user's desktop or laptop computer.

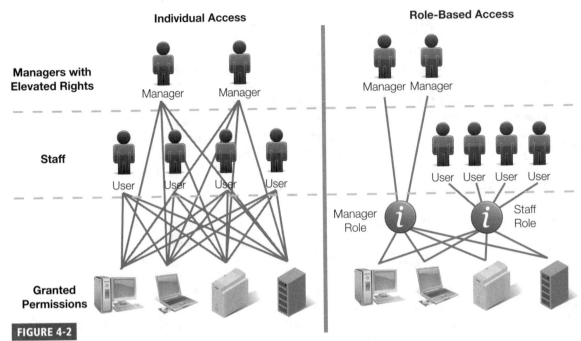

FIGURE 4-2

Role based access control concept.

> **NOTE**
>
> Authentication of a workstation and encryption of wireless traffic are Workstation Domain and LAN Domain issues. The assignment of a workstation identity and configuration of the wireless protocol is a Workstation Domain issue. The authentication and encryption of the traffic is a LAN Domain issue.

Usually, when an end user seeks to access information, he or she authenticates in the User Domain. Once he or she is known, the end user is often authorized to the workstation itself. Each workstation has an identity much like an end user. Not only can you restrict end users to specific workstations, you can also restrict what workstations are allowed on your network. This is particularly important when connecting to a network wirelessly because wireless access may be available to the public. Most wireless access points restrict which devices can access the internal network. Wireless access points also should encrypt the traffic between the authorized wireless device and the access point into the LAN.

The Workstation Domain defines the controls within the workstation itself, such as limiting who can install software on the workstation. Some end users share a workstation. Therefore, it is important that settings are stable, and that one end user cannot affect another. To achieve this, end users often have limited rights on workstations. That means they can typically access the software that's been installed, they have some rights to configure the software to their needs, but they do not have unlimited rights to make changes that could affect another user. This also ensures that an end user does not inadvertently infect the workstation with a virus or malware. Most domain controls ensure that appropriate antivirus software is loaded and runs on each workstation.

A central management system typically manages workstations such as Microsoft System Center Configuration Manager. These management systems have evolved over time and help an organization save time, money, and greatly improve response time. Can you imagine having to visit hundreds or thousands of desktops individually to apply a patch or install a piece of software? Fortunately, those days are long over. Central management systems are capable of many functions, including:

- **Inventory management**—An **inventory management** system tracks workstations as they connect to the LAN. This builds an inventory of what workstations exist and how often they connect to the LAN.

- **Discovery management**—Detects software that is installed on a workstation. **Discovery management** can also detect information on a workstation. This is highly specialized software that is not routinely used. Information inventories are useful when investigating security incidents and to ensure regulatory compliance. For example, discovery of files that contain Social Security numbers would be useful when investigating an incident or to check for compliance.

- **Patch management**—A **patch management** system ensures that current patches are installed on workstations. It's particularly important to apply security patches in a timely manner to address known vulnerabilities.

- **Help desk management**—A **help desk management** system provides support to end users through a help desk. Help desk technicians may remotely access a workstation to diagnose problems, reconfigure software, and reset IDs.

- **Log management**—A **log management** system extracts logs from a workstation. Typically, log management software moves logs to a central repository. Administrators scan these logs to find security weaknesses or patterns of problems.

- **Security management**—A **security management** system manages workstation security. This may include ensuring end users have limited rights and that new local administrator accounts are not present. The unexpected addition of local administrator accounts may be an indication that a security breach has occurred.

LAN Domain

The **LAN Domain** encompasses the equipment that makes up the LAN. A LAN typically has network devices that connect a local office or buildings. A LAN can be either simple or complex. If you have a wireless network device at home, you have a simple LAN. Let's say you have a home cable modem connected to a wireless device, which is usually called a wireless router. The wireless router creates a LAN, bridging your cable modem to your home computer. This wireless router is your LAN access point to the Internet.

The following are definitions for common network devices found on LANs:

- **Hub**—Connects multiple devices within a LAN. A **hub** has ports, and as traffic flows through the device, the traffic is duplicated so all ports can see the traffic. You use a hub to connect computers or segments.

- **Switch**—A **switch** is similar to a hub but can filter traffic. You can set up rules that control what traffic can flow where. Unlike hubs that duplicate traffic to all ports, a switch is typically configured to route traffic only to the port to which the system is connected. This reduces the amount of network traffic, thus reducing the chance that someone will intercept communications. The ability to configure a switch to control traffic is a real advantage over a hub. Many organizations do not allow the use of hubs and prefer switches for enhanced security.
- **Router**—A **router** connects LANs, or a LAN and a WAN.
- **Firewall**—A software or hardware device that filters traffic in and out of a LAN. Many **firewalls** can do deep-packet inspection in which the firewall examines the contents of the traffic as well as the type of traffic. You can use a firewall internally on the network to further protect segments. Firewalls are most commonly used to filter traffic between the public Internet WAN and the internal private LAN.

A LAN in the business world is far more complex than a home LAN, and has many layers of controls. Let's look at two general types of LANs, flat and segmented networks.

A **flat network** has few controls, or none, to limit network traffic. When a workstation connects to a flat network, the workstation can communicate with any other computer on the network. Think of a flat network as an ordinary neighborhood. Anyone can drive into the neighborhood and knock on any door. This doesn't mean whoever answers the door will let the visitor in. However, the visitor has the opportunity to talk his or her way in. In the case of flat networks, you can talk your way in by being authorized or by breaching a server, such as guessing the right ID and password combination. Flat networks are considered less secure than segmented networks because they rely on each computer (i.e., each home on the block) to withstand every possible type of breach. They are also less secure because every computer on the network can potentially see all the network traffic. This means a computer with a **sniffer** can monitor a large portion of the communication over a LAN.

NOTE

Many standards require network segmentation. Payment Card Industry Data Security Standard (PCI DSS), for example, requires network segmentation to further protect credit cardholder information.

A **segmented network** limits what and how computers are able to talk to each other. By using switches, routers, internal firewalls, and other devices, you can restrict network traffic. Continuing the analogy from the previous paragraph, think of a segmented network as a gated community. To access that neighborhood, you must first approach a gate with a guard. The guard opens the gate only for certain traffic to enter the community. Once inside, you can knock on any door. A segmented network acts as a guard, filtering out unauthorized network traffic.

Why do you want to segment a network? The basic idea is that by limiting certain types of traffic to a group of computers, you are eliminating a number of threats. For example, if you have a database server with sensitive information that by design should only receive database calls (such as **Structured Query Language [SQL]** traffic), why allow **File Transfer Protocol (FTP)** traffic? If the server is not properly configured, the FTP service could be used as a way to break into the computer. By eliminating the FTP traffic, you have effectively eliminated that particular threat. You should still make sure the server is properly configured to prevent such an attack. However, you reduced the likelihood of a successful breach because the attacker must first breach the segment (i.e., get by the guard at the gate) and then breach the database server (i.e., break down the door). Security is never absolute, but segmenting your network makes it more difficult to breach a computer.

LAN-to-WAN Domain

The **LAN-to-WAN Domain** is the bridge between a LAN and a WAN. A LAN is efficient for connecting computers within an office or groups of buildings. However, to connect offices across the country or globally you need to connect to a WAN. Generally, routers and firewalls are used to connect a LAN and WAN. The Internet is a WAN. The Internet, like many WANs, is public and considered unsecure.

How do you move data from an unsecure WAN to a secure LAN? Typically, you begin by segmenting a piece of your LAN into a **demilitarized zone (DMZ)**. The military uses the term DMZ to describe creating a buffer between two opposing forces. The DMZ sits on the outside of your private network facing the public Internet. Servers in the DMZ provide public-facing access to the organization, such as public Web sites. They are especially hardened against security breaches because the servers are easily accessible to the public and hackers. Sitting between the DMZ and internal network are firewalls that filter traffic from the DMZ servers to the private LAN servers. Often, the DMZ sits between two layers of firewalls. The first firewall allows limited Internet traffic into the DMZ, and the second highly restricts traffic from the DMZ servers into the private network.

There are a number of different network architecture designs that can be used to connect your internal private LAN with the external Internet WAN. The key point is to understand that you need some layer of firewalls to limit traffic between these domains. Creating a network segment like the DMZ as buffer between the LAN and WAN is a good way to protect your private network.

WAN Domain

The **WAN Domain**, for many organizations, is the Internet. Alternately, large organizations can lease dedicated lines and create a private WAN. However, as connectivity to the Internet has become more reliable, many organizations have switched from private WANs to using the Internet to connect offices over all over the world.

A challenge for companies using the Internet to connect offices is how to keep communications secure and private. A common solution is a **virtual private network (VPN)**. By setting up network devices at both offices, you can create an encrypted tunnel through the Internet. The tunnel protects communication between the offices from eavesdropping. You can use a dedicated network device whose only function is to create and manage VPN traffic. These devices are "VPN concentrators." Many firewalls also have the capability to create and maintain a VPN tunnel.

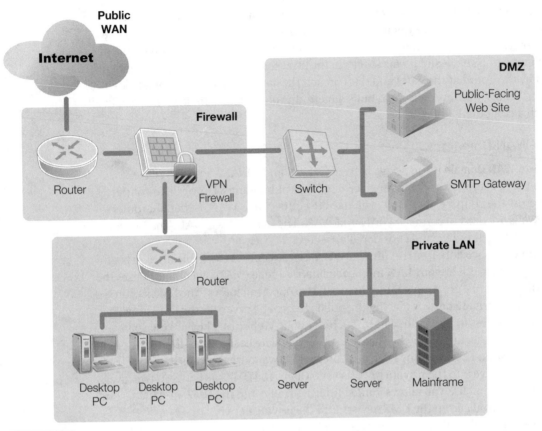

FIGURE 4-3

Basic LAN-to-WAN network layers.

Large organizations can lower communication costs by using VPN tunnels instead of leasing private lines for WANs. Beyond cost there's also the issue of time. Leased lines for WANs can take weeks to months to order, sign contracts, install, and set up. Most companies already have an Internet connection. They can add VPN-compatible devices at both ends to establish a VPN tunnel in days. For small and medium-size companies, it's the only practical solution given the cost and technical complexities.

Remote Access Domain

The **Remote Access Domain** is nothing more than an enhanced User Domain. The only difference is that you are traveling from a public unsecure network into the private secure company network. You have all the issues you have in the User Domain plus special remote authentication and network connectivity issues.

Remote authentication has always been a concern because the person is coming from a public network. Do you truly know that individual is an employee, or is he or she a hacker pretending to be an employee? There's less of a concern when accessing the network within the office. The office might have guards at the entrance, locked doors, badges, and visibility of people sitting at workstations. Over the Internet, how do you know who's on the other side of the wire? Most organizations today feel that an ID and password combination is not an adequate authentication method for remote access.

Many companies require **two-factor authentication** for remote access. Two-factor authentication requires an end user to authenticate his or her identity using at least two of three different types of credentials. The three most commonly accepted types of credentials are as follows:

- **Something you know**—Refers to something only you are supposed to know, such as your ID and password combination. You should never share your password with anyone.

- **Something you have**—Refers to a unique device that you must have in your physical possession to gain access. An example is a security token that flashes a unique number every 30 to 60 seconds. No two tokens ever display the same number at the same time. Unless you have the token in your possession and enter the right number, you cannot authenticate to the network.

- **Something you are**—Refers to some sort of biometric feature such as a fingerprint scanner.

Many organizations today require two-factor authentication for remote users. The authentication factors may be an ID/password combination (something you know) plus some type of token or smart card (something you have) to authenticate remote access. This provides a high level of confidence that the remote user is an employee. Some tokens can be loaded directly to the company laptop. The laptop becomes something you must have to connect remotely.

Remote network connectivity has the issues previously discussed with WAN Domains: how to keep communications secure and private. A VPN is typically the solution. You can configure a VPN to permit only predefined workstations to be connected. Earlier we discussed that a VPN can be used to connect two sites such as a remote office to the corporate headquarters. Each site has a dedicated hardware device that creates an encrypted tunnel through the Internet. This is typically called a site-to-site VPN connection. A remote user can also create a VPN tunnel. Instead of having VPN hardware at home, you have a desktop or laptop with software called a VPN client. This VPN client communicates with the VPN hardware to create the same type of encrypted tunnel through the Internet. This is typically called a client-to-site VPN connection. In both cases VPN is used to secure the communication through the Internet. Figure 4-4 illustrates the site-to-site and client-to-site connectivity.

The combination of enhanced remote authentication and network connectivity can be powerful tools to ensure a network's protection. Yet these tool also extend the business network anywhere in the world. Consider this scenario: Don, an executive, receives a call on a Saturday to approve a change to a vital business shipment. For Don to approve the shipment, he must review the changes on an internal system and electronically sign off on the changes. However, he is away for the weekend with his family.

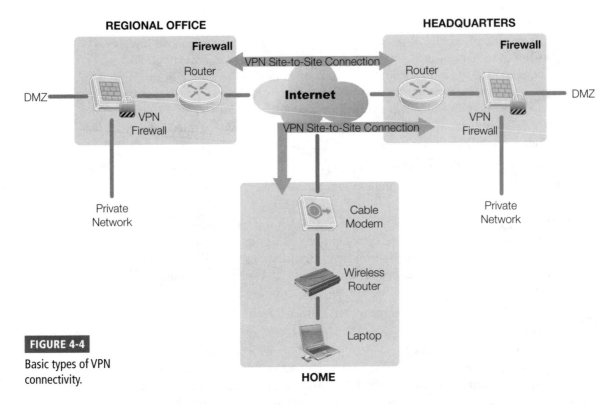

FIGURE 4-4

Basic types of VPN connectivity.

Fortunately, Don has his laptop in the hotel and he has an Internet connection. He signs onto his company laptop and connects to the network using his ID/password and a token he carries on his key chain. A VPN tunnel is established, and his laptop is authorized onto the network. Don can now access the system the same way he does from his desk in the office. The encrypted communications are secure and private. He can review the shipment change and approve its release. This approach maintains the authentication, confidentiality, integrity, and nonrepudiation of the transaction. The use of the ID/password and token achieves authentication and nonrepudiation for any transactions Don decides to execute. The confidentiality and integrity of the communication is achieved through encrypting the tunnel.

System/Application Domain

As complex as networks are, they essentially secure communication between an end user and some application software. What collects, processes, and stores data is ultimately software. Business software is typically an "application." **System software**, such as a server operating system, runs business applications. The **System/Application Domain** refers to all the system and application software-related issues.

Application software is at the heart of all business applications. Application software can run on a workstation or server. For example, an application can display a screen by which customers and employees can select products and enter data. Once the information is collected, the application transmits the transaction to a server. The server stores the information in a database to be processed later or instantly processes the transaction, stores the results, and displays information back to the end user. Later an employee can extract data from this ordering application into a spreadsheet to track the total number of orders each month by product type. The application that took the orders, the spreadsheet that tracked the orders, and perhaps the e-mail client used to announce record sales for the month, are all examples of application software.

Information Security Business Challenges and Security Policies That Mitigate Risk Within the Seven Domains

The previous section provided a foundational understanding of each of the seven domains. In this section, you will examine the business challenges and risks in each domain. You will also learn how the proper application of security policies can mitigate many of these risks.

> **NOTE**
>
> Chapters 9 and 10 take a detailed look at many security policies that affect the seven domains of a typical IT infrastructure.

User Domain

For an organization to be efficient requires the proper alignment of people, processes, and technology. An organization relies on its people to understand processes and technology. Good employees are not expected to blindly execute processes. The organization also needs its employees to understand the context of the process and the guiding principles of the organization. When the unexpected occurs, the employee can then react appropriately and consistently within the business goals and values.

Employee efficiency starts with well-defined policies that reflect the organization's reasonable expectations. Security policies must closely align with business requirements. This situation allows employees to understand the importance of the policy to the organization. It also ensures that security policies support business goals. One of the major business challenges is getting employees to follow policies. There are several ways good security policies can mitigate this risk, as follows:

- **Awareness**—Policies require employees to receive formal security awareness training. Most importantly, this training lets employees know where to go for help when the unexpected arises. The training also sets expectations on the handling of sensitive information to protect such as ensuring customer privacy.

- **Enforcement**—Security controls flow from security polices. These controls are designed to enforce how the business wishes to operate. Among the most important security controls are those that enforce segregation of duties. The term "separation of duties" means a single person cannot execute a high-risk transaction, for example, wiring large sums of money out of a bank. Typically, this requires one person to request the wire and a manager to approve the transfer.

- **Reward**—Refers to how management reinforces the value of following policies. An organization should put in place both disciplinary actions for not following policies and recognition for adhering to policies. This could be as simple as noting the level of compliance to policies in the employee's annual review.

Another business concern is handling sensitive information in physical form, such as reports. Many organizations have a "clean desk policy." This policy generally requires employees to lock up all documents and digital media at the end of a workday and when not in use. Compliance checks are relatively easy because any report or CD left out overnight is a violation of policy. This protects customer privacy and reminds employees of the sensitivity of company information. It also sets the right image for customers and vendors who may be visiting the office.

A major business concern is having processes that can run repeatedly and consistently. This reliability is essential for producing high-quality products and services. Security policies mitigate related risks by clearly defining roles and responsibilities. As we discussed earlier in the chapter, methods like RBAC help ensure that only the right person has the authority to execute the process.

Security policies also ensure that contractors and consultants are properly vetted before gaining access to company information. This includes performing background checks. Employees and non-employees alike must follow security policies.

Not all business processes can be standardized. Employees sometimes transfer knowledge by word of mouth, such as how to run some nonstandard transaction. The potential for significant failure in these processes may exist. At a minimum, when a failure occurs, the security policies ensure the process and related data can be restored.

Workstation Domain

Locking your front door but leaving your window wide open is not good security. Let's assume you have good authentication and you know who is signed onto your network. However, if a workstation is breached, you could have malicious software compromising your network whenever the authorized user connects.

The ramifications of a security breach are more severe for some organizations that are regulated. There is an expectation that leading practices are being applied to prevent such breaches. Security policies help identify those practices and ensure they are applied to protecting the workstation. That includes ensuring that all workstations that access the network are patched and have antivirus software installed. The business may not be aware of many of these basic common controls expected by regulators. The security policies ensure such controls are in place and help ensure regulatory compliance.

FYI

"Spyware" is a type of program that attempts to covertly gather and transmit confidential user information without your knowledge or permission. Spyware applications can hide inside freeware or shareware programs. Spyware can also be loaded through accessing malicious Web sites. Once installed, spyware can monitor end user activity and can gather information about passwords, credit card numbers, and information access by the end user. This information can then be transmitted to a hacker Web site without the end user knowing it.

Effective security is often a matter of determining some basic security configuration rules and applying them consistently across your enterprise. Applying such security without disrupting the business is a concern. The days of sending a technology person to each desk to configure a workstation for most organizations are long past. Security policies can help establish a reliable automated patch management process. Security policies can specify the type and frequency of patches to apply. The policies often require IT to test patches in a lab setting before applying them to workstations. Changes are made at night so there is a minimal impact on the company's day-to-day operations.

Security policies also reduce the risk of spyware by requiring limited access on a workstation. Usually an end user does not have administrative rights on a workstation. This means the end user cannot inadvertently install programs like spyware.

If they cannot breach your company's network directly, hackers often attempt to breach a workstation and infect it in some manner. The attempt is to either capture information from the workstation or use the workstation as a way to access the protected network. Security policies are good at outlining the rules for protecting workstations. One good example is encrypting laptop hard drives. This has become standard practice in many industries. With the increase in mobile computing, sensitive data leaves networks more easily and more often. As a result, many companies that handle sensitive information encrypt their employee's laptop hard drives. In that way, if the laptop is lost or stolen, the sensitive data is protected.

Many security policies require the encryption of data whenever the information leaves the protection of the network. This include encrypting data over the Internet, in e-mails, and on mobile devices such as universal serial bus (USB) drives, CDs, personal digital assistants (PDAs), and laptops. Case in point, in 2007, a health care contractor for Electronic Registry Systems Inc. (ERS) in Ohio was the victim of a burglary. A thief stole the contractor's laptop, which contained medical information on 25,000 patients. The information included names, addresses, Social Security numbers, medical record numbers, diagnoses, and treatment information. The data on the contractor laptop was not encrypted and therefore the records of 25,000 patients were compromised. Had the laptop been encrypted, which is considered a best practice in many industries, the data would have been safe.

Security policies that set encryption standards need to ensure the vendors and contractors follow the same policies that employees are required to follow.

LAN Domain

Many organizations have discovered that granting mobile access to business applications can increase productivity and revenue. A LAN is all about connectivity for the business. The easier you can be connected to a LAN, the faster you can start accessing and exchanging data. Wireless and mobile computing have changed the way we see LANs. This new view affects our perception of LAN and Remote Access Domain issues.

Wireless connectivity allows you to view the LAN more broadly than the computer on your desktop. Handled devices allow you to extend your LAN network out of the office and into the business. In other words, you can connect to the network and access or exchange information where the product or service is being made or delivered. Here are a few examples of how using wireless technology can extend the LAN into the business:

- **Health care**—Health care providers can access real-time patient information or medical research from a patient's bedside. These devices enhance collaboration for more accurate diagnoses. These devices can also track medical equipment to ensure availability at critical times.

- **Manufacturing**—Wireless connectivity allows employees to share real-time data on the factory floor.

- **Retail**—Wireless access to a LAN helps retailers place intelligent cash registers where there is no network wiring. This network access allows retailers to manage inventory, check customers out faster, and print the latest promotion coupons from the register.

> **NOTE**
>
> LANs today can also carry video feeds, such as those from security cameras. As LANs are extended, security policies must be extended to cover the new risks.

> **NOTE**
>
> Bandwidth is a measurement that quantifies how much information can be transmitted over the network. When a LAN reaches its maximum bandwidth, it becomes susceptible to many kinds of transmission errors and delays.

Extending the LAN has many advantages over just connecting a standard PC. LANs today can carry voice, video, and traditional computer traffic. Voice over Internet Protocol (VoIP) allows you to place and receive phone calls over a LAN or WAN. This has become popular for both home and business because of the cost savings over traditional telephone systems. Rather than incurring high flat-rate fees and per-minute call charges, most VoIP services charge a low flat-rate fee. We continue to see new companies enter the market offering less expensive voice and video solutions over the Internet.

Organizations often view LANs much like utilities such as electricity, water, or gas. The organization expects the LAN to be always available and always have capacity. It's also thought of as a commodity that should be inexpensive to install and run. This puts tremendous pressures on LAN resources. Bandwidth within the LAN, for example, decreases as new services such as VoIP and video are offered.

Security policies are helpful by defining and enforcing what is acceptable use over the LAN. It is not uncommon to have security policies limit the use of live video feeds. Video can take up significant bandwidth. Thousands of employees watching a major sports event from a TV feed over the Internet, for example, could impact an end user trying to process a customer order. On March 19, 2010, the *Phoenix Business Journal* reported that Integra, a Portland-based telecom, had a 15 percent increase in network traffic. The spike was attributed to the NCAA Division I Men's Basketball tournament. The company said the surge was related to customers streaming online video of the game. Similar policies limit listening to live music over the network. You can enforce many of these policies at the firewall, cutting off the source of video and music from the Internet.

Even with these business challenges, the benefits of extending a LAN beyond the workstation are enormous and include enhanced productivity, collaboration, and responsiveness.

LAN-to-WAN Domain

A major concern of organizations is protection of the servers in the DMZ. In other words, are the Web site servers protected? Organizations are particularly concerned about Web site availability and integrity. The Web sites for many organizations represent their public image and, for companies, their major sales channel.

Security policies set strict rules on how DMZ traffic should be limited and monitored. Security policies outline how the DMZ server should be configured and how often security patches should be applied. Security policies also outline how often external penetration testing is conducted. Penetration testing probes the network for weaknesses and vulnerabilities from the outside looking in. Penetration testing is required by many standards and is considered a best practice. For example, if you accept or process credit cards, PCI DSS requires penetration testing.

> **NOTE**
>
> An organization's reputation can be diminished by the appearance of **Web graffiti** on its Web site. Web graffiti is a result of **Web site defacement**, in which a Web site has been breached and its content altered, usually in a way that embarrasses the Web site owner. Web graffiti can contain abusive language or even pornographic images.

WAN Domain

When it comes to WANs, an organization is generally concerned about cost, reliability, and speed. As discussed earlier in the chapter, many organizations use virtual private networking to protect and secure communications over the Internet. But is that the right choice for all organizations?

Cost-wise, a VPN over the Internet is the right choice. The cost is fairly modest. Because most organizations already have Internet connectivity, IT can quickly deploy VPN technology. It could be as easy as installing devices and synching keys to establish a VPN tunnel.

> **NOTE**
>
> With virtual private networking, you "tunnel" through the public Internet to reach a specific site. Typically, two VPN devices establish a site-to-site VPN tunnel. Both devices are usually preconfigured with keys so only these devices communicate with each other. Once the tunnel is established, it can link entire LANs. A remote office, for example, can link to headquarters.

Reliability of a VPN depends on your Internet service provider (ISP). You can experience reliability issues even if your ISP guarantees a level of service while you're traveling over a public network. Think of the Internet like a road system. You have local roads, main arteries, and superhighways. Some ISPs advertise how many hops away from the Internet backbone they are. The "Internet backbone" represents the superhighway in our road system and can handle the fastest traffic. In theory, the fewer hops it takes to get to the backbone, the faster your access. A "hop" is a term meaning generally how many routers you have to pass through to get to your destination. If you have to go through a lot of back roads to get to your destination it takes a lot longer than if you live close a superhighway. Same holds true for the Internet traffic.

> **NOTE**
>
> Private WANs are point-to-point solutions that are not publicly shared and thus are usually not encrypted. Service providers of private WANs can guarantee upload and download bandwidth consistency.

When it comes to speed, using a VPN over the Internet may not be your best choice. This depends on your business requirements—how much data you need to send and how fast you need it to arrive. For example, if you require real-time information, speed is more important than if you send files for overnight processing. In addition, the type of data is important to consider in your selection of services. If you need to send large video feeds, speed and capacity are important. Generally, lower-cost broadband service does not always guarantee upload and download speeds. This makes predicting reliability a challenge. Also, all of that data is encrypted and then decrypted through the VPN tunnel. Encryption takes time and central processing unit (CPU) cycles.

Deciding on a public or private WAN solution for your organization depends on your requirements and budget. Small organizations have few options. For large enterprises, both WAN options are available.

Security policies outline how each connection type should be configured and protected. The security policies also outline roles and responsibilities. Keep in mind that the service provider typically configures private WAN security. Therefore, your security policies need to include how to deal with the vendor and how to validate the security configuration. Companies of any size can manage security for Internet-based VPN solutions in-house.

Remote Access Domain

When it comes to remote access, organizations are concerned about flexibility, reliability, and speed. As discussed, extending the LAN into the business where products are produced and services delivered has tremendous benefits. This is also true for extending the LAN anywhere in the world. This is where remote access concerns need to be addressed.

When it comes to flexibility, employees cannot be tethered to their desktops. Laptops have broken that tie, allowing employees to connect to the company network wherever there is an Internet connection. Wireless connections further extend the flexibility of laptops. Today, travelers and mobile employees often use a laptop with an air card to access the Internet and work network. An "air card" is a device that acts like a cell phone for a laptop, allowing the end user to obtain a broadband Internet connection. You can check e-mail, use instant messaging, and access the Internet anywhere in the world without having to find a hotspot.

Mobile devices and broadband are becoming very reliable. However, the speed and reliability with which they can access and exchange data depends on location and carrier. Much like cell phone coverage, mobile broadband coverage is spotty at times. However, despite their drawbacks, mobile devices offer many business benefits, including:

- Increased customer responsiveness
- Quick reaction to news and business-related events
- Advantage of real-time data access

This is one area in which security policies need to keep pace with technology and business requirements. Policies must be clear whether personal devices such as a smartphone should be permitted access to organization information. Although the trend is to permit only organization-owned PDAs access, many companies opt to reduce costs by allowing employees to use their personal devices. Some security policy questions that must be addressed for handheld device use include:

- Who owns the device?
- Who has the right to wipe the device if it's lost or stolen?
- How do you encrypt data on the device?
- How do you apply patches?
- Who's allowed to have such a device connected to the company network?

With any emerging technology, well-defined security policies help an organization think through its risk decision. Security policies ensure risk assessments are performed and look at leading practices. This is vital so the organization can understand not only the benefits of new technology but also the risks.

System/Application Domain

An organization has two main concerns when it comes to information collected, stored, and processed: Is the information safe? Can you prevent confidential information from leaving the organization? These seem like fairly easy questions but are complicated to answer.

This chapter has discussed many ways to keep information safe. Security policies ensure risks are evaluated throughout the seven domains. Security policies ensure alignment to business requirements. When risks exist, security policies ensure a risk assessment is performed so that management can make a balanced decision.

In this section, you will focus on the second business concern of how to prevent confidential information from leaving the organization. Security policies define what's often called either a **Data Loss Protection (DLP)** or a **Data Leakage Protection (DLP)** program. Both terms refer to a formal program that reduces the likelihood of accidental or malicious loss of data.

Company managers worry about secret business information ending up in competitors' hands. Managers must also protect customer privacy as required by law. A hacker does not have to be physically present to steal your business secrets, especially if the hacker is a disgruntled employee who might work in a data-sensitive area of the company. Your top salesperson might leave the company to work for a competitor and e-mail your entire sales database to his home Internet account. These are not theoretical losses to a business. You must ensure that all of your potential data leaks, both physical and digital, are plugged.

The concept of DLP comes from the acknowledgment that data changes form and often gets copied, moved, and stored in many places. This sensitive data often leaves the protection of application databases and ends up in e-mails, spreadsheets, and personal workstation files. Business is most concerned about data that lives outside the hardened protection of an application.

A typical DLP program provides several layers of defense to prevent confidential data from leaving the organization, including:

- Inventory
- Perimeter
- Encryption of mobile devices

Inventory

The DLP inventory component attempts to identify where sensitive data may be stored. This includes scanning workstations, e-mail folders, and file servers. The process requires actually inspecting the content of files and determining if they contain sensitive information such as social security numbers. Once identified, reports can be created to compare the security of files with security policies. For example, this helps prevent private customer information from accidentally being stored in a public e-mail folder. While this is an important capability, it has its limitations. The ability to understand the sensitivity of a file is very difficult to automate. Either you end up having too many false positives or end up missing the identification of sensitive data.

Perimeter

The DLP perimeter component ensures that data is protected on every endpoint on your network, regardless of the operating system or type of device. It checks data as it moves, including writing data to e-mail, CDs, USB devices, instant messaging, and print. If sensitive data is written to an unauthorized device, the technology can either stop and archive the file or send an alternate. It stops data loss initiated by malware and file sharing that can hijack employee information. Through the logging and analysis server, it monitors real-time events and generates detailed forensics reports.

You can also establish and manage security policies to regulate and restrict how your employees use and transfer sensitive data. It uses the same basic technology that is applied with the inventory component. It has the same limitations. Because you are dealing with data movement, you can add rules not often found in the inventory process, such as not permitting large database files to be e-mailed. Regardless of content, these rules can stop a hacker from sending a large volume of data out the door.

Encryption of Mobile Devices

In many ways, mobile devices like PDAs are mobile external hard drives. It's the same information that can sit on a workstation or server. When an executive receives an e-mail on an upcoming merger, or a doctor about a patient, the information needs the same protection as if it was on a workstation or server. The information on mobile devices is subject to the same regulatory requirements. This means you must also apply the same level of controls, such as encryption.

You need a DLP program because loss of confidential data hurts the business reputation, discloses competitive secrets, and often violates regulation. Well-defined security policies establish a formal DLP program within an organization.

CHAPTER SUMMARY

We learned in this chapter how to break up the technology infrastructure into manageable pieces called domains. We examined each of the domains to define why they exist, looked at related business concerns, and learned how to mitigate common risks. We understand that security policies have to be aligned to the business. Most importantly, we see how security policies can highlight regulatory and leading practice to guide the business in controlling these risks.

The chapter also examined the changing nature of business through technologies such as wireless and handheld devices. We understand the importance of security policies keeping pace with these business changes. We better understand the expanding role of the LAN to establish global connectivity through WANs. We learned techniques, such as VPN, to keep this communication protected and private. Finally, we talked about the importance of having a DLP program defined in our security policies. The DLP program helps us reduce the likelihood of data loss.

KEY CONCEPTS AND TERMS

Application software
Data Leakage Protection (DLP)
Data Loss Protection (DLP)
Demilitarized zone (DMZ)
Discovery management
Domain
E-mail policy
File Transfer Protocol (FTP)
Firewall
Flat network
Help desk management
Hub
Inventory management

LAN Domain
LAN-to-WAN Domain
Log management
Patch management
Privacy policy
Remote Access Domain
Remote authentication
Router
Security management
Segmented network
Sniffer
Structured Query Language (SQL)

Switch
System access policy
System software
System/Application Domain
Two-factor authentication
User Domain
Virtual private network (VPN)
WAN Domain
Web graffiti
Web site defacement
Workstation Domain

CHAPTER 4 ASSESSMENT

1. Private WANs must be encrypted at all times.

A. True
B. False

2. Which of the following attempts to identify where sensitive data is currently stored?

A. Data Leakage Protection Inventory
B. DLP Encryption Key
C. Data Loss Protection Perimeter
D. DLP Trojans

3. Voice over Internet Protocol (VoIP) can be used over which of the following?

A. LAN
B. WAN
C. Both
D. Neither

4. Which of the following is not one of the seven domains of typical IT infrastructure?

A. Remote Access Domain
B. LAN Domain
C. World Area Network Domain
D. System/Application Domain

5. Which of the seven domains refers to the technical infrastructure that connects the organization's LAN to a WAN and allows end users to surf the Internet?

6. Many of the business benefits of Internet access over mobile devices include which of the following?

A. Competitive advantage through real-time data access
B. Increased customer responsiveness
C. Prevention of unauthorized access to customer private information
D. A and B only
E. None of the above

7. A _____ is a term that refers to a network that limits what and how computers are able to talk to each other.

8. A LAN is efficient for connecting computers within an office or groups of buildings.

A. True
B. False

9. What policy generally requires that employees lock up all documents and digital media at the end of a workday and when not in use?

   A. Acceptable use policy
   B. Clean desk policy
   C. Privacy policy
   D. Walk out policy

10. What employees learn in awareness training influences them more than what they see within their department.

    A. True
    B. False

11. What kind of workstation management refers to knowing what software is installed?

    A. Inventory management
    B. Patch management
    C. Security management
    D. Discovery management

12. Always applying the most strict authentication method is the best way to protect the business and ensure achievement of goals.

    A. True
    B. False

13. Generally, remote authentication provides which of the following?

    A. Fewer controls than if you were in the office
    B. The same controls than if you were in the office
    C. More controls than if you were in the office
    D. Less need for controls than in the office

14. Remote access does not have to be encrypted if strong authentication is used.

    A. True
    B. False

15. Where is a DMZ usually located?

    A. Inside the private LAN
    B. Within the WAN
    C. Between the private LAN and public WAN
    D. Within the mail server

Information Security Policy Implementation Issues

O NCE A SECURITY POLICY IS CREATED OR REVISED, and agreed upon, the implementation process starts. The process of implementing security policies can be harder than creating the document itself. You should not underestimate this effort. Implementing security policies successfully takes a combination of soft skills in dealing with human nature and company culture and hard skills in project management. The number of tasks and considerations can seem overwhelming. It's important to take a systematic approach that keeps the implementation moving forward and supporters engaged.

Security policies specify ways to control risk and reflect the core values of the organization. This means security policies are as much about promoting a risk-aware culture and motivating workers as they are about implementing technical business requirements. Therefore it's important to keep in mind that a successful implementation must motivate, gain consensus, and compete with an individual's priorities. Gaining executive support is one of the keys to success. This means you must be able to communicate the value of the security policies. You must be able to explain why the business and individuals should care. This takes skill in influencing others and marketing the value of the security policies.

Security policy implementations vary by size and scope. Security policies can be large and complex with significant impacts to the organization. Implementations require strong project management skills to plan and deploy. There are many individual tasks and issues to resolve along the way. Maintaining a clear line of communication with the executives who approve the implementation and those affected by it is important. The implementation is not complete when polices are published. Like any good technology deployment, post-implementation tasks must be completed to ensure ongoing success. You can measure success by how well the security polices help to reduce risk to the organization. Implementing the policies is only the first step.

In this chapter, we review many of the issues and problems faced when implementing security policies. The chapter gives pointers on how to overcome these challenges and how to deal with human nature in the workplace. The chapter also gives guidance on how to manage security policy changes in your organization.

Chapter 5 Topics

This chapter covers the following topics and concepts:

- How to deal with human nature in the workplace
- What various organizational structures are
- How to overcome user apathy
- What the importance of executive management support is
- Why support from human resources is important
- How security policies influence roles, responsibilities, and accountability
- What happens when policy fulfillment isn't part of the job description
- How an entrepreneurial approach affects productivity and efficiency
- Why it's important to find the right measure of policy success
- How success depends on proper interpretation and enforcement

Chapter 5 Goals

When you complete this chapter, you will be able to:

- Describe how people are motivated in the workplace
- Describe different workplace personality types
- Compare advantages and disadvantages of different organization structures
- Describe the basic characteristics of organizational structure
- Explain how user apathy affects security policy implementation
- Explain the importance of executive and human resources support
- Describe the importance of a change model in implementing security policies
- Describe key tasks within a change model
- Explain key roles and responsibilities in implementing security policies
- Describe attributes of an entrepreneurial business unit
- Explain why interpretation and enforcement are key to success

Human Nature in the Workplace

A successful security policy implementation depends on people understanding key concepts and embracing the material. Understanding and influencing different personalities in the workplace will be important to achieving that success. Meeting the demands of a changing business environment is also important to a security policy implementation. Regulators frequently redefine limitations on organizations. As competition explodes globally, new channels of sales and products appear. These factors are usually accompanied by a change in technologies. Enormous efforts and resources are spent to document, debug, and map an organization's processes to these technologies. Over time, technology, frameworks, and standards evolve to become best practices. Workers might feel more connected if they have witnessed the birth of these practices during their careers. Yet success does not come by technology or process alone. Successful security policy implementation depends on the correct alignment of people, processes, and technology.

How much time and resources are placed on the people element? Too often, not enough.

This section explores human nature in the workplace. More precisely, it looks at different personality types and how they affect the adoption of security policies. A successful security policy implementation is defined in part when an employee understands the key concepts and can apply them broadly to situations that were not anticipated. Going beyond what one is told helps define a successful implementation of security policies.

Basic Elements of Motivation

What is motivation? We know it when we see it. It's the smile when we receive a cup of coffee, or it's the help desk employee who works persistently to fix our problem. It's being enthusiastic, energized, and engaged to achieve a goal or objective. A lack of motivation can be measured in poor customer services, and doing the minimum to get by, with mediocre results.

There are three basic elements of motivation: pride, self-interest, and success. When these three elements are combined in the workplace, you often see the following:

- Individual and team motivation
- Individuals going "above and beyond" their job requirements to be successful
- Satisfied customers
- An increase in bottom-line profits

Motivating employees is as important as mastering a technology. A motivated employee can deal with the unexpected. This is particularly important when dealing with unexpected security incidents.

Pride

Pride is part of our nature. Individuals are more likely to become motivated when they are working on something that is important. If our work is discarded or trivialized, we're less likely to put in a high-quality effort the next time. Conversely, if we understand the goal and objectives of our team and see how our individual efforts contribute, we feel a sense of obligation. It also builds team pride and spirit, which is important for future successes.

An important component of pride involves an understanding of the overall goals and objectives. Management is responsible for informing employees of their roles and how their efforts contribute to the larger goal. This communication creates a foundation for other discussions, such as performance appraisals and process improvement. Yet managers often overlook it.

Pride can be a powerful motivator. It can also create competition and a sense of self-worth. Managers must control competition so that the sole measure of success is not simply completing the task first. It must also promote helping each other so the "team" can succeed. Measuring success needs to include all the values important to the organization, including quality of service, customer satisfaction, and teamwork.

Being an early adopter of security policies will help lead an organization's successful implementation. Early adoption of security policies can be a source of pride for both the individual and the team.

Self-Interest

Self-interest, and sometimes self-preservation, is also part of human nature. Humans tend to repeat behavior that is rewarded. Having well-defined goals and objectives for individuals helps them understand what they must achieve. Those who achieve these goals receive rewards. Those who exceed these goals typically receive bigger or better rewards. Those individuals are "high achievers" or high performers. High achievers receive promotions more often and are models for others to emulate. To promote the importance of information and adherence to its policies, you should gain the support of high performers.

In a declining economic market, there's significant pressure on companies to cut jobs to save money. Self-preservation is an important part of human nature. When an organization lays off employees, it can motivate others to work harder. It can also de-motivate employees because they believe they could be laid off regardless of their performance. Either situation affects employee behavior.

Discipline also has an important self-preservation effect on our behavior. When an employee fails to perform, they may require disciplinary action. How management handles disciplinary actions either motivates or de-motivates an employee.

Everyone has strengths and weakness. Most people make mistakes and at some point will do something foolish. One management approach is to look at an employee's pattern of behavior more than individual errors in judgment. This approach has its limits, as in a case of sexual harassment or fraud. Excluding these extreme cases, though, when management accepts failures as part of individual and team growth, a culture of taking chances emerges.

> **NOTE**
>
> "Disciplinary action" can be anything from informal coaching over a cup of coffee, to a verbal warning, to the termination of employment. An employee is less likely to take chances and learn new techniques if errors in judgment usually lead to disciplinary action.

Taking chances and going beyond what's expected define high achievers and high-performance teams. Because security polices cannot define every event, their success depends on employees taking action by applying core principles to new situations. For example, an organization's security policy requires data to be encrypted on backup tapes and stored offsite. An employee is asked to back up some data to DVD and send it to a vendor for analysis. Assume the security framework doesn't include a procedure on how to create and send a DVD to a vendor in this particular situation. A successful security policy implementation would educate the employee on the importance of protecting customer data through encryption. The policy would also motivate the employee to look past existing procedures. This increases the likelihood that the employee might realize the risk and encrypt the DVD before sending it to the vendor. The employee in this scenario would not have violated policy by sending an unencrypted disk. However, a motivated employee might go beyond existing processes and apply the same core security policy principle used for offsite backups when sending a vendor a DVD of data.

Success

Wanting to be successful is part of human nature. Anyone who has played on a winning team knows the feeling. Imagine you played on a sports team that just won regional finals. It's simply a lot more fun being on the winning team than on the team that always comes in last. Even if you are a high performer, it's hard to get motivated if your team as a whole keeps losing. It is no different in the workplace. Individuals build confidence when frequently recognized for their successes. These individuals quickly become highly motivated. They can also afford to take chances and are more likely to build on their success by going beyond what's required. Success is measured as the perception of how well you perform your work, how you work as part of the team, ethical behavior, and perception of your customers.

You need to have some proficiency in soft skills to convince an organization to adopt security policies. The term "soft skills" refers to certain social personality traits such as the ability to communicate and project optimism. Mastering these soft skills is essential to influencing others. This is particularly important when trying to sell new security policy and control concepts. More and more, business relies on the agility of its workforce to adapt to the unexpected. These skills are just as highly valued as technical knowledge. In other words, the "people" part of the equation is also critical to implementing security policies. Soft skills contribute to being a high performer by allowing individuals to more effectively apply that knowledge. Successful implementation of security policies over time will change individual attitudes. If that success continues throughout the organization, a culture that is more security and risk aware may emerge. This culture shift makes it much easier in the future to identify and mitigate risk.

Pride, self-interest, and success issues overlap and interact. Sustaining motivation comes by creating the right balance between these basic elements. When you achieve balance, you not only motivate individuals but teams, departments, and entire organizations. Figure 5-1 depicts these three basic elements of motivation and their intersection.

Motivated employees are far more likely to embrace the implementation security policies. This leads to more risks being identified and mitigated for the organization.

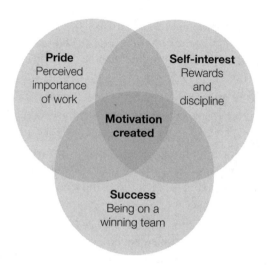

FIGURE 5-1

Three basic elements of motivation.

Personality Types of Employees

It's easy to see firsthand that individuals react differently in the workplace. What motivates one person does not always work for another. Understanding different personality types within a team is key to understanding how to motivate people. It's important to understand and appreciate the differences. This understanding allows you to leverage talents more effectively.

Let's illustrate this point with a simple example. Let's assume there are two individuals. One is very analytical with wonderful hard skills but does not work well with the customer. The other has wonderful soft skills but limited hard skills. Which is better? Answer: There's not a best type. When a team has only soft-skills members, it's hard to do the analysis to identify complex technical security risks to the business. Conversely, if you only had hard-skills members on your team, you may end up with a highly technical analysis that's hard to communicate to leadership to take action. The risk to business cannot be reduced unless security risks can be clearly identified and communicated in a way that gains leadership support.

> **NOTE**
>
> Understanding different personality types and creating a balance can be essential to an organization's success. This understanding also allows you to have a better idea of how to motivate people. For example, some personalities like public acknowledgment and rewards for their work. For others, it could be disastrous and seen as a public embarrassment.

HR Magazine identified eight classic personality types in the workplace. They are commanders, drifters, attackers, pleasers, performers, avoiders, analyticals, and achievers. In many ways their personality names speak to their individual traits. The following is a high-level summary of each of these traits:

- **Commanders**—Are demanding and not tactful. They come across at best as impolite, at worst rude and abrupt. They are forceful in an attempt to achieve stated goals. They can break through barriers that have prevented past success.

- **Drifters**—Are uncomfortable with structure and deadlines. They may have great soft skills but might not follow up and take a more laid-back attitude toward work assignments. What they lack in discipline may be offset by their creativity and thinking out of the box.

- **Attackers**—May seem angry or even hostile toward ideas and others on the team. They are critical of others' ideas and are egotistical. Although their biting attacks on other team members can be disruptive, they can also take on very unpopular tasks.

- **Pleasers**—Are very kind and thoughtful to others. They want everyone to "feel good" and will put their own self-interest aside for the good of the whole. They may shy away from enforcing rules that offend others, but they promote the concept of collaboration and teamwork.

- **Performers**—Like to be on center stage. They like to entertain and be the center of attention. They develop over time a wit and charm to capture people's attention. They may not be the highest producer and may be in the habit of self-promotion. They are often excellent public speakers and can establish new relationships important for the business.

- **Avoiders**—Like to fly under the radar and be in the background. They tend not to take chances or do anything that brings attention on them. They will do precisely what's asked of them but not much more. However, they are very dependable and their work quality is consistent.

- **Analyticals**—Like structure and deadlines. They measure their success in precise terms of the number of widgets produced in a given time at a given quality level. They tend to be obsessed with precision and attention to detail. They may not be the best at understanding human dynamics, so working with customers and emotions may be a problem. They are very comfortable with lots of information and have the ability to analyze issues and evaluate different types of risk.

- **Achievers**—Are very result oriented. They may have several traits of the other personality types. For example, they may be self-confident but not at the expense of others. They genuinely want the best result and may seek different ways to achieve it. Achievers can make good leaders.

It's rare that an individual is just one of these personality types. Typically, personality types blend and mix depending on many factors. Dominant traits over time can become your safe zone. A "safe zone" refers to the skills you are comfortable with to achieve a predictable outcome.

Understanding these personality traits is an advantage in implementing security policies. Often new security policies represent change. You can use the strengths of these personality traits to overcome objection to the change. For example, Analyticals could review detail logs and network designs to identify potential security threats. Performers can help deliver security awareness training. The Achiever may be the ideal individual to communicate with leadership. There is no set rule of how to tap the talent of each of these personality types. Understanding these types allows you to leverage people's strengths to more quickly implement security policies.

FYI

Personality assessments have existed for a long time. The Myers-Briggs Type Indicator (MBTI), for example, was first published in 1962. Assessments of personality types have become more widely used recently because computer-based testing makes them easier to deliver and their perceived accuracy has grown. Such an assessment should not, however, be the sole basis for hiring someone. A test can simply help you better understand a job candidate. Personality tests are also helpful when forming teams for long-term or highly important projects. Human resources (HR) books and Web sites are also good sources for personality type models.

Leadership, Values, and Ethics

Given all the material that has been written on the subject, entire libraries can be built around leadership, business values, and ethics. They are discussed in this section to help you better understand human nature in the workplace. This section focuses on how leadership affects employee behavior, and how good leadership can help ensure that employees adhere to policies.

Leaders must require proper behavior from employees and exhibit the same qualities in their own actions. A leader who demonstrates ethical behavior every day is more likely to see that behavior emulated by employees. Most employees have personal issues. Personality traits are formed over years based on upbringing and life experiences. Good leaders recognize the need to work within these personality types, guide their energy and passion, and get results. A leader's job is to work through others to achieve specific goals. Implementing security policies is all about working through others to gain their support and adhere to the policies.

There is no secret formula for motivating individuals. Some widely accepted leadership rules that also apply to security policies include:

- **Values**—Good leaders have core values. Leaders share their core values with employees. Good leaders will embrace the security policy and hold their teams accountable for its implementation.
- **Goals**—Good leaders have clear vision and set goals. They communicate these goals both to the team and to individuals. They communicate how contributions lead to success. People want to know they are working on something that matters. Good leaders will communicate how individual efforts are helping to protect customer information, which contributes to the health of the organization.
- **Teamwork**—Good leaders train their team to focus on goals and support each other's work. Success is measured not solely by individual successes but by the team's success. A good leader will encourage teamwork with the security staff to successfully implement and support security policies.

- **Ownership**—Good leaders instill a sense of ownership in each individual. That means listening. An individual who executes a process knows what works and what does not. Leaders should listen to ideas for improvement, and communicate back to individuals when their ideas are adopted. Good leaders will communicate ideas for security improvement back to the security team.

- **Support**—Good leaders accept failures. Things will go wrong. People will make mistakes. How a leader reacts to these mistakes sets a tone that can be healthy or destructive. How leaders react to errors in judgement can build long-term loyalty or promote mistrust. Leaders and the security team should collaborate on the best ways of reducing risk when a security breach or incident occurs. This also applies when security policies or controls are not achieving the desired outcome.

- **Reward**—Good leaders reward results, not personalities. A quick way to demoralize a team is to reward individuals based on who is liked versus who produces. What's commonly referred to as "company politics" can never be eliminated. However, the more a leader can measure real risk reduction because of security policies and controls, the fewer politics will be encountered.

 NOTE

Being realistic about the implementation of security policies and controls means working with leaders to understand what risks are real versus theoretical. This includes understanding the ability to respond to an incident.

Part of understanding human nature in the workplace is recognizing its complexity. You need to understand what motivates individuals and yourself. A leader can't simply issue commands and expect good results time after time. Nor can an executive simply mandate information security policies and expect staff to follow them. Good leaders demonstrate core values in their own actions, and communicate their expectations. They understand the human personality, ignite passions, and inspire people to achieve common goals. Managers and employees must understand these dynamics to approach implementation of security policies in a realistic and thoughtful manner.

Being thoughtful about the implementation of security policies and controls means balancing the need to reduce risk with the impact to the business operations. It could mean phasing security controls in over time, or as simple as aligning security implementation with the business's training events.

Organizational Structure

The way an organizational structure evolves over time affects the way people behave. Management must determine the behaviors and values it wants to promote. Then it can design an appropriate structure. The organizational structure chosen by management influences how security policies are put in place. It creates complex relationships and personal dynamics between different leaders, layers of approvals, and core values. An organization's structure reflects the relationship between teams (or departments), their responsibilities, and lines of authority. An organizational structure clearly indicates who's in charge and who reports to whom.

Figure 5-2 depicts a typical U.S. company organizational chart. You can learn a lot from an organizational structure. In this example, notice two lines of businesses. Assume that these businesses are distinct enough that they require a separate focus and leadership. This could be because the products are distinctive or the customer base has unique needs. For example, if they produced similar products they could organize themselves by geography, such as separating the U.S. from the Asian markets. Alternatively, they could produce two distinctive products for the same market such as consumer versus commercial product lines.

The key point is that an organizational structure gives you insight into leadership's perspective on the business and the type of challenges faced. You also get a sense of priorities. You see in Figure 5-2 that the business has decided to centralize the information technology (IT) function. This is typically called "shared services." This term relates to a department or team that provides similar services across an entire organization. By centralizing services, a business can reduce operating costs. For example, rather than building two almost identical data centers to service two business lines, both can share the same data center operated by the IT department. Within the IT department's structure you find a further breakdown on how services are provided to the two lines of business. Also notice the marketing department reports directly to the office of the president. This gives the department greater influence and perceived authority.

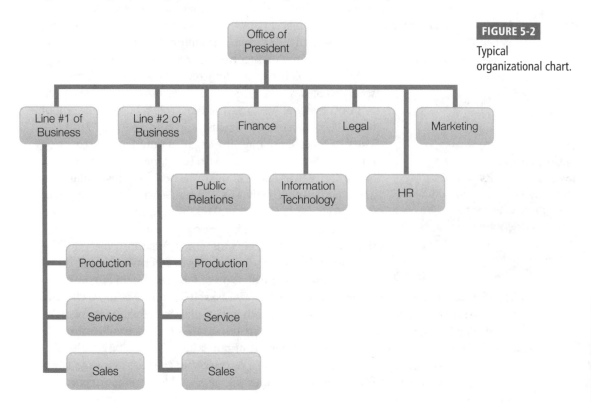

FIGURE 5-2

Typical organizational chart.

FIGURE 5-3

CISO reporting
directly to CFO.

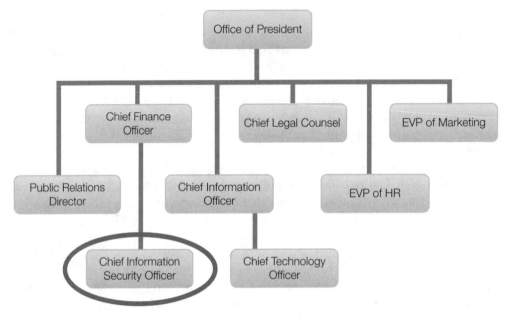

Let's examine how these dynamics influence the implementation of security policies. Assume the chief information security officer (CISO) reports directly to the chief finance officer (CFO), as shown in Figure 5-3. The CFO's role is traditionally a powerful position. Consequently, it's more likely that information security is perceived as a business concern rather than solely a technology issue. This allows information security policies to be given a higher priority across the enterprise.

Conversely, let's assume the CISO role reports three or four layers deep inside the IT department, as shown in Figure 5-4. The CISO would not have the organizational muscle to implement security policies with the same perceived influence or authority. This does not mean security policies couldn't be implemented effectively. The difference would be the approach used given the organizational realities. In this case, the CISO would most likely seek greater executive involvement rather than reliance on the CFO's influence and authority.

Ultimately, an organization has to determine how it wants to manage the division of labor and span of control. The **division of labor** means how you group various tasks. It's sometimes more effective to divide tasks into specialties. This way, the depth and quality is higher. As more tasks are divided into separate jobs, more specialties are created. As more specialties are created, more teams are formed. The result is the organization grows, along with operating costs. Employees are the most valuable resource but they are also expensive. They require salaries, training, supplies, facilities, benefits, and leadership support.

> **TIP**
>
> It's always a good idea to seek consensus and executive sponsorship for implementing security policies. It's even better to have strong organizational authority. In all cases, establishing the right tone at the top is essential to ensuring security policies receive the appropriate priority and visibility.

An organization needs to divide labor in a way that yields quality and keeps it competitive while controlling operating costs.

Another consideration is **span of control**, which relates to the number of layers and number of direct reports found in an organization. The span of control widens when a leader has many direct reports. This tends to flatten an organization. This is called a **flat organizational structure**. When the span of control widens, the leader is less connected to the details of what's going on. If a leader has to deal with a dozen direct reports, for example, it's doubtful he or she would have time to address many details. The leader would tend to focus on the big picture and the big risks.

There's no magic rule on the right number of direct reports. The appropriate span of control depends on the nature of the business, complexity of the issues, and number of problems needing the leader's attention. As the span narrows, the organization gains layers. This is called a **hierarchical organizational structure**. More layers tend to make an organization bureaucratic. Although the word "bureaucracy" can invoke thoughts of ineffective layers of work adding little value, hierarchical organizations are necessary. They allow specialties to thrive and produce high-quality products and services.

> ▶ **NOTE**
> An organization can have an overall hierarchical structure with pockets of flat organizational structures for specific teams and departments.

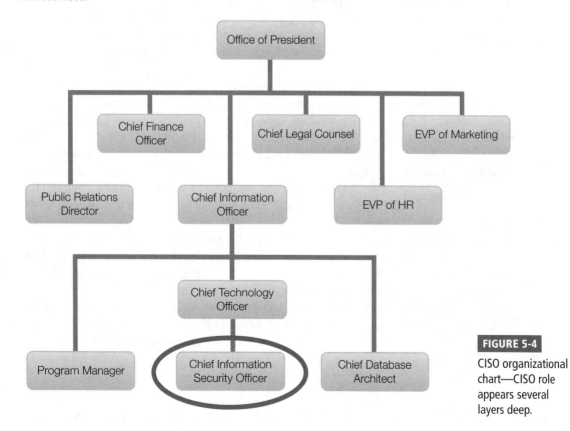

FIGURE 5-4

CISO organizational chart—CISO role appears several layers deep.

The difference between a flat and hierarchical organization is relative to its size and business model. Figure 5-2 indicates that an organization can be perceived as either flat or hierarchical. To understand the difference, you need to understand the number of layers between managers controlling the business and workers delivering products and services. For example, assume Figure 5-2 represents a carpet cleaning business with 20 workers. The lines of business could be commercial versus residential customers. The organization could be perceived as hierarchical. This is because the number of layers between the president of the company and workers could be perceived as excessive. Given the size and complexity of the business, one would expect a much smaller and flatter organization. Yet the same figure when applied to a larger business would be relatively flat. For example, assume Figure 5-2 represents a major domestic bank that offers retail banking and credit cards as lines of business. A major bank could have tens of thousands of employees. Yet Figure 5-2 reflects a relatively flat organization.

Flat Organizations

In a flat organization, the leaders are close to the workers that deliver products and services. A flat organization is generally defined as one with a limited number of organizational layers between the top and bottom ranks. As a result, leaders know their customers' and employees' needs and problems firsthand. This tends to produce faster decisions and more confidence to innovate. The right leader within this type of structure can be inspiring. This structure gives the leader the ability to connect with the workers and build trust.

From a security policy perspective, a flat organization can set the right tone from the top fairly easily. Senior leaders are directly engaged with the delivery of the security policy message. When leaders personally endorse security policies, the message is more powerful. Combine that with leaders who are engaged with and trusted by workers, and this approach becomes an enormous advantage in implementing security policies. In this situation, policies are more likely to be perceived as important and enforced. Engaged leaders in a flat organization often understand the perspectives of the workers better. This allows the leaders to guide the implementation of security policies in a way that resonates with the worker.

Flat organizations often have decentralized authorities. The span of control is so wide that leaders rely on the initiative of subordinates. There is no time to bring every problem to management for resolution. In some ways you need higher caliber teams that feel comfortable making independent decisions. Yet these decisions can lead to problems, especially when dealing with information security. Some problems include conflicting statements to regulators by the subordinate and senior leadership. It's important when defining security policing in a flat organization to clearly define when and how issues are to be escalated.

Hierarchical Organizations

For large organizations, hierarchical models are a necessity. The complexity required to keep a large organization running effectively requires a hierarchy of specialties. This means senior leaders are more detached from day-to-day operations. Can the same tone at the top be sent to all employees in a hierarchical organization? Yes, but it's more difficult than in a flat organization. The dynamics are different in a hierarchical organization.

Consider a help desk worker in an organization with 10,000 employees. The help desk worker is engaged with management within the team and department. Receiving a message on the importance of information security from the president of the company may have far less impact in a hierarchical organization. The message must still be sent but needs to be reinforced throughout the layers.

Have you ever watched children play the Gossip or Telephone game? Several children sit in a circle. The first child whispers a message into the ear of the next child. That child whispers what he or she heard into the ear of the next child, and so on. Once the message gets back to the first child, he or she states it. Not surprisingly, the final message has changed, sometimes greatly, from the original one. Communications in a hierarchical organization often follow the same pattern. It's easy to send a message from the top to the lower ranks of an organization. The challenge is how to avoid the message changing. You want the same passion and importance placed on the message consistently through the layers of the organization.

 NOTE

Many organizations require sign-off approval on training materials and other collateral to ensure the message is correct. The process often includes key leaders in several departments who examine the materials. However, one key leader who disagrees with the content can undermine everyone.

To be successful in implementing security policies in a large organization, you must continually sell the message at each layer. You must build support at the top, middle, and bottom ranks. You must choreograph the review, approval, and release process so you continue to be part of the messaging. Remember, the message can change as it moves through the layers of the organization. For example, when dealing with senior leaders, a core part of the message could be cost avoidance and reduction in operating risks. Messages to other layers might have greater emphasis on regulatory compliance or meeting customer expectations of privacy. It's important to tailor the benefit message to resonate with the audience. If workers can connect with the importance and priority they are more likely to follow the policy.

Advantages of a Hierarchical Model

There are some distinct advantages to a hierarchical model. The importance of specialization has been discussed. In a hierarchical model, communication lines are more clearly defined. When you encounter a problem, there is most likely a group that specializes in that area that can help solve it. The depth of knowledge in a subject area tends to be greater. This allows managers to predict and avoid problems before they occur.

Managers can also create "centers of excellence." These are small, specialized teams that focus on specific problems within an organization to help provide high-quality products and services. Assume, for example, an organization faces a growing problem of credit card fraud. A hierarchical organization that uses specialty teams would be able to use one or a combination of these teams to create a center of excellence to reduce fraud.

 WARNING

The larger the organization, the faster it can grow. For example, the more teams involved in producing a product or service means more teams will be needed to coordinate their activity. It's important that an organization does not grow for the sake of growth. It's especially important that security policies keep pace with organization growth, which drives a greater exchange of information sharing.

Disadvantages of a Hierarchical Model

There are also some disadvantages in a hierarchical model. One such disadvantage is accountability. A hierarchical model relies on work passing between a number of teams to ultimately produce a product or service. A communications breakdown between these groups could cause errors or delays.

Accountability could also be a problem. When many component teams are involved, whose fault is it if something doesn't work? This becomes even more difficult when the teams cross organization boundaries such as between large departments. This is a classic example in the IT world. The IT department is usually held accountable for application failures. However, did the business fail to provide the IT department the necessary information and budget? There may not be a clear answer, which is precisely the problem.

There's no one structure that fits all organizations. What's important is to fit the organization's structure to its business, size, and technology. Another important consideration is the fit to its leaders. If a leader is successful and leans towards a flat organization, a flat structure will emerge. On the other hand, if a leader's success is tied to hierarchical organizational benefits, that structure emerges. What's most important is recognizing these differences and adjusting your security policy approach accordingly.

In the end, it's people within the organization who will make the implementation of security policies and controls successful. How they are motivated to adopt the security principles within these policies indicates how easily you can introduce change. When you navigate an organizational structure to build support for security policies, you are talking to people, not boxes on an organizational chart. It's important to listen, accept suggestions, and realize you will need to overcome concerns and user apathy towards information security. It will be important to build support with executive leaders who may have differing views of risk and different management styles. Successful implementation of security policies will depend on how well you can navigate these people issues.

The Challenge of User Apathy

In its basic form, **apathy** is indifference and lack of motivation. An employee who is apathetic often "goes through the motions." This attitude results in poor performance and doing the minimum to get by. In the case of information security, it's hard to imagine that doing the minimum keeps information safe.

Policies by their nature cannot predict every situation. It's the nature of policies to rely on the talents of individuals to deal with the unexpected. Combining an apathetic worker with an unexpected security incident can result in disaster. A simple delay in reporting a potential incident, for example, could mean the difference between preventing an incident or having to deal with its aftermath. An apathetic worker can miss the opportunity to prevent sensitive information from getting into the wrong hands, leaving thousands of angry customers whose personal privacy has been breached.

Management must work closely with workers or teams that are apathetic to security polices. As a manager, you need to listen to the employees' issues and try to re-engage them. Security awareness and messaging is not a one-time event. It's important to reinforce the message as much as possible. If you can engage employees and show them why security is relevant to their jobs, there's a greater chance employees will adhere to policies. Security awareness programs help to keep workers engaged with the information security message, thereby helping to prevent apathy.

Well-defined security policies assume a certain level of noncompliance and even worker apathy. You build redundancy into security policies to detect and react to security breaches. In this way, you don't have to rely on any one individual to maintain security. A good example is automated escalation. If an administrator is paged about a potential security breach and fails to respond within a given time limit, an escalation page is sent to a supervisor. Security policies can require such escalation.

Overcoming the effects of apathy on security policies is a combination of the following:

- **Engaged communication**—Get leaders to listen to reasons for worker apathy. Adjust the implementation strategy to better explain the importance of the policy within the context of the individual role.

- **Ongoing awareness**—Continually reinforce the message of the value and importance of information security. Good security awareness can be a preventative measure against apathy.

- **Setting the right expectations**—Ultimately workers are expected to follow policy as part of their jobs. Setting expectation and monitoring adherence can encourage compliance.

- **Creating some layers of redundancy**—Some layers of redundancy are good. Avoid sole reliance on any individual or single technology when practical to do so.

The Importance of Executive Management Support

Implementing security policies starts with executive management. Without executive support, policies are just words. To have meaning they must be given the right priority and be enforced. That's when the benefits and value of security policies are realized for an organization. Implementing security policies creates a culture in which risk awareness takes work and resources. Unfortunately, some executives see involvement with security policies and risk awareness as an IT issue, and a distraction given their other priorities. However, executive management support is critical to the success of security policy implementation and acceptance throughout the organization.

The Standish Group published a major study in 1995 on why projects fail. The results of the study are just as valid today as they were then to explain executive behavior related to projects. The study looked at projects worth over $1 million. It concluded that of those projects that failed, the lack of executive support accounted for 7.5 percent. Of those projects that succeeded, 13.9 percent attributed their success to executive management support. When it comes to engaging the user within the business as a core factor for success or failure of the project, the numbers are even higher. Successful projects viewed user involvement as a factor in their success 15.9 percent of the time. Unsuccessful projects attributed the lack of user involvement as the cause of their failure 12.8 percent of the time. The numbers are less important than the fact that executive management support and engagement with the business, or the lack of it, is a major reason for project success or failure.

Selling Information Security Policies to an Executive

Understanding executive perception of these successes and failures is important. These perceptions must be overcome when soliciting support from executives. An online business site reported that projects fail due to eight common perceived missteps:[1]

- **Unclear purpose**—Unclear purpose refers to the clarity of value the project brings. In the case of security policies, it's important to demonstrate how these policies will reduce risk. It's equally important to demonstrate how the policies were derived in a way that kept the business cost and impact low.

- **Doubt**—Doubt refers to the need for change. You need to explain why what's in place today is not good enough. Change is perceived as a distraction from the core business. You need to convince the executive that the benefits outweigh disruption. Doubt may also be a factor if an organization has had several false starts. If several attempts have been made to implement a security policy with little success, you must convince them that this time is different. Even when the message and benefits are clear, it is also a matter of credibility with the executive.

- **Insufficient support from leadership**—Insufficient support from leadership refers to the broad support for the project. In the case of policies, a leader doesn't like surprises and wants to know he or she is not alone. You need to explain both the depth and breadth of support for the policies. To avoid surprises, be sure to articulate any pushback you are getting from other leaders. This will help avoid surprises and the executive can be an advocate to sway his or her peers. When problems are encountered, be sure to anticipate where your support will emerge or evaporate.

- **Organizational baggage**—Organizational baggage refers to how the organization executes based on past unsuccessful efforts. Unlike doubt, which is a personal credibility issue, this category focuses on the organization's ability to execute. If an organization continues to have problems implementing policies of any kind, how will security policies be any different? This type of organization usually fails to stay on course. Organizations that reorganize twice a year or have frequent leadership changes fall within this category.

- **Lack of organizational incentives**—Lack of organizational incentives refers to the inability to motivate behavior. Value is only derived from policies when they are enforced. An organization must have the will and process to reward adherence. The organization must have a low or zero tolerance for security policy violations.

- **Lack of candor**—Lack of candor refers to not having open, candid conversations. In the case of policies, you need to be clear what can and cannot be achieved. You need to listen and explain how the business's input was considered and adopted or rejected. Executives need a sense that they were part of a process and not just the recipients of the result.

- **Low tolerance for bad news**—Low tolerance for bad news refers to how executives react to missteps. You can count on an error in judgment at some point in implementing security policies. You need to prepare executives for the inevitable. You also need to gauge how they will react.

- **Unmanageable complexity**—Unmanageable complexity refers to how complex and realistic the project is. The ability of the organization to support the security polices will be an important topic of conversation.

Before, During, and After Policy Implementation

There's an art and science to obtaining support from executives for security policies. It's as much about confidence and credibility as it is about the facts. It's important to stay engaged and in communication with executives before, during, and after security policy implementation. Sometimes you will see initial optimism waning over time. Support can dissipate, so it's important to listen to and reinforce core messages to continually build support throughout the implementation.

One pitfall you want to avoid is trying to turn an executive into a knowledgeable security expert. Executives generally have neither the time nor interest, and need to rely on your expertise. What they do expect is that you have packaged the implementation steps into clearly understood and manageable tasks that minimize costs and effort. Their staff will also report back to them the results of your efforts. Therefore, you must be clear about what you expect and what the business must deliver.

The following is a checklist for packaging implementation tasks and to help stay on point when discussing security policies:

- **Things to do**—What exact tasks are to be performed and by whom?
- **Things to pay attention to**—How does the business know if it is successful?
- **Things to report**—What should be reported and when?
- **Roles and responsibilities**—Who's responsible for what?
- **Things to be aware of**—Why is the security policy in place?
- **Things to reinforce with employees**—What is the messaging to the staff?

Investing in planning prior to implementation will build a strong relationship with executives. It should also build true support. Executives who truly support you will continue their support when things do not go as planned. Messaging to executives needs to include their accountability for information security. Their role is essential to create a genuine effort to protect information. In the end, it's their organization that is affected when a breach occurs.

The Role of Human Resources

Well-defined HR policies provide the framework that governs employee relations. HR policies state core business values and what is expected. They can also prevent misunderstandings. Managers are more likely to engage a worker on sensitive topics, such as lack of performance, when there's a clear process they can follow to stay out of trouble. Like any written record, the HR policies can be used against an organization in a lawsuit. Poorly drafted policies become evidence to support an employee's contention that he or she acted within company expectations.

Although HR policies must demonstrate commitment to secure business practices and clearly state values, they must be flexible and definsible in a court of law while meeting business objectives. They must also establish processes for management to follow. You often find HR policy language intentionally vague. This avoids language that could be interpreted as an employment contract or unintended promise. You find what are sometimes called "weasel words" such as "generally," "typically," or "usually." These words are used so that managers and attorneys have the flexibility to interpret and apply policies broadly. In contrast, security policies must be precise, establishing clear expectations of behavior that can be enforced.

Security policy enforcement can be achieved using automated security controls that prevent an inappropriate action from happening. It's better to stop a security policy violation immediately through automation than to deal with its aftermath. However, how do you enforce security policies when automated controls are not available or ineffective? A classic example is when a worker views inappropriate sexual material on a company computer. Let's assume it can clearly be shown as willful versus accidentally stumbling onto an inappropriate Web site. This example starts to show reliance that security policies have on HR policies to define acceptable behavior and to enforce adherence through disciplinary actions.

Relationship Between HR and Security Policies

Security policies must be well grounded within HR policies. Don't look for precision in HR policies. They are better viewed as a foundation on which to build. They establish broad rules of acceptable behavior. These rules cover such topics as expectation of privacy when using company computers to declaring zero tolerance for certain inappropriate behaviors. Security policies can then operationalize these core values and define controls to enforce them. Just as security policies must align to business processes, they must also align to HR policies.

> **NOTE**
>
> The acceptable use policy (AUP) is often based in part on HR policy. The HR policy would prohibit gambling on company property. The AUP would define acceptable use of computers to prohibit gaming. Security controls based on the AUP would block gaming sites on the Internet. Violations of policy would most likely be referred to HR.

The relationship between HR and security policies can be seen in Figure 5-5. This figure depicts several key touch points. Let's use the previous example of viewing inappropriate material on a company computer. Figure 5-5 illustrates the relationship between HR and security policies. First, An HR policy would state the core value. This could be as simple as "Computers are for company use only." Or it could detail the type of material prohibited. The security policies could then align by outlining acceptable uses of the Internet. Preventative security controls can be designed to block unacceptable sites. A worker who finds a way around these controls may be discovered through detective controls that scan company computers for unauthorized software and information. If such material is found, management can determine what disciplinary action, if any, is necessary. Management would look to HR policies for guidance. After working with HR, management might decide a formal warning or even termination is appropriate. This illustrates the close alignment needed between HR and security policies.

Lack of Support

The ability to take disciplinary action to enforce security policies is not the only reason to seek support from HR. A lack of support can also make implementing security policies difficult or impossible. You need to remember that HR is a primary point of contact with workers. It can serve as a point of communication with the employees and a place to resolve conflicts. The following outlines several key areas of support provided by HR regarding security policy implementation:

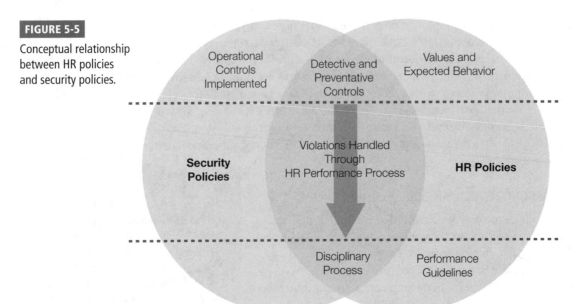

FIGURE 5-5

Conceptual relationship
between HR policies
and security policies.

- **HR policy and values**—Aligns with the organization's values
- **Security awareness**—Provides access to new employees to promote security awareness
- **Exit interview**—Provides access to departing employees to better understand what is working and what is not; important to continuously improve information security policies and controls
- **Field complaints**—As a point of contact to defuse complaints
- **Disciplinary action**—Provides the process needed to take disciplinary action
- **Source of authority**—Provides authority for establishing certain security controls

Both HR policy and value language can be vague by design. You need HR support to make sure you are interpreting the language correctly. This makes sure you align not just to the words but also to the spirit of HR policies. These interpretations become the basis of key security policies such as monitoring employee behavior on company equipment. If you don't have the right interpretation of HR policies, it's difficult or impossible to design effective security controls to prohibit certain behavior.

Security policies rely on employees understanding and cooperating with the rules. Security awareness is one of the best ways to achieve this understanding. A good security awareness program starts when a new employee walks in the door. It's reinforced at least annually and as an employee is promoted into new responsibilities. A lack of HR support makes it impossible to provide security awareness to new employees and when their jobs change.

Continuous improvement relies on people telling you what is and isn't working. A good source for this information is when a person is departing a company. You ask current employees what they think. But do you know if they are just telling you what you want to hear? They may not want to make waves. Individuals departing a company tend to be more candid with less to lose. Most HR departments conduct what is called an "exit interview." They ask basic questions about the work environment and why the person is leaving. It's also a good opportunity to ask a few well-selected questions on security. This could help you understand the strengths and weaknesses of the information security program. A lack of HR support means you never get to ask the question to know where your security weaknesses may lie.

An important part of HR's job is to field complaints from employees. No matter how good you are at explaining security policies, at some point you will ruffle someone's feathers. Count on them calling HR to complain. To get HR on your side, they need to know exactly how and why you are implementing security policies. They are skilled in listening and communicating with employees on sensitive matters. They can support you to help defuse problems. They can explain how the policies align with company values. They can reinforce key security awareness messages. A lack of support has the opposite effect. Complaints can escalate and get out of hand. Worse yet, if HR takes the employee's side, you may find yourself backing down on security policies or weakening the security awareness message.

You have learned how HR support relates to disciplinary action. If security policies are not enforced, employees inevitably perceive them as unimportant. Management needs the broad mandates within HR policies to assess employee performance. This includes how well people follow security policies. Without this HR support, security policies become optional and unenforceable.

Security policies, like any policy, must have a mandate. Someone in authority has to say "This is important" and "You have to do it." Often this comes from executive leadership. On occasion you can point to key values within HR policies as an additional source of authority. Doing so also provides a perceived mandate that helps gain support among executives. A lack of HR support makes it more difficult to obtain executive approval for security policies and easier to have them challenged.

In summary, it's difficult or impossible to implement security policies without HR support. Fortunately, HR in most organizations understands its role in helping implement security policies. It's rare to find an HR department that attempts to hinder implementation of security policies. More likely, you will find different degrees of support. The relationship with HR is an important one for the information security team to develop.

Policy Roles, Responsibilities, and Accountability

A comprehensive security policy is a collection of individual policies covering different aspects of the organization's information security. Implementation of these different security policies is an ongoing effort. It's rare that an organization goes from having no security policies to implementing a complete set. More commonly, a constantly churning set of policies will be under consideration. New policies will be added. Old policies will change in scope, depth, and breadth. The amount of change will depend on the industry, business drivers, complexity of the technology being deployed, and regulators. But change is inevitable.

TIP

When you implement security policies you are implementing change. This can include implementing business perspectives and organizational values. This means sometimes you are implementing culture change as much as security controls. Be sure to select a change management model that speaks to the need to influence leaders as much as to technical implementation of controls.

Many players are involved in the process of security policy implementation. The roles and responsibilities are different depending on where you are in the life cycle of a security policy. The term "life cycle" in this chapter refers to the creation, implementation, awareness, and enforcement of security policies. These different tasks require different roles and responsibilities.

There are many theories on how to approach change and an individual's role in the change process. The key point is to understand everyone's role from the perspective of a change model. You need to clearly define everyone's role when developing and changing policies. You also need to recognize different roles when it comes to enforcing policies after they have been implemented.

Change Model

There are lots of change models to choose from. You may be able to adapt some when implementing security policies. This section focuses on Kotter's Eight-Step Change Model. John Kotter, a professor at Harvard Business School, developed the model. He introduced the model in 1995 in a book titled *Leading Change*. The model has been widely adapted for a number of purposes. This model addresses the need to create executive support for implementing change. This is a critical success factor in implementing security policies.

Professor Kotter states that to be successful in implementing change in a company at least 75 percent of management needs to "buy into" it. The early stages of creating vision and urgency around the need for security policies will be critical later to build the coalition of executives needed to make change happen.

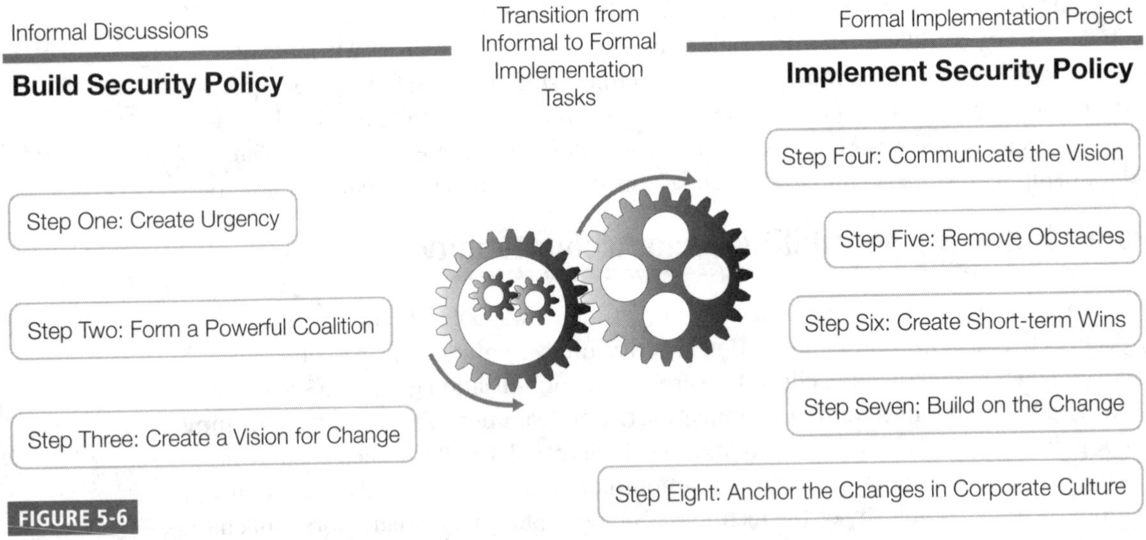

Informal Discussions

Build Security Policy

Transition from Informal to Formal Implementation Tasks

Formal Implementation Project

Implement Security Policy

Step One: Create Urgency

Step Two: Form a Powerful Coalition

Step Three: Create a Vision for Change

Step Four: Communicate the Vision

Step Five: Remove Obstacles

Step Six: Create Short-term Wins

Step Seven: Build on the Change

Step Eight: Anchor the Changes in Corporate Culture

FIGURE 5-6

Basic policy implementation approach.

Let's examine the model in relation to implementing security policies. The model divides an effective change process into eight steps:

1. **Create urgency**—For change to happen there must be an urgent need. The greater the sense of urgency the more likely that change will occur.
2. **Form a powerful coalition**—For change to happen leadership must back you. You need the authority and influence of leadership to make true change happen.
3. **Create a vision for change**—Change needs to be understandable. It must be clear what you are asking of people and what value the change will bring.
4. **Communicate the vision**—Once you have support, you need to communicate your intent widely. You need to let everyone know what's coming and keep it a priority in their minds.
5. **Remove obstacles**—There will be barriers to your success. You need to remove these barriers while continually moving "change" forward.
6. **Create short-term wins**—Success, no matter how small, breeds more success. If you can achieve a number of short-term successes, you can silence critics and build toward long-term goals.
7. **Build on the change**—Real change takes time and continued effort. Do not declare victory too soon.
8. **Anchor the changes in corporate culture**—To make anything stick, it must become habit and part of the culture.

Figure 5-6 shows how this model can be adapted to implementing security policies. You would cycle through this model each time you added a new security policy or made a major change to an existing policy. This model ensures that before you start a formal implementation you have the leadership support needed to succeed. This figure also highlights the separation between informal and formal tasks. When we adapted Kotter's model for the purposes of this chapter, we created a separation between informal and formal implementation tasks. This is to emphasize the importance of preparing for policy implementation through informal discussions versus starting a formal project approach right away. There are two major benefits to having these informal tasks. First, you gain executive support. Having a formal project before you have executive support is presumptuous and will create unnecessary resistance. Second, it establishes a collaborative setup that allows you to change and modify your approach. It also builds ownership into the process for the executive giving you advice.

Responsibilities During Change

Implementing security policies is easier if you manage it from a change model perspective. It helps you establish a collaborative style that allows business leaders to understand and buy into what you are trying to accomplish. The process starts with an informal set of steps that builds awareness and understanding. With a clear purpose beyond your security policies, you can build the executive support needed to succeed.

Using the steps in Kotter's Eight-Step Change Model, the following sections explain the roles and responsibilities involved in the change process.

 WARNING

Be sure not to overplay the urgency by exaggerating the amount of risk that the policy will reduce or by focusing on unlikely events. Overplaying urgency damages an ISO's credibility.

Step 1: Create Urgency

It is the responsibility of the **information security officer (ISO)** to convey urgency to business leaders. This is selling the need for information security. An effective way of doing this is to understand the business risk the security policy addresses and convey the need in business terms. The greater the business risk reduction, the greater the urgency perceived by the business.

Step 2: Create a Powerful Coalition

It's important to get executive support. Leaders are responsible for reducing risk to their organization. It's the responsibility of the ISO to know who the key stakeholders are. "Stakeholder" is a term referring to individuals who have an interest in the success of the security policies. It is the responsibility of the ISO to reach out to stakeholders, explain the policy change, and listen to concerns. It is the responsibility of stakeholders to analyze the impact of the policy change. There's no rule of thumb about how detailed this analysis must be. It could be as simple as a phone conversation about the proposed change or as complicated as a formal report. In any case, it's the responsibility of the stakeholder to offer an opinion as to how the security policy impacts the organization.

The size of the stakeholder group varies depending on the scope of the policy change and the size of the organization. When the number of stakeholders in any group is too large, the ISO can take a sampling approach. For example, assume a policy change affects the entire organization, which is composed of more than 1,000 managers. It's not practical to ask each manager how the policy would affect every team. Therefore, the ISO would sample a population of managers. The ISO can target those types of managers who would be more affected than others. A larger sample size is better than a small sample size. The following is typical list of key stakeholders to contact:

- Department executives
- Business managers responsible for following the policy
- Legal
- Teams that monitor regulatory compliance
- HR
- Internal Audit

Step 3: Create a Vision for Change

The security policy must be understandable. It is the ISO's responsibility to write the policy in terms the business understands. The ISO can tune the message so the value of implementing the policy makes sense. After compiling everyone's input, the ISO creates a coherent security message and policy. The message should include high-level explanations of the policy to sell the vision. It is the responsibility of the stakeholder to validate the ISO's assumptions and raise objections.

It's not appropriate for a stakeholder to wait until just before a security policy is implemented to object. The ISO is responsible for ensuring all objections are transparent and either resolved or escalated. It's the responsibility of the ISO to make every effort to resolve an objection. The objection could be pointing out a legitimate problem that requires a change to the security policy or control.

It might not be possible to make everyone happy. However, everyone needs to have a say. Remember, success depends on a genuine effort to implement the spirit of the policies. Everyone reports to someone in an organization. It is the ISO's role to escalate conflicts to some authority who can resolve them. In the end you are trying to get the majority of leaders on your side.

TIP

Find a leader in your organization who can be an agent of change. These are leaders who don't always follow the pack and can think out of the box. They can guide you through the organizational politics involved in implementing change.

Step 4: Communicate the Vision

The policy change must be widely communicated. It is the ISO'S responsibility to create the message. The ISO must also formally lay out communication plans. A communication plan outlines the messages to be conveyed, how they will be conveyed, and to whom they are conveyed. For example, the communication plan may include a combination of posting notices about the policy change on the organization's intranet plus internal e-mails sent by department leaders to their staffs. The ISO also needs to transition the implementation of security policies from informal discussions to a formal project plan. The project plan needs to outline dates, timelines, resources, and organizational support needed to be successful.

Stakeholders, particularly executive leaders, are responsible for communicating the change with their endorsement. Whether a leader raised an objection or not, leaders have an obligation to communicate and endorse any approved policy. This tone at the top is an important responsibility for an executive to perform. Executives are also responsible for setting team priorities to implement security policies.

TIP

The collateral created to sell the policy vision should be used in security awareness training. It will express the business need for the policy as well as the technical security components.

Step 5: Remove Obstacles

Obstacles to implementation must be identified and removed. It is the ISO's responsibility to be the central point of contact and to track implementation problems. It is the stakeholder's responsibility to collect and report problems with the implementation. It is everyone's responsibility to report problems with security policies to their leadership. Many information security teams set up intranet sites so security issues can be reported directly to the security team.

Step 6: Create Short-Term Wins

It's important to demonstrate value as early as possible. The ISO is responsible for identifying how success is measured. The ISO works with line management to collect metrics for assessing the policies' effectiveness. It is usually the responsibility of these line managers to make sure such metrics are captured and are meaningful.

Step 7: Build on the Change

It takes time to change an organization's culture. The ISO must continually monitor security policy compliance. The ISO reports to leadership on the current effectiveness of the security policies. The ISO will also have to ask the business to accept any residual risk or come up with a way to reduce it. Residual risk is the amount of risk that remains after you implement security controls. For example, let's assume a virus scanner can catch 99 percent of all known viruses. That leaves 1 percent of the viruses undetected. The business needs to know about this risk. The business leaders are then responsible for accepting this risk or paying for more technology to stop the remaining 1 percent.

Step 8: Anchor the Changes in Corporate Culture

Make the values in the security policies part of the culture. This takes time and is achieved by changing employees' attitudes. The ISO needs to be a strong communicator. It is his or her responsibility to come up with ways to reinforce the security message without creating a distraction for the business.

Roles and Accountabilities

The organization is ultimately accountable for information security. When something catastrophic occurs, with lawyers and regulators engaged, the organization's leaders have to explain what happened. In fact, officers of the organization may be held personally liable. They may pull the top technology executive (the CIO) along for the ride. But executives are the ones who fund technology and determine how much risk they are willing to pay to reduce.

The concept of holding business leaders ultimately accountable for information security is reinforced by the amount of money spent on technology. The amount of money spent protecting information security and how it is protected are both business and shareholder issues. Technology costs are a major part of many organizations' budgets and are controlled by the business. A report from Financial Insights suggests that capital market firms spent $95.5 billion on technology in 2007. Added to these enormous technology expenditures are an increasing number of privacy laws requiring tighter controls around data. Regulations like Sarbanes-Oxley (SOX) require business executives to personally attest to the security controls related to financial statements.

Although business leaders may be ultimately responsible, they rely on key technology roles to keep them out of trouble. These roles are accountable for implementing security policies, monitoring their adherence, and managing day-to-day activities. Although their titles may vary within an organization, typically you find different individuals accountable for each of the following roles:

- **Information security officer**—The individual accountable for identifying, developing, and implementing security policies. The information security officer is also accountable to ensure corresponding security controls are designed and implemented.

- **Executive**—A senior business leader accountable for approving security policy implementation. An **executive** is also responsible for driving the security message within an organization and ensuring the security policy implementation is given appropriate priority.

- **Compliance officer**—An individual accountable for monitoring adherence to laws and regulations. A **compliance officer** often uses adherence to security policies as a measure of regulatory compliance.

- **Data owner**—Typically someone in the business who approves access rights to information. **Data owners** are accountable for ensuring only the access that is needed to perform day-to-day operations is granted. They would also be responsible to ensure there a separation of duties to reduce risk of errors or fraud.

- **Data manager**—An individual typically responsible for establishing procedures on how data should be handled. **Data managers** also ensure data is properly classified.

- **Data custodian**—An individual responsible for the day-to-day maintenance of data. **Data custodians** back up and recover data as needed. They grant access based on approval from the data owner. You can view their accountability as generally maintaining the data center and keeping applications running.

- **Data user**—The end user of an application. **Data users** are accountable for handling data appropriately. They are accountable for understanding security policies and following approved processes and procedures. Data users have an obligation to understand their security responsibilities and not to violate policies.

- **Auditor**—An individual accountable for assessing the design and effectiveness of security policies. **Auditors** can be internal or external to the organization. They offer formal opinions in writing. These opinions review the completeness of the policy design and how well it conforms to leading industry practices. Auditors also offer opinions on how well the policies are being followed and how effective they are. Auditors do not report to the leaders they are auditing. This allows them to provide a valuable independent second opinion. For example, internal auditors in publicly traded companies typically report findings to the audit committee and line management. External auditors may issue findings to executive management and the audit committee. The audit committee is a subcommittee of the board of directors.

Implementing security policies typically starts with the ISO. The ISO identifies needs and establishes a standard approach to adding and changing policies, such as the adoption of Kotter's Eight-Step Model. Once security policies are implemented, the ISO monitors all roles. When a security policy violation occurs, the ISO drives accountability. The ISO influences management to enforce policies and hold individuals accountable.

ISOs need to make sure they build security policies collaboratively. The key is to create an open and candid conversation on risk. If the discussions on risk are perceived as valuable, executives are more willing to commit their time. This means the ISO needs to hold stakeholders accountable to participate. No one should be able to opt out. Accountability changes once the security policies are implemented. End users are accountable for following policies. The ISO's central role is to coordinate these activities.

When Policy Fulfillment Is Not Part of Job Descriptions

There is no rule of thumb about how often an employee's performance should be appraised. Many organizations perform annual assessments, although some perform assessments twice a year. This is in addition to individual appraisals between employees and their managers.

The basis for these appraisals starts with the employee job description. When a job description does not include adherence to policies, it's more challenging to implement security policies. In most cases, gross violation of policies is considered during an individual's performance appraisal regardless of the job description. Absent gross violations, policies may not be mentioned. It's not enough that an employee simply follows security policies. Policies cannot cover every situation. The ideal situation is having a workforce that is aware of security threats and can appropriately react to the expected.

However, if a job description does not include policy fulfillment, the employee could perceive it as someone else's problem. To understand threats, employees must take a genuine interest in security awareness education. They need to apply this material to their jobs. They need to ask questions and challenge the status quo. When an employee sees an opportunity to improve security, he or she needs to be an advocate for such change. This is the ideal situation.

Today's employees, however, are overworked. They have constant limits on their time and resources. Too often in today's challenging business climate there's little or no mention of security policies during an employee's appraisals. The exception is when a gross violation of policy or a major incident occurs. Minor violations may be overlooked. Even major security policy and control deployments may not be considered important. Security policy fulfillment is an abstract concept to many. Given a choice, most employees will focus on what their manager thinks is important instead of learning an abstract concept.

You learned earlier in the chapter how self-interest is a powerful motivator of behavior. When there's no reward associated with promoting security policies, such activity competes with other interests. The unfortunate reality is that many times the effort given is the bare minimum. It's not because executives or managers don't believe it's important. It's because there's little time and no perceived benefit.

There's no easy answer on how to overcome this. If you can't change job descriptions you need to create a perceived benefit. The culture of compliance can help by creating peer pressure. Also, it's useful to engage employees so feel some ownership in the security policies' success. This can be as simple as soliciting ideas for improvement and publicizing those suggestions selected. Provide public recognition for individuals who exhibit the desired behavior. This could be as simple as a thank-you letter from a top executive in the organization. In short, create a reward outside the job description.

Impact on Entrepreneurial Productivity and Efficiency

Entrepreneurship can be defined many ways. Let's talk about some key attributes. Entrepreneurship focuses on innovation and growth. Startup companies are full of entrepreneurial spirit out of necessity. They must innovate to enter a crowded market and they must grow to survive. Well-established organizations have long passed this stage. As an organization matures, so does its business model. Those true entrepreneurs that started the company, or saw it through its high growth periods, often leave. They are usually replaced with very talented professional managers.

Therein lies the struggle between how to manage a business versus how to "grow" it. This is not an abstract problem. It has significant implications for security policies that must reflect the core values of the business.

A company in its early startup stages or in high-growth mode focuses on agility and innovation, and tends to have a greater acceptance of risk. This is when you see a dominant entrepreneurial culture emerge. When a business has a large percentage of leaders who share this entrepreneurial mindset, you will also see a greater level of risk acceptance. They challenge the status quo and push the limits of policies to achieve their goals.

Conversely, as the company matures and this population of entrepreneurs leaves the company, they are often replaced with professional managers. These may be very talented individuals coming from the finest business schools. But you do see a different culture emerge with a greater focus on how to sustain and manage a business. This translates into less risk taking and a clearer definition about how business should be run. During this latter maturity stage, the business starts growing its bureaucracy.

It's not suggested that one approach is better than the other. That will depend on the business and situation. But an information security professional must recognize which attitude dominates his or her organization. All organizations have dominance of one over the other. Security policies must be written and implemented to accommodate this mindset and tolerance for risk.

Although there is always a dominant culture, an organization can by design be a mix of these two mindsets. The mix typically comes in when a mature company is "testing the waters" into a new business line.

Consider, for example, a company that has little or no sales presence on the Internet. It wants to start a new unit to test for feasibility by selling a limited number of products online. Let's assume the test period is 24 months. The business intends to evaluate the success or failure of the effort. The business wants to keep costs low—it may completely disband the new unit and abandon the idea within the next 24 months. It brings in leaders with startup experience, and a clash of cultures occurs almost immediately.

The new unit's staff is under tremendous pressure to demonstrate small successes quickly. They have little tolerance for delays. They face pressure to get their applications onto the Internet quickly and access to information on demand. This situation promotes a tendency to take short cuts within existing processes, which can increase risk.

Applying Security Policies to a Entrepreneurial Business

Security policies need to reflect the dominant view of risk within an organization. In other words, you cannot have two sets of policies—one for those who are more entrepreneurial and one for those who like to take less risks. You need to establish security policies that reflect the overall tolerance for the enterprise. Establish through policy those tolerances as acceptable behavior. Then create risk acceptance processes and mitigating controls for behavior that falls outside the tolerance area.

That's exactly what is called for in the example of an entrepreneurial unit startup in a more mature organization. Although the policies would apply to this unit no differently than any other unit, their execution and mitigating controls may be different. For example, you could segment the network in a way that isolates those systems and applications being placed on the Internet. You could also grant them elevated privileges and have the additional risk accepted by the business.

This does not mean that the controls associated with an entrepreneurial unit are bypassed or disabled. A business cannot accept unreasonable risks or risks that place the company in noncompliance to regulations. It does mean that your service model to an entrepreneurial unit must change. You must adopt a service model that reflects the same agility that the unit needs to stay in business. This could mean assigning an ISO directly to that business unit. Dedicating resources to the business would improve responsiveness. It would also increase costs.

Entrepreneurial businesses, like any other, need the discipline that comes with security policies to control risks. The service model associated with these businesses needs to be responsive and agile to avoid impacting their productivity. The security policies also need to support processes that can quickly escalate risks to the business for acceptance or mitigation.

Tying Security Policy to Performance and Accountability

Determining if a business adheres to its security polices is an important measurement of success. It's often reported to senior leadership to show risks are being controlled. It's also reported to regulators to show a commitment to being compliant. You should remember that security policies target risk, and the reduction in risk to the business is the measurement of success.

To determine if the implementation of security policies is successful, take performance measurements and measurements of accountability. These two measurements combined provide a good indicator if the business adheres to its security policies.

Regarding accountability, you need to measure if employees are following the policies. Selecting the right performance measurement can be tricky. A common pitfall is to measure success as a percentage of implemented policy coverage. It's easier to demonstrate the value security policies bring to the business when the business sees its operational risk being reduced. Therefore, the best measurement of whether employees are following policies is the actual reduction in risk that occurs.

For example, let's say you have a security policy that requires all servers to be patched. More precisely, you must apply all critical security patches within so many days of their release. For this discussion, assume you know what a critical security patch is and can measure when it's applied. Reporting that 90 percent of your servers have received the patch may sound good. But how much of the risk has been reduced? If 80 percent of your business runs through the 10 percent that has not been patched, your business is very much at risk. When measuring performance or effectiveness of policies, always ask, "How much actual risk to the business has been reduced?"

Let's consider a second example. Assume a business experienced disruptions and outages on 3 percent of its call center desktops last month. You have a security policy requiring a virus scanner on all desktops. You determine some desktops are missing the scanner. Other desktops have an out-of-date scanner. You determine the problem is a new virus that's hard to remove. You come up with a plan to install a different virus scanner. You track your deployment of the solution and declare victory once the solution is deployed to all desktops. A better performance measurement of success would have been to track the reduction in disruptions or outages on call center desktops. It's important to know if the solution actually solved the problem. In other words, did the business realize the value of the policy enforced by having real risk reduced? Maybe not, if the solution doesn't work in all cases or if the solution ended up causing a different kind of disruption or outage on the desktop. In either case, the value to the business is when the disruptions or outages stop.

 TIP

When tying policy adherence to performance measurement, focus on measuring risk to the business as opposed to implementation of policies and controls.

You can get a basic understanding if individuals are being held accountable for adherence to security policies by examining policy violations, incidents, and security awareness. These basic measurements are as follows:

- **Number of security violations by employees reported**— You should investigate any unexplained increase in this number to determine why an abnormal number of security violations occurred. One reason could be lack of training.

- **Number of incidents that could have been avoided**— When a security breach occurs, you need to determine the root cause. This root cause can tell you if a contributing factor was a policy failure.

- **Completion and competency rate for security awareness**— You should track which individuals have completed security awareness training. Additionally, the training should measure the level of competency with the material. This training needs to be refreshed and retaken at least annually.

TIP

When reporting trends, explain how the numbers were collected and the business context. For example, a rise in security policy violation may be expected if a new policy was just released or if the reporting capability was recently improved.

Success Is Dependent Upon
Proper Interpretation and Enforcement

Security policies state how the organization is to protect its information. They describe how to conduct business functions and transactions with a desired outcome. They set the stage for building security controls to enforce policy tenets. A comprehensive security policy is the "who does what to whom and when" document. It should reflect core values such as the importance of protecting customer privacy. Policies have powerful words that can reduce real business risk. The power of security policies to reduce risk comes from people taking action. Some of these people will design and implement automated controls.

You learned that policies must be enforced. Employees tend to treat unenforced policies as optional guidelines. The most effective enforcement of security policies is through management. It is the responsibility of managers to provide oversight of employees' work. Therefore, it's a natural extension of a manager's duties to enforce security policies. It's also highly effective. Managers set the values that employees emulate. When these leaders "walk the talk" and treat information security as an important priority, it's more likely employees will do the same.

In addition, managers are in the best position to identify policy violations and correct behavior on the spot. Security violations and minor infractions aren't always reported. If, however, employee coaching takes place on the spot, such behaviors can be corrected quickly. Ultimately, that's one of the important goals of reporting infractions. Effective security policy enforcement stops violations and helps change the culture.

However, enforcement assumes employees understand the meaning of security policies beyond the words themselves. Well-written security policies convey key concepts that can be applied to situations that the policies never anticipated. Concepts such as protecting customer privacy are universal in that they can be applied to a number of business situations. Interpreting security policies against new business situations and new technologies ensures the business gets the maximum benefit. The documents are not designed to change every time a new situation arises. They are designed to guide people through key risk decisions when faced with new situations.

FYI

The U.S. Constitution is similar to a security policy in that the Constitution represents core values that withstand the test of time. The U.S. Constitution is an "enduring" and "living" document. Although the core values remain the same, underlining laws change based on circumstances. Enforcement of its principles comes from interpretation in the context of new situations. The founding fathers could not have envisioned the Internet. Yet the laws related to Internet copyright find their roots in the U.S. Constitution.

Well-written security policies can be enduring because they define core values that apply to an array of business and technology situations. The interpretation of security policies must be tracked and recorded. Because interpretations become the basis for managing risk, these need to be tracked in a central registry. The benefits of a central policy interpretation registry include the following:

- Creates a system of record on how to manage risk
- Provides solutions for individuals with similar problems
- Creates a historical record for research; especially important in answering regulator questions
- Provides input into creating or changing policies based on volume of interpretations in a particular area
- Promotes communication between leaders on risk topics as interpretation is passed around for review and approval
- Can be monitored to anticipate the changing security needs of the organization

Providing the wrong policy interpretation could have serious consequences. Take the question of how a policy applies to a new law or regulation, for example. Policy interpretations require grasp of the core business and security principles and the leadership experience to understand their limitations. A central group might handle security policy interpretations. A well-defined process typically includes several layers of review before an interpretation is formally published. Depending on the impact that the interpretation might have, other areas may be included in the review such as HR, legal, and compliance teams.

CHAPTER SUMMARY

In this chapter, we defined key issues to be considered when implementing security policies. This included how personality types in the workplace can affect how you implement security policies. It's important to understand different personality types in the workplace to better motivate and influence workers to embrace security policies. Proper motivation can overcome user apathy. Executive support is important to get resources and to drive the security message and visibility needed to be successful.

This chapter demonstrated how post-implementation activities are just as important as those leading to policy implementation. We learned that success is measured by the value the security policies bring to the business in terms of risk reduction. We also examined how security policies are effective only if they are used. This means they must be enforced. The core values and ways to look at risk within security policies can be applied to a wide array of business situations and new technologies. Successful security policy implementations can change mindsets and an organization's culture. They can further reduce risks as individuals are better equipped to deal with the unexpected threats.

KEY CONCEPTS AND TERMS

Apathy	Data owner	Hierarchical organizational structure
Auditor	Data user	
Compliance officer	Division of labor	Information security officer (ISO)
Data custodian	Executive	
Data manager	Flat organizational structure	Span of control

CHAPTER 5 ASSESSMENT

1. Which of the following is a basic element of motivation?

  A. Pride

  B. Self-interest

  C. Success

  D. B and C

  E. All of the above

2. Which personality type often breaks through barriers that previously prevented success?

  A. Attackers

  B. Commanders

  C. Analyticals

  D. Pleasers

3. Avoiders like to _____ and will do _____ but not much more.

4. As the number of specialties increases so does _____.

5. In hierarchical organizations, the leaders are close to the workers that deliver products and services.

    A. True
    B. False

6. User apathy often results in an employee just going through the motions.

    A. True
    B. False

7. Which of the following is a method for overcoming apathy?

    A. Avoiding redundancy
    B. Issuing company directives
    C. Engaging in communication
    D. Requiring obedience to policies

8. Why is HR policy language often intentionally vague?

9. In the case of policies, it is important to demonstrate to business how polices will reduce risk and will be derived in a way that keeps costs low.

    A. True
    B. False

10. Interpreting security policies against new business situations and new technologies ensures the business gets the maximum benefit from the policies over time.

    A. True
    B. False

11. Kotter's Eight-Step Change Model can help an organization gain support for _____ changes.

12. When a catastrophic security breach occurs, who is ultimately held accountable by regulators and the public?

    A. Company officers
    B. The CIO
    C. The ISO
    D. The data owner

13. Which of the following are attributes of entrepreneurs?

    A. Innovators
    B. Well educated in business management
    C. More likely to take risks
    D. A and C
    E. B and C

14. A company can have two sets of enterprise security polices, if necessary, to address the needs of individual business units.

    A. True
    B. False

15. Which of the following is the best measure of success for a security policy?

    A. Number of security controls developed as a result
    B. The number of people aware of the policy
    C. Reduction in risk
    D. The rank of the highest executive who approved it

ENDNOTE

1. Glaser, John. "Management's Role in IT Project Failures: Senior Managers Obviously Have Great Interest in Seeing That Projects Become Successful. Yet Despite Best Intentions, All Too Often They Wind Up Playing a Pivotal Role in Ensuring Project Failure." (Allbusiness.com, October 2004). *http://www.allbusiness.com/technology/technology-services/237595-1.html* (accessed on April 26, 2010).

PART TWO

Types of Policies and Appropriate Frameworks

IT Security Policy Frameworks

A N INFORMATION TECHNOLOGY (IT) security policy framework is the foundation of an organization's information security program. The framework consists of a library of documents. Organizations can use the framework to help build processes and acquire technology to enforce policies. The framework is also useful for putting security personnel in place to operate and maintain the program.

Organizations cannot afford to be reactive or operate in an ad-hoc fashion regarding information security. There's increased accountability and liability with regulations. There's increase demand from senior leadership to demonstrate value. There's a push and drive from security professionals to measure success. However, before you can measure anything you need a benchmark. A benchmark allows you to gauge if you've reasonably covered the risks. It's something you can measure against to demonstrate value. The benchmark, and that gauge of success, is a security framework. It captures the experience and knowledge of security professionals from all over the world. It provides a road map to guide an organization through the maze of security issues.

This chapter covers the components of an IT security policy framework. It also helps you understand how to create a framework that meets your organization's needs. The chapter covers the business and assurance consideration. The chapter also discusses the issues with unauthorized access and their ramifications. Through these discussions you learn better the value and construction of security frameworks.

This chapter covers the following topics and concepts:

- What an IT security policy framework is
- What a program framework policy or charter is
- Which business factors you should consider when building a policy framework
- Which information assurance factors and objectives to consider
- Which information systems security factors to consider
- What best practices are for IT security policy framework creation
- What some case studies and examples of IT policy framework development are

Chapter 6 Goals

When you complete this chapter, you will be able to:

- Describe the role of a policy framework in an information security program
- Describe the different types of policies used to document a security program
- Explain the role of policies, standards, guidelines, and procedures
- Explain the organization of a typical standards and policies library
- Explain the personnel roles in a typical security department

What Is an IT Policy Framework?

An **IT policy framework** includes policies, standards, baselines, procedures, and guidelines. The framework resembles a hierarchy or tree. At the top of the tree is a charter or program framework policy, followed by additional policies. Then there are several standards. Under standards are many guidance and procedure documents. Getting the framework right is key to a successful security program.

Figure 6-1 offers one view of how you might structure an information security policy and standards library.

Building a policy framework is also like growing a tree. The roots and branches of the tree are established; you water the tree and allow it sufficient time to grow. Eventually it provides coverage for everyone. Over time, tree branches die off, leaves fall to the ground, new branches grow, and the tree needs pruning. A policy framework works in the same way. You give it ongoing attention to nurture the process and document content. This assures that it provides the coverage your organization needs and demands.

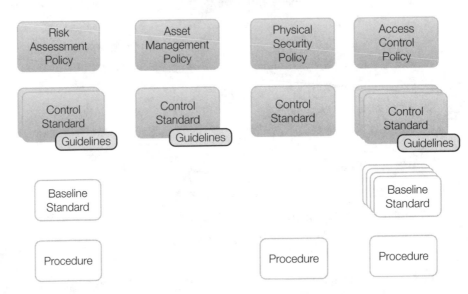

FIGURE 6-1

A policy and standards library framework.

> **NOTE**
> You will often hear the framework documents referred to as "policies." In practice, the framework includes policies, standards, and other documents. Each type of document has a specific purpose.

Your security posture defines your organization's risk tolerance. It describes how you plan to protect business information and resources. The posture is documented in the security policy framework documents.

What Is a Program Framework Policy or Charter?

The program framework policy, or **information security program charter**, is the "capstone" document for the information security program. The charter is a required document. This document establishes the information security program and its framework. This high-level policy defines:

- The program's purpose and mission
- The program's scope within the organization
- Assignment of responsibilities for program implementation
- Compliance management

The chief executive officer (CEO) usually approves and signs the charter. The charter establishes the responsibility for information security within the organization. This responsibility is often placed on an individual known as the chief information security officer (CISO). The CISO is responsible for the development of the framework

FYI

The CISO may also be known by many other titles, depending upon the culture of the organization. The CISO role is functionally aligned to the top ranking individual who has full-time responsibility for information security. Some examples include:

- Director of Information Security
- Chief Security Officer
- Director of Risk and Compliance
- Information Security Program Manager

for IT security policies, standards, and guidelines. The CISO also approves and issues these documents. One of the CISO's primary roles is to ensure consistency with regulations. The regulations may be at the local, state, or federal level. The CISO also sets up a security awareness program. The program helps employees understand and live up to the organization's information security policies, standards, guidelines, and procedures.

Purpose and Mission

This part of the policy states the purpose and mission of the program. You should define the goals of the IT security program and its management structure.

Integrity, availability, and confidentiality are common security-related needs. These needs can form the basis of the program's goals. For example, let's assume an organization maintains mission-critical databases. The goals could address how to reduce errors, data loss, and data corruption. In another example, most e-commerce systems maintain confidential personal data. In this case, the goals might include stronger protection against unauthorized disclosures.

You should create a structure that addresses program and organizational goals. Your policies should mirror your organization's mission and goals. They should describe the operating and risk environment of the organization within this structure. Important issues for the structure of the information security program include:

- Management and coordination of security-related resources
- Interaction with diverse communities
- The ability to communicate issues of concern to upper management

Scope

A policy's scope specifies what the program covers. This usually includes resources, information, and personnel. In some instances, a policy may name specific assets, such as major sites and large systems.

Sometimes, you must make tough management decisions when defining the scope of a program. For example, you may need to decide how the program applies to contractors who connect to your systems. The same concept applies to external organizations.

TIP

Define the responsibilities of computer services providers versus the managers of applications who use the computer services. The policy can also serve as the basis for establishing employee accountability.

NOTE

An employee can unintentionally violate a policy. For example, an employee may lack knowledge or training. This can result in noncompliance.

Responsibilities

A policy should state the responsibilities of personnel and departments related to the program. This includes the role of managers, users, and the IT organization. This is also referred to as the program's delegation of authority.

Compliance

Compliance is the ability to reasonably ensure conformity and adherence to both internal and external policies, standards, procedures, laws, and regulations. A program-level policy should address enforcement of the policy. For example, what happens if someone doesn't comply with computer security policies?

The program-level policy is a high-level document. It usually does not include penalties and disciplinary actions for specific infractions. However, this policy may authorize the creation of other policies or standards that describe violations and penalties. One common strategy for handling this issue is to have the information security policy refer to disciplinary procedures found elsewhere, such as in a human resources policy that broadly covers disciplinary actions.

Industry-Standard Policy Frameworks

Policy frameworks provide industry-standard references for governing information security in an organization. They allow you to leverage the work of others to help jump-start your security program efforts. The following areas determine where framework policies are helpful:

- Areas where there is an advantage to the organization in having the issue addressed in a common manner, such as shared IT resources
- Areas that affect the entire organization, such as personnel security
- Areas for which organization-wide oversight is necessary, such as compliance
- Areas that, through organization-wide implementation, can result in significant economies of scale, such as unified desktop computer management

No two organizations are alike. For-profit companies may have different goals and concerns than nonprofit organizations or government agencies. Different needs require different solutions. Therefore, security professionals have a wide variety of policy frameworks to work with. It's up to each organization to determine the best policy framework that meets the needs of the organization and the threats they face.

Three frameworks stand out because of their scope and wide acceptance within the security community:

- **Control Objectives for Information and related Technology (COBIT)**—A widely accepted set of documents that is commonly used as the basis for an information security program. COBIT is an initiative from the Information Systems Audit and Control Association (ISACA) and is preferred among IT auditors. COBIT was addressed in Chapter 3.

- **ISO/IEC 27000 series**—An internationally adopted standard for any information security management program in virtually any organization

- **National Institute of Standards and Technology (NIST) Special Publications, such as (SP) 800-53, "Recommended Security Controls for Federal Information Systems and Organizations"**—Geared to U.S. government agencies and their subcontractors

Many of the regulatory bodies use these standards to develop security guidance and auditing practices. By relying on those who have paved the way for you, you can help to assure compliance with regulations that affect your organization without reworking all of your compliance processes. The following sections offer details on how to use the ISO/IEC 27002 and NIST SP 800-53 standards to describe your policy framework.

ISO/IEC 27002 (2005)

The International Organization for Standardization (ISO) and the International Electrotechnical Commission (IEC) develop and publish international standards. These standards are published as ISO/IEC numbered designations. It's common to see these standards abbreviated as ISO. For example, the **ISO/IEC 27002** standard is often shortened to ISO 27002.

 NOTE

ISO is actually not an acronym. It is short for "isos," which is the Greek word for equal.

ISO/IEC 27002 is titled "Information Technology–Security Techniques–Code of Practice for Information Security Management." This is a popular industry standard for establishing and managing an IT security program. ISO/IEC 27002 outlines 12 main areas that compose the framework:

1. **Risk assessment and treatment**—Describes how to perform periodic risk assessments. This area also offers options for risk treatment, including:
   - Applying appropriate controls to reduce the risks
   - Knowingly and objectively accepting risks, as long as they clearly satisfy the organization's policy and criteria for risk acceptance
   - Avoiding risks by not allowing actions that would cause the risks to occur
   - Transferring the associated risks to other parties, such as insurers or suppliers

2. **Security policy**—Describes how management should define an information security policy. Organizations usually maintain detailed security policies in a library. Information security standards, procedures, and guidelines support the library.

3. **Organization of information security**—Describes how to design and implement an information security governance structure. This section describes the need for an internal group that manages the program, including the governance of business partners.

4. **Asset management**—Describes inventory and classification of information assets. The organization should understand what information assets it holds, and manage its security appropriately. This section covers responsibility for assets and information classification.

5. **Human resources security**—Describes security aspects for employees joining, moving, or leaving an organization. The organization should manage system access rights. The organization should also provide security awareness, training, and education. Section 5 covers these employment phases:
   - Prior to employment
   - During employment
   - Termination or change of employment

6. **Physical and environmental security**—Describes protection of computer facilities. Valuable IT equipment should be physically protected against malicious or accidental damage or loss, overheating, loss of main power, and so on. This section covers:
   - Secure areas
   - Equipment security
   - Critical IT equipment, such as cabling and power supplies

7. **Communications and operations management**—Describes management of technical security controls in systems and networks. This section includes these topics:
   - Operational procedures and responsibilities
   - Third-party service delivery management
   - Protection against malicious and mobile code
   - Backups
   - Network security management
   - Media handling
   - Exchange of information
   - Electronic commerce services
   - Monitoring

8. **Access control**—Describes restriction of access rights to networks, systems, applications, functions, and data. This section addresses controlled logical access to IT systems, networks, and data to prevent unauthorized use. The following topics are covered:
   - Business requirements for access control
   - User access management

- User responsibilities
- Network access control
- Operating system access control
- Application and information access control
- Mobile computing and remote employee access

9. **Information systems acquisition, development, and maintenance**—Describes building security into applications. Information security must be taken into account in the Systems Development Life Cycle (SDLC) processes for specifying, building/acquiring, testing, implementing, and maintaining IT systems. These activities include the following:
   - Security requirements of information systems
   - Correct processing in application systems
   - Cryptographic controls
   - Security of system files
   - Security in development and support processes
   - Technical vulnerability management

10. **Information security incident management**—Describes anticipating and responding appropriately to information security breaches. Information security events, incidents, and weaknesses should be promptly reported and properly managed. This section of the standard covers:
    - Reporting information security events and weaknesses
    - Managing information security incidents and improvements

11. **Business continuity management**—Describes protecting, maintaining, and recovering business-critical processes and systems. This section describes the relationship between IT disaster recovery planning, business continuity management, and contingency planning, ranging from analysis and documentation through regular exercising/testing of the plans. Controls are designed to minimize the impact of security incidents that occur despite the preventive controls from elsewhere in the standard.

12. **Compliance**—Describes areas for compliance, which include:
    - Compliance with legal requirements
    - Compliance with security policies and standards, and technical compliance
    - Information systems audit considerations

ISO/IEC 27002 covers the three aspects of the information security management program: managerial, operational, and technical activities. All three must be present in any IT security program for comprehensive coverage. For more information about ISO/IEC 27002, visit *http://www.iso27001security.com/html/27002.html.*

TABLE 6-1   A summary of NIST SP 800-53.

CONTROL AREA	DESCRIPTION
Access Control	Limit information system access to: • Authorized users • Processes acting on behalf of authorized users • Devices (including other information systems) • The types of transactions and functions that authorized users are permitted to exercise
Awareness and Training	Ensure that managers and users of information systems are aware of the security risks associated with their activities. Ensure adequate training for personnel to carry out their assigned information security-related duties and responsibilities.
Audit and Accountability	Create, protect, and retain information system audit records. Records include those for monitoring, analysis, investigation, and reporting of unlawful, unauthorized, or inappropriate information system activity. Users are accountable for their actions.
Security Assessment and Authorization	Periodically assess the security controls in information systems to determine if the controls are still effective. Develop and implement plans of action that correct deficiencies and reduce or eliminate vulnerabilities in information systems. Continually monitor information system security controls to ensure their effectiveness.
Configuration Management	Establish and maintain baseline configurations and inventories of information systems throughout their life cycles. Establish and enforce security configuration settings for devices in use.
Contingency Planning	Establish, maintain, and implement plans for: • Emergency response • Backup operations • Post-disaster recovery
Identification and Authentication	Identify information system users. Verify the identities of those users, as a prerequisite to allowing access to information systems.
Incident Response	Establish an incident handling process for information systems. Track, document, and report incidents to appropriate officials and/or authorities.
Maintenance	Perform periodic and timely maintenance on information systems. Provide effective controls to conduct information system maintenance.
Media Protection	Protect information system media, both paper and digital. Limit access to information on information system media to authorized users.

TABLE 6-1 *continued*

CONTROL AREA	DESCRIPTION
Physical and Environmental Protection	Limit physical access to information systems, equipment, and operating environments to authorized people.
	Protect the support infrastructure for information systems.
	Protect information systems against environmental hazards.
	Provide environmental controls for all information systems.
Planning	Develop, document, periodically update, and implement security plans for information systems. Describe the security controls in place or planned for the information systems. Include the rules of behavior for accessing the information systems.
Personnel Security	Determine that individuals in positions of responsibility are trustworthy and meet established security criteria for those positions, including third-party service providers.
	Maintain the protection information systems during and after terminations and transfers.
	Employ consequences for people failing to comply.
Risk Assessment	Periodically assess the risk to operations, assets, and people when using information systems or transmitting information.
System and Services Acquisition	Allocate sufficient resources to protect information systems.
	Employ system development life cycle processes that incorporate information security considerations.
	Ensure that third-party providers employ adequate security measures to protect information, applications, and/or services.
System and Communications Protection	Monitor, control, and protect information transmitted or received by information systems at perimeter and important boundaries of the information systems.
	Employ architectural designs, software development techniques, and systems engineering principles for effective information security.
System and Information Integrity	Identify, report, and correct information and information system flaws in a timely manner.
	Provide protection from malicious code at appropriate locations within information systems.
	Monitor information system security alerts and advisories and take appropriate actions in response.
Program Management	Ensure the ongoing operation of the Information Security program.

NIST Special Publication (SP) 800-53

NIST is an agency of the U.S. Department of Commerce. NIST develops information security standards and guidelines for implementing them. **NIST SP 800-53**, "Recommended Security Controls for Federal Information Systems," was written using a popular risk management approach.

Organizations often rely on NIST publications for reference and to develop internal IT security management programs. NIST SP 800-53 uses a framework similar to ISO/IEC 27002. However, NIST SP 800-53 includes 18 areas that address managerial, operational, and technical controls. Table 6-1 summarizes NIST SP 800-53.

For more information about NIST SP 800-53, visit *http://csrc.nist.gov/publications/PubsSPs.html*

What Is a Policy?

Policies are an important part of an information security program. They are best defined as high-level statements, beliefs, goals, and objectives. Policies help protect an organization's resources and guide employee behavior. Security policies help you address critical computer security issues. With effective policies in place, your organization will have better protection of systems and information.

Security policies also provide the "what" and "why" of security measures. Procedures and standards go on to describe the "how" of configuring security devices to implement the policy. For example, Marcus Ranum, a security industry expert and author of *The Myth of Homeland Security*, defines a firewall as:

> . . . the implementation of your Internet security policy. If you haven't got a security policy, you haven't got a firewall. Instead, you've got a thing that's sort of doing something, but you don't know what it's trying to do because no one has told you what it should do.

The IT security program begins with statements of management's intentions. These intentions are documented as policies. Policies describe the following:

- Details of how the program runs
- Who is responsible for day-to-day work
- How training and awareness are conducted
- How compliance is handled

The following is an example of a high-level policy that establishes an IT security program:

> Executive Management endorses the mission, charter, authority, and structure of Information Security. The Company's Executive Management has charged Information Security with the responsibility for developing, maintaining, and communicating a comprehensive information security program to protect the confidentiality, integrity, and availability of Company information resources.

Write policies as broad statements that describe the intent of management, defining the direction for the organization. Make these statements nonspecific as to *how* that will be accomplished. You should include details about how to meet the policy in a family of documents below the high-level policy.

What Are Standards?

You have many choices when deciding how to protect your computer assets. Some choices are based on quantifiable tradeoffs. Other choices involve conflicting tradeoffs and questions related to your organization's strategic directions. When making these choices, the policies and standards you establish will be used as the basis for protecting your resources—both information and technology—and for guiding employee behavior.

Standards are formal documents that establish:

- Uniform criteria that you can evaluate and measure
- Methods to accomplish a goal
- Repeatable processes and practices for compliance to policies

Security standards provide guidance towards achieving specific security policies. Although security policies are written at a high level, there's insufficient detail to explain how people should support them.

Security standards are often related to particular technologies or products. They are used as benchmarks for audit purposes and are derived from:

- Industry best practices
- Experience
- Business drivers
- Internal testing

Standards come in two forms: control or issue-specific standards and system-specific technical or baseline standards.

Issue-Specific or Control Standards

Issue-specific standards focus on areas of current relevance and concern to your company. Be prepared for frequent revision of these standards because of changes in technology and other related factors. As new technologies develop, some issues diminish in importance while new ones continually appear. For example, it might be important to issue a standard on the proper use of a cutting-edge technology even if the security vulnerabilities are still unknown.

A useful structure for issue-specific or baseline standards is to break the document into basic components. Those components are described in the following sections.

Statement of an Issue.   This section defines a security issue and any relevant terms, distinctions, and conditions. For example, an organization might want an issue-specific policy on the use of Internet access. The standard would define which Internet activities you permit and those you don't permit. You may need to include other conditions, such as prohibiting Internet access using a personal dial-up connection from an employee's desktop PC.

Statement of the Organization's Position.   This section should clearly state an organization's position on the issue at hand. To continue with the example of Internet access, the policy should state which types of sites are prohibited. Examples of these sites may be pornography, brokerage, and/or gambling sites. The policy should also state whether further guidelines are available, and whether case-by-case exceptions may be granted, by whom, and on what basis.

Statement of Applicability.   This section should clearly state where, how, when, to whom, and to what a particular policy applies. For example, a policy on Internet access may apply only to the organization's on-site resources and employees and not to contractors with offices at other locations.

Definition of Roles and Responsibilities.   This section assigns roles and responsibilities. Continuing with the Internet example, if the policy permits private Internet service provider (ISP) accesses with the appropriate approvals, identify the approving authority in the document. The office or department(s) responsible for compliance should also be named.

Compliance.   Gives descriptions of the infractions that are unacceptable and states the corresponding penalties. Penalties must be consistent with your personnel policies and practices and need to be coordinated with appropriate management,

Points of Contact .   This section lists the names of the appropriate individuals to contact for further information. It may also identify other applicable standards or guidelines. For some issues, the point of contact might be a line manager. For other issues, it might be a facility manager, technical support person, systems administrator, or security program representative.

System-Specific or Baseline Standards

System-specific standards, or baseline standards, are focused on the secure configuration of a specific system, device, operating system, or application. Many security policy decisions apply only at the system level.

Examples include:

- Who is allowed to read or modify data in the system?
- Under what conditions can data be read or modified?
- What firewall ports and protocols are permitted?
- Are users allowed to access the corporate network from home or while traveling?

What Are Procedures?

A procedure is a written instruction on how to comply with a standard. A procedure documents a specific series of actions or operations that are executed in the same manner repeatedly. If properly followed, procedures obtain the same results under the same circumstances. Procedures support the policy framework and associated standards by codifying the steps that are proven to yield compliant systems.

Procedures should be:

- Clear and unambiguous
- Repeatable
- Up to date
- Tested
- Documented

Examples of procedures include:

- Incident reporting
- Incident management
- User ID addition/removal
- Server configuration
- Server backup
- Emergency evacuation

A single standard often requires multiple procedures to support it. The people responsible for supporting or operating technical equipment in compliance with a standard are often the same people who document procedures to meet compliance requirements. Security department personnel may assist with documenting procedures. Once approved, the security department publishes procedures within the policy and standards library with appropriate controls over who has access to them.

 NOTE

Some procedures may be proprietary or contain trade secrets. These procedures may not be suitable for broad access by all employees.

Figure 6-2 illustrates an example of an extract of a policy and standards library. The figure highlights an access control policy, which is one of many security-related policies.

Exceptions to Standards

Situations arise in which your organization cannot meet one or more standards immediately. You must recognize **exceptions** to standards to determine where problems may exist.

Periodic reviews of these exceptions can also lead to improvements to the standards when many exceptions point to a general inability to meet compliance goals. Paying attention to exceptions is vital to assuring that the policy framework remains relevant and current.

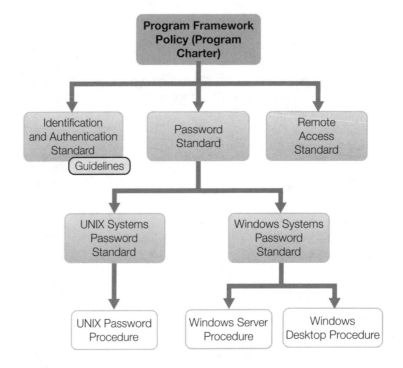

FIGURE 6-2

A possible access control policy branch of a policy and standards library.

What Are Guidelines?

IT security managers often prepare guidelines, or guidance documents, to help interpret a policy or a standard. Guidelines may also present current thinking on a specific topic. Guidelines are generally not mandatory—failing to follow them explicitly does not lead to compliance issues. Rather, guidelines assist people in developing procedures or processes with best practices that other people have found useful. A guideline can also clarify issues or problems that have arisen after the publication of a standard.

You can think of guidelines as "standards in waiting." They are used where possible, and feedback on guidelines is given to IT security managers responsible for policy and standards maintenance. Guidelines provide the people who implement standards or baselines more detailed information and guidance (hints, tips, processes, etc.) to aid in compliance. These documents are optional in a library but are often helpful.

Business Considerations for the Framework

Chapter 2 focused on business considerations that drive the need for security policies. An organization's collection of security policies, and therefore the entire security framework, shows its commitment to protecting information.

As with security policies in general, a few considerations for implementing a framework include:

- **Cost**—Cost of implementing and maintaining the framework
- **Impact**—Impact of the controls required by the framework on employees, customers, and business processes

Creating a policy framework from the ground up takes time and effort. It's important for management to budget for these expenses. In addition, as the number of documents in the framework grows, you may need a content management system to manage the documents. Many organizations already use Microsoft SharePoint Server or a similar product to manage all business-related documents. You can use the same system to manage documents in a policy framework.

Employees often resist change, especially changes that affect how they need to perform their jobs. However, a comprehensive policy framework can help employees do their jobs more efficiently. The framework includes guidelines that employees can follow, and procedures that specify how to perform tasks. Essentially, a policy framework provides a structure within which employees can work more efficiently.

A policy framework also helps management adhere to compliance requirements. As mentioned in Chapter 3, your security policy framework enables you to show regulators that you are using best practices. Many regulations provide specific details that must be included in your security policies. It's often helpful to create a "cheat sheet" that cross-references your security documents with the standards. For example, an entry might state that "HR Policy 2010-033 entitled 'Pre-Employment Screening' satisfies PCI DSS requirement 12.7." This will come in very handy if you are ever audited; you can use the cheat sheet to show auditors the exact sections of policy that implement each requirement.

Complying with the Sarbanes-Oxley Act

As technology further expands, laws and regulations eventually follow to compel positive action to protect information systems.

In 2002, the U.S. Senate passed the Sarbanes-Oxley (SOX) Act, which gained the attention of U.S. corporate CEOs. The act passed in the wake of the collapse of Enron, Arthur Andersen, WorldCom, and several other large firms. SOX requires publicly traded companies to maintain internal controls. The controls ensure the integrity of financial statements to the Securities and Exchange Commission (SEC) and shareholders. The act also requires that CEOs attest to the integrity of financial statements to the SEC.

Because of this mandate, controls related to information processing and management are now highly scrutinized. Since the law took effect, the need for a comprehensive library of current operating documents is underscored.

ROLE	ACTIVITY
TABLE 6-2 Roles related to a policy and standards library.	
CISO	Establishes and maintains security and risk management programs for information resources
Information resources manager	Maintains policies and procedures that provide for security and risk management of information resources
Information resources security officer	Directs policies and procedures designed to protect information resources; identifies vulnerabilities, develops security awareness program
Owners of information resources	Responsible for carrying out the program that uses the resources. This does not imply personal ownership. These individuals may be regarded as program managers or delegates for the owner.
Custodians of information resources	Provide technical facilities, data processing, and other support services to owners and users of information resources
Technical managers (network and system administrators)	Provide technical support for security of information resources
Internal auditors	Conduct periodic risk-based reviews of information resources security policies and procedures
Users	Have access to information resources in accordance with the owner-defined controls and access rules

Roles for Policy and Standards Development and Compliance

Developing and maintaining a policy framework is a major undertaking. In large organizations, it usually requires many people. Table 6-2 lists roles commonly found in the development, maintenance, and compliance efforts related to a policy and standards library.

Information Assurance Considerations

To develop a comprehensive set of security policies, start with the goals of information security: confidentiality, integrity, and availability. As you learned in Chapter 1, information assurance (IA) tenets also include nonrepudiation and authentication.

One of the prime objectives of the information security program is to assure that information is protected. Ensuring confidentiality means limiting access to information to authorized users only. The integrity of the information must also be maintained

FYI

The goals of information security—confidentiality, integrity, and availability—are often referred to as the CIA triad. Some systems security professionals refer to the CIA triad as the "A-I-C" triad (availability, integrity, and confidentiality) to avoid confusion with the U.S. Central Intelligence Agency, which is commonly referred to as the CIA. Either abbreviation is acceptable. However, if you use CIA, make sure people understand you're referring to "confidentiality, integrity, and availability."

so that it can be trusted for decision-making. A system is considered to have integrity when you can trust that any modifications to the data were intentional changes made by authorized users or business processes. Availability ensures the information is accessible to authorized users when required. Nonrepudiation ensures that an individual cannot deny or dispute being part of a transaction. Finally, authentication is the ability to verify the identity of a user or device.

To meet information assurance needs, your framework should include policies for the following:

- Automation of security controls, where possible.
- Implementation of appropriate accounting and other integrity controls.
- Controls that handle potential conditions that appear while a system is operating. This should include error handling that won't reduce the normal security levels it's expected to support. Fail-secure rather than fail-safe is better for protecting information systems.
- Development of systems that detect and thwart attempts to perform unauthorized activity.
- Assurance of a level of uptime of all systems.

The following sections address the tenets of IA from a policy framework perspective.

Confidentiality

To meet confidentiality requirements, your security objectives must be specific, concrete, and well-defined. Let's use the goal of confidentiality as applied to e-mail as an example. You might have an objective of ensuring that all sensitive information be protected against eavesdropping. Implement this by requiring that users encrypt all e-mails containing sensitive information. This is a concrete, specific, and well-defined objective.

Write objectives so they are clear and achievable. Security objectives should consist of a series of statements that describe meaningful actions about specific resources. These objectives are often based on meeting business functions. In addition, they should state the security actions needed to support the requirements.

Integrity

To meet integrity requirements, define operational policies that list the rules for operating a system. Using e-mail as an example, this operational policy defines approved behaviors by people using a corporate e-mail system. The policy indicates who (by job category, organization placement, or name) can do what (modify, delete, etc.) to what kinds of e-mail and under what conditions. This includes controls over sending sensitive data via e-mail, such as the use of encryption, and when and how it might be appropriate.

> **NOTE**
>
> The more fine-grained a policy is, the easier it is to automate enforcement. For example, if an e-mail server requires a specific configuration to be considered secure, a monitoring tool or agent on the server can report on the configuration and relay this to compliance personnel.

Managers must make decisions when developing policies because it is unlikely that all security objectives will be fully met. Consider the degree of granularity needed for operational security policies. "Granularity" indicates how specific the policy is regarding resources or rules. The more granular the policy, the easier it is to enforce and to detect violations. A more granular policy involves security controls over a specific element of technology. It might describe all the settings needed to configure a device or system securely. Checking it only requires ensuring that the settings are still in place. A less granular policy does not provide many details about a specific control, which allows people to determine how to comply. Less granular policies are more difficult to prove compliance because each situation differs.

A formal policy is published as a distinct policy document. A less formal policy may be written in a memo. An informal policy might not be written at all. Unwritten policies are extremely difficult to follow or enforce. On the other hand, very granular and formal policies are an administrative burden. In general, best practice suggests a granular formal statement of access privileges for a system because of its complexity and importance.

Availability

To meet availability needs, your policy framework may include documents that require your systems be accessible to internal and external users. External users require different forms of access than internal users. For example, an external user might be required to use a virtual private network (VPN) to access the internal network. Another policy might deal with uptime, in that your systems must be operational 99.99 percent of the time.

Authentication

Identification of authorized users is the primary authentication concern. You may need policies that address the following:

- Requirements for ensuring proof that users are who they say they are
- Different levels of authentication for different users; for example, a username and password combination for internal users and two-factor authentication for contractors and other external users

Other authentication policies may require users to change their passwords periodically, limit the number of times a user can enter an incorrect password before the account is locked, and so on.

Nonrepudiation

To meet nonrepudiation needs, the policy framework must describe the controls surrounding transaction assurance. As you read previously, authentication provides you with the assurance that the person on the other end of the transaction is who they claim to be. However, that is a lot different than providing you with the ability to prove to a third party that the other person initiated a transaction. Nonrepudiation controls, such as the use of digital signatures, provide this flexibility. A digitally signed document can be prepared with strong encryption and a public key infrastructure. This type of document enables you to prove, in court if need be, that the document came from the purported sender. The sender will not be able to deny (or repudiate) that they created the document.

Information Systems Security Considerations

The success of an information security program depends on the policy produced and on the attitude of company management toward securing information IT systems. The policy framework helps ensure that all aspects of information security are considered and controls are developed. As a policymaker, it's up to you to set the tone and the emphasis on the importance of information security.

Unauthorized Access to and Use of the System

The proliferation of technology has revolutionized the ways information resources are managed and controlled. Long gone are the days of the "Glass House," full of mainframe computers under tight centralized control. Internal controls from yesteryear are inadequate in controlling today's decentralized information systems. Relying on poorly controlled information systems brings serious consequences, including:

- An inability of the organization to meet its objectives
- An inability to service customers
- Waste, loss, misuse, or misappropriation of scarce resources
- Loss of reputation or embarrassment to the organization

To avoid these consequences, risk management approaches are needed. Risk is an accepted part of doing business. Risk management is the process of reducing risk to an acceptable level. You can reduce or eliminate risk by modifying operations or by employing control mechanisms.

The dollars spent for security measures to control or contain losses should never be more than the estimated dollar loss if something goes wrong. Balancing reduced risk with the costs of implementing controls results in cost-effective security. The greater the value of information assets, or the more severe the consequences if something goes wrong, the greater the need for control measures to protect it.

Unauthorized Disclosure of the Information

Maintaining the confidentiality of information is critical to many organizations in the age of knowledge workers. When you consider the economic activity of the world's more advanced nations, most of the productive output of workers is information, rather than the widgets of yesterday. Consider two examples:

- Market research companies spend thousands of dollars and countless hours gathering business intelligence for their clients. Often, the sole output of these projects is a report summarizing the results. If this got into the hands of the client's competitors, it would destroy the competitive advantage created by the report. It could also reduce the economic value of the information to the client, and potentially jeopardize the market research firm's client relationship.

- Manufacturing companies may now produce many of their products in overseas factories where labor is inexpensive. However, they still do the "knowledge work" of developing product plans, formulas, and other trade secrets in developed nations. If those plans got into the hands of competitors, it would be quite simple for the competitor to ship the plans to an overseas factory and produce the same product without any of the research and development expense.

Disruption of the System or Services

The demands for timely and voluminous information are increasing. One major protection issue is the availability of information resources. In some cases, service disruptions of even a few hours are unacceptable. Think about how much revenue Amazon.com or eBay.com loses for every hour of downtime. Reliance on essential systems requires a plan for restoring systems in the event of disruption. Organizations must first assess the potential consequences of an inability to provide their services and then create a plan to assure availability.

Modification of Information

If information is modified by any means other than the intentional actions of an authorized user or business process, it could spell disaster for the business. This underscores the importance of integrity controls, which prevent the inadvertent or malicious modification of information. Consider, for example, a product-testing firm that spends many hours testing the optimal settings for a piece of safety equipment used in factories. If a power surge alters the data stored in the testing database, the company might use the incorrect data to recommend equipment settings, jeopardizing the safety of factory workers.

Destruction of Information Resources

In addition to unauthorized modification of information, security controls should also protect against the outright destruction of information, whether intentional or accidental. The most common control used to protect against this type of attack is the system backup. By storing copies of data on backup tapes or other media, the company has a fallback option in the event data is destroyed. Consider the case of an insurance company that stores policy information on servers in a data center. If that data center is destroyed by fire, off-site backup tapes can be used to re-create it. Without those backup tapes, the company would have no way of knowing which policies it had issued, putting the entire business in jeopardy.

Best Practices for IT Security Policy Framework Creation

Your policies need high visibility to be effective. When implementing policies, you can use various methods to spread the word throughout your organization.

Use management presentations, videos, panel discussions, guest speakers, road shows, summits, question/answer forums, and newsletters. Introduce computer security policies in a manner that ensures that management's support is clear, especially where employees feel overwhelmed with policies, directives, guidelines, and procedures.

You should also integrate IT security policy into and be consistent with other organizational policies, such as personnel policies. A way to help ensure this is to coordinate their development with other departments in the organization.

Formulating viable computer security policies is a challenge and requires communication and understanding of the organizational goals and potential benefits that will be derived from policies. Through a carefully structured approach to policy development, you can achieve a coherent set of policies. Without these, there's little hope for any successful information security systems.

Case Studies in Policy Framework Development

This section provides three case studies that help you understand how to develop or implement a policy framework. You will look at cases from the private sector, the public sector, and the critical infrastructure protection area.

Private Sector Case Study

In 2008, Nadia Fahim-Koster, director of Piedmont Healthcare IT Security, reassessed the security compliance of the hospital using a well-established approach. The director decided to start with baseline metrics for IT security risk. This would help her determine whether the systems were already in compliance. It would also provide a baseline when assessing systems in the future. If systems were not in compliance, her IT team could adjust security configurations and controls to bring them into compliance.

However, the director faced the following challenges:

- A large, diverse network of systems with over 7,000 devices
- An incomplete inventory of all IT assets and their configurations
- No easy way to classify assets
- A broad Health Insurance Portability and Accountability Act (HIPAA) standard that left elements of reporting open to interpretation

She assembled an IT team to work on the project. They began with asset discovery to have a complete and up-to-date inventory of systems. Next, they looked at system configurations to determine if they complied with regulations and existing hospital policies.

The director decided to measure Piedmont Healthcare's IT security controls using NIST SP 800-53. The team established a framework for classifying and measuring security controls across the Piedmont Healthcare network.

"Selecting the NIST framework as our measurement framework meant that we had to classify all of our IT assets the same way," explained Fahim-Koster. "Once this was completed, we could begin to capture the existing security controls and perform a gap analysis to see where we needed to make improvements."

Using the NIST framework, Piedmont classified its servers as high, medium, or low impact based on the type of information they contained. When IT personnel determined the gaps in compliance controls, they could prioritize which servers to address first and prioritize which controls to use.

Public Sector Case Study

In 2006, the State of Tennessee determined the need for a comprehensive information security program. One of the main goals was to protect the state's revenues, resources, and reputation. The state accomplished this by researching, selecting, and implementing risk management methodologies, security architectures, control frameworks, and security policies.

The policies for Tennessee were based on the ISO/IEC 17799 (now ISO/IEC 27002) standard framework. The policies comply with applicable laws and regulations. The policies in the framework are considered the minimum requirements to provide a secure computing operation for the state.

The framework defines the information security policies for the State of Tennessee and the organizational structure required to communicate, implement, and support these policies. The policy framework was developed to establish and uphold the controls needed to protect information resources against unavailability, unauthorized or unintentional access, modification, destruction, or disclosure.

The policies and framework cover any information asset owned, leased, or controlled by the State of Tennessee. They control the practices of external parties that need access to the State of Tennessee's information resources. The policies were developed to protect:

- All state-owned desktop computing systems, servers, data storage devices, and mobile devices
- All state-owned communication systems, firewalls, routers, switches, and hubs
- Any computing platforms, operating system software, middleware, or application software under the control of third parties that connect to the State of Tennessee's computing or telecommunications network
- All data stored on the State of Tennessee's computing platforms and/or transferred by the state's networks

Critical Infrastructure Protection Case Study

Critical infrastructure is a prime target for attacks. Sectors like the electrical grid and telecommunications system rely on one another to operate. On September 11, 2001, when the Verizon telephone network near Wall Street stopped working, the financial markets stopped operating moments later.

One of the thorniest issues in maintaining critical infrastructure is that 85 percent of it is privately held. The government has a responsibility to develop effective and efficient information-sharing partnerships.

Building on the successes of private industries to develop information-sharing infra-structures among themselves, the U.S. federal government established a framework for the two-way flow of timely and actionable information between public and private participants.

Under the National Infrastructure Protection Plan (NIPP) initiatives, the government established an information-sharing approach that works horizontally and vertically. Using secure networks and coordination mechanisms, the process allows information sharing and collaboration within and among sectors. The federal system also enables multidirec-tional information sharing between government and industry that reduces redundancy in reporting as much as possible.

These processes incorporate private sector security partners into the national intelligence cycle. Sector partners' confidence that the integrity and confidentiality of their sensitive information will be protected is increasing. Both the government and the sector partners work to assure that information sharing can produce actionable information regarding threats, incidents, vulnerabilities, and potential consequences to critical infrastructure and key resources (CI&KR).

The policy framework used to implement and operate the partnerships for improving information sharing was guided by considering a number of important elements:

- Current, reliable, accurate, and actionable information is critical to private sector decisions to protect their business.

- Private sector entities have spent years establishing strong collaborative information-sharing relationships with state and local authorities to facilitate the sharing of time-sensitive threat and vulnerability information.

- The private sector operates within multiple information-sharing frameworks. Some organizations have established trust with local and state agencies and wish to continue using those relationships to share information related to vulnerabilities, threats, and so on.

- When homeland security, law enforcement, and terrorism-related information is shared, it sometimes reflects the regulatory environment in which the private partner operates. In times of crisis, laws that regulate the private sector may not violate and should not get in the way of effective information sharing.

- The private sector relies on multiple information sources, including professional and local organizations, private information providers, news outlets, colleagues, open intelligence sources on the Web, and company management throughout the world.

CHAPTER SUMMARY

Policy framework development is needed for the establishment and ongoing operation of the organization's security program. This program begins with documentation in the form of policies, standards, baselines, procedures, and guidance for compliance. The library of documents is arranged as a hierarchy with the highest level consisting of a charter. The next level includes policies, followed by an increasing number of standard and baseline documents. These documents are supplemented with guidelines to aid in implementation. Finally, many procedure documents that explicitly describe how to implement a security control or process are included. The library should be developed and managed by dedicated personnel who are experts in the subject matter related to the organization's industry or mission.

Any effective IT security program includes top-down sponsorship to establish and enforce these policies and standards. Because information security never stands still for long, most of the documents in a policy and standards library must be considered living documents that are updated as technology and the environment changes.

KEY CONCEPTS AND TERMS

Compliance

Exception

Information security program charter

ISO/IEC 27000 series

Issue-specific standard

IT policy framework

NIST SP 800-53

System-specific standard

CHAPTER 6 ASSESSMENT

1. An IT policy framework charter includes which of the following?

   A. The program's purpose and mission
   B. The program's scope within the organization
   C. Assignment of responsibilities for program implementation
   D. Compliance management
   E. A, B, and C only
   F. A, B, C, and D

2. Which of the following is the first step in establishing an information security program?

   A. Adoption of an information security policy framework or charter
   B. Development and implementation of an information security standards manual
   C. Development of a security awareness-training program for employees
   D. Purchase of security access control software

3. Which of the following are generally accepted and widely used policy frameworks? (Select three.)

   A. COBIT
   B. ISO/IEC 27002
   C. NIST SP 800-53
   D. NIPP

4. Security policies provide the "what" and "why" of security measures.

   A. True
   B. False

5. _____ are best defined as high-level statements, beliefs, goals, and objectives.

6. Which of the following is not mandatory?

   A. Standard
   B. Guideline
   C. Procedure
   D. Baseline

7. Which of the following includes all of the detailed actions and tasks that personnel are required to follow?

   A. Standard
   B. Guideline
   C. Procedure
   D. Baseline

8. Risk management is the process of reducing risk to an acceptable level.

   A. True
   B. False

9. List the five tenets of information assurance that you should consider when building an IT policy framework. _____

10. Preservation of confidentiality in information systems requires that the information not be disclosed to _____.

11. When building a policy framework, which of the following information systems factors should be considered?

   A. Unauthorized access to and use of the system
   B. Unauthorized disclosure of information
   C. Disruption of the system
   D. Modification of information
   E. Destruction of information resources
   F. A, B, and E only
   G. A, B, C, D, and E

How to Design, Organize, Implement, and Maintain IT Security Policies

I N CHAPTER 6, you learned about policy frameworks. A framework includes policies, standards, baselines, procedures, and guidelines. We introduced you to some widely accepted frameworks to help you develop your own library of documents. You also learned about the roles people perform to create the library.

Viewing the IT security program at the framework level gives you a macro or holistic view of the program's span. At this level, you see overarching statements about a particular security topic but few details. It's essential to establish the framework properly because it's the basis for further work on the library.

If the policy framework from Chapter 6 is at the macro level, Chapter 7 gives you a micro look into each document within that collection.

Chapter 7 Topics

This chapter covers the following topics and concepts:

- Which policy and standards design elements you should consider
- How to organize the contents of an IT policy framework
- What to consider when implementing the policy and standards library
- What the policy change control board is
- How to maintain the policy and standards library over time
- What best practices are for policies and standards maintenance
- What some case studies and examples of IT security policy management and maintenance are

Chapter 7 Goals

When you complete this chapter, you will be able to:

- Describe the characteristics of a "good" policy or standard that meets the organization's needs
- Describe the core security principles that policy writers should keep in mind while developing policies
- Explain the need for and structure of a policy and standards library for organizing the collection of documents
- Explain the review and approval process for policies, standards, procedures, and guidance documents
- Explain the document publication and training and awareness processes needed for policies and standards
- Explain the role and activities of the policy change control board
- Describe the processes needed for maintaining and updating policies and standards

Policies and Standards Design Considerations

All documents in a policy and standards library are meant for people to read and consume. Policies and standards are not guidelines that offer suggestions. They are a collection of concrete definitions that describe acceptable and unacceptable human behavior. There are consequences for failing to follow approved standards. Developing them is not a trivial undertaking.

There's little point in writing documents that people cannot understand or that make compliance highly difficult or impossible. The best kinds of documents are clearly worded and address the six key questions who, what, where, when, why, and how.

These questions provide a consistent direction in writing policies and standards. Journalists traditionally ask these six questions as they research and write news stories. Most readers, of news articles and policy documents alike, are busy. They need concise and precise information. Lack of clarity forces readers to make assumptions. Often those assumptions are wrong. When you answer these questions within the first few sections of your documents, you increase the reader's comfort level and increase the likelihood of compliance.

 NOTE

Most often, the questions related to where, when, and how are more appropriate for procedures or guidelines rather than policies or standards. Try to keep your policies and standards at the what, who, and why levels of detail.

The characteristics of a good policy or standard depend on many factors. These factors are collectively described as the "culture" of the organization. Some organizations have a strong "command and control" culture. This dictates that policies and standards are written as strong, imperative statements, for example, "You must log off at the end of each work day." Other organizations use subtler phrases and tone, intended to persuade those who must follow the policy. It's important to avoid using "squishy" language or loose terms when developing your documents. If you allow people to interpret your requirements on their own, they might look for ways to opt out of them. It's simply human nature.

Principles for Policy and Standards Development

Because no two organizations or risk assessment outcomes are the same, there are no universal recipes for building an IT security program. Instead, "principles" help you make decisions in new situations using proven experience and best practices. By considering several principles, you can derive control requirements and help make implementation decisions.

Use the following principles to help you develop policies, standards, baselines, procedures, and guidelines. These are the common core security principles recommended for industry best practices, regardless of the organization's business nature:

- **Accountability principle**—The personal responsibility of information systems security should be explicit. Some roles in the organization are accountable only for the work they perform daily. Other roles are accountable for their own work, plus all the work performed by their team of employees. Accountability helps to assure that people understand they are solely responsible for actions they take while using organization resources. You can think of accountability as a deterrent control.

- **Awareness principle**—Owners, providers, and users of information systems, and other parties should be informed of the existence and general context of policies, responsibilities, practices, procedures, and organization for security of information systems.

- **Ethics principle**—Information systems and the security of information systems should be provided and used in accordance with the ethical standards applicable to your operating environment.

- **Multidisciplinary principle**—Policy and standards library documents should be written to consider everyone affected, including technical, administrative, organizational, operational, commercial, educational, and legal personnel.

- **Proportionality principle**—Security levels, costs, practices, and procedures should be appropriate and proportionate to the value of the data and the degree of reliance on the system. They should also be proportional to the potential severity, probability, and extent of harm to the system or loss of the data. In other words, don't spend $1,000 to protect $500 worth of assets.

- **Integration principle**—Your documents should be coordinated and integrated with each other. They should also integrate with other relevant measures, practices, and procedures for a coherent system of security.

- **Defense-in-depth principle**—Security increases when it is implemented as a series of overlapping layers of controls and countermeasures that provide three elements to secure assets: prevention, detection, and response. This is referred to as **defense in depth**. It is both a military concept and an information security concept. Defense in depth dictates that security mechanisms be layered so that the weaknesses of one mechanism are countered by the strengths of two or more other mechanisms.

- **Timeliness principle**—All personnel, assigned agents, and third-party providers should act in a timely and coordinated manner to prevent and to respond to breaches of the security.

- **Reassessment principle**—The security of information systems should be periodically reassessed. Risks to technology change daily and periodic reassessments are needed to assure that security requirements and practices are kept current with these changes. Standards also need reassessments, at least annually, to assure they represent the current state of affairs.

- **Democracy principle**—The security of an information system should be balanced against the rights of customers, users, and other people affected by the system versus your rights as the owners and operators of these systems. In other words, consider your users or partners when requiring information that could place their privacy rights at risk.

- **Internal control principle**—Information security forms the core of an organization's information internal control systems. Regulations mandate that internal control systems be in place and operating correctly. Organizations rely on technology to maintain business records. It's essential that such technology include internal control mechanisms. These maintain the integrity of the information and represent a true picture of the organization's activities.

- **Adversary principle**—Controls, security strategies, architectures, and policy library documents should be developed and implemented in anticipation of attack from intelligent, rational, and irrational adversaries who may intend harm.

- **Least privilege principle**—People should be granted only enough privilege to accomplish assigned tasks and no more.

- **Separation of duty principle**—Responsibilities and privileges should be divided to prevent a person or a small group of collaborating people from inappropriately controlling multiple key aspects of a process and causing harm or loss. For example, in an accounting department, the person preparing invoices for payment should not be the same person writing the checks for payment.

- **Continuity principle**—Identify your organization's needs for disaster recovery and continuity of operations. Prepare the organization and its information systems accordingly.

- **Simplicity principle**—Try to favor small and simple safeguards over large and complex ones. Security is improved when it's made simpler.

- **Policy-centered security principle**—Policies, standards, and procedures should be established as the formal basis for managing the planning, control, and evaluation of all information security activities.

Types of Controls for Policies and Standards

With principles in hand, you can begin to map what you want to accomplish with common security controls. Security controls are measures taken to protect systems from attacks on the confidentiality, integrity, and availability of the system. Sometimes, safeguards and countermeasures are used synonymously with the word "control." Controls are chosen after the risk assessment of the assets is complete. Once you have identified and assessed the risks to your assets, you can select the appropriate control to counter the threat, mitigate, or reduce the risks.

Security Control Types

Security controls can be described according to two different categorization schemes: one based upon what the control is and the other based upon what the control does.

The first category includes administrative, technical, and physical control categories. They describe what the control actually is, such as a named process, a standard, a firewall, a locked door, and so on:

- **Administrative controls** are the policies, standards, and procedures that guide employees when conducting the organization's business. Pre-employment screening of personnel and a change management process are also examples of administrative controls.

- **Technical security controls** are the devices, protocols, and other technology used to protect assets. These include antivirus systems, cryptographic systems, firewalls, and more.

- **Physical security controls** are the devices used to control physical access. Examples here are fences, security guards, locked doors, motion detectors, and alarms.

The second set of controls describes what controls do. These controls include the following:

- **Preventive security controls** prevent intentional or unintentional security threats. Examples include network access policies, firewall rules, and locks on wiring closets and server room doors.

- **Detective or response controls** act like alarms and warnings. These controls kick in *after* an incident begins. Examples include motion detectors, log files, files that contain system audit information, etc.

- **Corrective controls** help you respond to and fix a security incident. Corrective controls are also used to limit or stop further damage. Some examples include cleaning a virus off a system, closing a firewall port, and blocking an Internet Protocol (IP) address.

- **Recovery controls** help you put a system back into operation once an incident ends. Disaster recovery and tape backups fit into this category.

There is significant overlap between security control categories. Some controls can be administrative and preventive or technical and corrective, or any combination. This overlap occurs on purpose for implementing the principle of defense in depth.

You can find catalogs of security controls for virtually every security topic. One such catalog is called Control Objectives for Information and related Technology, or COBIT for short. COBIT is an IT governance framework developed by ISACA that includes supporting tools to help bridge the gaps between control requirements, technical issues, and business risks. Chapter 3 covered COBIT, and you can visit the ISACA Web site at *http://www.isaca.org* for more information.

Document Organization Considerations

Organizing your library of documents requires a numbering scheme that people can readily understand in context. You can create your own numbering scheme or use an existing one. Should you decide to use an existing framework like ISO/IEC 27002, you can begin with the taxonomy it provides.

> **NOTE**
>
> **Taxonomy** is the practice and science of classification. A hierarchical taxonomy is a tree structure of classifications for a given set of objects or documents.

Figure 7-1 offers an example that you might consider using for your taxonomy.

Think of Figure 7-1 as a sideways tree. The program-level policy or information security charter on the left side is the "root." It establishes the tree and delegates the authority for managing the tree to the information security department of the organization. Let's call it IS (for information security), POL (for policy), and add "001" because it's the first document: IS-POL-001.

FIGURE 7-1

A possible policy
and standards library
taxonomy.

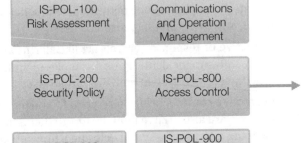

Framework Policies

IS-POL-100
Risk Assessment

IS-POL-700
Communications
and Operation
Management

IS-POL-200
Security Policy

IS-POL-800
Access Control

Program-Level Policy

IS-POL-300
Organization of
Information Security

IS-POL-900
Information Systems
Acquisition, Dev, and
Maintenance

IS-POL-001
Information Security
Program

IS-POL-400
Asset Management

IS-POL-1000
Information Security
Incident Management

IS-POL-500
Human Resources
Security

IS-POL-1100
Business Continuity
Management

IS-POL-600 Physical
and Environmental
Security

IS-POL-1200
Compliance

To the right, you find the collection of program framework policies that were described in Chapter 6. This framework uses ISO/IEC 27002 topics for policy types. They are numbered in groups of 100 to allow for growth. Each of these policies stands on its own and serves as the first major branches of the tree. From these branches, standards and their supporting documents appear.

Looking at the Access Control (IS-POL-800) framework policy as an example, you can see control standards labeled IS-CSTD-810 through 840. The CSTD label is short for "Control Standard." Figure 7-2 shows just this part of the policy and standards library.

Baseline standards are then numbered to maintain the consistency of the taxonomy and support the control standards upon which they're based. The baseline standards are specific to technology and numbered as IS-BSTD-821 and 822, where BSTD stands for Baseline Standard. These two standards define the requirements for password

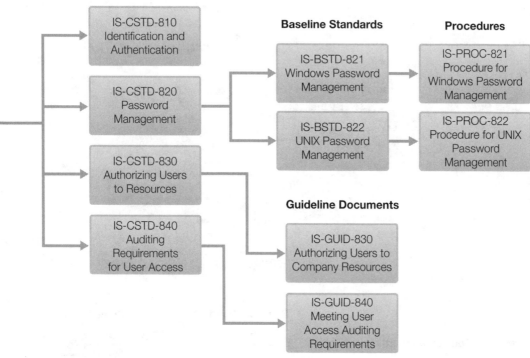

management as they pertain to the Windows operating system and the UNIX operating system. In this example, the numbering follows the parent standard's numbering, IS-CSTD-820.

Procedures link to the baseline standards that they support. For example, IS-PROC-821 and 822 are directly mapped to the 821 and 822 baselines. In most cases, there is a one-to-one mapping of baselines and procedures in support of the control standard. Figure 7-3 shows a close-up of baseline standards and procedures in the policy and standards library tree.

Guideline documents are most often tied to a specific control standard, as shown in Figure 7-4. Guideline documents (GUIDs) are useful where there may not be any technology for enforcing controls, but the guidelines provide useful information for process management or controls.

FIGURE 7-2

Control standards branch out from the Access Control (IS-POL-800) framework policy.

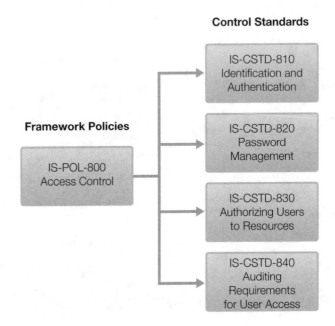

FIGURE 7-3

Baseline standards and procedures provide additional branches of the library tree.

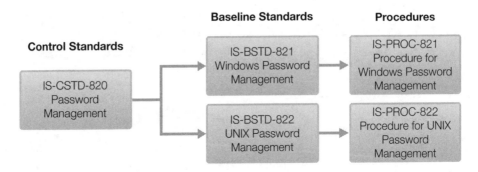

TIP

Whatever numbering scheme you adopt, leave plenty of room for adding new documents. You don't want to get into a position where you can't add a new document without starting a new numbering scheme. Carefully think through a numbering scheme before you decide to use it.

When people look for a specific document, the name of the document should tell them all they need to know. After they gain some experience with the taxonomy, they'll know where to look.

Sample Templates

In this section, you will look at some suggested document formats for policies and standards. You can use these as is or create a template that best reflects your organization's needs.

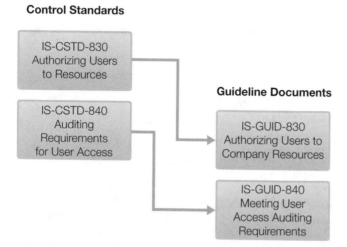

Control Standards

Guideline Documents

Sample Policy Template

The following outline of a policy document helps you organize the content for your program-level policy and framework policies:

POLICY NAME AND IDENTIFYING INFORMATION

1. PURPOSE

This document establishes a policy for . . .

2. BACKGROUND

This document was developed because . . .

3. SCOPE

This policy applies to the use of . . .

4. OPERATIONAL POLICY

4.1. Section 1

4.2. Section 2

4.3. Section 3

4.4. Section 4

5. ROLES AND RESPONSIBILITIES

The following entities have responsibilities related to the implementation of this policy:

6. APPLICABLE LAWS/GUIDANCE

7. EFFECTIVE DATES

This policy becomes effective on the date that [xxx] Chief Information Officer (CIO) signs it and remains in effect until officially superseded or canceled by the CIO.

8. INFORMATION AND ASSISTANCE

    Contact the . . . for further information regarding this policy.

9. APPROVED

    [Director of Information Security Policies]   Date of Issuance

10. ASSOCIATED RESOURCES

    This policy is augmented by . . .

The following is a sample policy statement for access control that would appear in the "Operational Policy" section of a framework policy:

> Personnel must be positively authenticated and authorized prior to being granted access to <Organization> information resources. Access based on an individual's role must be limited to the minimum necessary to perform his or her job function.
>
> Access to critical information resources must be controlled through a managed process that addresses authorizing, modifying, and revoking access, and periodic review of information system privileges."

Sample Standard Template

The following outline of a standards document helps you organize the content for your control and baseline standards:

STANDARD NAME AND IDENTIFYING INFORMATION

1. PURPOSE

    This document establishes a standard for . . .

2. BACKGROUND

    This document was developed to support . . .

3. SCOPE

    This standard applies to the use of . . .

4. STANDARD STATEMENT(S)

    4.1. Section 1

    4.2. Section 2

    4.3. Section 3

    4.4. Section 4

5. ROLES AND RESPONSIBILITIES

    The following entities have responsibilities related to the implementation of this standard:

6. GUIDANCE

Links to guidance documentation for this standard . . .

7. EFFECTIVE DATES

This standard becomes effective on the date that [xxx], Chief Information Officer (CIO), signs it and remains in effect until officially superseded or canceled by the CIO.

8. INFORMATION AND ASSISTANCE

Contact the . . . for further information regarding this standard.

9. APPROVED

[Director of Information Security Policies]   Date of Issuance

10. ASSOCIATED RESOURCES

This standard is augmented by . . .

The following are sample statements for access control that would appear in the "Standard Statement(s)" section of a control standard:

Access to all <Organization> information resources must be controlled by using user IDs and appropriate authentication methods as required by the Information Classification Standard and the Information Handling Standard.

Access to all <Organization> information resources connected to the <Organization> network must be controlled by using user IDs and appropriate authentication.

In order to ensure individual accountability, the use of any user ID must be associated with a specific individual. Passwords must never be shared between users.

The following is a sample statement for UNIX account management that would appear in the "Standard Statement(s)" section of a baseline standard:

Default system accounts must be locked (except root). The password field for the account must be set to an invalid string and the shell field in the password file must contain an invalid shell. /dev/null is a good choice because it is not a valid logon shell.

Sample Procedure Template

The following outline of a procedures document helps you organize the content for any procedures needed to implement baseline standard controls:

PROCEDURE NAME AND IDENTIFYING INFORMATION

EFFECTIVE DATE

Date the procedure becomes effective. This can be the same as or later than the approval date in order to allow time for training and implementation if necessary.

1. PROCEDURE

   Insert procedural steps in the table . . .

   1.1. Section 1.1

   1.2. Section 1.2

   1.3. Section 1.3

   1.4. Section 1.4

2. STANDARD

   Indicate the name and number of the baseline standard to which this procedure relates . . .

3. FORMS

   List any form numbers and names and their location if there are any needed to conduct this procedure.

4. PROCEDURE HISTORY

   List all previous known versions (including obsolete procedure numbers or titles if known) and their effective dates.

5. INFORMATION AND ASSISTANCE

   Contact the . . . for further information regarding this standard.

6. APPROVED

   [Director of Information Security Policies]   Date of Issuance

7. KEYWORDS

   Indicate any cross references, aliases, phrases, or terms that describe the procedure. Define all acronyms, abbreviations.

8. ASSOCIATED RESOURCES

   This standard is augmented by . . .

The following is a sample procedure snippet for data destruction on media that could appear in the "Procedure" section of a procedure document:

Disk sanitization involves securely erasing all the data from a disk so that the disk is, except for the previous wear, "new" and empty of any previous data. For example, a disk connected to a Linux system may be sanitized by repeating the following command three to seven times (or more):

```
dd if=/dev/random of=/dev/hdb && dd if=/dev/zero of=/dev/hdb
```

This command first writes a random pattern to disk /dev/hdb, then writes all zeros to it. Any disk that needs to be sanitized, including any flash memory device or former PC or Macintosh disk may be attached to a Linux (or other Unix) system and erased using the above command, replacing /dev/hdb with the appropriate disk device name.

Sample Guideline Template

Although there are generally no standard templates for guidelines, you can use or adapt the following:

GUIDELINE NAME AND IDENTIFYING INFORMATION

1. PURPOSE

    This document provides guidance and advice in helping to meet the control requirements from Standard(s) . . .

2. BACKGROUND

    This document was developed to support . . . .

3. SCOPE

    This guidance applies to the use of . . . .

4. GUIDANCE SECTION(S)

    4.1. Section 1

    4.2. Section 2

    4.3. Section 3

    4.4. Section 4

5. ROLES AND RESPONSIBILITIES

    The following entities have responsibilities related to the implementation of this standard: . . .

6. EFFECTIVE DATES (may or may not be needed)

7. INFORMATION AND ASSISTANCE

    Contact the . . . for further information regarding this document.

8. APPROVED

    [Director of Information Security Policies]   Date of Issuance

9. ASSOCIATED RESOURCES

    This guideline is augmented by . . .

The following is a sample guideline snippet for the use of encryption within a university setting. This text could appear in the "Guidance Section" section of a guideline document:

"University personnel and student organizations:

- Should use industry-standard encryption algorithms to protect their data.
- Should not attempt to develop their own proprietary encryption algorithms and should carefully scrutinize any claims made by vendors about the security of proprietary encryption algorithms.

Considerations For Implementing Policies and Standards

Implementing your policies and libraries entails three major steps:

- Reviews and approvals for your documents
- Publication of the documents
- Awareness and training

Reviews and Approvals

Throughout the research and interview processes with operational users and their managers, you should have prepared them for changes that the information security (IS) department will be mandating for compliance. This give-and-take process helps to improve the quality of the document content. It also helps with buy-in from those who are subject to the rules and controls you'll be implementing based on the risk analysis and assessment work completed.

Once written, you need to share your documents again with those who helped you develop them. Give those employees an opportunity to review the documents well before you implement them. These reviews allow you to assess the impact of the policy or standard on the organization before deploying it in a potentially disruptive fashion.

 TIP

If you cannot implement controls immediately, postpone the implementation date. Let people know that new controls are coming at a future specific date. Depending on the size of the organization, the grace period can be from a few months to one year.

These reviews sometimes require you to revise parts of a policy or standard to allow for current conditions. Sometimes you may need to postpone implementing some controls until the environment is better prepared for compliance. Early in your overall policy development project, you should work with your organizations' audit group to determine how soon after policy publication they will audit based on the policy. By allowing a grace period for compliance, you are helping to ensure that the policies will be enforceable. A grace period gives personnel time to implement any project, processes, or internal communications necessary for compliance.

Allow sufficient time for gathering and addressing concerns. Once you gain the concurrence of those subject to the policies, it's vital to gain approval from their managers or their management team. Often, executive managers appoint delegates for standards reviews and rely on recommendations before they approve or reject changes. If you've done a good job with those subject to the specific standards, approvals should be timely.

Ultimately, your goal is to gain senior executive approval of the policy or standard. The executive approver may be the chief information security officer (CISO), if the role exists. That person is unlikely to give approval if all parties have not reviewed the document. Internal reviews within the IS department should help mitigate some of the executive approver's concerns once the document reaches him or her for approval. Here are some suggested people who should be given the opportunity to become a second or third layer of review:

- **Technical personnel**—You may need to call upon the expertise of technical staff with specific security and/or technical knowledge in the area about which you are writing.

- **Legal**—The legal department should have input into the policy development process. They can provide advice on current legislation that requires certain types of information to be protected in specific ways. Your legal department should also review policy and standards documents once they are complete.

- **Human resources (HR)**—The HR department may need to review and/or approve your policy or standard if your document addresses topics covered by existing HR policies. E-mail usage and physical security are examples. Make sure you reference the HR policy rather than repeat content. Simply repeating content can lead to future inconsistencies.

- **Audit and compliance**—Internal audit personnel will monitor compliance with a policy once it is in force. If you work with external compliance groups, consult with them as needed.

Although these review steps may seem onerous, early buy-in is needed to assure there are no surprises when policy changes take effect. It's better to put in the time and effort early in the process to avoid rework later.

Once policies and standards are approved, you need to distribute them in ways that work best in your organization.

Publishing Your Policies and Standards Library

Publishing your policy and standards library depends on the communications tools available in your organization. Many organizations use some form of an intranet for internal communications. Different departments may have their own sub-section of the intranet, and IS should have its own. An intranet generally has a front page or portal that announces new content on the site. It also includes news, other announcements, access to standard forms, and so on.

Sometimes, intranet sites use a back-office engine for managing content, like Microsoft SharePoint Server. Departments can use SharePoint for the documents and contact information they wish to share, and then publish the content to the intranet for anyone to access.

If your organization uses a content management tool for departmental Web sites, you might consider using that for publishing your documents. Documents must be readily obtainable at any time, with a copy placed on the internal network shared drives or the organization intranet. Some of the best practices for publishing your documents are to create separate Web pages for each document and provide a link to the document itself on that Web page. The page should contain:

- Identifying information
- Overview of the document
- Last revision date and the name or initials of the person who revised the document
- Next scheduled document review date
- Keywords for the intranet search engine to simplify locating your documents
- Links to related documents
- A link to an Adobe Portable Document Format (PDF) version of the document

▶ **NOTE**

"Wiki" is the Hawaiian word for "quick." Wiki software (also called a WikiWeb or wiki application) is software that runs a Web site for users to collaboratively create and edit Web pages using a Web browser. A wiki can run on one or more distributed Web servers. The content, including all current and previous revisions, is usually stored in either a file system or a database.

The medium you choose for developing your policy content may determine the level of difficulty you'll encounter in the review cycle. Word processing documents are appealing because they're easy to use and convenient. However, for review purposes, word processing documents aren't always efficient. A better method is to use a collaboration tool, like a WikiWeb, for developing common templates, completing content online, and requesting collaboration from your peers or other stakeholders in real time. With a Wiki, you can allow interactive collaboration and decide if changes that other people suggest are acceptable or not. When you're ready with a final draft, you can create a set of PDF documents that comprise the policy and standards library. You then publish the library in a way that's best for your organization.

In 2008, a new class of software was introduced called Governance, Risk, and Compliance, or GRC, tools. These tools are available from a number of companies. Each company uses a unique approach to policy management and publication. Functions that are commonly found in a GRC tool include:

- Assessing the proper technical and non-technical operation of controls, and mitigating/remediating areas where controls are lacking or not operating properly (governance)

- Assisting in quantification, analysis, and mitigation of risk within the organization (risk)

- Authoring, distribution, and policy and controls mapping to the governing regulation, as well as tracking exceptions to those policies/regulations (compliance)

GRC tools are typically delivered as modules that plug in to a central GRC engine. Usually, you can license a policy and standards module. With this module, you can use the workflow features to develop and share your documents for reviews and approvals, publish the library as Web pages, and search for relevant documents. Some organizations use the tools for:

- Awareness training using quizzes
- E-mails to users that notify them of new content or changes to existing policies
- E-mails that notify people that new content is ready for them to review or approve
- Tracking changes to documents to ensure that important content is not lost or erroneously changed

The following GRC tools, as well as several others, are widely used:

- Archer SmartSuite Framework, *http://www.archer-tech.com*
- Symantec Control Compliance Suite, *http://www.symantec.com/business/control-compliance-suite*
- Modulo Risk Manager, *http://www.modulo.com/risk-manager*

▶ **NOTE**

As part of a continuous improvement effort, plan to review and update published policies and other framework documents periodically. You'll learn about document review and maintenance later in this chapter. Chapter 15 covers policy compliance monitoring and change management techniques.

Awareness and Training

Implementation requires not only educating personnel on each of the core elements, but also on changing their role to emphasize protecting data and systems.

A security awareness program is one of the key factors for the successful implementation of an organization-wide security policy. Awareness tools should describe and outline the specific mandate for all employees to secure organization assets. These tools should also explain the core elements of the security policies and standards. The program is aimed at generating an increased interest in the information security field in an easy-to-understand yet effective way.

Gaining management awareness and buy-in should be your first step. Without management support and commitment, it's unlikely that your efforts to educate the masses later on will succeed. As you're selling the program to your executive sponsor(s) and gaining approval for issuing your documents, use that time to leverage their authority with managers and direct reports to ensure compliance. With that level of buy-in secure, the task of gaining buy-in from the rest of the organization is made that much easier.

Awareness programs are often divided into two parts: awareness and training. The purpose of awareness is to provide employees with a better understanding of security risks. The importance of security primarily focuses on the daily operation of the organization. Training should cover many potential security problems in detail, as well as introduce a set of easy-to-understand rules to reduce the risk of problems.

Although training and awareness are the focus of Chapter 12, here are a few techniques that many others have found useful in "getting the message out":

- The mantra for any awareness and training must be "Security is everyone's responsibility."
- It's vital that employees clearly understand that uneducated and untrained employees can endanger sensitive information, and render useless any technical security measure or process in place.

- It's vital to have a good strategy that draws people and motivates them to learn how they can improve information security. Everyone has a particular learning style. Some people are visual learners. Others learn by listening. Still others need hands-on exercises that make it personal to them. Mixing up the modes of learning by using different media, different messages, and content-communications tools helps assure that most people will understand and retain the information.

- People tend to be interested in stories about computer security, especially computer crimes. Making use of this may help people understand that they are going to be the new "gatekeepers" of critical organization data. Use stories and examples from within your organization, too. Don't focus only on the horror stories of bad security practices. Show and tell people about the benefits of being good corporate citizens and the potential rewards for compliance.

- As much as possible, use examples that make security a personal choice. Develop scenarios where people need to make a choice as to what they might do in a particular situation. Relate these situations to actual ones people might encounter from day to day.

Furthermore, you can help people perceive actual personal benefits from the security program, such as the new skills they will gain. For example, mention to them how this information can help them increase the security of their personal computers at home and their own information.

Varying the methods of education can increase the success of your awareness and training program. Ensure you have a fresh, ever-evolving, and dynamic education program. The following sections offer suggestions for broadening awareness and educating staff about security.

 TIP

Rather than a formal newsletter, you could set up an Information Security Awareness area on your intranet. You could maintain several pages of information that are linked and easily updated.

Security Newsletter

One interesting and valuable way to reach and educate your staff is a security newsletter. The main idea is to provide users with an interesting and engaging way of understanding the points outlined in the policy and standards library. You can send it via e-mail or post it on your intranet.

If you develop your newsletter in-house, you may need to ask for help from others in the information security group. Also consider getting input from people outside the group who have security-related perspectives to share with the rest of the organization. An alternative is to subscribe to third-party security newsletters that you tailor to your organization. One such company is the Computer Security Institute (CSI). CSI offers *FrontLine*, a quarterly four-page newsletter that increases employees' awareness of critical security topics. Once you subscribe to *FrontLine*, CSI will customize the newsletter for your organization and make it appear that you published it. To learn more about *FrontLine*, visit the CSI Web site at *http://www.gocsi.com/frontline*. You can view a sample newsletter in PDF format.

The following sections describe parts of a typical security newsletter.

Security Articles

Sometimes people appreciate reading detailed, in-depth information on a specific topic that helps them understand the subject more clearly. For example, if in a security awareness campaign you covered e-mail threats, you could include an associated article in the next newsletter while the topic is still fresh in the employees' minds.

The following are possible article topics:

- **Password security**—Discuss the importance of passwords and their crucial role in the protection of the data. Other articles might include how to properly maintain user IDs and passwords, password creation and maintenance, and best practices.

- **Acceptable Internet use**—Discuss the possible dangers posed by Internet connectivity and information that employees should be aware of while browsing the Web from work.

- **Why are they targeting us?**—This could be an interesting topic to describe the motivation of different attackers and the purpose behind attacks. This can provide users a better understanding of the importance of having proper information security measures implemented

- **Your role in the protection of the organization**—Think of as many scenarios as you see fit. The idea for these articles is to explain the most important aspects of information security in an informal yet effective way. You could cover social aspects combined with brief technical explanations if needed.

What Is . . . ?

This section of the newsletter educates or informs staff and acts as an information security glossary. It includes various security terms explained in non-technical, easy-to-understand terms. General security topics such as Trojan horses, worms, and firewalls can be covered individually, as well as other topics or concepts that you think are useful, must-know, or that can help with compliance to standards and policies.

Ask Us

You can include an "Ask Us" section in your newsletter. Over time, you can create a Frequently Asked Questions (FAQ) document that summarizes the questions and answers to give users a richer experience when interacting with the IS department.

The questions and corresponding answers could be included in the next issue of the newsletter, so that it will not only be a collective information source to a large group of people, but also stimulates the asking of further questions.

Security Resources

A "Security Resources" section might include short news pieces that cover some aspect of information security in an easy-to-understand form. The idea is to help users understand the importance of security awareness via security news, news of the latest security breaches, losses suffered by companies due to security problems, and so on.

technical TIP

Create a social network or even a satellite system of security experts and **evangelists** throughout your organization. These people will act as advocates for information security and help their specific departments or groups answer questions related to their obligations for compliance. You can start with people who show an above-average level of security interest or skills. Identify and promote these groups as a social network that speeds the adoption of security. Start by tracking the people who stand out during awareness sessions or other training opportunities.

Contacts

Make sure to include the contact details for the IS department so that users will know precisely whom to contact in case of a problem. Publish the intranet uniform resource locator (URL) to your site everywhere you can to help remind people that help may be a click away.

Policy Change Control Board

A policy and standards library does not exist in a vacuum. To remain effective and relevant, ongoing changes and maintenance are required. Sometimes the changes you are asked to make affect people other than those requesting the changes.

 NOTE

Security personnel need to be aware of policy and standards change requirements. They also need to understand the impact of the change on the IT environment. Because systems, applications, and networks are integrated, a change to one component can affect other components.

It's important that changes are not made unilaterally or cause unexpected consequences. To avoid these situations, form a policy change control board or committee. You can organize this group ad-hoc, meeting as needed for reviews and approvals. It can also be a standing committee or working group that meets regularly to address changes, additions, and enhancements to policies and standards. You can develop a standard that creates the board and establishes membership requirements. Minimally, you should include people from information security, compliance, audit, HR, leadership from other business units, and project managers (PMs). PMs set the agenda for the meetings, take meeting minutes, assign action items, and follow up on deliverables.

The objectives of the policy change control board are to:

- Assess policies and standards and make recommendations for change
- Coordinate requests for change (RFCs)
- Ensure that changes to existing policies and standards support the organization's mission and goals
- Review requested changes to the policy framework
- Establish a change management process for policies and standards

The policy and standards change management process ensures that policies and standards are refreshed when needed. It deals with new developments in technology and changes in the business environment. When potential changes are identified, change management determines whether the changes should be made or if a new policy or standard is needed. There also needs to be a "lessons learned" process that allows for problems to be resolved and changes made to the policies and standards being designed.

> **NOTE**
>
> A "lessons learned" process ensures that mistakes are made once and not repeated. Lessons learned can come from anyone and anywhere.

The policy change control board assesses and approves RFCs. An RFC typically responds to known problems but can also include improvements. A challenge when handling an RFC is to determine whether it should be approved or whether a transitional policy or standard will resolve the issue.

Business Drivers for Policy and Standards Changes

Additionally, there are business drivers for policy and standards changes, which may include the following:

- **Business-as-usual developments**—Over time, an organization might realize that meeting policy or standards requirements is impossible, too costly, or unnecessary given changing business conditions.

- **Business exceptions**—As the business changes, new systems or processes are introduced. They may vary from what a policy or standard requires.

- **Business innovations**—New opportunities for revenue growth or cost reduction can lead to innovative changes that were previously not considered. Standards may need to adapt to these innovations or be adjusted to permit innovations.

- **Business technology innovations**—New technology often comes with unknowable risks until you gain experience using it. Standards may need revisions to allow for the use of the new technology or for use in new ways that were not envisioned when the standards were developed.

- **Strategic changes**—An organization may change its business model and come under new regulatory requirements. For example, an organization might purchase a bank to reduce the costs of credit card processing. In this case, changes to an existing standard are far-reaching and may affect every standard in place.

Some change requests result in a complete redevelopment of the policy and standards library, or at least in one facet of the policy and standards development cycle.

Maintaining Your Policies and Standards Library

As pointed out in Chapter 6, the policies and standards library is like a tree, and over time, requires pruning and maintenance. The policy change control board helps determine what changes should be made to which documents. Other needs for changes can come about from issues related to specific users or groups, and documents may need trivial or isolated changes. One of the tasks of the board is to determine which requests they will address and which ones are normal maintenance requests.

Updates and Revisions

An update many be considered a non-substantive edit. Examples include updating a position title or a department name, correcting a typo, and repairing broken Web site links.

Revisions may be of minor or major significance:

- A minor revision usually has low significance. An example is clarifying the wording within a sentence or paragraph.
- A major revision significantly changes the policy. Examples include new requirements, new limitations, or expanded responsibilities. These types of changes should be sent to the policy change control board for consideration.

Throughout the chapter, you were provided with some best practices for developing your documents, numbering them appropriately, publishing your documents, and spreading the word about them. If you follow this guidance, the change process should take minimal effort. If every change requires a complete revisiting of the library, you have a much bigger problem on your hands.

Assuming that you follow the same development and review cycles for your updates and gain the necessary buy-in from those who are affected by changes, the most time-consuming activity will be communicating your changes to the organization. Using the techniques and tools for communication and media, you should be able to rely on the same processes you developed for ongoing awareness and training.

To help you determine what changes or maintenance you'll need to perform, use the information provided by:

- **Exceptions and waivers**—Look for common problems related to compliance. If the standard cannot be met very often, it's because there is a problem with the standard (or policy).
- **Requests from users and management**—Make it easy to obtain feedback on people's actual experience with complying with the standards. Major requests should be formally documented and sent to the policy change control board. However, don't ignore the feedback about what's causing people concern or prompting questions about the document.
- **Changes to the organization**—Companies come and go. Mergers and acquisitions happen constantly. Should you find yourself in a situation where your organization has bought or sold a division and you need to revisit the polices and standards for the combined organization, use the tools and techniques you've learned in this chapter to help resolve conflicts or fill in gaps that come about from the change.

Best Practices for Policies and Standards Maintenance

The following list of activities and advice comes from leading practices in policy and standards development and management experts. It was culled from years of experience and is being collected here so you can avoid many of the pitfalls others have experienced when developing a library:

- Ask yourself the key questions of who, what, where, when, why, and how as you set out to research and develop policies and standards.

- Base your decisions on core information security principles to support business objectives. Because there are no universal recipes for developing policies and standards, you need to rely on principles to advance the cause.

- Establish a cohesive and coherent document organization taxonomy that leaves you with room for growth and changes.

- Use common templates for each type of document and stick with them. Nothing leads to confusion more than different document styles that are intended to meet the same purposes.

- Use a collaboration tool for developing documents that allows others access to drafts early in the development cycle. It should be easy to solicit reviews and comments.

- Establish a repeatable review process for your draft documents. The process should consider a representative sample of people who will be affected by new policies and security controls.

- Publish your library in a form that your organization is already using. Introducing new technology for distributing policies and standards at the same time you publish the documents may cause unnecessary confusion.

- Use a broad variety of communications and awareness media and techniques to reach a wide audience. Keep your message consistent and easy to understand.

- Establish a policy change control board to help identify major changes to the library and to keep it up to date.

- Use adaptations of your development, review, approval, publication, and training processes for changes to the library. Creating one-off processes that are different for changes than they are for development can lead to extra work and extra time to keep the library relevant and current.

Case Studies and Examples of Designing, Organizing, Implementing, and Maintaining IT Security Policies

The following three case studies review how to develop or implement a policy framework. You will look at cases from the private sector, the public sector, and the critical infrastructure protection area.

Private Sector Case Study

During an internal review, American Imaging Management (AIM) decided it needed to improve its due diligence practices. AIM decided to expand its corporate security program. The company began by performing a risk assessment on its current security program.

The assessment used the ISO 27001 gap assessment methods. When complete, AIM delivered a recommended course of action. These activities were intended to address and remediate areas that were either under- or over-controlled.

Using the Plan-Do-Act-Check cycle from the ISO standards, AIM's activities included:

- Defining more detailed roles and responsibilities
- Identifying all relevant security requirements (legislative, regulatory, and contractual)
- Defining all supporting policies, standards, and procedures
- Defining and establishing a security awareness program
- Expanding the organization's vulnerability management program
- Collaborating with the business continuity/disaster recovery (BC/DR) team to integrate security program objectives
- Improving the incident response program
- Implementing an internal security control audit program

By the end of the project, AIM was able to create a road map for building a security program that could be registered to the ISO 27001 standard.

Public Sector Case Study

To improve security in California's IT infrastructure, the Office of the State Chief Information Officer (OCIO) issued a new policy that includes employee remote access security standards for working from home or off-site. The policy also requires that state agencies complete a compliance form.

The policy was issued to help state agencies develop secure remote access for employees and minimize security risks. The corresponding standard highlights important measures that IT agencies must adopt to certify their remote access programs. It includes controls related to the use of up-to-date operating system software and security software for every remote connection.

The standard also requires that all computing equipment connected to the state's IT infrastructure network for remote access purposes be state-owned and securely configured. Remote access users can only connect through secure encrypted channels—virtual private networks—authorized by agency management. The security measures also apply to paper files and mobile devices like personal digital assistants (PDAs).

According to the information policy letter, agency heads must comply with the following:

- Make sure authorized users permitted to use remote access are trained for their roles and responsibilities, security risks, and the requirements in the standard

- Adopt and implement the requirements in the standard and certifying their agency's compliance

- Annually complete and submit the Agency Telework and Remote Access Security Compliance Certification form to the Office of Information Security

California was among the first governments in the country to establish enterprise-wide policies for remote access, joining states such as Virginia and Arizona, and the federal government.

Critical Infrastructure Example

In December 2005, the Justice and Home Affairs Council asked the European Union Commission to propose a European Programme for Critical Infrastructure Protection (EPCIP). In response, the commission adopted a Communication and a proposal for a Directive. It set out to identify and designate European critical infrastructure for improving its protection.

The Communication established the principles, processes, and instruments to implement EPCIP. The objective of EPCIP is to improve the protection of critical infrastructure in the European Union (EU) by implementing the European legislation set out in the Communication. The proposed EU program, called "Prevention, Preparedness, and Consequence Management of Terrorism and other Security Related Risks" was adopted on February 12, 2007.

The legislative framework for the EPCIP included:

- Procedures to identify and designate European critical infrastructure

- A common approach to assessing the need to improve the protection of the infrastructure

- Measures to assure the implementation of EPCIP, including:
  - An EPCIP action plan
  - The Critical Infrastructure Warning Information Network (CIWIN)
  - Establishing Critical Infrastructure Protection (CIP) expert groups at EU level
  - Establishing CIP information sharing processes
  - Identification and analysis of interdependencies

CHAPTER SUMMARY

This chapter addressed techniques for designing, organizing, implementing, and maintaining an IT security policy and standards library. You learned characteristics of policies and standards that make them easy to understand. Core security principles were covered, which are important to remember when developing security documents. Training and awareness programs help you enforce policies and get buy-in from employees.

You also learned about the review and approval processes that are part of creating and maintaining library documents. A policy change control board, for example, is an efficient way to maintain policies and standards. It also helps minimize unforeseen impacts on the organization. Finally, you learned about some leading practices that others have found useful for developing and maintaining a policy and standards library.

KEY CONCEPTS AND TERMS

Defense in depth
Evangelist
Taxonomy

CHAPTER 7 ASSESSMENT

1. When writing policies and standards, you should address the six key questions who, what, where, when, why, and how.

   A. True
   B. False

2. All policy and standards libraries follow a universal numbering scheme for consistency between organizations.

   A. True
   B. False

3. Guideline documents are often tied to a specific control standard.

   A. True
   B. False

4. Which of the following is not an administrative control?

   A. Development of policies, standards, procedures, and guidelines
   B. Screening of personnel
   C. Change control procedures
   D. Logical access control mechanisms

5. Which of the following are common steps taken in the development of documents such as security policies, standards, and procedures?

   A. Design, development, publication, coding, and testing
   B. Feasibility, development, approval, implementation, and integration
   C. Initiation, evaluation, development, approval, publication, implementation, and maintenance
   D. Design, coding, evaluation, approval, publication, and implementation

6. Which departments should review policies and standards before official approval? (Select four.)

   A. Technical
   B. Legal
   C. HR
   D. Maintenance
   E. Audit

7. Controls are implemented to do which of the following?

   A. Create new standards.
   B. Protect systems from attacks on the confidentiality, integrity, and availability of the system.
   C. Eliminate all risk and eliminate the potential for loss.
   D. Support guidelines.

8. Which type of control is associated with responding to and fixing a security incident?

   A. Deterrent
   B. Compensating
   C. Corrective
   D. Detective

9. List examples of physical security control items. _____

10. Security _____ are the technical implementations of the policies defined by the organization.

11. A(n) _____ is a plan or course of action used by an organization to convey instructions from its senior-most management to those who make decisions, take actions, and perform other duties on behalf of the organization.

12. The principle that states security is improved when it is implemented as a series of overlapping controls is called _____

13. Security principles are needed in the absence of complete information to make high-quality security decisions.

    A. True
    B. False

14. "Access to all Organization information resources connected to the <Organization> network must be controlled by using user IDs and appropriate authentication" is a statement you might find in a procedure document.

    A. True
    B. False

15. Which of the following does a policy change control board do? (Select two.)

    A. Assesses policies and standards and makes recommendations for change
    B. Determines the policy and standards library numbering scheme
    C. Implements technical controls as business conditions change
    D. Reviews requested changes to the policy framework

IT Security Policy
Framework Approaches

A SECURITY POLICY FRAMEWORK is a comprehensive way of looking at information risks. You can look at security frameworks as a systematic way to identify, mitigate, and reduce these risks. The data can be at rest or moving through a process. The core objective of these frameworks is to establish a strong control mindset. A framework supports business objectives and legal obligations. It also promotes an organization's core values.

In this context, risk represents an event that could affect the achievement of these goals. For an organization to truly have control over these risks, a strong system of internal security controls must be in place. Security policies and procedures should be understood and followed. These security policies and controls must extend beyond the IT department and into the business process. The framework manages risk at an enterprise level. It helps an organization deal with conflicting priorities, resource constraints, and uncertainty. An effective IT security policy framework also enables management to deliver value to the business.

This chapter reviews various security policy frameworks. The chapter discusses policy strengths and their positioning in the market. Additionally, the chapter examines key elements from the frameworks such as roles, responsibilities, separation of duties, governance, and compliance.

Chapter 8 Topics

This chapter covers the following topics and concepts:

- How to choose an IT security policy framework
- How to set roles, responsibilities, and accountabilities for personnel
- Why separation of duties within an organization is important
- What a structured approach to security policy governance and compliance entails
- What best practices for IT security policy framework approaches are
- What some case studies and examples of IT security policy framework approaches are

Chapter 8 Goals

When you complete this chapter, you will be able to:

- Identify the top security policy frameworks
- Understand the type of roles needed to support these frameworks
- Explain the responsibilities of these roles
- Describe how roles create a separation of duties
- Describe how roles create a layered approach to security
- Understand the need and importance of governance and compliance
- Understand how these frameworks are applied in the real world through case studies

IT Security Policy Framework Approaches

How do you choose among the many IT security policy frameworks promoted by government agencies, corporations, and many others? There's no simple answer. Your choice will depend on your industry, as well as your management view of risk and any bias within your organization. You should focus on selecting the standards that are widely accepted. This ensures a regulator's acceptance of the risk management approach. Also, you'll find readily available resources to support accepted standards.

Figure 8-1 depicts a simplified framework domain model. Notice that a significant portion is dedicated to the governance and management of risks. This establishes the principle that managing risk and understanding business is a core competency. More comprehensive frameworks recognize that the effectiveness of controls rely on the understanding of the business process. Understanding the business process allows you to better identify risks and design effective controls.

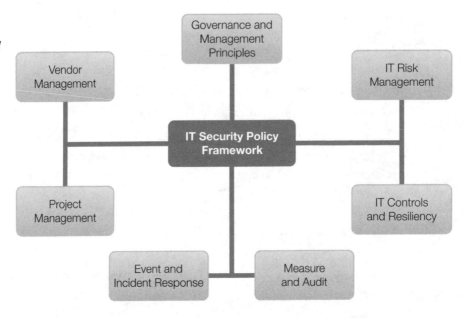

FIGURE 8-1

Simplified IT security policy framework domain model.

Your first step is to determine the scope of coverage for your framework. Then, you can use it as a filter to make sense of the various frameworks to choose from. Even a simplified framework domain model can help you recognize your organization's key areas of concern. You can create a framework that addresses specific weaknesses and aligns to your business requirements. Once you understand those requirements, you can use the following steps to select industry frameworks to consider:

1. Review industry regulatory requirements. For example, a government agency is required to implement the Federal Information Security Management Act of 2002 (FISMA).

2. Look to your auditors and regulators for guidance. For example, major external audit firms may have adopted **Committee of Sponsoring Organizations (COSO)** and **Control Objectives for Information and related Technology (COBIT)** as part of their controls testing.

3. Select frameworks that have maintained broad support in the industry over time. These are the frameworks that could be considered industry best practices.

Find out which frameworks are used by peer organizations. This can validate your approach. Many industries tend to share the same risk and leverage the same frameworks. Table 8-1 is a sample of IT security policy frameworks. These are best practice frameworks. This is not a comprehensive list, as there are other heavily used frameworks, including industry-specific frameworks. The frameworks in Table 8-1 represent different, widely adopted framework approaches.

Even the short list of IT security policy frameworks shown in Table 8-1 provides a wide array of approaches and choices. Organizations often combine these frameworks to draw upon each of their strengths.

For example, a single organization could adopt the following:

- COSO for financial controls and enterprise risk management structure
- COBIT for IT controls, governance, and risk management
- ITIL for IT services management
- PCI DSS for processing credit cards

The combination of frameworks in this example provides a comprehensive view of business risk and information security. The combination would represent an organization's security and risk framework. It starts with COSO, which provides a strategic and financial view of risk. COBIT links business requirements with technology controls. ITIL provides best practices for delivery of IT services. PCI DSS provides highly specific technology requirements for handling cardholder data. You could also substitute ISO for any of these layers or mix and match other frameworks to create a comprehensive policy approach.

The power of the frameworks in Table 8-1 is their flexibility and modularity. They are flexible in that they can align with each other or be implemented by themselves. They are modular in that you can pick and choose the component or set of objectives you wish to implement. An exception to this rule is PCI DSS. An organization required to adhere to PCI DSS must implement all of its requirements.

Risk Management and Compliance Approach

To deliver value, a framework must be able to identify and manage risk. Although the previously mentioned frameworks all have unique approaches, they share some of the same characteristics:

- They are risk-based
- They speak to the organization's risk appetite
- They deal with operation disruption and losses

The **risk appetite** refers to understanding the level of risk-taking within the business. This approach understands the business and its processes and goals. It's the overall risk the organization is willing to accept. A key measurement is the cost of risk mitigation. The risk appetite is driven by the amount of risk reduction the business is willing to fund.

The goal of these frameworks is to reduce operation disruption and losses. The frameworks reduce surprises. They ensure risks are systematically identified and reduced, eliminated, or accepted.

The ISACA Risk IT framework extends COBIT and is a good example of a comprehensive risk management approach. You can implement the ISACA Risk IT framework alone or as part of a COBIT implementation. Figure 8-2 is an overview of the Risk IT process model. The Risk IT framework is built on three domains: Risk Governance, Risk Evaluation, and Risk Response. Each of these domains has three process goals. Each process goal is broken down into key activities. For this discussion, this section will focus on domains and process goals.

> **NOTE**
>
> A framework that is risk-based focuses on the highest risk to the organization's objectives. This includes considering business objectives, legal obligations, and the organization's values.

TABLE 8-1 Sample of IT security policy frameworks.

FRAMEWORK	SPONSORING ORGANIZATION	DESCRIPTION
COSO	COSO *http://www.coso.org*	COSO is a framework for validating internal controls and managing enterprise risks. COSO is heavily focused on financial operations and risk management. It's a widely recognized standard for providing reasonable assurance that an organization's financial controls are working appropriately.
COBIT	Information Systems Audit and Control Association (ISACA) *http://www.isaca.org*	COBIT is a framework and supporting toolset that aligns business and control requirements with technical issues. COBIT is an international governance and controls framework and a widely accepted standard for assessing, governing, and managing IT security and risks. COBIT is extended with a series of other ISACA publications such as Risk IT, which extends COBIT for IT risk management. COBIT maps to many major frameworks such as COSO, ISO, and ITIL.
ISO	**International Organization for Standardization (ISO)** *http://www.iso.org*	ISO has produced a vast array of standards supporting a number of different industries and business models. The ISO standards related to information security and IT risk are widely accepted as the leading international standards. The following is a sample of key ISO publications: • ISO 20000—IT Service Management System • ISO 27001—Information Security Management • ISO 27002—Code of Practice for Information Security Management • ISO 38500—Corporate Governance of Information Security • ISO 9000—Quality Management

FRAMEWORK	SPONSORING ORGANIZATION	DESCRIPTION
ITIL	Information Technology Infrastructure Library (ITIL) http://www.itil-officialsite.com	ITIL is a widely accepted international framework and set of best practices on delivering IT services. ITIL contains a comprehensive list of concepts, practices, and processes for managing IT services
NIST	**National Institute of Standards and Technology (NIST)** http://csrc.nist.gov/publications/PubsSPs.html	The Federal Information Security Management Act (FISMA) requires federal agencies to follow a common set of security standards. These standards are provided by NIST and are known as the Federal Information Processing Standards (FIPS). FIPS is a series of special publications (SP 800) such as SP 800-53, "Security Controls for Federal Information Systems and Organizations."
OCTAVE	Computer Emergency Readiness Team (CERT) at Carnegie Mellon University http://www.cert.org/octave	**OCTAVE** (Operationally Critical Threat, Asset, and Vulnerability Evaluation) provides a framework for information security assessment and planning. OCTAVE is a framework developed by CERT. The framework consists of tools, techniques, and methods
PCI DSS	Payment Card Security Standards Council https://www.pcisecuritystandards.org/index.shtml	Payment Card Industry Data Security Standard (PCI DSS) is a security framework for any organization that accepts, stores, or processes credit cards. The PCI DSS has 12 core requirements that are further broken down into 200 individual security controls.

TABLE 8-1 *continued*

The **Risk Governance** domain provides the business view and context for a risk evaluation. This ensures that risk activity aligns with the business goals, objectives, and tolerances. This includes aligning to business strategy. This domain ensures that the full range of opportunities and consequences are considered.

The **Risk Evaluation** domain ensures that technology risks are identified and presented to leadership in business terms. Formal risks are analyzed and processes are created to assess impact. This domain also creates a risk repository of all known risks. This further enhances the risk analysis and reporting.

FIGURE 8-2

The Risk IT framework process model is built on three domains.

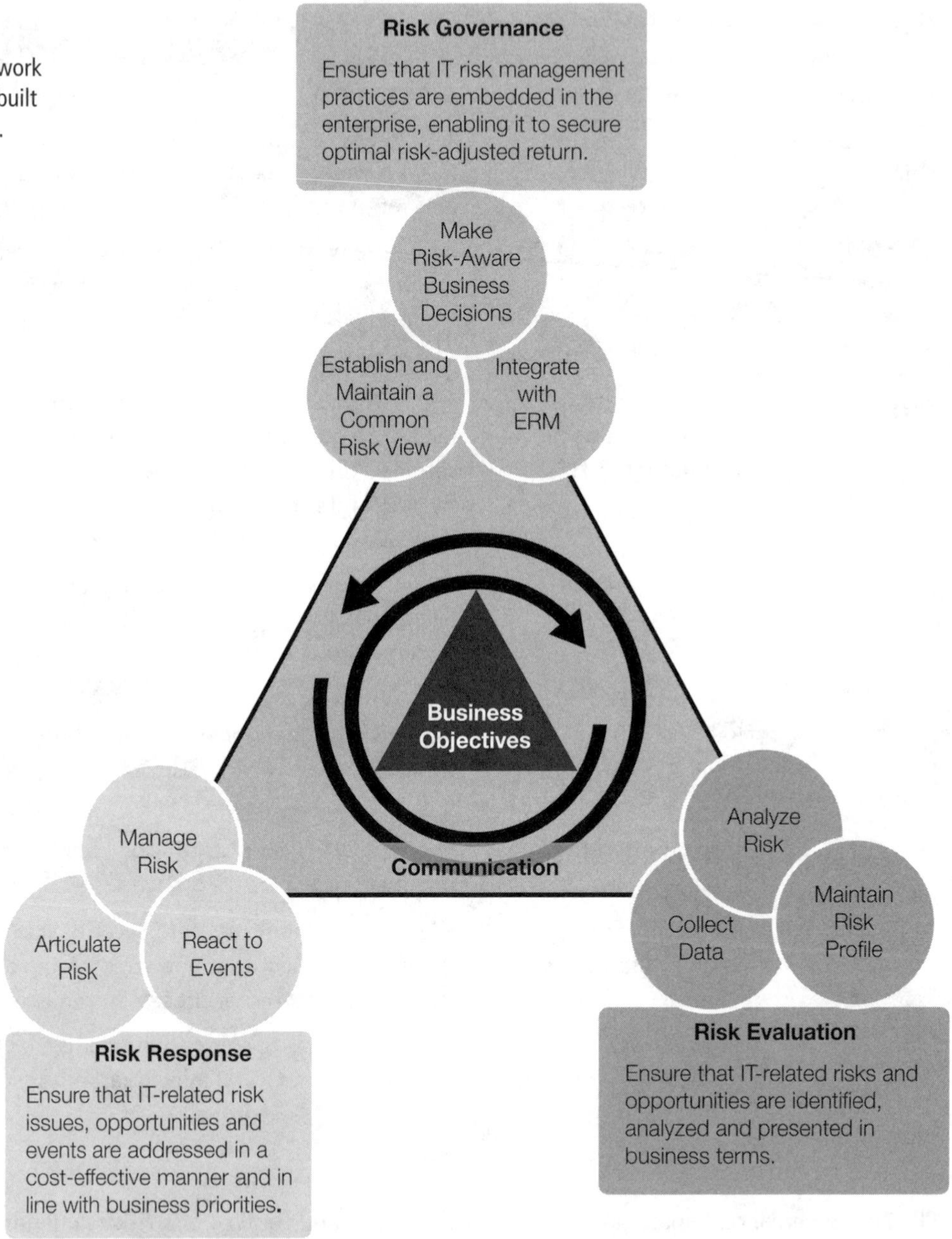

Risk Governance

Ensure that IT risk management practices are embedded in the enterprise, enabling it to secure optimal risk-adjusted return.

Make Risk-Aware Business Decisions

Establish and Maintain a Common Risk View

Integrate with ERM

Business Objectives

Communication

Manage Risk

Articulate Risk

React to Events

Analyze Risk

Collect Data

Maintain Risk Profile

Risk Response

Ensure that IT-related risk issues, opportunities and events are addressed in a cost-effective manner and in line with business priorities.

Risk Evaluation

Ensure that IT-related risks and opportunities are identified, analyzed and presented in business terms.

The **Risk Response** domain ensures risks are reduced and remediated in the most cost-effective manner. This domain coordinates risk responses so that the right people are engaged at the right time. This prevents risks from increasing in magnitude. Processes are established to manage risk throughout the enterprise to an acceptable level.

These domains build on each other, creating flexibility and agility. You can discover a potential threat in the Risk Evaluation domain and quickly assess its impact using the Risk Governance domain. In addition, the framework can quickly identify and coordinate a response to any risk.

The Physical Domains of IT Responsibility Approach

When implementing an IT security policy framework, remember to align the framework to the business process. For example, ISO 27002 provides clear guidance and best practice recommendations on controls. This creates a clear linkage between the control and the business process. This allows you to see all the controls implemented to protect an end-to-end business process. This approach minimizes controls and prevents "silo" thinking about threats. Organizations use the frameworks to reduce costs and to meet regulatory compliance.

For example, assume you are assessing backup and recovery processes. If you follow the process, you can identify risks during the hand-off between technologies. Perhaps you can no longer restore a tape that's been archived for several years. The backup technology in your data center was upgraded to a different format. Taking a look at the off-site inventory independent of the recovery aspect might miss this risk. Mapping out the process that controls the life of a backup tape is a better way to look at controls. A simple mapping might follow the tape from creation, transport, off-site storage, recall, recovery, and destruction.

Roles, Responsibilities, and Accountability for Personnel

To select, implement, and support a security policy framework requires involvement from the entire organization. As you follow a business process end-to-end through the seven domains of an IT infrastructure, you can quickly see the number of roles involved in protecting information. Each individual has specific responsibilities from administration for ensuring data quality.

The Seven Domains of a Typical IT Infrastructure

Chapter 4 introduced the seven domains of a typical IT infrastructure. Within the seven domains are special roles responsible for the data quality and handling. The following individuals work with the security teams to ensure data quality:

- Head of information management
- Data stewards
- Data custodians
- Data administrators
- Data security administrators

 NOTE

Individuals do not work in isolation. They are supported by organizational roles. The organizational roles implement a framework that establishes the standards for identifying and managing risk. Collectively, these roles and the organizational support help define the risk culture.

8

IT Security Policy Framework Approaches

The **head of information management** role is the single point of contact responsible for data quality within the enterprise. This person deals with all aspects of information. This person establishes guidance on data handling and works closely with the business to understand how information drives profitability. A business person as opposed to a technologist typically fills this role.

Data stewards are the individuals responsible for ensuring data quality within the business unit. Data stewards are the owners of the data. They approve access. They work closely with information management to ensure the business gets maximum value from the data. They define the business requirements for data and create descriptions of what the data is and how it will be used.

Data custodians are individuals in IT responsible for maintaining the quality of data. These individuals make decisions on how the data is to be handled given the requirements from the data steward. Whereas the data steward's primary role is to design and plan, the custodian's primary role is implementation.

Data administrators are responsible for executing the policies and procedures such as backup, versioning, uploading, downloading, and database administration.

Data security administrators have a highly restricted role. They grant access rights and assess threats to the information assurance (IA) program.

Organizational Structure

An organizational structure can tell you a lot about how risk is managed. It defines priorities through the teams' specialties. It defines how the organization perceives its threats. It also indicates how agile the response might be. Figure 8-3 defines a theoretical information security organization in the private sector. Notice the layer of executive governance of the security function in this example. Executive governance provides oversight for the security process and authority to execute.

The board of directors establishes an **audit committee** to deal with audit issues and non-financial risks. The chief information officer (CIO) reports to the audit committee about technology issues. The chief information security officer (CISO) may also report issues directly to the audit committee. Alternatively, the CISO may report to the CIO. Then the CIO's role is to report the security issues. The CISO may have a legal requirement to report to the board directly. For example, the Gramm-Leach-Bliley Act (GLBA) requires reporting to the board on the status of the GLBA program. That report is created and presented to the audit committee by the CISO. Keep in mind that the board of directors creates the audit committee. Consequently, issues on security coming to the board would generally go through the audit committee.

The **executive committee** helps set priorities, removes roadblocks, secures funding, and acts as a source of authority. The **security committee** members are leaders across the organization. This gives the security team its authority. The security committee acts as a steering committee for the information security program. The CISO is usually the chairperson. The CISO sets the committee agenda and facilitates discussions. The security committee reports its issues and budget requests to the executive committee. The executive committee aligns the security committee with the organization's goals and objectives.

The security committee might have a less formal relationship with the audit committee and the **operational risk committee**. The committees exchange information and on occasion agree to joint initiatives. Although less formal, these are key relationships. For example, the operational risk committee provides important information on the risk appetite of the organization. Knowing the risk appetite can help the security committee understand business requirements and priorities at an operational level.

The security management role is held by the CISO. The security committee is the key committee for the CISO. This is where the CISO can set the agenda and direction of the security and risk program.

Security administration in Figure 8-3 refers to centralized access management. Centralized access management refers to creating and maintaining user IDs, which includes granting users access rights. This also includes building roles and ensuring appropriate levels of segregation of duties. The team most likely works with project managers and developers to ensure application security requirements are met. Depending on the volume of projects, this function could be separated from security policy management.

The policy and compliance team is responsible for creating, reviewing, approving, and enforcing policy. This team works with legal to capture policy regulatory requirements. The policy and compliance team provides interpretation of policies.

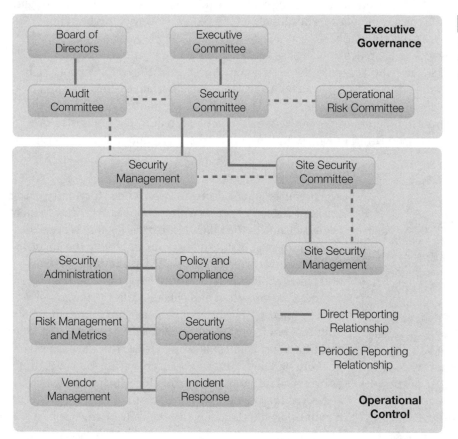

FIGURE 8-3

Information security organizational structure.

They approve deviations from policies. This team interfaces with regulators, providing evidence of compliance. The team monitors the effectiveness and adherence to policies.

The risk management and metrics team reviews the business processes and identifies potential risks and threats. The team works closely with the business to understand potential for fraud. Team members communicate with the other security teams to provide them with their assessment and analysis. They similarly use the other security teams as a source for metrics. By combining various metrics, they develop a scorecard that indicates key risks and the effectiveness of the security function. They also create reports for the CISO to present to various leaders.

A security operations team monitors for intrusions and breaches. Team members monitor firewalls and network traffic. When a breach is discovered, they activate the incident response team (IRT). The IRT responds to breaches and helps the business recover. Furthermore, the IRT assesses how the breach occurred and makes recommendations for improvement. The IRT performs forensic examinations, investigations, and interfaces with law enforcement agencies.

The vendor management team manages security concerns with vendors and third parties. Before data leaves the organization and is processed by a third party, this team would have performed an assessment on that vendor. This team is responsible for ensuring that the vendor's environment meets the control requirements of the originating organization. That typically includes certification that the vendor's security has been reviewed and meets industry standards, such as a SAS 70 report.

Figure 8-3 is a theoretical model based on combining a number of the best practices frameworks. This hybrid organizational structure illustrates the need for support from leadership and business. The number of teams and specialization depends on volume of activity, complexity of environment, and funding. The key point is that these teams do not operate in isolation. An organizational framework creates specialties that have the agility to respond quickly, while continuously working to reduce risk to the business.

Organizational Culture

The organizational culture influences how IT security policies are implemented. It starts with the tone at top—how senior leaders deal with the CISO. Security professionals are skilled in gathering threat information and analyzing the impact to the organization. They are skilled at identifying threats and vulnerabilities and then presenting these findings.

> **⚠ WARNING**
>
> Frameworks and best practices do not always translate into value to the business. A best practice may not work for every organization. There's no substitute for common sense. That's not to suggest that all best practices are optional. Once you select a framework, there must be a compelling reason not to implement a component. The easiest way to lose credibility is to fall back on the statement, "It's policy."

These are important and difficult skills to master. Equally important is the ability to navigate the organizational culture. These soft skills are especially important for a CISO. The CISO must connect and build trust with the business. Without building trust, the IT security team may be viewed as overhead rather than a partner in reducing risk.

Successfully dealing with the organization's culture means understanding how to drive value to the business.

This means working with the business to draft comprehensive security strategies to increase the business's capability. For example, the business may strive to be a virtual organization with extensive remote access. This means working on how to extend the perimeter to remote laptops versus focusing on why the risks for such a plan could be too high.

The key point is not to be out of step with the organizational culture. You must drive security solutions into the organization in a way that will resonate and be perceived as delivering value to the business.

Separation of Duties

A fundamental component of internal control is the **separation of duties (SOD)** for high-risk transactions. The underlying SOD concept is that no individual should be able to execute a high-risk transaction, conceal errors, or commit fraud in the normal course of their duties. You can apply SOD at either a transactional or organizational level.

Layered Security Approach

The **layered security approach**, which means having two or more layers of independent controls to reduce risk, can be a SOD. Layered security leverages the redundancy of the layers so if one layer fails to catch the risk or threat, the next layer should. By this logic, more layers should mean better risk reduction. However, more layers can be burdensome and expensive. There needs to be a balance between cost and return in risk reduction.

The classic example of an SOD is when it's applied at the transactional level. If you have a high-risk transaction, or combination of transactions, then you want to separate them between two or more individuals. For example, suppose a business sets up vendor accounts and issues checks based on the goods received. That business has three distinct processes: setting up a vendor account, receiving goods, and paying the vendor. Having one individual control all three processes may prove too big a temptation for fraud. Such people could set themselves up as vendors and issue checks based on goods never received as one example. This type of fraud is reduced by assigning responsibility for these processes to separate roles.

Domain of Responsibility and Accountability

Typically, SOD applies to transactions within a domain. It's management's responsibility within a domain to identify high-risk transactions and ensure adequate SOD. Ensuring adequate SOD means that you identify opportunity for fraud within these transactions. It also means identifying the potential for human error within these transactions. Applying SOD can reduce both fraud and human errors.

The concept of SOD can also be applied across domains at an organizational level. Some organizational processes and functions come with risk. For example, ensuring an organization is compliant with regulations is vital and a high risk. As in the previous transaction example, you would not have one team responsible for all three tasks of designing, implementing, and validating solutions that ensure compliance. Typically, you create an organizational SOD between those teams that implement and validate compliance.

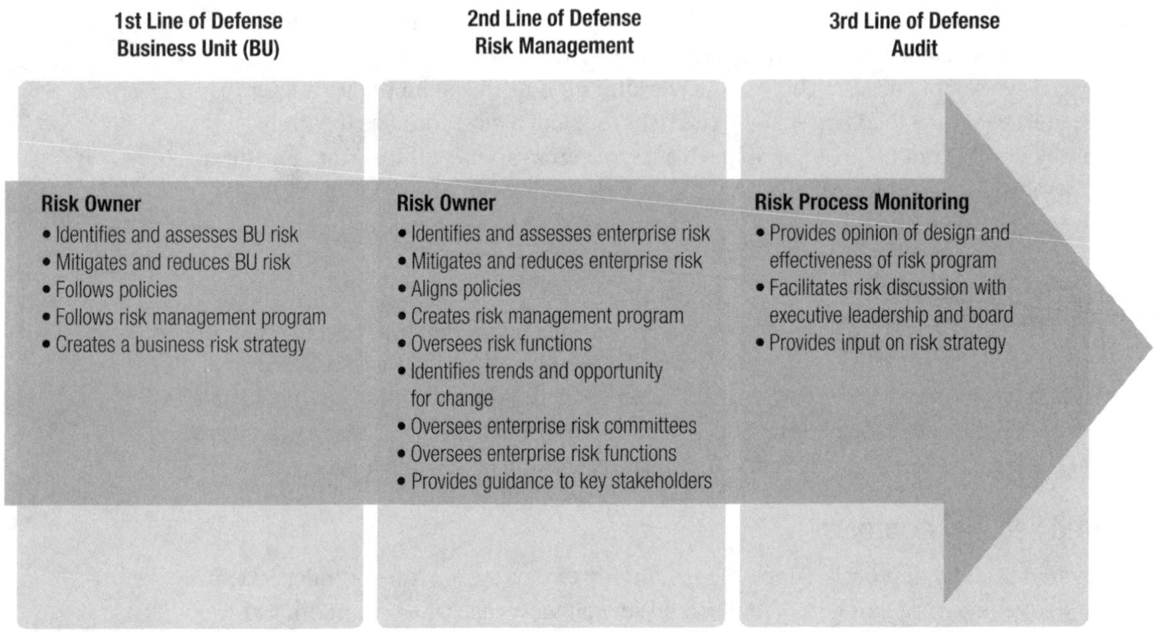

1st Line of Defense Business Unit (BU)	2nd Line of Defense Risk Management	3rd Line of Defense Audit
Risk Owner • Identifies and assesses BU risk • Mitigates and reduces BU risk • Follows policies • Follows risk management program • Creates a business risk strategy	**Risk Owner** • Identifies and assesses enterprise risk • Mitigates and reduces enterprise risk • Aligns policies • Creates risk management program • Oversees risk functions • Identifies trends and opportunity for change • Oversees enterprise risk committees • Oversees enterprise risk functions • Provides guidance to key stakeholders	**Risk Process Monitoring** • Provides opinion of design and effectiveness of risk program • Facilitates risk discussion with executive leadership and board • Provides input on risk strategy

FIGURE 8-4

Three-lines-of-defense model.

Implementing an organizational SOD is less about fraud and more about reducing potential errors in vital processes and functions.

In the financial services sector, some organizations have adopted a three-lines-of-defense model. This risk management model is a good illustration of an organizational layered approach that creates a separation of duties. Figure 8-4 depicts a three-lines-of-defense model to risk management.

First Line of Defense

The first line of defense is the business unit (BU). The business deals with controlling risk daily. They identify risk, assess the impact, and mitigate the risk whenever possible. The business is expected to follow policies and implement the enterprise risk management program. The BU owns the risk and develops short-term and long-term strategies. Ownership means they are directly accountable to ensure the risk is mitigated or reduced.

Second Line of Defense

The second line of defense is the enterprise risk management program. A risk management team owns the risk process. This team is responsible for managing risk at an enterprise level. The team provides guidance and advice to the first line of defense. They align policies and ensure that the risk management program aligns with company goals. The team has management oversight of risk committees and risk initiatives.

The second line is responsible for engaging the business to develop a risk strategy and gauging the risk appetite of the organization. Participants have an obligation to report to the board material noncompliance and risks that put the organization's strategic goals in jeopardy.

Third Line of Defense

The third line of defense is the independent auditor. That role provides the board and executive management independent assurance that the risk function is designed and working well. Additionally, the auditor acts as an advisor to the first and second lines of defense in risk matters. The third line must keep his or her independence but also have input on risk strategies and direction.

Several views exist on how closely involved the third line of defense can be in advising leadership without losing independence. If the third line of defense advises a course of action, is he or she the right person to determine the success of that action? Many audit organizations develop rules to avoid this conflict. Views differ on whether external auditors belong in the third line of defense or actually compose a fourth line.

This model clearly demonstrates how organizational roles can be used to create a separation of duties. In this case there is oversight, checks, and re-checks across three layers of the organization. In an ideal world, the first line of defense would self-assess and identify all the risks. It's not realistic to expect such precision. The basic idea is that what's not caught in the first line is caught in the second line. What the first and second lines do not catch, the third line catches. By the time you reach the third line, whatever risks still exist should not be significant and are therefore manageable.

Governance and Compliance

Even in the best of situations, an organization can be challenged to provide evidence that policies are implemented, enforced, and working as designed. The process includes collecting, testing, and reporting evidence. This can be tiresome and time consuming, especially when an organization struggles to address what may seem to be endless audit findings. These audits can lead to retesting and more control deficiencies and risks identified.

Implementing a governance framework can allow the organization to identify and mitigate risks in an orderly fashion. Once in place, the ability to quickly respond to audit requests drastically improves. The framework provides the ability to measure risk in a few ways:

- In context of how well the organization has implemented leading practices
- In context of how much of the organization's risk is covered by the resulting implemented controls

A well-defined governance and compliance framework provides a structured approach. It provides a common language. It is also a best-practice model for organizations of all shapes and sizes. A well-recognized framework standard provides a solid ground for discussing risk. It's a foundation from which information security policies can be governed.

 NOTE

Controls and risk become more measureable with a framework. Being able to measure the enterprise against a fixed set of standards and controls is powerful. It tells the regulators you are in compliance. It helps prioritize and becomes an unemotional gauge for funding risk remediation efforts. Most importantly, it helps reduce uncertainty.

IT Security Controls

Regulatory compliance is a significant undertaking for a number of organizations. Some organizations have full-time teams dedicated to collecting, reviewing, and reporting to show adherence to regulations. This diverts resources that could have been applied to protect the business.

The IT policies framework helps reduce this cost by defining security controls in a way that clearly aligns with policies and regulatory compliance. The better an organization can inventory and map its controls to policies and regulation, the lower its costs to demonstrate compliance.

From a controls design view, best practices frameworks provide the mapping to major regulations such as the Sarbanes-Oxley (SOX) Act. As a result, the adoption of these frameworks is a quick way to demonstrate adequate coverage of regulatory IT requirements.

However, good design and effective coverage of regulatory requirements does not mean the controls are working. The more an organization can automate, the lower the cost to demonstrate compliance. This is because automation reduces the time to gather documentation, test controls, and gather evidence. Two key areas of automation are documentation and testing.

Automating documentation for IT security controls simply means capturing the policy and regulatory requirements at the time the control was designed and implemented. The level of automation does not require sophistication. The core requirement of the automation is that the information is searchable. Documenting the information in multiple places in a format that cannot be searched is not automation. When the information is centralized and searchable, it's much easier to explain to a regulator how the organization is compliant. The ability to search a list of controls also makes it easier to determine which controls need to be tested. There's a vast array of low-cost documentation library solutions that can be used for this purpose.

> ⚠️ **WARNING**
>
> One problem with a statistical sample is that you have to select a sufficient number to make the sample relevant. Auditors follow sampling guidelines to ensure a sufficient number. Another problem is that a statistical-based opinion is an educated guess. Even if you use good sampling methods, it's still a guess. The samples selected could have missed a potential problem or weakness. When you automate, you usually do not have that limitation.

Automating the testing of IT controls is harder but yields the greatest benefit. The type and level of automation will depend on the technology, the control, and the complexity of the IT environment. For example, many tools can compare a file of active employees from an HR database to a list of active accounts. If the control to remove an individual is working, you should not see former employees with active accounts. Providing the same level of assurance manually would be far more costly and prone to errors. Manual verification in a larger population of users would be statistically based. You couldn't check every account manually. You would instead sample past and current employees. Depending on the number of errors an auditor found, an opinion would be made as to the overall population of active accounts.

Automated testing tools are often shared across the enterprise to improve operational effectiveness. For example, assume the automated testing of a control identifies a defect. The defect is reported and fixed. During the next test, another defect is found, reported, and fixed. The cycle continues. The individuals responsible for security control often adopt the testing tool to validate their own controls. In the real world, these individuals are very motivated to avoid repeated audit findings. As a result, automation of compliance tests builds collaboration and improves operational effectiveness.

NOTE

With so many different regulations to consider, it is nearly impossible to test without some level of automation. It is important to keep automated testing in mind when designing controls. The more you can consolidate and centralize automated testing, the lower the cost to support compliance.

Testing for compliance is more complex than the few simple examples provided. Although the complexity and volume is much larger, the key concepts are the same. It's the complexity of the technology and infrastructure that prevents wide-scale automated compliance testing today. Not all controls can be tested automatically. However, the goal should be to design controls that can be tested with automated tools.

IT Security Policy Framework

Business requirements lead to controls, which lead to reduced risk. Regardless of framework, the core objective of reducing risk remains the same. The frameworks listed in Table 8-1 can address many business risks. There are many other types of non-technology risks, well beyond the scope of these frameworks, such as credit or market risks. These are risks associated with customers being unable to pay, or market changes in which there's no longer a demand for the product or service.

Business risks are defined as five specific risks, as follows:

- **Strategic**—**Strategic risks** are a broad category focused on an event that may change how the organization operates. Some examples might be a merger or acquisition, a change in the industry, or change in the customer. The key point is that it's an event that effects the entire organization.

- **Compliance**—**Compliance risks** relate to the impact to the business of failing to comply with legal obligations. Noncompliance can be willful, or it can result from being unaware of local legal requirements. This could include regulatory requirements or legally binding contracts. Let's say a company accepts the rules associated with processing credit cards but fails to implement PCI DSS. The card companies, under a binding contract, can force the merchant to stop taking credit cards.

- **Financial**—**Financial risk** is the potential impact when the business fails to have adequate liquidity to meet its obligations. This is when you fail to have adequate cash flow. For example, the consequences of failure to pay loans, payroll, and taxes would be financial risks. This lack of available funds can be due to a poor credit rating or operations too risky for banks to fund. Regardless of the reason, if you were unable to meet your financial obligations, that would be a financial risk.

- **Operational**—**Operational risks** are a broad category that describes any event that disrupts the organization's daily activities. The Office of the Comptroller of the Currency (OCC) defines operational risk as "the risk of loss resulting from inadequate or failed internal processes, people and systems, or from external events."[1] In technology terms, it's an interruption of the technology that affects the business process. That could be a coding error, slow network, system outage, or security breach.

- **Other**—"Other risks" is a broad category that relates to all other non-IT specific events. For example, political unrest could occur in another country where the organization has a call center. The political unrest is a non-IT event. Lack of personnel showing up for work could impact IT operations. A reputational risk can also be an example. A reputational risk results from negative publicity regarding an organization's practices that could lead to a loss of revenue or litigation.

Best Practices for IT Security Policy Framework Approaches

Governance, risk management, and compliance (GRC) is the discipline that systematically manages risk and policy compliance. "Governance" describes the management oversight in controlling risks. Governance includes the process and committees formed to manage risk. Governance reflects leadership tone at the same time. This means that governance reflects the core values of the organization towards risk, including the ability to enforce policy, the importance given to protecting customer data, and the tolerance for taking risks.

"Risk management" describes the formal process for identifying and responding to risk. The concept beyond this part of GRC is a close alignment of business process and technology. This approach ensures risks are assessed and managed within the context of the business. Risk management also reflects leadership's risk appetite. How far is leadership willing to go to ensure third-party vendor protection of the organization's data? This view of risk can be reflected in leadership acceptance of risk, ranging from accepting vendor representation to insisting on on-site audits.

"Compliance" refers to processes and oversight necessary to ensure the organization adheres to policies. Compliance also includes regulatory compliance. An organization's internal policies should address external regulatory concerns. Therefore, for organizations with well-defined policies, the focus is mainly on internal policies. If you can show evidence of adherence to internal policies, you can demonstrate regulatory compliance. The ability to demonstrate regulatory compliance is further enhanced when an organization can demonstrate the adoption of a best practices policy framework.

A framework helps create an enterprise view of risk. Many organizations have complex business and technology environments. The need to align these environments is critical. Organizations also find themselves facing increased pressure from regulators to demonstrate compliance. As a consequence, adoption of best practices provides leaders, regulators, shareholders, and the public the assurance each group requires.

Another framework approach is **enterprise risk management (ERM)**. This framework aligns strategic goals, operations effectiveness, reporting, and compliance objectives. ERM is a methodology for managing a vast array of risks across the enterprise.

FYI

A GRC study by the Enterprise Management Association (EMA) published in 2008 identified the top three best practices frameworks. They are:

- ISO 27000 series
- COBIT
- COSO

ERM is not a specific set of technologies. As an example, the ERM function may look at credit or market risk and attempt to determine if the pricing strategy or compensation to the sales force is creating risk to the business. ERM is not an IT security policies framework. It is a good integration point for IT security issues to be considered in context to other risks.

What Is the Difference Between GRC and ERM?

The terms GRC and ERM are sometimes used interchangeably, but that's incorrect. The difference is not in their goals. They both attempt to control risk. You can view ERM more as a broad methodology that leadership adopts to identify and reduce risks. There are similarities worth noting, as both approaches:

- Define risk in terms of the business threats.
- Apply flexible frameworks to satisfy multiple compliance regulations.
- Eliminate redundant controls, policies, and efforts.
- Proactively enforce policy.
- Seek line of sight into the entire population of risks.

GRC is more a series of tools to centralize policies, document requirements, and assess and report on risk. Because GRC is tools-centric, many vendors have created GRC offerings. It's not surprising that with vendors aggressively selling solutions, GRC has more momentum than ERM. That's not to suggest there aren't tools to support the ERM process. Many of the GRC tools can be used to support the ERM methodology. But as a methodology, ERM adoption is driven by the organization's leadership.

The lines between GRC and ERM do blur. In the real world, ERM teams deal with governance and compliance issues all the time. They use many of the same tools and techniques. More and more, GRC teams are reaching out to risk committees and teams to align efforts at a leadership level.

The important distinction is that ERM focuses on value delivery. This shifts the discussion from organizations' budgetary requirements for risk mitigation, compared with how their expenditures enhance value. ERM takes a broad look at risk, while GRC is technology-focused. This broad view of risk considers technology as one aspect of risk among many. This can be either a benefit or a drawback depending on the leadership ability to understand IT risk. One of the benefits is that a successful implementation of ERM leads to risk management being fused into the business process and mindset.

Case Studies and Examples of IT Security Policy Framework Approaches

The case studies in the section reflect actual risks that were exploited in the real world. Each case study examines potential causes. By looking at these policies in the context of security policies, you can identify how they might be avoided.

The case studies examined in this section include:

- **PCI DSS**—Relates to leveraging PCI DSS to prevent credit card data being stolen
- **FISMA**—Relates to a court case in which an executive department was sued for lack of FISMA compliance
- **COBIT**—Relates to an energy company using COBIT to better control technology growth and business risks

Private Sector Case Study

A franchisee of a national hamburger chain in the southern United States was notified by Visa U.S.A, Inc. and the U.S. Secret Service of the theft of credit card information in August 2008. The franchisee has a chain of eight stores with annual revenue of $2 million.

The chain focused on the technology of its point-of-sale (POS) system. A leading vendor that allowed for centralized financial and operating reporting provided the POS system. It used a secure high-speed Internet connection for credit card processing. The company determined that neither the POS nor credit card authorization connection was the source of the breach. Although the POS was infected, the source of the breach was the network. Each of the franchisee's stores provided an Internet hotspot to its customers. It was determined that this Wi-Fi hotspot was the source of the breach. Although considerable care was given to the POS and credit card authorization process, the Wi-Fi hotspot allowed access to these systems. It was determined the probable cause of the breach was malware installed on the POS system through the Wi-Fi hotspot. The malware collected the credit card information, which was later retrieved by the thief.

This was a PCI DSS framework violation. The PCI DSS framework consists of over 200 requirements that outline the proper handling of credit card information. It was clear that insufficient attention was given to the network to ensure it met PCI DSS requirements. For discussion purposes, the focus is on the network. The PCI DSS outlines other standards that may have been violated related to the hardening of the POS server itself. The following four PCI DSS network requirements appear to have been violated:

- Network segregation
- Penetration testing
- Monitoring
- Virus scanning

PCI requires network segments that handle credit cards be segmented. It was unclear whether there was a complete absence of segmentation or if weak segmentation had been breached. PCI DSS outlines the standards to ensure segmentation is effective. If the networks had been segmented, this breach would not have occurred.

PCI requires that all public-facing networks be penetration tested. This type of testing would have provided a second opportunity to prevent the breach. This test would have uncovered such weaknesses within a Wi-Fi hotspot that allowed the public to access back-end networks.

PCI also requires a certain level of monitoring. Given the size of the organization, monitoring might have been in the form of alerts or logs reviewed at the end of the day. Monitoring could include both network and host-based intrusion detection. Monitoring may have detected the network breach. Monitoring may also have detected the malware on the POS system. Both types of monitoring would have provided opportunities to prevent the breach.

PCI requires virus protection. It was unclear if this type of scanning was on the POS system. If it was not, that would have been a PCI DSS violation. Such scanning provides one more opportunity to detect the malware. Early detection would have prevented the breach.

The PCI DSS requirements are specific and adopt many of the best practices from other frameworks such as ISO. The approach is to prevent a breach from occurring. Early detection of a breach can prevent or minimize card losses. For example, early detection of the malware in this case study would have prevented card information from being stolen. Some malware takes time to collect the card information, which must then be retrieved. Quick reaction to a breach is an opportunity to remove the malware before any data can be retrieved.

Public Sector Case Study

In October 2006, New York University (NYU) published in its *Law Review* an article related to a case involving a government agency accused of violating FISMA. The case involved beneficiaries of the Individual Indian Money Trusts (IIMT) managed and administered by the Department of the Interior (DOI). The beneficiaries were concerned that their personal data was being exposed over the Internet because of the agency's failure to implement adequate security controls, as required by FISMA. The information they were concerned about included personal financial and banking records.

The beneficiaries asked the court to force the DOI to disconnect the IIMT system from the Internet. The court agreed with the beneficiaries. The judge stated he was "alarmed and disturbed" by DOI's failure to adequately protect the beneficiaries' sensitive and personal data.

The court found a series of violations including failure to respond to network attacks, lack of monitoring, and lack of adequate intrusion-detection tools. They found logs were not being reviewed for 45 days, and systems were being deployed with no intrusion-detection software loaded. What compounded the concerns is that DOI had been certified as being FISMA-compliant.

There were clear NIST framework violations. NIST is the standard required by FISMA. For discussion purposes, the focus is on the network. NIST publications outlined other standards that were violated, such as effective security management and oversight. The following three NIST framework network policies were clearly violated:

- Self-reporting
- Penetration testing
- Monitoring

There is a portion of the FISMA certification that relies on self-reporting. This part of the process appears to have been violated in that the agency did not fully disclose its control weaknesses. The article did not indicate if this was an intentional omission or not. Nonetheless, had the self-report component of FISMA been working, the control weaknesses would have prevented the agency from being certified. This lack of certification would have required a second look at how the agency handles sensitive information. This might have prevented the lawsuit and any potential data breach.

The NIST framework outlines the guidance on penetration testing. Such testing would have clearly demonstrated the controls' weaknesses. This type of testing and assessment would provide another opportunity to correct the network control deficiencies prior to a breach.

The NIST framework outlines the requirements for effective network monitoring. These requirements require logs to be reviewed in a timely manner. Log reviews are essential in identifying potential hackers. Hackers tend to probe a network for weaknesses prior to a breach, but effective monitoring can detect probing. This type of monitoring provides another opportunity to correct the network control deficiencies before a breach.

Critical Infrastructure Case Study

Adnoc Distribution is an energy company with revenue of more than $3 billion. In 2008, Adnoc was expanding its energy business from petroleum into new areas, such as natural gas. The company's IT environment was also growing, supporting expanded business markets and field projects. The amount of IT resources was not proportionally increased. This resulted in internal confusion and served to degrade IT services. Many of the IT processes were not standardized, which contributed to the problem. Generally, IT was considered an operating cost that did not require additional investment. Pressures on IT to deliver continued to increase as services continued to decline.

To reverse this trend, management selected COBIT as a means to add discipline, improve service, and increase customer satisfaction levels. COBIT also brought the IT governance necessary to better align with the business's goals and provide effective oversight of the IT investments. The project was considered successful.

Some key areas of improvement noted after the COBIT implementation included:

- Value delivery
- Resourcing of IT
- Communication

With limited resources, delivering value can be a challenge. By better aligning with the business objectives and priorities, IT was able to focus resources on the project with greatest benefit to the business. COBIT was able to improve the **value delivery** by directing the IT resources more effectively into the areas vital to business goals. Confusing priorities were eliminated, implying a cost savings. Resources are wasted and costs rise when projects are started, stopped, restarted, and abandoned. COBIT ensures the appropriate controls were in place so management can exercise effective prioritization and delivery of technology solutions. COBIT was also flexible in that it aligned with other framework standards at Adnoc such as ISO.

As the business saw value in what IT was delivering, it made funding the technology easier. The resources devoted to IT depend on the perceived and actual value of solutions delivered. As COBIT better aligns an IT department with the business, the perceived value is improved. This is because the business sees IT as providing solutions for important problems.

A major benefit of COBIT is the alignment between the business and technology. What's comes from this alignment is better communications. Tangible benefits accrue to an organization when business and IT can effectively communicate needs and risks. This communication allows for risks to be systematically identified and mitigated. It also allows tailoring of solutions to meet the business need. COBIT ensures processes are in place so issues can be quickly identified and resolved.

CHAPTER SUMMARY

This chapter examined various IT security policy frameworks. The frameworks share many of the same concepts and goals of controlling risk. However, their approach and scope of coverage differs. The chapter walked through methods to identify which best practice is appropriate for an organization. Implementation approach to framework will vary by type of framework and organization culture.

The chapter examined separation of duties from a roles and organizational view. The organization view was used to create three lines of defense to enhance the risk management program. Finally, the importance of the frameworks was highlighted in case studies. These case studies illustrated how implementing a policies framework to control risk prevents breaches and ensures compliance.

KEY CONCEPTS AND TERMS

Audit committee

Committee of Sponsoring
    Organizations (COSO)

Compliance risk

Control Objectives for
    Information and related
    Technology (COBIT)

Data administrator

Data security administrator

Data steward

Enterprise risk management
    (ERM)

Executive committee

Financial risk

Governance, risk management
    and compliance (GRC)

Head of information
    management

International Organization for
    Standardization (ISO)

Layered security approach

National Institute of Standards
    and Technology (NIST)

OCTAVE

Operational risk

Operational risk committee

Risk appetite

Risk Evaluation

Risk Governance

Risk Response

Security committee

Separation of duties (SOD)

Strategic risk

Value delivery

CHAPTER 8 ASSESSMENT

1. The security committee is the key committee
for the CISO.

A. True
B. False

2. Which of the following is not an IT security
policy framework?

A. COBIT
B. ISO
C. ERM
D. OCTAVE

3. Which of the following are PCI DSS network
requirements?

A. Network segregation
B. Penetration testing
C. Virus scanning
D. All of the above
E. A and B only

4. Which of the following are common
IT framework characteristics?

A. Risk-based management
B. Aligned business risk appetite
C. Reduced operation disruption and losses
D. Established path from requirements
    to control
E. All of the above
F. A and C only

5. Which of the following applies to both GRC
and ERM?

A. Defines an approach to reduce risk
B. Applies rigid framework to eliminate
    redundant controls, policies, and efforts
C. Passively enforces security policy
D. Seeks line of sight into root causes of risks

6. The underlying concept of SOD is that
individuals execute high-risk transactions
as they receive pre-approval.

A. True
B. False

7. A risk management and metrics team is generally the first team to respond to an incident.

A. True
B. False

8. Which of the following approves business access to data?

A. Data steward
B. Data guardian
C. Data administrator
D. A and C
E. All of the above

9. Which of the following is not a key area of improvement noted after COBIT implementation?

A. Value delivery
B. Decentralization of the risk function
C. Better resourcing of IT
D. Better communication

10. A security team's organizational structure defines the team's _____.

11. Implementing a governance framework can allow an organization to systemically identify and prioritize risks.

A. True
B. False

12. The more layers of approval required for SOD, the more _____ it is to implement the process.

13. Monitoring detects which of the following?

A. A network breach
B. Hackers probing the network
C. A and B
D. None of the above

14. All organizations should have a full-time team dedicated to collecting, reviewing, and reporting to demonstrate adherence to regulations.

A. True
B. False

 ENDNOTE

1. "Supervisory Guidance on Operational Risk Advanced Measurement Approaches for Regulatory Capital" (Office of the Comptroller of the Currency, July 2, 2003). *http://www.occ.treas.gov/ftp/release/-003-53c.pdf* (accessed April 30, 2010).

User Domain Policies

A TENET OF TELECOMMUNICATIONS SAYS the more people who access a network, the more valuable the network becomes. This is called Metcalfe's law. Let's use a telephone system as an example. If only two telephones were on the system, the value of the system is limited. Only two people can talk at any given time. But add millions of phones and people, and suddenly the value of the network rapidly increases.

This same rapid, accelerated growth factor holds true when it comes to information security risks. As the number of people accessing your network increases, so does the number of risks. As the user population increases, so does the need to access information. This need translates into complex security controls that must be provided. Inevitably, this complex jumble leads to gaps in protection of the information. A known gap in information security is a risk that cannot be mitigated. Organizations must accept these types of risks. The unknown gaps are more dangerous because they deal with the unexpected. People who follow User Domain policies are best equipped to deal with the unexpected.

This chapter examines different types of users on networks. It reviews individual need for access and how those needs lead to risks that must be controlled. We will also discuss how security policies mitigate risks in the User Domain. The last part of the chapter presents several case studies to illustrate the alignment between types of users, risks, and security policies.

This chapter covers the following topics and concepts:

- What the weakest link in the information security chain is
- What different types of users there are
- How to govern different types of users with policies
- What acceptable use policies (AUPs) are
- What the significance of a privileged-level access agreement (PAA) is
- What security awareness policies (SAPs) are
- What best practices for User Domain policies are
- What some case studies and examples of User Domain policies are

Chapter 9 Goals

When you complete this chapter, you will be able to:

- Understand why users are considered the weakest link in implementing security policies and controls
- Understand the different users in a typical organization
- Explain how different users have different information needs
- Define an AUP
- Define a PAA
- Explain how a SAP can reduce risks
- Identify several best practices related to User Domain policies
- Understand through case studies how security policies can reduce risk

9

User Domain Policies

The Weakest Link in the Information Security Chain

Security experts consider people the weakest link in security. Unlike automated security controls, different people have different skill levels. People can also let their guard down. They get tired or distracted, and may not have information security in mind when they do their jobs. Automated controls have advantages over people. An automated control never sleeps or takes a vacation. An automated control can work relentlessly and execute flawlessly. The major advantage people have over automated controls is the ability to deal with the unexpected. An automated control is limited because it can mitigate only risks that it has been designed for.

> **NOTE**
>
> The term "employee" in this chapter broadly describes people hired by an organization or who contract with an organization to provide services. "Employee" refers to an ordinary employee, a consultant, or a contractor.

This section looks at different ways in which humans earn the distinction of "the weakest link in the security chain." As you'll learn, social engineering, human mistakes, and the actions of insiders account for many security violations. However, lack of leadership support for security policies is another reason security measures fail. As a future security leader, keep in mind why employees at every level must accept and follow security policies.

Social Engineering

People can be manipulated. **Social engineering** occurs when you manipulate or trick a person into weakening the security of an organization. Social engineering comes in many forms. One form is simply having a hacker befriend an employee. The more intimate the relationship, the more likely the employee may reveal knowledge that can be used to compromise security.

> **NOTE**
>
> There are many different techniques that fall under "social engineering." However, they all rely on a person revealing sensitive information.

Another method is pretending to be from the IT department. This is sometimes called **pretexting**. A hacker might call an employee and convince him or her to reveal sensitive information. For example, a hacker asks an employee to enter data the hacker knows won't work. The hacker then simply asks for the employee's ID and password to "give it a try." Hackers who use pretexting are usually highly skilled in manipulating people. They can present simple or elaborate stories that seem compelling to an unsuspecting employee.

> **NOTE**
>
> For social engineering to be successful, an attacker needs the employee to violate policies. That's why you should add "social engineering" to a security awareness training program. Chapter 2 covers awareness training, and security awareness policies are covered later in this chapter.

Social engineering can be more economical for the hacker than trying to break through an automated control like a firewall. Breaking through automated controls can take weeks, months, or years. You may never be able to bypass the control. If you do bypass the control, you still might not get access to the information you want. Just because you break through a firewall does not mean you can access the server containing the information you want to steal. It may be easier to randomly call employees and pose as an IT department employee. This can be accomplished within a short time and only takes one individual letting his or her guard down to be successful.

Human Mistakes

> **NOTE**
>
> A survey conducted by Help Net Security found that employee carelessness is ranked fourth in the top 10 information security threats of 2010.

One characteristic all humans share is that they make mistakes. Mistakes come from carelessness, lack of knowledge, or inadequate oversight or training. Regarding security, humans may perceive a threat that does not exist. Humans might miss a real threat that is obvious.

Carelessness can be as simple as writing your password on a sticky note and leaving it on your keyboard. It can also be failing to read warning messages but still clicking OK. Carelessness can occur because an employee is untrained or does not perceive information security as important. Careless employees are prime targets of hackers who develop malicious code. These hackers count on individuals to be their point of entry into the network.

Another form of carelessness is intimidating people into weakening security controls out of convenience. This can happen when a supervisor or an executive, for example, asks an employee to take shortcuts or to bypass normal control procedures. The employee feels compelled to follow the instructions of his or her superior.

Carelessness can also be a result of a lack of common computer knowledge. Technology often outpaces an employee's skills. Just as some employees acquire solid understanding of a system or application, it's upgraded or replaced. Too much change in an organization is unsettling and can lead to portions of your workforce being inadequately trained. An untrained worker can create a security weakness inadvertently, such as by failing to log off a system and leaving information on the screen exposed.

It's not just users who can be careless or make mistakes. Programmers make mistakes in their code that can be exploited by hackers. This includes programmers of systems and applications. The situation is understandable given how complex operating systems have become. Operating systems continue to grow in size. That means the number of lines of code continue to grow. For example, Microsoft Windows XP eventually grew to over 40 million lines of code. Microsoft Windows 7 has so many teams contributing code that it's hard to calculate the total size. Regardless, given the size and complexity of these operating systems error in code is inevitable. These errors can lead to security weaknesses that attackers exploit. Once these exploits are identified, vendors react quickly to publish code patches to mitigate the threat.

You can use security policies to help developers reduce vulnerabilities during application development. Security polices can establish secure coding standards. The policies require penetration testing for high-risk applications. The best time to reduce risk is when an application is being written. Security policies can define how you perform vulnerability reviews during the development life cycle. Collectively, these polices can help you protect an application against attack.

Insiders

A significant threat to information security comes from the user who is an insider. The term **insider** refers to an employee, consultant, contractor, or vendor. The insider may even be the IT technical people who designed the system, application, or security that is being hacked. The insider knows the organization and the applications. An IT department insider knows what is logged and what is checked and not checked. This person may even have access to local accounts shared between administrators. As a result, the IT insider has an easier time bypassing security controls and hiding his or her tracks. Insiders can hide their tracks by deleting or altering logs and time stamps. Knowing where the logs are kept and how frequently they are checked is a great advantage to an insider.

Application Code Errors

There are differing views on the number of average errors per line of code written. Some general rules of thumb use 10 to 20 defects per 1,000 lines of code while others estimate as many as 50 defects per 1,000. Commercial software tends to have fewer errors than code written in-house—as low as .5 to 3 defects per KLOC. A KLOC is a unit of measure that stands for 1,000 lines of code. For example:

- An application with 2 million lines of code and a rate of 20 defects per KLOC would expect to have 40,000 coding errors.
- This is calculated based on 20 (defects per KLOC) multiplied by 2 million (lines of code) divided by 1,000 (the KLOC).

Thousands of new vulnerabilities are discovered in code each year. The number of new vulnerabilities recorded in 2009 by IBM was 6,601. You can safely assume that the vulnerabilities for new products are not found immediately. The new vulnerabilities discovered each year are a combination of errors in new and existing systems and applications.

> **NOTE**
>
> The motivation of an insider is not always greed. An individual may feel disgruntled for a variety of reasons—from feeling mistreated to being passed over for some promotion. The person may have some disappointment in life outside of work. The person may simply have a sense of entitlement, "taking" the rewards he or she feels have been earned.

Regular employees with a long history in the organization may also pose a risk. These employees may be in a position of trust. These individuals have a sense of how the organization responds to incidents and can tailor their attack accordingly.

A 2009 study by Verizon's Business RISK team reviewed 90 of the company's 2008 security cases. The team found 20 percent were caused by insiders. That was up by 2 percent from the previous year. A joint study between the United States Secret Service and Carnegie Mellon University was published in May 2005. That joint study surveyed 500 security and law enforcement executives. It found that 29 percent of their incidents originated from insiders. The survey also indicated that the vast majority of insiders were either previously or currently employed full-time in a technical IT job within the organization. The majority of insider attacks come from systems administrators, programmers, engineers, and IT specialists.

One motivation is money. Let's consider someone trying to steal 100,000 credit card numbers. Some estimate stolen credit cards can be sold for $2 to $6 each on the black market. Let's assume a hacker offers $20,000 to an employee for insider help. The employee copies the card information or provides a way to get into the system. Paying for information becomes a more economical approach than taking the time to hack through automated defenses with uncertain results. The return in this example would be $200,000 to $600,000 for a $20,000 investment.

Sometimes the insider gives you information for a lot less money. This is especially true in overseas locations such as India and the Philippines. Companies have outsource arrangements for call centers in those countries because of lower labor costs. According to JobStreet.com, an average call center agent in the Philippines with four years experience makes an average of $338 per month, or $4,056 per year. It's easy to see how offering a few months' worth of salary for information can be enticing.

Insiders breaching security can have a devastating effect on an organization's reputation and viability. For example, Jerome Kerviel was a trader at a major European bank. He was blamed for losing $7.9 billion. Kerviel was an insider who placed unauthorized trades, putting the bank at serious risk. He covered up the trades by falsifying records and hacking into company computers to hide the trades. This reportedly went on for almost two years until he was caught in 2008.

Security policies and controls can help limit damages and threats. Security policies ensure access is limited to individual roles and responsibilities. This means the damage from using an insider's credentials is limited to that function. Additionally, a policy may require that an individual's access be removed immediately upon leaving the organization. These types of user controls can reduce risk.

Six Types of Users

The User Domain, one of seven domains of a typical IT infrastructure, consists of a variety of users. Each user type has unique access needs. As the different types of users in the domain grow, so does the security complexity. At a minimum, each type of user has unique business needs and thus requires unique rights to access certain information. Within each of these major types of users, the rights are further refined into subtypes. Each subtype might be further broken up, and so on. For example, your organization might have many types of administrators. The number depends on the size of the organization, complexity, and team specializations. You may further separate rights between Oracle and Microsoft SQL database administrators. Figure 9-1 is an example of types and subtypes of users.

> **NOTE**
>
> Chapter 4 discussed the seven domains of a typical IT infrastructure.

You can build better security policies and controls by understanding user needs. To illustrate this point, this chapter focuses on six basic user types, as follows:

- **Employees**—Ordinary staff members of the organization
- **Systems administrator**—Employees who work in the IT department to provide technical support to the systems
- **Security personnel**—Individuals responsible for designing and implementing a security program within an organization
- **Contractors**—Temporary workers who can be assigned to any role
- **Guests and general public**—A class or group of users who access a specific set of applications
- **Auditors**—Individuals who evaluate controls for design and effectiveness

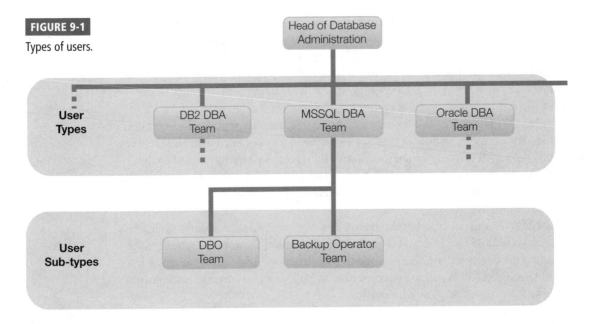

FIGURE 9-1

Types of users.

Table 9-1 outlines each of these user types in context of their business and access needs. The table focuses on six basic user types. The same approach can be applied to any user accessing information on the network.

Employees

Employees represent the broadest category of users within an organization. Organizations are composed of departments and lines of business. An employee may be full-time or part-time. An employee may be in a customer-facing role or a corporate function. Regardless of their job in the organization, employees have unique information needs.

Successfully implementing security policies depends on knowing who has access to the organization's information. Security policies require users to have unique identities to access systems, applications, and/or networks. This is typically accomplished by the employee entering a unique user ID and password.

Employees' access must be managed through the life cycle of their career with the organization. There is always pressure to grant and extend user access to increase productivity. No one wants to wait weeks for a new hire to be granted access. Additionally, when a change to the business occurs, you might need to change employee access. Although there's significant pressure to grant employees new access rights, the same pressure may not exist to remove access. Consider the following example:

An employee with many years of experience within an organization worked her way to a role with a high level of trust with her management. She entered the organization at an entry-level position. She was eventually promoted to the role of supervisor and then manager. The employee transferred within the department. Throughout the changes in her role, the prior access was never removed. This is someone who understands the inner workings of the department and has intimate knowledge of the technology. She is often asked to train others.

Security policies require access to be removed when an individual changes roles. Without good security policies you may find longtime employees with excessive access rights. They collect new access as they change roles and continue to retain access from their prior roles. Department leadership might not perceive this as a problem, especially when an employee uses this broad access to "save the day" during a crisis. Looking ahead, people may believe there's no time to ask for additional access during an emergency. An individual who is able to execute transitions quickly might prevent the problem from escalating.

TABLE 9-1 Typical domain users' need for access.		
TYPE OF USER	**BUSINESS NEED**	**ACCESS NEED**
Employees	Need to access specific applications in the production environment	Access is limited to specific applications and information.
Systems administrators	Need to access systems and databases to support applications	Access is broad and unlimited in context of the role. For example, database administrators may have unlimited access to the database but not the operating system.
Security personnel	Need to protect network, systems, applications, and information	Access to set permissions, review logs, monitor activity, and respond to incidents.
Contractors	Temporary worker needing the same access as a full-time worker in the same role	Access is the same as for full-time worker.
Guests and general public	Need to access specific application functions	Access is assigned to a type of user and not to the individual.
Auditors	Need to review and assess controls	Access often includes unlimited read access to logs and configuration settings.

Excessive access rights represent a serious security risk. As individuals change roles their access rights must be adjusted. Prior access rights that are no longer needed must be removed. New access rights must be properly approved and granted. This is for the employee's protection as much as for the organization's. When a security incident occurs, one of the first steps is to identify who may have had access. This is accomplished by reviewing individual access rights. Employees can avoid suspicion if they have no access to the affected systems, applications, and information. Removing unneeded access also reduces overall security vulnerabilities. In the event an ID and password is compromised, a hacker's access rights would be contained within the employee's current role. Consider the following example:

> In a bank, a teller may be able to initiate the process of sending money between banks from one account to another. This is an important service provided to commercial customers. Before the money is sent, however, the bank manager must approve the transfer. This dual control creates a separation of duties (SOD) to reduce fraud. If the employee was once a teller and retained his access rights, the bank is at risk. The employee in this scenario could start and approve the transfer of money. The ability to perform both roles violates the SOD security policies for these types of transactions. Additionally, having such access becomes an unnecessary temptation for fraud in which employees could target rarely used accounts to wire themselves funds.

Good security policies make clear that individuals only have the access needed for their jobs. Security policies outline how rights are assigned and approved. This includes the removal of prior access that is no longer needed. This accomplishes the following:

- Reduces the overall security risk to the organization
- Maintains separation of duties
- Simplifies investigation of incidents

Systems Administrators

Systems administrators may need unlimited rights to install, configure, and repair systems. With this elevated access comes enormous responsibility to protect credentials. A systems administrator's credentials are a prime target for hackers. As a result, organizations should consider additional layers of authentication for administrators when feasible, such as certificates and two-factor authentication.

Security policies reduce risk by requiring monitoring of the systems administrator's activity. The systems administrator should only use broad access to perform assigned duties. Let's consider a database administrator. She needs access to apply patches, resolve issues, and configure applications. Yet she normally does not access customer personal information stored within the database. Logging administrator activity is one way to verify that access rights are not being abused. Logs record if administrators granted themselves access beyond the scope of their roles. Logs record the names of people who access customer personal information. Although you may not be able to prevent a systems administrator from accessing customer information, you can review the logs to detect the event.

With elevated access, systems administrators could just turn off the logs. However, the act of turning off or altering logs is also trackable. Many systems write an entry when the log service starts and stops. Additionally, logs can be sent to a log server. A **log server** is a separate platform used to collect logs from platforms throughout the network. Access to log servers is highly restricted. Analyzing logs can help you detect gaps in logs, which are an indication the log service was turned off. Analyzing logs can also help detect if they have been altered. Knowing that your activity is being monitored is a deterrent in itself. Security policies outline the requirements of what is logged and how often the logs are reviewed.

There's a widely accepted approach that states systems administrators' access rights should be limited to their daily routine tasks. Through a separate process, systems administrator's rights can be elevated when they need to install, configure, or upgrade the system. The approach assumes that tasks associated with the elevated rights occur infrequently. Therefore, the additional process is not burdensome. Some systems administrators resist this approach. Having unfettered access makes their job easier in that they don't have to request access before performing certain tasks. It can be hard to predict what their access needs are. As a result, they may feel asking for permission is cumbersome and creates unnecessary delays.

You can consider limiting administrator rights a leading practice in regulated industries. The approach is widely accepted in the financial services industry. Some of the advantages of granting elevated rights to administrators as needed include the following:

1. It reduces the overall security risk to the organization. In the event the systems administrator's credentials are compromised access would be limited.

2. It dramatically reduces the volume of logs to be reviewed to detect when an administrator abuses his or her access rights.

3. It improves the alignment and understanding between technical tasks and business requirements.

   a. This approach records the business reason for the elevated rights being granted, which addresses why the security administrator accessed certain files.

   b. This information can also be used to identify patterns of control weaknesses.

It's not practical to log every access a busy systems administrator performs daily. The volume of logs would be excessive. Reviewing these logs would lack context. You may be able to determine that an administrator accessed a file but there's no business context. In other words, given the volume of log files, it would difficult at best to determine which files they should or should not have accessed that day. The approach described above allows you to understand why the access rights were used. By the nature of the request, you know what files they should access and the business reason why. For example, if you found that a security administrator had accessed a financial spreadsheet, was it to fix a corrupted file or because he or she wanted to illegally access information used to buy or sell stock? When an administrator is fixing a problem, you have a record of the reason why he or she accessed the file. Knowing the business reason gives you the context.

The process for capturing business requirements and elevating privileges are well established. Security policies outline the process of temporarily granting elevated rights, which is often called a firecall-ID process. A **firecall-ID process** provides temporary elevated access to unprivileged users. The name implies the urgency behind granting the access to resolve a problem quickly. During a firecall-ID process, the issue or problem is defined in a trouble ticket. The **trouble ticket** is a complete record of what access was granted and the business reason. The ticket is then assigned to someone to fix the problem. When the problem is assigned, the individual is granted elevated privileges. The individual completes the work and closes the ticket. When the ticket closes, the individual's elevated rights are removed. Figure 9-2 depicts a basic firecall-ID process.

A firecall-ID process is an accepted way to grant temporary access for a number of activities, such as one-time events like special financial reporting. With this approach, you configure more detailed logging without generating excessive volume. This is because you will record more detail but only when the elevated rights are turned on.

Security Personnel

Security personnel are responsible for designing, implementing, and monitoring security programs. In larger organizations, the roles may be separated between those who define versus implement the policies. Security personnel develop security awareness and training programs. They also align security policies with other parts of the organization such as legal and HR.

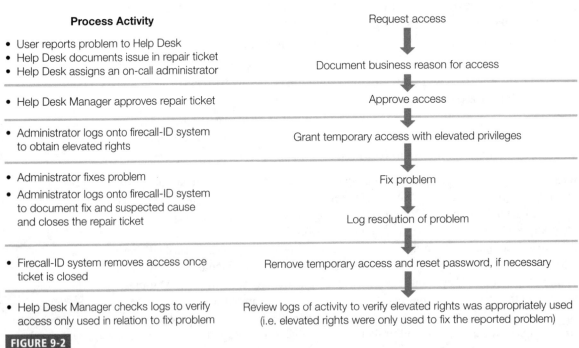

FIGURE 9-2

Basic firecall-ID process.

Security staff must understand and implement different types of controls, such as management, operational, and technical. They have to wear many hats. On any given day, security staff may handle a variety of tasks. One day they may work with procurement to review a new software package for vulnerabilities. They may be woken up in the middle of the night to respond to a security breach. In many organizations, the security team is understaffed, so they must carefully prioritize the work load to focus on the greatest risks. The following are examples of the diversity of issues that security teams deal with:

- Audit coordination and response, and regulator liaison
- Physical security and building operations
- Disaster recovery and contingency planning
- Procurement of new technologies, vendor management, and outsourcing
- Security awareness training and security program maintenance
- Personnel issues, such as background checks for potential employees and disciplinary actions for current employees
- Risk management and planning
- Systems management and reporting
- Telecommunications
- Penetration testing
- Help desk incident response

These individuals need access to information that shows them how security controls are working. This often means they have read access to logs and configuration information. As with systems administrators, with this broad access comes enormous responsibilities to protect their credentials. The credentials of these individuals are also a prime target for hackers.

Contractors

Contractors are temporary workers. They can be assigned a role like a regular employee. The two major advantages of a contractor are in cost and skills. These individuals comply with the same security policies as any other employee. There may be additional policy requirements on a contractor such as special non-disclosure agreement and deeper background checks.

Contractors allow you to ramp up your workforce during peak periods. Contractors generally save organizations money over the long term. Although you pay contractors more than similar employees' wages, you usually need contractors for shorter periods of time. In addition, contractors generally do not receive paid benefits, such as sick leave and vacation time.

Contractors can bring a variety of special skills to an organization. These skills can be valuable to a specific project or initiative. Maintaining these skills within your full-time staff may not be cost effective. For example, assume you are deploying a new technology to prevent data leakage. The project is to install a leading vendor package designed to prevent sensitive information from being e-mailed out of the organization.

Your staff may be unfamiliar with the package and the technology. You can hire a contractor who has installed this product numerous times. The contractor has knowledge based on prior installations that cannot be achieved through training.

Contractors must be fast learners. Within a short time, they are expected to know your security policies. They also have to adapt to the organization culture. The firm placing the individual often completes background checks for contractors. If that is the case, it's important to verify that the background checks are as thorough as those performed by the hiring organization. The other challenge relates to security awareness. Depending on the length of the engagement, there may be limited time to conduct the same caliber of awareness training as you do with existing employees.

Guests and General Public

Guests and the general public are a special class of users. Unlike other types of users who are assigned unique IDs and passwords, you might not know the identity of an individual accessing a public-facing Web page. This is common on the Internet. There are many applications on the Internet that are freely accessible to the public. When an individual wants access to one of these applications, an ID and password is not needed.

> **NOTE**
>
> The term "**harden**" refers to eliminating as many security risks as possible. You do this by reducing access rights to the minimum needed to perform any task, ensuring access is authenticated to unique individuals, removing all nonessential software, and other configuration steps that eliminate opportunities for unauthorized access.

For example, let's assume a Web site contains a zip-code lookup application in the demilitarized zone (DMZ). You enter a zip code to find out which city is in the zip code area. Assume the Web site is freely available. The cost of the site is supported by advertisers placing ads on the Web page. When someone types in a zip code, the corresponding city name appears. This is accomplished through a query to a back-end database that matches the entered zip code with the appropriate city. Credentials are exchanged between the Web site server and back-end database server. Rather than seeing an individual accessing the database, the security controls may only see the credentials of the Web site server. This in itself does not create a security exposure if the application, network, and database are hardened.

The zip-code lookup application ensures that only a five-digit zip code can be entered, which prevents a **Structured Query Language (SQL) injection** attack. SQL injection is a common form of hacker attack in which a SQL command is placed inside an input field. Hackers hope that when the input field is passed to the database query they can execute their own commands on the database. Network controls ensure that only traffic from the DMZ application to the database server is permitted. These network controls (such as a firewall) would also ensure that the only traffic permitted is a SQL query from the DMZ application to the specific back-end database server. The back-end database server accepts a connection only from the DMZ application. The back-end database server also permits only one type of SQL query, which reads the zip code entered and returns the associated city to be displayed. Figure 9-3 depicts these layers of controls at the DMZ application, network, and database layers.

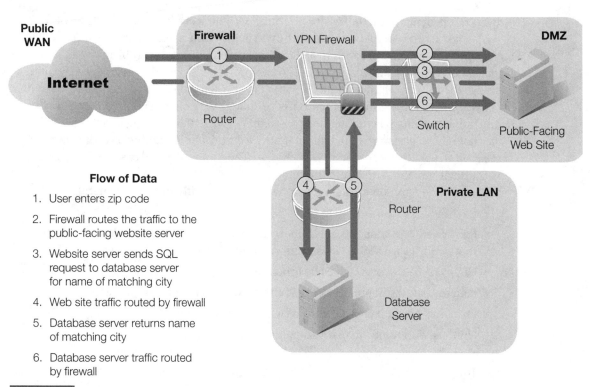

Flow of Data

1. User enters zip code

2. Firewall routes the traffic to the public-facing website server

3. Website server sends SQL request to database server for name of matching city

4. Web site traffic routed by firewall

5. Database server returns name of matching city

6. Database server traffic routed by firewall

FIGURE 9-3

Example of a DMZ application connecting to back-end server.

In this specific Web site example, you can see that the application, network, and database would be well protected. It's not so easy in the real world. In the real world, applications share Web site space and back-end database servers. A breach in one application can lead to a breach in another. Not all applications effectively test and limit what a user can enter. An application's internal controls can be sound but the application becomes compromised by a vulnerability in the operating system. Security policies outline the type of controls and hardening methods used to protect a server in the DMZ.

It's important to remember that guests and the general public have different skill sets than your employees. These individuals have not had the benefit of security awareness training. Their computer skills may be limited. The design of your application and associated security controls must be hardened. You need to assume users may input data that makes no sense. Validation and error checking is important. It's also a safe assumption that when you have a public-facing application, at some point a hacker will probe for security weaknesses.

When dealing with guests and the general public, you grant access rights to a class of users rather than individuals. You can accomplish this in several ways. You can assign credentials to applications, servers, or types of database connections. You can also assign rights to a generic user ID or service account. Assigning credentials in the form of a hard-coded ID and password stored within an application is less secure. Security policies typically prohibit this approach to application credentialing. The problem is that if an application is compromised, the ID is also compromised. It also makes it very difficult to change the ID's password without recoding or reconfiguring the application. As a result, a password used in this manner tends not to change very often. This creates a security vulnerability. A much better method of assigning credentials is using a method that does not rely on passwords, such as assigning a certificate. Assigning a certificate to an account, application, or server is fairly easy. The complexity and cost comes in setting up the environment to maintain the certificates.

The following are some best practices when dealing with guest and general public access:

- From a policy standpoint, it is important to have a well-defined risk process that performs a detailed assessment of guest and general public access
- Highly restrict access to specific functions
- Penetration test all public-facing Web sites to detect control weaknesses
- Don't hard-code access credentials within applications
- Limit network traffic to point-to-point communications

Auditors

There are many different types of auditors. For example, financial auditors focus on financial operations. They look at the completeness, fairness, and representation in the organization's financial statements. They look at the underlying processes and operations that produced the financial data. Financial auditors look at any potential control weaknesses that may call into question the accuracy of the financial statements.

Technology auditors are often referred to as IT auditors. They look at an organization's technology controls and risks. They assess the controls for design and effectiveness. They ask questions such as "Do the controls address all the vulnerabilities and are they working well?" They also look at how well an organization assesses technology risk in context of the business processes.

Although financial and technology audit teams have distinct responsibilities, they often collaborate. This is referred to as an integrated audit. In an **integrated audit**, more than one audit discipline is combined for a single audit. For example, let's assume a company purchases large amounts of equipment for its manufacturing process. The accuracy of the company's financial statements depends in part on properly reporting these expenditures. Financial auditors look at the underlying financial data and accounting methods used to reflect these investments. Financial auditors may look at the depreciation method used. They might even challenge the completeness of the data. On the other hand, IT auditors focus on the underlying technology that captures, records, and calculates the financial results. IT auditors look at the security controls and the integrity of the data.

This includes who can change the calculations or formulas. IT auditors also look at how system and application changes are monitored. The combination of these audits can determine whether the information and/or formulas were altered by unauthorized users. Combining financial and IT audits provides greater confidence that financial statements are true and accurate. This is the assurance that an executive needs to provide to regulators and the public.

 NOTE

The authority to conduct audits depends on the type of organization. For example, government agencies are subject to audits through legal statutes and directives. A private company may be subject to audit requirements set by its board of directors. Many publicly traded companies adopt an audit committee structure. This is a subcommittee of the board of directors formed to focus on audit matters.

In a public company, an auditor reports findings to the business unit management and to the audit committee. This dual reporting serves several goals. It ensures that line management knows about control weaknesses so immediate action can be taken. It also ensures that risks get visibility at the highest level of the organization. Reports to the audit committee usually come in three forms:

- Risks and issues since the last report
- Major incidents and risks
- Risk trends

Security policies detail the controls in granting auditors access. For an IT audit this typically means access to security reports, logs, and configuration information. Auditors primarily need read access. Auditors have specialized tools that help analyze samples taken and record their findings. Within these specialized applications they are granted appropriate rights to capture the evidence and write audit reports.

Why Govern Users with Policies?

Organizations want a single view of risk. Decision-making becomes easier, as does talking with regulators or shareholders. Security policies offer a common way to view and control risks. In addition, regulations require the implementation of security policies. A few examples include the Sarbanes-Oxley (SOX) Act of 2002 and the Health Insurance Portability and Accountability Act (HIPAA), discussed in Chapter 3. This is not unique to the United States. Global organizations face an array of similar laws and regulations, such as the European Data Protection Directive.

Having well-defined policies that govern user behavior ensures key risks are controlled in a consistent manner. These policies provide evidence of compliance to regulators. Regulators are increasingly looking at how security policies are applied. It's not enough to have written policies. Regulators also want to see evidence that these policies are enforced.

Acceptable Use Policy (AUP)

It is important to set clear expectations for what's acceptable behavior while using an organization's technology assets. An AUP defines the intended uses of computers and networks, including unacceptable uses and the consequences for violation of policy. An AUP also prohibits accessing or storing offensive content. The following topics are typically found in an AUP:

- Basics of protecting an organization's computers and network
- Managing passwords
- Managing software licenses
- Managing intellectual property
- E-mail etiquette
- Level of privacy an individual should expect when using an organization's computer or network
- Noncompliance consequences

A good AUP should also be accompanied with awareness training. This training should address realistic scenarios an individual might face. The following situations are a few examples of what might show up in AUP awareness training:

- A coworker asks you to log on to the network or an application because he or she is waiting for access to be approved. What should you do?
- You receive a politically sensitive joke via e-mail. Should you forward the e-mail?
- The person next to you spends many hours a day surfing the Internet for stock tips. What should you do?

The Privileged-Level Access Agreement (PAA)

 NOTE
The federal government uses PAAs in the defense industry. However, few organizations outside the defense industry have adopted PAA use.

When administrative rights are breached or abused the impact can be catastrophic to the organization. A **privileged-level access agreement (PAA)** is designed to heighten the awareness and accountability of those users who have administrative rights. The PAA is a formal agreement signed by an administrator acknowledging his or her responsibilities. The agreement basically says the administrator will protect these sensitive credentials and not abuse his or her authority. The PAA is an enhanced form of security awareness specifically for administrators.

The PAA is typically a one- to two-page document. It reads as a formal agreement between the administrator and the organization. The PAA generally contains the following from the administrator's perspective:

1. Acknowledgement of the risk associated with elevated access in the event the credentials are breached or abused

2. Promise not to share the credentials entrusted to his or her care

3. Promise to only use the access granted for approved organization business

4. Promise not to attempt to "hack" or breach security

5. Promise to protect any output from these credentials such as reports, logs, files, and downloads

6. Promise to promptly report any indication of a breach or intrusion

7. Promise not to tamper with, modify, or remove any security controls without authorization

8. Promise not to install any backdoor, malicious code, or authorized hardware or software

9. Promise not to violate intellectual property rights, copyrights, or trade secrets

10. Promise not to access or store inflammatory material, such as pornographic or racist content

11. Promise not to browse data that is not directly related to assigned tasks

12. Promise to act in good faith and be subjected to penalties under breach of contract and criminal statutes

In many respects, these items are already covered by security policies and awareness training. The PAA reinforces the importance of these terms with administrators.

Security Awareness Policy (SAP)

Hackers and disgruntled employees are the exception, not the rule. Most individuals want to do a good job. They can if they know what the rules are. It's difficult to hold an individual accountable if they have not been instructed as to what is or is not acceptable. That is the core reason behind a security awareness program. The basic benefits of security awareness policies ensure workers are informed of the following:

- Basic principles of information security
- Awareness of risk and threats
- How to deal with unexpected risk
- How to report suspicious activity, incidents, and breaches
- How to help build a culture that is security and risk aware

Security policy is not just a good idea—it's the law! There are many regulations that require security policies and a security awareness program. Many state laws also require security awareness. Having a security awareness program is considered in most industries a best practice. The following list highlights a number of federal mandates that require an organization to have a security awareness programs:

- HIPAA
- Gramm-Leach-Bliley Act
- Sarbanes-Oxley Act
- Federal Information Security Management Act (FISMA)
- National Institute of Standards and Technology (NIST) Special Publications 800-53, "Recommended Security Controls for Federal Information Systems"
- 5 Code of Federal Regulations (C.F.R.)
- The NIST Guide for Developing Security Plans for Information Technology Systems
- Office of Management and Budget (OMB) Circular A-130, Appendix III
- The NIST Computer Security Handbook

Laws can outline the frequency and target audience of awareness training. For example, 5 C.F.R. requires security awareness training before an individual can access information. Also a refresher course must be taken annually. The following outlines the 5 C.F.R. requirements:

- **All users**—Security basics
- **Executives**—Policy level and governance
- **Program and functional managers**—Security management, planning, and implementation; also risk management and contingency planning
- **Chief information officers (CIOs)**—Broad training in security planning, system and application security management, risk management, and contingency planning
- **IT security program managers**—Broad training in security planning, system and application security management, risk management, and contingency planning
- **Auditors**—Broad training in security planning, system and application security management, risk management, and contingency planning
- **IT function management and operations personnel**—Broad training in security planning and system/application security management, system/application life cycle management, risk management, and contingency planning

For information security policies to deliver value, they must explain how to manage risk and proactively address threats. A well-planned security awareness program can be a cornerstone to accomplish this objective.

Communication of security policy through a security awareness program is vital. Even the best policy is of little use if no one is aware of it. Security awareness changes behavior. Security awareness consists of a series of campaigns aimed at improving understanding of security policies and risks. Security awareness is not a onetime event. It's a campaign that strives to keep reinforcing the message in different ways.

Best Practices for User Domain Policies

A **best practice** is a leading technique, methodology, or technology that through experience has proved to be very reliable. Best practices tend to produce a consistent and quality result. The following short list of best practices focuses on the user and is found in security policies. These best practices go a long way toward protecting users and the organization. Policies should require the following practices:

- **Attachments**—Never open an e-mail attachment from a source that is not trusted or known.
- **Encryption**—Always encrypt sensitive data that leaves the confines of a secure server; this includes encrypting laptops, backup tapes, e-mails, and so on.
- **Layered defense**—Use an approach that establishes overlapping layers of security as the best way to mitigate threats.
- **Least privilege**—The principle of least privilege is a concept that basically says individuals should only have the access necessary to perform their responsibilities.
- **Patch management**—Be sure all network devices have the latest security patches including user desktop and laptop computers. Patch management is an essential part of a layered defense. Even when you do everything right, there may be a vulnerability in the vendor's system or application. An effective patch management program mitigates many of these risks.
- **Unique identity**—All users accessing information must use unique credentials that identify who they are; the only exception is public access of a publicly facing Web site.
- **Virus protection**—Virus and malware prevention must be installed on every desktop and laptop computer.

Case Studies and Examples of User Domain Policies

The case studies in this section reflect actual risks that were exploited in the real world. Each case study examines potential root causes. By looking at these case studies in the context of security policies, you identify how they can be avoided.

Private Sector Case Studies

The case studies examined in this section relate to security policy violations, acceptable use issues, and a lack of separation of duties. The studies involve the compromise of corporate laptops, and the collapse of Barings Bank in 1995.

Corporate Laptops Compromised

Two corporate laptops in an investment firm were identified as points of attack against an online financial management portal. An outside security team was brought in to investigate. It was determined that keylogger software was installed on the laptops without the employee's knowledge. **Keylogger software** captures the keystrokes of a computer's users. The malicious code captured the ID and password credentials to the online financial management portal. Anyone who used these laptops could have their credentials compromised. It was determined that various IDs and passwords had been captured for eight months. The software captured credentials to a number of financial management sites. It also recorded that the laptops were used to access adult content Web sites.

User Domain-level security policies in this situation that might have been violated include:

* Acceptable use
* Virus protection
* Least privilege

There was a clear violation of acceptable use. Using the laptops to visit adult Web sites may have been the source of the breach. Although the case study did not indicate the original source of the breach, these sites are well known to be sources of infection. It's a strong possibility that by visiting these sites the laptops were infected with the keylogger software.

The virus protection on the laptops was not adequate to prevent the infection. Virus scanners cannot stop all infections. It's especially hard to prevent newer, more sophisticated attacks. However, keylogger software as described in the case study is well known. It is possible that the virus scanner on the laptops was not up to date to detect this type of infection. If so, this would be a violation of security policies.

There may have been a least privilege security policy violation. The keylogger software would typically use the credentials of the individual signed on to the laptops to write keystrokes to a text file. The text file of keystrokes would then be retrieved or automatically forwarded to the hacker's server. In this case, the text file containing the keystrokes was written to a system directory. This may be an indication that the user had excessive rights. Security policies would prohibit typical users, such as those in a financial role, from being an administrator on their laptop. Administrative privilege has access to system files and directories.

The Collapse of Barings Bank, 1995

Barings Bank was one of the oldest investment banks in Britain. The bank was founded in 1762. The bank was sold for less than $2 in 1995 after it was discovered that an employee had lost over $1.3 billion of the bank's assets on the market. The bank could not cover its liabilities, having only $615 in reserve capital. The case is used today as a classic example of the need for user oversight and effective separation of duties controls.

The bank's losses resulted when an arbitrage trader was placed in multiple roles to manage trades, as well as to ensure trades were properly settled and reported. The arbitrage trader was the floor manager for the Barings' trading desk in Singapore. This is a front-office role that allowed the employee to make trades. The arbitrage trader was also the head of settlement operations in Singapore. This is a back-office role that allowed him to effectively review and approve his own trades daily. It also allowed him to falsify records and alter reports being sent to the home office in London. There was a special account he used to cover up his trades. He would create trades that would show profit in other accounts while effectively moving the losses to this one account. He then made sure that this one account with the losses was not reported to the home office. This meant while the bank consistently lost millions it actually looked profitable.

This shows a lack of separation of duties. The business should not have permitted a single individual to hold both positions. The business should have ensured the appropriate accounting and reporting systems were in place. This was not just a failure of the business but also a failure of the security policies on a number of levels. User Domain-level security policies in this situation typically require:

- **Risk assessment**—A risk assessment is performed on major applications to identify risk of fraud.
- **Controls design**—Controls are designed based on the core principles in the security policies and weaknesses found during the risk assessment.
- **Access management**—Effective access management develops roles to ensure separation of duties and reports violations to leadership.
- **Escalation**—Risks and threats to the business are escalated to the business unit, senior leadership, and as needed, to the board.

A risk assessment should have been performed when the application was first implemented and periodically thereafter. This was clearly a high-risk application and business process that represented significant income and risk to the bank. Security policies would require a threat assessment looking at external and internal sources. The risk assessment would have examined leading industry practices. This would have identified the clear need to separate access rights between front and back offices. The result would be a good understanding on the type of access and reporting controls needed.

The controls design process required by security policies would implement the needed security controls within the application and the business process. These controls ensure separate security roles would be implemented for front and back office. The controls also identify key monitoring reports necessary to detect fraud. Had the home office received monitoring reports on accounts, including the one hiding the losses, the fraud would have been detected. The trader did falsify reports, which means either there was a controls design failure or at least a privilege principle violation. Either the controls design failed to produce the report or the control allowed the trader to delete off-key monitoring information.

Access management processes detect when controls on separation of duties are violated. At the time the trader access was requested for both the front- and back-office applications, a separation of duties violation would have been detected. This assumes such a control was put in place. Ideally, the request for access that violates separation of duties should be immediately denied. Even if the trader was somehow granted the access, a detective control flags the violation to be resolved by the business unit leadership.

Escalation is used when risks are being addressed. In this case, escalation could have occurred during the performance of a risk assessment, controls design, or access management process. Anywhere within these security processes the risk should have been detected and reported to management for resolution. In ordinary situations, the CISO is required to escalate events and risks if a business unit is not responsive. The escalation path varies depending on the organization. These types of separation of duties risks are reported to executive leadership, the chief risk officer, or both. The reporting of such risks are picked up by the auditors who follow up to see how the risk was resolved. This provides the auditor evidence that the escalation process is working effectively.

To further understand how the bank's losses occurred, let's examine what arbitrage trading is. Arbitrage is the simultaneous buying and selling of an asset in two different markets at two different prices. It's this price difference between the two market prices where you make a profit or take a loss. Because there's typically very little difference in prices between the markets, the trader must make very large trades to make any meaningful profit and to cover the cost of the trade itself.

In the case of Barings, the trader was trading in the billions of dollars, betting that the Tokyo stock market (known as the Nikkei) would rise. Instead of buying and selling, this trader just bought positions to sell at a later time. This was not an arbitrage trade. He was betting that he knew what the market was going to do. The losses started small. He kept increasing the trades in the hope to make up the losses and so on. Eventually the trades put billions at risk. This went on for a year before he could no longer sustain the fraud.

It's not unusual for fraud to go on for years before its detected. That's why security policies typically require an active risk assessment program. You should review high risk applications in light of new and emerging threats.

Public Sector Case Study

The *Wall Street Journal* reported in April 2010 that spies had hacked into the Pentagon's $300 billion Joint Strike Fighter project computers. Several terabytes of data was stolen. The Joint Strike Fighter, also known as the F-35 Lightning II, relies on 7.5 million lines of computer code. According to the U.S. Government Accountability Office, that's more than triple the number of lines used in the current top Air Force fighters.

The public may never know the details given the highly sensitive nature of the breach. The article did note that the intruders entered through vulnerabilities in the networks of contractors helping to build the jet. The intrusion had been going on since at least 2008. The article went on to say it's difficult to protect against vendors with uneven security. Also the Pentagon is getting more engaged with the vendor to improve security.

Although the details of the breach are not public, we do know that there was a vendor management problem. For whatever reasons, the vendor networks did not meet the control requirements of the Pentagon and as result the system was breached.

The problems highlighted in the article apply equally to private and public sectors. Vendors are critical to many organizations. Yet organizations depend on vendors providing the same level of controls that organization would provide for itself.

That's why security policies require vendor assessment to gain that assurance. A vendor assessment is a specialized risk assessment that looks at the vendor's environment if there is risk to the data if you use their services. For example, the organization acquiring the service of a vendor compares the organization's User Domain policies and controls to the vendor's. Any differences are further examined to determine if they represent a control weakness. These controls weaknesses could be exploited to compromise the organization's data.

Critical Infrastructure Case Studies

The case studies examined in this section relate to security policy violations regarding virus controls and patch management, and policy violations regarding password sharing. The studies include a look at a water treatment plant control system, and disgruntled employee breaches.

Water Treatment Plant Control Systems Compromised

In 2005, the U.S. federal government reviewed a cyberattack to a water treatment plant, which is part of the national **critical infrastructure**. The government uses the term critical infrastructure to identify assets that are essential for the society and economy of the United States to function. The public utilities are considered part of this national critical infrastructure.

The attack was not specifically targeting the treatment facility. An employee within the company stopped at a coffee shop one morning before work. While there he connected to the public wireless system and began surfing the Web. A hacker scanned his laptop for vulnerabilities and breached it. The hacker loaded a worm onto the employee's laptop. Later that morning, the employee connected to the water treatment plant's network to begin working. Within minutes, the worm started infecting a number of servers and other desktop and laptop computers connected to the network.

The worm spread to the **Supervisory Control and Data Acquisition (SCADA)** servers. A SCADA system is both hardware and software that collects critical information to keep a facility operating. In the case of the water treatment plant, the SCADA system collects information on the quality of water before the water is released to the public. The same SCADA system monitors the distribution of the water throughout the city. The SCADA data is analyzed and fed back into the facilities systems to adjust the water treatment and distribution processes.

The laptop should have been sufficiently hardened and patched so that the breach at the coffee shop could not happen. The employee in this case did nothing wrong. He was authorized to have the laptop and was browsing sites related to his work and industry. Those sites were not the source of the breach. User Domain-level security policies that may have been violated include:

- Virus protection
- Patch management
- Least privilege

The review determined that a lack of virus protection was the culprit. Security policies require not only that a virus scanner be installed on every laptop and desktop computer but also that the virus scanner is updated frequently. It is not unusual to find virus scanners updated daily to ensure they can detect the latest threat. In this case, the virus scanner was installed but was out of date.

There was also a patch management issue. The laptop should have been sufficiently hardened to prevent the breach that allowed the worm to be installed. Just as in the case of the virus scanner, security patches should be up to date on the user's laptop to close any known vulnerabilities. Because patches are applied with the same frequency as virus protection, security policies require a process to determine when the patches should be applied. This process usually involves monitoring for patches daily, determining how critical the threat is, and scheduling the updates. Sometimes the vulnerability is so great or widespread that the patch should be applied immediately. More often patches are bundled and are applied on a set schedule such as monthly or quarterly. In this case, concerns were raised that the laptop was not properly patched. It's not unusual to find an organization that lacks an effective patch management to be years behind in applying patches.

There also may have been a least-privilege security policies violation. Once connected to the internal company network, the worm spread within minutes to key systems like the SCADA system. This is an indication that the employee had elevated rights on many of these servers. It could also be an indication that the servers lack the same patch management as did the laptop. In any case, reducing the employee's access could help slow the worm.

Although not part of the User Domain, network segmentation might have reduced the spread of the worm to the SCADA system. Security policies typically require network segmentation of high-risk systems. Network teams detected the worm quickly once the network was infected. If the SCADA system was isolated from the user network, the infection to the key system would have been prevented.

In this case it's fortunate that the malicious code was not targeting the water treatment facility itself. The employee whose laptop was infected at the coffee shop could have worked in any industry and for any company. The incident shows the potential for serious harm to the public. If the infected code was smart enough to alter the SCADA data, the hacker might have gained control over the water treatment process itself. The hacker might manipulate the process to release unsafe water or to cut off water to parts of the city. There are manual controls and human intervention that prevent these types of manipulation. Nonetheless, as industries become more reliant on good information to drive automated systems the need for effective security policies and controls increases.

Disgruntled Employee Breaches Former Employer's Systems

An application developer lost his job as a result of downsizing. Within three weeks after his termination he used a coworker's ID and password to gain remote access to his former employer's network. He launched two separate attacks. In the first attack, he altered the company's public Web site to insert pornographic images. He also sent an e-mail to all the registered users. The e-mail let the customer know its information had been hacked and referred the customer to the altered Web site. The former employee launched a second attack six weeks later. This attack reset all the passwords for the network users and altered 4,000 prices with false information.

There's no indication that the systems or applications were not properly hardened. For discussion purposes, assume the systems and application were not hacked due to some vulnerability. In other words, the former employee simply accessed the systems using someone else's ID and password. User Domain-level security policies in this situation typically require:

- Unique identity
- Least privilege

The initial breach occurred when the former employee used a coworker's ID and password to remotely access the network. This was a violation of the security policies requiring each user to have a unique identity. The coworker violated security policies when he or she shared the password with the former employee. Regardless of whether the disgruntled employee was still employed at that time, the coworker should never have shared the password. The security policies required awareness training for all employees to educate them on this basic security principle. Security policies prohibit the sharing of passwords with anyone, including management. In the real world, an individual's ID and password might be shared to debug a problem. Although the practice is not encouraged it does occur. In this event, the password must be immediately reset once the problem is resolved. If the former employee did not have access to the coworker's password the breach would not have occurred.

There's also an indication of a security policies violation related to least privilege. The coworker's ID allowed access to Web site content, customer passwords, and pricing records. Web site development, customer support, and product pricing are typically separate roles. As such, the coworker access should have been limited to a specific role. It is possible that Web site access was part of the role related to pricing. That role might have the ability to change product pricing and post those changes on the Web site. In any case, a role related to pricing should not have access to customer passwords to perform his or her duties. These controls weaknesses should have been detected by the security team when the application was installed.

CHAPTER SUMMARY

This chapter examined the risk associated with the User Domain, part of the seven domains of an IT infrastructure. As the number of users grows on the network, their diverse needs also grow. Security policies are a structured way of managing the user related risks in this complex environment. The chapter reviewed the many different types of users and discussed unique roles such as administrator, security, and auditor. With these roles often comes elevated privilege and enormous responsibilities.

Security policies are an effective way to reduce risks and govern users. They help identify the higher risk activities such those performed by systems administrators. They also help establish processes to reduce these risks, such as targeted awareness training and Privileged Assess-level Agreements. In the end, security policies can educate users, reduce human error, and be used to better understand how incidents occurred.

KEY CONCEPTS AND TERMS

Best practice

Contractors

Critical infrastructure

Escalation

Firecall-ID process

Harden

Insider

Integrated audit

Keylogger software

Log server

Pretexting

Privileged-level access
   agreement (PAA)

Security personnel

Social engineering

Structured Query Language
   (SQL) injection

Supervisory Control and Data
   Acquisition (SCADA) system

Systems administrator

Trouble ticket

CHAPTER 9 ASSESSMENT

1. Pretexting is when a hacker breaks into a firewall.

   A. True
   B. False

2. What can keylogger software capture?

   A. Usernames
   B. Passwords
   C. Web sites visited
   D. All of the above

3. You can use a _____ process to grant temporary elevated rights.

4. Security awareness is required by which of the following?

   A. Law
   B. Customers
   C. Shareholders
   D. All of the Above

5. A(n) _____ looks at risk and issues an independent opinion.

6. A privileged-level access agreement (PAA) prevents an administrator from abusing elevated rights.

   A. True
   B. False

7. Which of the following does an acceptable use policy relate to?

   A. Server-to-server communication
   B. Users accessing the Internet
   C. Encryption when transmitting files
   D. A and B

8. A(n) _____ has inside information on how an organization operates.

9. Social engineering occurs when a hacker posts her victories on a social Web site.

   A. True
   B. False

10. Typically in large organizations all administrators have the same level of authority.

   A. True
   B. False

11. A CISO must _____ risks if the business unit is not responsive.

IT Infrastructure Security Policies

I T INFRASTRUCTURE SECURITY POLICIES are broader in scope and depth than User Domain policies. As discussed in Chapter 9, User Domain policies focus on human access and data handling. The number of user-related policies can be limited because you can define specific user access requirements. There is also a practical matter of human capacity. When writing policies for the typical user, you must consider the capacity to learn and retain the information.

In contrast, the IT infrastructure is vast. The number of devices and possible access points are far greater. A single server may have hundreds of ports. Each port on a server is an access point that needs to be protected. Security policies define how to protect data, regardless of where the data flows or is processed. This diverse set of technology must be individually configured. It must also function flawlessly.

The key purpose of infrastructure security policies is to provide technical knowledge for configuring technology in a coordinated fashion. This coordination has both human and technical aspects. The human aspect ensures changes are well coordinated throughout the IT infrastructure. For example, policies ensure that network and database administrators coordinate activities when a new database server is added to the network. The technical aspect ensures devices collectively protect data as it flows from device to device. For example, remote access, network, and authentication policies act collectively. They ensure that data passed from a worker's home is encrypted through a virtual private network firewall and securely routed to an internal database server.

In this chapter, we discuss common IT infrastructure policies. It's not possible in one chapter, or even in one book, to cover all the possible security policies an organization needs. This chapter illustrates key points by selectively discussing some policies in more detail. The intent of this chapter is to create an under-standing of the basic structure of an IT infrastructure policy. In addition, the chapter discusses the most common security policies that relate to different infrastructure domains.

This chapter covers the following topics and concepts:

- What the basic anatomy of an infrastructure policy is
- What common Workstation Domain policies are
- What common LAN Domain policies are
- What common LAN-to-WAN Domain policies are
- What common WAN Domain policies are
- What common Remote Access Domain policies are
- What common System/Application Domain policies are
- What common telecommunication policies are related to the IT infrastructure
- What some IT infrastructure security policy best practices are
- What some case studies and examples of IT infrastructure security policies are

Chapter 10 Goals

When you complete this chapter, you will be able to:

- Explain the basic anatomy of a policy
- Understand types of security control requirements for IT infrastructure domains
- Identify the differences between core domain policy requirements
- Describe common policies by domain
- Describe best practices in creating and maintaining domain policies
- Use case study examples to explain how to use domain policies

Anatomy of an Infrastructure Policy

Many security policies look alike. They often follow the same look and feel. This makes them easy to read and understand. The challenge is how to organize policies as a collection. Policies need to be easily accessible and align to how an organization manages its IT environment.

You can organize policies by either domain or functional area. Consider the seven domains of a typical IT infrastructure in Figure 10-1. This is one logical way to view requirements and policies. For example, the Workstation Domain deals with pirated software. The Remote Access Domain deals with virtual private network (VPN) tunnels. Different domains can have different security requirements.

The problem with organizing policies by domain is that many issues pertain to multiple domains. For example, virus control is a concern for workstations and servers. The requirements may vary a bit. However, the core need and control solutions would be the same.

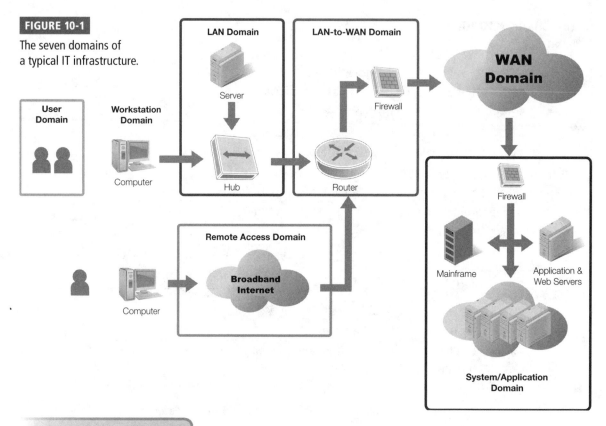

FIGURE 10-1

The seven domains of a typical IT infrastructure.

> **NOTE**
>
> To keep the discussion at a high level, this chapter discusses policies as they align to a typical IT infrastructure. This allows us to discuss domain requirements that drive policies. It does not mean this is the best way for every organization to organize its policies.

There are few crisp bright lines between these domain areas. You especially need to watch for requirements between domains that conflict.

A common approach is to organize policies to align with industry-standard frameworks. Examples of these frameworks include those provided by ISO and Control Objectives for Information and related Technology (COBIT). This is the most practical approach. First, many samples are easily accessible over the Internet. Secondly, once policies align to best practice frameworks, it becomes easier to demonstrate compliance to regulators. Industry-standard frameworks comply with regulations. By adopting the policies that use core concepts from these frameworks, you then demonstrate compliance.

The basic anatomy of a policy starts with understanding the different types of documents that capture the domain security control requirements. Four common documents are:

- **Control standards**—Policy documents describing core security control requirements
- **Baseline standards**—Technical documents describing security controls for a specific technology

- **Procedure documents**—Processes to implement control and baseline standards
- **Guidelines**—Optional documents that include parameters and recommend policies, standards, or procedures

Different organizations use different terms. Some people refer to control standards as core "policy statements." A baseline standard is also called a technology "minimum security baseline (MSB)." The key point is policy documents make a distinction between core policy requirements and requirements unique to technology. For example, a core requirement may be to change passwords every 30 days. You might have two different baseline documents describing how to configure Microsoft versus UNIX servers to achieve the core requirement.

The number of documents can vary greatly between organizations. Some organizations combine related issues into a single policy document. For example, a workstation policy may combine preventing pirated software with virus protection requirements. Other organizations may treat this as two separate policy standards. The number of documents an organization uses depends on its need and capacity to deploy.

The goal is to develop a cohesive set of documents that do not require constant revisions to stay current and relevant. When there is overlap, reference the corresponding document rather than duplicating content. A few common reasons why policy documents vary from one organization include:

- Organizations use unique sets of technical tools and hardware.
- Risk management practices are often customized to an organization.
- The size of IT departments varies according to business needs.

Format of a Standard

Typically, standard and process documents have a well-defined format. A common format includes the following sections:

- **Document Number**—Uniquely identifies the document and usually categorizes the document as a policy, standard, procedure, or guidance
- **Title**—Identifies the topic of the document
- **Version/Date**—Identifies the version and date of the document
- **Purpose**—Provides measureable objectives and goals
- **Background**—Explains why the standard was put in place
- **Standard/Process**—Describes the standard or process to be implemented
- **Roles and Responsibilities**—Identifies who is responsible for implementation and adherence
- **Effective Dates**—When the standard must be implemented
- **Information and Assistance**—Teams within the organization that can explain the standard and assist in coordinating its implementation
- **Approval**—Who approved this standard
- **Associated Resources**—Any related resources

TIP

Be sure to select a format that is searchable. The section headers are typically the key words that will help sort through information within a standard. It may also be important to include fields that track versions and dates of changes.

The exact format may vary from between organizations. For example, some organizations may describe whom the standard affects in a separate scope section. In our example, this is bundled under roles and responsibilities. Other possible sections are Revision History, Key Terms, and Supporting Attachments. The format varies by need and source of material. Often, samples of policy templates are based on industry-standard frameworks or vendor-supplied samples. These samples usually define the initial format. The format changes over time to adapt to an organization's individual need.

Standards need to be highly structured to be understood quickly. It is common for an individual to scan a dozen standards looking for particular piece of information such as scope or responsibility. A well-defined format will allow that individual to quickly sort through a large amount of data and focus on information of interest.

Workstation Domain Policies

Workstation Domain policies relate to any computing device used by an end user. It often refers to the user's desktop or laptop computer. A "workstation" can be any user device that accesses data such as smartphones.

These devices might not be operating within a protected office or data center. As a result, policies must protect the physical and logical security of these devices. Even in an office environment, physical security is important. Cleaning crews and visitors may have access to an office. Additionally, devices often have connectivity outside the network. Laptops, desktop, and smartphones all have browsers. That makes these devices particularly vulnerable to Internet threats.

Mobile devices, by their nature, are distributed. This means policies need to address unique monitoring and patching challenges in a distributed environment. How you connect, monitor, and patch a mobile device is a different challenge than doing the same from a desktop in an office or a server in a data center.

Control Standards

Control standards for workstations establish core security requirements to harden these devices. The standards define how to manage the devices in a distributed environment. The standards need to be clear as to what responsibilities users have versus central administrators. You often align workstation policies to functional responsibilities.

A Malicious Code Protection standard, for example, is a central responsibility. The standard tries to keep a workstation free from viruses and other malware. The policy is a preventive and detective control. It tries to prevent an infection through installing scanning software. It also requires the user to detect and report symptoms of an infection. Examples of some control statements in this type of policy are as follows:

- Anti-malware software must be used on all devices connected to the <Organization> network. IT staff is responsible for ensuring that all devices have an approved version of anti-malware software installed. They are also responsible for ensuring a mechanism is in place to keep malware definitions current.

- No executable software, regardless of the source, may knowingly be installed without prior IT staff approval.

- IT staff must verify that all software is free of malicious code before installation.

- Users must not intentionally disable anti-malware software without prior approval.

- IT staff must scan data that will be transferred from the <Organization> network to a customer. Scanning must indicate that the data is free of malicious code before the transfer may occur.

The Malicious Code standard is a good example of a policy that protects devices. Table 10-1 outlines other workstation related control standards. This is not an exhaustive list. This table depicts common control standards that focus on protecting and managing workstation devices. Notice the sheer breadth of policies required to properly secure a workstation.

Baseline Standards

With core policies defined, the focus then turns to how to configure the devices. Baseline standards provide the specific technology requirements for each device. IT staff uses documented procedures to implement baseline standards. These configurations by devices ensure the following:

- Secure connectivity for remote devices
- Virus and malware protection
- Patch management capability
- Backup and recovery
- Hardening of the device

This is not an exhaustive list. It does depict the configuration considerations for each workstation. This is especially important given the distributed nature workstations.

You can find a variety of these baseline standards from different organizations around the world. The Center for Internet Security (CIS) offers Security Configuration Benchmarks. These benchmarks include examples for the private sector, government agencies, and educational institutions. You can download the benchmarks from *http://cisecurity.org/en-us/?route=downloads.benchmarks*. CIS also offers auditing tools to its members to assess compliance with these benchmarks.

 TIP

Before you create content for your policy and standards library, research published industry standards. It is more efficient to modify a standard than to create your own from scratch. You can find policies, standards, and guidelines in the public domain. The license terms of many of these examples permit their modification and use by others.

10

IT Infrastructure
Security Policies

TABLE 10-1 Additional types of Workstation Domain control standards.

TYPE OF CONTROL STANDARD	DESCRIPTION
Access Control for Portable and Mobile Systems	Establishes restrictions for employer-owned portable and mobile workstations.
Acquisitions	Describes security controls for acquiring new devices. This standard might include minimum hardware requirements for security such as cryptographic co-processors.
Configuration Management Control	Defines the requirements for approving changes to a workstation. This includes configuration and patch management.
Device Identification and Authentication	Defines how the network identity of the devices will be established.
Session Lock	Defines the requirements to prevent access to the workstation after a defined period of inactivity. The session lock remains in effect until the user re-authenticates to the workstation.
Software Use	Describes installation of software on workstations. Also describes methods to protect the organization from unapproved software being installed.
System Use Notification	Describes the on-screen display of system notification message. This is common to establish a legal notice that you are accessing a protected system. Examples of message are: • You are accessing an organization-owned workstation. • System usage may be monitored, recorded, and subject to audit. • Unauthorized use of the system is prohibited and subject to criminal and civil penalties.
Unsuccessful Logon Attempts	Defines a limit on the number of consecutive invalid access attempts such as three failed logons within 10 minutes per user. Also describes actions the workstation will take when the limit is exceeded, such as locking the account.

The following are examples of baseline documents you may need to prepare:

- **Host hardening** standards for each workstation product family, such as Microsoft Windows, UNIX, Mac OS, and smartphones
- Virus scanner configuration standards
- Patch management agent standards
- Automated backup standards for workstations
- Wireless security standards

Procedures

For each baseline standard, you need a related procedure document. That does not mean every device configuration requires a unique procedure. Many of these configuration activities reuse the same procedure. The key to these procedures is to ensure that the administrators know how to access and apply the baseline configuration. If the tools and methods are substantially different, the process may be unique enough to require its own procedure.

An example of a procedure is a configuration procedure for workstations. This procedure provides the explicit settings for configuration files such as registries. This process might cover Windows, UNIX, Mac OS, and other desktop operating systems.

Guidelines

Guidelines for implementing control standards are useful to planners and managers. The following guideline documents are useful when dealing with workstations:

- **Acquisition Guidelines**—Recommendations for sources to acquire new workstations such as preferred vendors.
- **Guidelines on Active Content and Mobile Code**—Describe the threats and countermeasures over **active content**. This includes a discussion on mobile code such as JavaScript and Active X controls. Furthermore, it describes the security expectations for the development or use of such code.

LAN Domain Policies

The LAN Domain refers to the organization's local area network (LAN) infrastructure. A LAN allows two or more computers to connect within a small physical area. The small area could be a home, office, or a group of buildings.

LAN security policies focus on connectivity, such as defining how devices attach to the network. The policies also define how to control traffic, such as through segmentation and router filtering.

LAN configuration issues are similar to those for workstations. However, the primary difference is administration. The LAN Domain is often centralized to a small group of network administrators. This means devices are less distributed and are under tighter control.

> **NOTE**
> The same individuals that use network policies often write them. This is an advantage because it reduces training and interpretation errors.

Control Standards

Control standards for the LAN Domain address a wide array of connectivity issues such as firewall controls, denial of service protection, and Wi-Fi security control. Wireless connectivity is also a part of the Workstation Domain. This is a good example of a cross-domain security issue. It also underscores the importance of configuring workstations and servers to protect data as it leaves a workstation and travels on a network.

A Firewall control standard, for example, describes how LAN firewalls handle network traffic. This kind of traffic filtering includes Web, e-mail, and Telnet traffic. The standard describes how to manage and update the firewall. The following are examples of statements adapted from the National Institute of Standards and Technology (NIST) Special Publication 800-41, "Guidelines on Firewalls and Firewall Policy":

The firewall must always block the following types of traffic:

- Inbound traffic from a non-authenticated system with a destination address of the firewall system. This type of packet usually represents a probe or attack against the firewall.

- Inbound traffic with a source address indicating that the packet originated on a network behind the firewall. This type of packet may represent a spoofing attempt.

- Inbound traffic containing Internet Control Message Protocol (ICMP) traffic. An attacker can use ICMP traffic to map the networks behind some firewalls. Therefore, ICMP traffic should not be allowed from the Internet or any untrusted external network.

In this example, ICMP represents a protocol within Internet Protocol (IP). This protocol does not carry data but does carry information about the network. A simple ping command echoes back network information. It is an example of an ICMP protocol.

A Denial of Service (DoS) Protection standard describes controls that protect against or limit the effects of DoS attacks. This standard attempts to prevent using the organization network as a launching point against another network. Here is an example of control statements from this type of standard:

Configure routers and firewalls to forward IP packets only if those packets have the correct source IP address for the <Organization> network.

Only allow packets to leave the network with valid source IP addresses that belong to the <Organization> network. This will minimize the chance that the <Organization> network will be the source of a denial of service attack.

The firewall and DOS examples illustrate how technical LAN security requirements can be established. These are high-level examples. In the real world, LAN policies are usually long and detailed. Table 10-2 contains additional examples of LAN control standards.

Table 10-2 mentions the term **audit** several times. Why are audits so important? Any security-relevant event needs to be written to a log. Qualified personnel review these logs to determine if a security problem has occurred. These individuals determine who, what, where, and when activity caused the problem. Audit logs determine compliance issues, hardware misconfiguration errors, and application software security problems. They are useful in reconstructing actions that took place during a security incident. Audit logs should be well protected and only accessed by those people authorized by management.

TABLE 10-2 Additional types of LAN Domain control standards.

TYPE OF CONTROL STANDARD	DESCRIPTION
Audit Events	Describes important events that must be audited and reported such as breaches to routers, firewalls, and servers
Configuration Change Control	Describes the change control management process for requesting changes, approving changes, implementing changes on the network
Controlled Maintenance	Defines the schedules on LAN-attached devices for routine preventative and regular maintenance
Controls over Media	Defines protection, access to media, labeling, storage, transport, sanitization, and disposal
Device Identification and Authentication	Describes the security requirements for identifying LAN-attached devices for authentication, routing, and filtering
Intrusion Detection and Prevention	Describes the requirements for host- and network-based intrusion detection and prevention tools
Protection of Audit Information	Describes the controls needed to protect audit information and tools from unauthorized access, modification, disablement, and deletion
Router Security Controls	Describes minimal security configuration for all routers and switches
Security Assessments	Describes the need to conduct assessments of the security controls in the LAN. These assessments determine the extent that controls are implemented correctly, operating as intended, and producing the desired outcome
Trusted Time Stamps	Describes the need for trusted time stamps and timeservers for audit record generation such as Network Time Protocol
Wi-Fi Security Controls	Defines the authorized uses of Wi-Fi on organization property

Baseline Standards

Two key areas of LAN Domain controls are connectivity and controlling network traffic. Baseline standards are particularly important because they establish connectivity between devices. This connectivity is important to ensure data protection in transit. To accomplish this, configure each device with an identity and method of authenticating network traffic it receives. This is no small task given the volume of network traffic generated.

10

IT Infrastructure
Security Policies

The network typically contains mixed traffic, such as sensitive business transactions, routine user-related transactions, and, potentially, hacker traffic. Separating business and routine user transactions depends on properly configuring network devices. These transactions do not attempt to be in conflict and thus are reasonably easy to identify and separate.

A greater challenge is how to configure devices to ensure hackers cannot masquerade as valid transactions. Another concern is hackers monitoring sensitive transactions in the clear. A hacker can configure a network card to "promiscuous mode." When a network card is in promiscuous mode, it captures all the network traffic on a segment. Normally, a network card only captures traffic addressed to its device. In other words, a device in promiscuous mode allows you to listen to all the traffic messages between every device on the segment. With this information, a hacker can create his or her own messages in an attempt to masquerade as valid sensitive transactions.

 NOTE

Baseline security standards configure devices to maintain message and transaction integrity. Establishing secure point-to-point connectivity is an important part of the baseline standards.

NOTE

Baseline standards determine how to monitor network traffic. It is important to log network traffic during an event. Use of network IDS or IPS systems is also highly advisable.

Another important concern of baseline LAN standards is network traffic monitoring. Regardless of how good firewalls and routers are, they have their limitations. These devices prevent attacks against known and predicted threats. Intrusion systems provide a broad range of protection. They look for patterns of attack. Just as a virus scanner looks for patterns to indicate a file has infected, an intrusion system looks for network traffic patterns to detect a network attack. An intrusion system can be detective or preventive. An **intrusion detection system (IDS)** recognizes a network attack and sends an alert. An **intrusion prevention system (IPS)** recognizes a network attack, stops the attack, and sends an alert. Audit logs also play an important role in monitoring network traffic. Configuring devices to generate logs about network events help you to determine later what occurred during an attack.

The following are examples of baseline standards that configure devices to address connectivity and monitoring activity:

- **Wi-Fi Access Point (AP) Security Standard**—Defines secure wireless connectivity to network

- **Intrusion Detection System (IDS) and Intrusion Prevention System (IPS) Standard**—Defines configuration of intrusion monitoring for the network

- **Baseline OS Configuration(s) Standard**—Defines hardening of servers, including server authentication and communication protocol

- **Remote Maintenance Standard**—Defines secure connectivity to devices for remote administration

- **Audit Storage and Records Standard**—Defines configuration of auditing tools and logs to record network events

- **Firewall Baseline Security Standard**—Defines configuration of network filters by firewall, version, and manufacturer type

- **Router Baseline Security Standard**—Defines configuration of network filters by router, version, and manufacturer type
- **Server Baseline Configuration(s)**—Defines configuration of servers to support network connectivity such as Dynamic Host Configuration Protocol (DHCP) and authentication protocols

Procedures

Many of the same procedures issues exist between domains, such as configuration and patch management. There is a greater emphasis in the LAN Domain on detecting and responding to network attacks. An attack on a workstation is isolated. An attack on the network threatens the entire organization. You can see this difference reflected in several network procedures, as follows:

- **Response to Audit Processing Failures**—Procedure to respond to failure of network monitoring and audit tools such as logs filling up
- **Firewall Port/Protocol Alerts**—Procedure to respond to security alerts such as the time frame for responses and escalation paths
- **Monitoring Wi-Fi APs**—Procedure for configuring and monitoring Wi-Fi access points
- **Audit Record Retention**—Procedure for preserving audit records

Guidelines

The number of threats against a network can be substantial. The ability to assess these threats takes a combination of technical knowledge and experience. Guidelines can transfer that experience and knowledge by walking an individual through core principles and different ways to look at LAN risks.

These guidelines are useful to planners, systems administrators, network administrators, and their managers. These individuals must assess LAN threats and build appropriate countermeasures. The following guidelines documents illustrate this point:

- **Security Assessments Guidelines**—Provides guidance on how security assessments should be conducted, how rate threats, and how to escalate resolution
- **Firewall Architecture and Management Guidelines**—Provides guidance on firewall architectures and when they should be used
- **Router Architecture and Management Guidelines**—Provides guidance on router types and architectures and when they should be
- **IDS and IPS Architecture and Management Guidelines**—Provides guidance on IDS and IPS architectures, types, and when they should be used to reduce false alerts
- **Wi-Fi Security Guidelines**—Provides information on Wi-Fi systems architectures, types, and when they should be used

LAN-to-WAN Domain Policies

The LAN-to-WAN Domain refers to the technical infrastructure that connects an organization's LAN to a wide area network (WAN). The main concern is controlling network traffic between the outside network, or the WAN, to the private network, or the LAN. The LAN-to-WAN Domain denotes, for many organizations, its connection to the Internet. This connection represents significant risk. The Internet has a direct connection to an organization's private network and resources. Protection relies on the organization's ability to layer controls that filter out unwanted network traffic.

An important policy concern is how to filter traffic between the Internet and the internal network. Additionally, many organizations have an Internet presence. This has the additional challenge of serving content on the Internet to customers and businesses. These public-facing Web sites often provide access to internal resources such as databases for product information. As a result, they are a prime target for hackers.

The LAN-to-WAN key standards define the security requirements to harden Internet-facing servers, filter traffic between these networks, and monitor for breaches in security. Although there are other policy requirements, such as defining what data the public can access, these standards generally represent core requirements.

Control Standards

> **NOTE**
>
> An Internet proxy is a server that acts as an intermediary between users and the Internet. The server receives requests and responses and filters unwanted traffic.

The industry has well-defined standards that require access control to the Internet. As such, the standards tend to be specific about technologies and architecture choices. For example, these standards often require the use of an Internet proxy and specific demilitarized zone (DMZ) architecture.

A Content Filtering standard is an example of a filtering policy. It describes the control requirements for employee access to Web sites using employer-owned devices. The following is a control statement you might find in this type of standard. This standard was adapted from the SANS Technology Institute document, "Employee Internet Use Monitoring and Filtering Policy":

> IT staff shall periodically review and recommend changes to Internet and protocol filtering rules. HR staff shall review these recommendations and provide suggestions for changes, if necessary. Changes to Internet and protocol filtering rules will be recorded in the Internet Use Monitoring and Filtering Policy.

Here are several additional examples of policies that deal with LAN-to-WAN connectivity and filtering:

- **External Information System Services Connect Standard**—Requires that providers of external services to establish a secure connection. This standard applies to all external parties such as business partners and outsourced providers. It also establishes service level agreements and how to measure and report security control compliance.

- **DMZ Control Standard**—Establishes the controls for publicly accessible devices to place them in a DMZ.
- **User Internet Proxy Standard**—Establishes controls for using an Internet access proxy (a **user proxy**) for all inbound and outbound Internet traffic.

Baseline Standards

A LAN-to-WAN Domain baseline standard focuses on perimeter devices that separate the WAN from the LAN. The following are some examples:

- **Content-Blocking Tools Configuration Standard**—Requirements that describe what types of Web content should be blocked and how updates are approved
- **Intrusion Detection and Prevention Tools Configuration Standard**— Requirements for each product with particular emphasis on those place in the DMZ
- **Proxy Server Configuration Standard**—Requirements for maintaining the **access control list (ACL)** for the device that controls access to the Internet from the LAN
- **Firewall Configuration Standard**—Describes DMZ and firewall architecture

Procedures

Many of the same procedures issues exist between domains such as configuration and patch management. In the case of WAN-to-LAN connectivity there, a greater emphasis on managing changes and detecting and responding to network attacks. For example, you can be view the DMZ as the "front door" to your private network. Changes to configuration in this domain can have serious impact on the publicly facing Web site or the ability to prevent an instruction. It is not uncommon to see procedures in this domain require senior level approval and extensive testing before changes are applied.

Guidelines

Guidelines in this domain are useful for individuals who must determine how much Internet access should be permitted. Controls and baselines create crisp lines on minimum standards. The guidelines establish additional choices while balancing the additional risk. The following guideline documents are examples:

- **DMZ Guidelines**—Recommends additional services to be placed in the DMZ and, depending on those services, additional security requirements
- **Intrusion Detection and Prevention Systems Guidelines**—Recommends how to design an IDS system of sensors, collection stations, and alert mechanisms to eliminate or reduce false positives
- **Content-Filtering Guidelines**—Recommendations on content-filtering options, ways to maintain the list of banned sites, and ways to request access to blocked sites when needed

WAN Domain Policies

A WAN is a network that covers a large geographical area. The Internet is an example of a WAN. A private WAN can be built for a specific organization to link offices across the country or globally. These types of WANs are constructed using dedicated leased lines, satellites, and/or microwave communications.

Typically, the LAN-to-WAN domain addresses many of the WAN connectivity standards. As a result, this domain's standards tend to focus primarily on the WAN build-out and supporting components. Some organizations may not have any WAN-specific standards or policies. This is because many of the topics are often included in other domains.

Control Standards

When you do see WAN-specific standards, they address WAN management, Domain Name Services (DNS), router security, protocols, and Web services. The standards might call out specific security requirements for WAN devices such as routers, switches, and wireless devices.

A WAN controls standard might include the following statements:

The IS department shall approve all access points to the WAN.

The IS department shall approve all physical and logical connections to the WAN that provide access to individuals or groups.

The IS department shall approve all WAN-related address changes and configurations.

Employees who plan to connect to the <Organization> network must first sign an agreement to abide by the requirements outlined in the WAN Security Standard.

A DNS control standard might be included in the WAN standard. This standard describes the requirements for obtaining a domain name for use by external parties. The following are examples of control statements you might find in this standard, adapted from the U.S. Department of Energy DNS policy:

Prior to development of a new Web site or Web-based application, you should notify the IT domain name manager of a request for a domain name. The CIO is the only <Organization> executive with the authority to approve a request for registration of a new domain name. Approval will be granted in the form of a signed memorandum and should include the following information:

- An explanation of how the domain will be used
- A justification for using a new domain name
- The server name and IP address where the DNS will be registered
- Name, telephone/fax numbers, and e-mail address for points of contact (POC) for the person(s) who will administer the domain name and for the person who will be responsible for the payment of the fee
- Date of last vulnerability scan on targeted server(s)

Others standards related to the WAN domain may include:

- **WAN Router Security Standard**—Describes the family of controls needed to secure the connection from the WAN router to the internal network
- **Web Services Standard**—Describes which controls are needed for use of **Web services** from external partnerships and suppliers. This may include the use of Web services security (SAML, XML message integrity and confidentiality) and controls over the Web services gateway device(s).

Baseline Standards

The lines between baseline and control standard can blur in this domain. The reason is that the topics tend to focus on specific technology solutions such as router, protocols, and Web services. Many organizations tend to focus on a small set of network vendors such as Cisco Systems or Juniper Networks. Because the standards are often written with these technologies in mind, you can find a convergence of control and baseline standards into one document versus two.

Procedures

Procedures in this domain tend to focus on configuration and maintain of the WAN. This may include specific configuration procedures for WAN devices such as routers and firewalls.

These procedures track very closely to change management procedures found in the LAN-to-WAN domain. For most organizations, the network team working on the LAN will be the same network team working on the WAN. As a result, you find the same procedures being used for LANs and WANs.

Guidelines

Web services are an example of a WAN guideline. It describes when and how Web services may be used. DNS management guidelines are another example that offers recommendations on the use of DNS within the LAN and WAN environments.

Remote Access Domain Policies

The Remote Access Domain refers to the technology that controls how end users connect to an organization's LAN remotely. An example is someone needing to connect to the office network from his or her home or on the road.

The focus of security standards in this domain is on remote user authentication and secure connections. Creating a remote computing environment that is secure is a challenge. Beyond authentication and connectivity, you need to secure the remote device. Some standards require all remote users to use employer-owned laptops. This allows the organization to control the remote device itself. These types of business choices drive what standards you see in this domain.

Control Standards

The Remote Access Domain standards include standards related to VPN connections and multi-factor authentication. For example, a Virtual Private Network standard describes the security requirements for establishing an encrypted session. The following are examples of control statements you might find in this standard. They are adapted from the SANS Institute's "Virtual Private Network Policy" document:

> Employees with VPN privileges must not share their VPN credentials to <Organization> internal networks with unauthorized users.

> VPN use must be controlled using one-time password authentication. This may include a token device or a public/private key system with a strong passphrase.

> VPN users will be automatically disconnected from the <Organization> network after 30 minutes of inactivity.

Other Remote Domain policies may include physical and technical standards. Physical standards may outline the policies for working from home. These policies may require users to lock up company documents at home and ban family members from access to company assets. Other technical security standards may include the need for two-factor authentication.

Baseline Standards

The control standards establish the broad requirements. Often in this domain, there are multiple technologies involved in establishing a secure connection with a remote user. Here are a few examples of standards that focus on configuration:

> **NOTE**
>
> RADIUS is a networking protocol for centralized authentication, authorization, and accounting (AAA) for computers to connect and use a network service. RADIUS is often used by Internet service providers (ISPs) and organizations to manage access to networks.

- **VPN Gateway Options and Requirements Standard**—Outlines the security configuration features for the specific VPN concentrators used by the organization
- **VPN Client Software Options and Requirements Standard**—Outlines the security configuration features for the specific VPN remote client software
- **RADIUS Server Security Requirements Standard**—Describes the security configuration of the Remote Authentication Dial In User Service (RADIUS)

Procedures

Procedures in this domain are useful to remote users and those responsible for supporting that environment. Because you have a diverse set of users remotely accessing your network from anywhere in the world, support procedures need to be clear and concise. One example is a VPN Configuration and Support Guide, which lists the configuration settings and steps to debug a VPN connection.

Guidelines

Guidelines for implementing control standards are useful to network administrators and access administrators who have responsibilities for remote access. These guidelines may outline various remote computing environments, such as working from home, and methods of security. Remote Access Domain guidelines often reinforce security awareness training.

System/Application Domain Policies

The System/Application Domain refers to the technology and application software needed to collect, process, and store company data.

This domain covers a broad range of topics from the systems that process information to data handling. This domain covers all the security issues associated with applications. Consequently, the type of standards in this domain are diverse.

Control Standards

With such a diverse set of security issues, many of the standards within this domain focus on classifying assets and assigning accountability. Accountability includes who owns key decisions over the assets and who maintains the security controls. This distinction between the owner and custodian of assets is in many standards.

The Information Classification standard, for example, helps employees determine the classification of information. This type of control standard also helps you identify procedures to protect the confidentiality, integrity, and availability of data. The following are example control statements in an information classification standard:

All <Organization> employees and contractors share in the responsibility for ensuring that <Organization> information assets receive an appropriate level of protection by observing this Information Classification policy:

- Managers or information "owners" shall be responsible for assigning classifications to information assets according to the standard information classification system presented below.
- Where practicable, the information category shall be embedded in the information itself.
- All <Organization> associates shall be guided by the information category in their security-related handling of <Organization> information.

The Production Data for Testing control standard is an example of a policy dealing with data handling. This standard outlines the controls needed to prevent the use of production data for testing purposes. This standard may require that the data be sanitized or scrubbed before being used for testing.

Other related standards require cryptography and public key infrastructure (PKI). These standards describe approved uses of cryptography and are often driven by the data classification assigned. A PKI standard describes the environment under which the organization will use PKI.

Other standards related to the System/Application Domain include those listed in Table 10-3.

Baseline Standards

The baseline standards in this domain deal with technology configurations and technical requirements. The following is a sampling of standards:

- **Public Key Infrastructure Certification Authority (CA) Standard**—Describes the PKI infrastructure. Also describes how certificates are managed using CAs.
- **Approved Cryptographic Algorithms and Key Lengths Standard**—Describes the encryption algorithms and keys used, such as approved key lengths for symmetric and asymmetric cryptography.
- **Physical Security Baseline Standards**—Describe the physical security technologies deployed. Examples are badge readers, electronic locks, and cameras and other monitoring systems. Each technology needs a baseline standard to describe which features should be implemented for what purposes, and how to handle and manage the information generated by those devices.
- **Developer Coding Standards**—Describe how to write and test security of applications.

Procedures

For each baseline technical standard, you may need to create a procedure document for administrators and developers to implement the control requirements. You could also have procedures for incident handling, monitoring, and reporting. Some organizations have procedures for using penetration-testing tools.

As with other domains, change management is an important procedure. In this particular domain, the project management life cycle (PMLC) plays a central role. The PMLC typically outlines the procedures a team follows to implement an IT project, such as developing a new software application. The PMLC is a specific series of steps and procedures. These steps have safeguards that ensure the prior step's deliverables are complete.

TABLE 10-3 Additional types of System/Application Domain control standards.

TYPE OF CONTROL STANDARD	DESCRIPTION	EXAMPLES
Separation of Environments	Establishes the need to separate the development environment from the production environment Outlines the rules and conditions for promoting application software between environments	Logical or physical access control Prohibition of compilers on production computers
Physical Security Control Standards	Includes a number of standards for physical security and datacenter access controls	Physical access authorizations Physical access control Monitoring physical access Visitor control Access records Power equipment and power cabling Emergency power, lighting, and shutoff Fire protection Temperature and humidity controls Water damage protection Delivery and removal of assets
Developer-Related Standards	Specifies secure coding and developer standards	Developer workstation and account configuration management—limits or grants the rights to developers to change their workstation configurations Developer security testing control requirements Secure coding standards include published programming standards and developer training requirements Information accuracy, completeness, validity, and authenticity Malicious code protection Error handling

Guidelines

With such a diverse set of security issues, the standards cannot define every situation. Guidelines are useful as education vehicles and offering recommendations. For example, software developers might have guidelines for secure coding of .NET, Java, and other leading languages. The guidelines promote secure coding habits and educate developers on specific threats.

Telecommunications Policies

The telecommunications area refers to the use of telephone equipment and voice services that do not fit into the other domain areas. For purposes of this chapter, the telecommunications discussion focuses on devices such as telephones, fax machines, modems, and smartphones.

Control Standards

An essential control standard in this category is Voice over IP (VoIP). These standards describe the security considerations and controls that apply to a VoIP network. Because of the ease of access to and prolific nature of VoIP connections, there are growing technology risks. The telephone system was once isolated within an organization. Now telephone service uses the same network as any other application. This expanded use of the network brings new security challenges and vulnerabilities. A VoIP standard describes countermeasures to prevent unnecessary risk and compromise corporate information.

The following are some control statements that might appear in this standard. They are adapted from the U.S. Federal Aviation Administration's "Voice Over Internet Protocol (VoIP) Security Policy" document:

> The integration of voice and data into a single physical network is a complex process that may introduce vulnerabilities and risk. To mitigate these risks, the following must be adhered to:

 NOTE

The key point of telecommunication standards is to define the protocols and devices to be used. Once defined, the standards address how to handle data on those devices. Remember, VoIP deals with digital information. These digital conversations can be captured, stored, and played back.

- VoIP systems and networks must adhere to a common security configuration recommended by <Organization>'s security requirements.
- VoIP equipment used to transmit or discuss confidential or restricted information must be protected with FIPS 140-2 encryption standards.
- VoIP systems must follow security guidance on the segregation of data and voice networks.

Fax machines standards are another example of telecommunication policies. This standard outlines the controls necessary for the transmission and receipt of faxed information such as company confidential or restricted information.

Baseline Standards

Telecommunications equipment and devices usually have specific technology require-ments. The baseline standards focus on securing equipment and on configuration issues. Here are some examples of baseline standards:

- **Smartphone Enterprise Server Configuration Requirements Standard**— Describes security characteristics for the enterprise server that delivers corporate e-mail to smartphones

- **Use of Bluetooth Communications Standard**—Describes controls for the use of Bluetooth technology on employer-issued mobile computing devices

- **VoIP Security Product Requirements Standard**—Documents security controls for specific VoIP equipment selected by the organization

Procedures

For each baseline technical standard, you may need to create a procedure document for telecommunications personnel to implement control requirements. Procedure documents might give details for reporting a lost or stolen employer-issued smartphone. Other procedure documents outline how to configure an employer-issued mobile device and VoIP product security.

Guidelines

Guidelines for implementing control standards are helpful to personnel who are responsible for the security of telecommunications devices and equipment. Consider using employer-issued mobile phone and other device security guidelines for employees and administrators. Some organizations also use VoIP systems architecture and security guidelines.

Best Practices for IT Infrastructure Security Policies

The volume of infrastructure policies can be quite large, depending on your organization's need. For example, the more diverse the technologies deployed, the greater the number of baseline standards required. It is important to define the requirements for standards in a methodical way.

In this chapter, we discussed the requirements based on domains. More than one approach works. Many organizations first select a framework, such as ISO or COBIT. They then develop requirements and standards based on the framework.

Do not reinvent the wheel. There are rare instances where you will need to develop original content to create a new policy. More often, you modify an existing sample obtained from a reliable source. Before you create content for a specific topic, see what others have already done and adapt that work to your specific needs. Some sources for security policies and standards include the following:

10

**IT Infrastructure
Security Policies**

- The U.S. government offers hundreds of standards through NIST.
- Private organizations, such as SANS, sell prewritten security policies. SANS sells a CD with over 1,400 prewritten security polices based on ISO.
- Professional associations offer security policy examples to their membership. Some associations are the Institute of Internal Auditors (IIA) and the Information Systems and Control Association (ISACA).
- Contact the vendors of your IT products to find out if they offer sample security policies.

Do not impose strict access controls to your policies and standards. Make them freely available to everyone expected to follow them. These documents reinforce security awareness messages.

Keep content cohesive. When developing a document, focus only on the subject it covers. If you need to refer to other topics contained in other documents, do not repeat the content. Simply reference the other related documents in the one you have developed.

Keep content coherent. Maintain the same "voice" throughout a single document. Do not add more information than is necessary to convey the information. Do not stray from the message.

Make your library as searchable as possible. When implementing your policies, make it easy to locate relevant documents by indexing them with keywords and phrases.

Federate ownership to where it best belongs. Over time, you will find that nonsecurity personnel are adept at producing policy documents. This is especially true for creating procedures they use every day. If you work on building alliances with data center operators and administrators, you can often obtain their help in preparing policy documentation.

Case Studies and Examples of IT Infrastructure Security Policies

The case studies in this section examine how industries and state governments develop and implement infrastructure security standards. These case studies illustrate the influence that industry standards have on internal infrastructure policies. These examples reference leading industry standards to create and implement internal policies. This approach is true for both private and public sector.

Private Sector Case Study

A small correspondent bank wishes to exchange check information electronically with a large bank. This is permitted under a law enacted in October 2003 commonly known as the Check 21 Act. By exchanging information electronically, it can expedite cashing checks for customers. Both banks use the X9.37 standard created by Accredited Standards Committee X9 (ASC X9). The ASC X9B Working Group develops industry standards related to data and information security. The intent of the standards is to reduce financial data security risk and vulnerability. The banking and finance sector couldn't exist without effective interbank communications based on standards.

The problem was that the correspondent bank could not bundle its checks into one bundle for processing by the larger bank. Multiple bundles of checks increase cost. Exceptions were handled separately or bundled into smaller exception groups.

A company called All My Papers developed a software solution. This company specializes in financial services software. All My Papers was able to recode the check bundles to be compatible with the X9.37 standard being used by both banks. This resulted in a single bundle being processed by the large bank. Bundle recoding reduced costs. It also helped ensure compliance with the Check 21 Act.

This solution required a change to how the correspondent bank implemented the X9.37 standard. This drove both a baseline standard change and a series of procedures changes.

This case study illustrates that applying an industry standard does not guarantee compatibility. Industry standards can have components that are subject to interpretation. As a standard matures, more deployments can be reviewed for lessons learned.

Public Sector Case Study

A recent State of Maryland initiative is an example of external influences on infrastructure security policies. The governor of Maryland created a "Best in the Nation Statewide Health Information Exchange and Electronic Health Records" initiative. By 2012, the state must create a statewide technology infrastructure to support the electronic exchange of health records. This infrastructure will support health service providers doing business in Maryland. The goal of the initiative is to reduce costs and improve the quality of patient treatment.

The Information Technology Support Division (ITSD) is the state's IT department. The Department of Health and Mental Hygiene (DHMH) is responsible for meeting the governor's health goals. ITSD is responsible for the technology aspect of the initiative. The ITSD already supports DHMH technology environment.

Some of the core ITSD requirements include:

- Expand network performance and capacity.
- Provide continuous operations.
- Provide a secure infrastructure.
- Provide remote access.
- Real-time access to patient medical information.

DHMH developed a staged implementation strategy. The strategy starts with pilot applications. After assessing performance and security, the pilot applications evolve to fully functional operations. This includes ITSD providing continuous security support.

This government initiative directly impacts infrastructure policies. ITSD is responsible for developing and maintaining information security policies, standards, and procedures for DHMH. This new infrastructure affects state-owned computing environments. While not implicitly stated, any private company wishing to participate and access this network must also adopt these infrastructure standards.

This is also a good example of not reinventing the wheel. It's reasonable to assume that ITSD based the new statewide policies on the Health Insurance Portability and Accountability Act (HIPAA). HIPAA can be viewed as the core security control standards. The implementation of these core controls result in numerous baseline standards for the state's new infrastructure, such as new and modified LAN and WAN security standards.

Critical Infrastructure Case Study

The Telecommunications Industry Association (TIA) is an accredited standards committee of ANSI. Their standards often become international ISO/IEC standards. TIA standards are used by both the public and private sectors.

The medical center at the University of Kentucky turned to the ANSI/TIA-1179 standard for its build-out of a new medical facility. The standard defines the physical and logical security around installing networks and cables in commercial buildings. This standard helps define an organization's infrastructure.

A case study was presented in 2003 of the implementation of the standard. Implementation required significant security considerations. This means the university needed to change its infrastructure policies to be compliant with the standard. One of the stated goals was to be compliant with HIPAA. By adopting this industry standard, the university demonstrated compliance.

The case study also noted the "convergence" of critical systems, such as security and biomedical. The case study clearly noted the need for strong security and supporting policies. By their nature, these policies required the support of the medical staff to adopt new security procedures.

CHAPTER SUMMARY

In this chapter, we discussed security documents that relate to each domain of a typical IT infrastructure. You learned there is more than one approach to creating standards. It is important to separate core policy language from specific technology configuration. One way to approach this is to have two separate documents, such as control standards and baseline standards. Supporting documents include procedures and guidelines. Collectively, these documents represent a comprehensive way of addressing risk.

We examined both the form and substance of many standards. In fact, the volume of policy and standard topics is enormous. Organizing this material in searchable and useful manner is important. We also discussed how to categorize various documents in the library and how to describe their relationships. Finally, we examined best practices that included a number of sources for policy and standard material. Organizations rarely create new policies from scratch. It is far better to leverage best practices security frameworks and related policies.

KEY CONCEPTS AND TERMS

Access control list (ACL)	Intrusion prevention system (IPS)
Active content	User proxy
Audit	Web services
Host hardening	
Intrusion detection system (IDS)	

CHAPTER 10 ASSESSMENT

1. The steps to implement security controls on a firewall would be documented within which of the following?

   A. Policy
   B. Control standard
   C. Baseline standard
   D. Procedure

2. A DMZ separates a LAN from which of the following?

   A. Phone network
   B. Internet
   C. Cellular network
   D. VoIP Network

3. Visitor control is an aspect of which of the following?

   A. Network security
   B. Personnel security
   C. Workstation security
   D. Physical security

4. Which of the following can you use to segment LANs?

   A. Routers and firewalls
   B. Routers and gateways
   C. Gateways and servers
   D. Servers and workstations

5. Without a policy that leads to controls that restrict employees from installing their own software on a company workstation, a company could suffer which of the following consequences?

   A. Malware on the network
   B. Lawsuits from software licensing issues
   C. Loss of productivity
   D. All of the above

6. Good sources for security policies and standards include which of the following?

   A. U.S. Government
   B. Private companies selling standards
   C. Professional organizations
   D. Vendors
   E. All of the above

7. Two-factor authentication is a typical control used by employees to remotely access which of the following?

   A. Workstation
   B. LAN
   C. DMZ Web site
   D. WAN

8. Which document outlines the specific controls that a technology device needs to support?

   A. Control standard
   B. Baseline standard
   C. Procedure
   D. Policy

9. The User Proxy control standard is needed for the _____ domain.

10. The content for the documents in the policies and standards library should be written so they are _____ and_____.

11. Production data should be sanitized before being used in a test environment.

    A. True
    B. False

12. Organizations should always create new policies tailored to their needs rather than adopt industry norms found on the Internet.

    A. True
    B. False

Data Classification and Handling Policies and Risk Management Policies

DATA SUSTAINS AN ORGANIZATION'S business processes and enables it to deliver products and services. Stop the flow of data, and just as quickly you disrupt the ability to deliver products and services. If the loss of data lasts long enough, the viability of the organization itself comes into question. That's how vital data is for many organizations today.

Data classification is a useful way to rank the importance of data to an organization. There are also standardized methods of understanding the importance of business processes to the organization. When you combine these techniques, you can define handling policies. These policies help prevent disruption of services. This is particularly important during a natural or man-made disaster, such as an earthquake or fire. At these times rapid response is important.

This chapter discusses data classification techniques used by the government and within the private sector. The chapter discusses how to identify mission-critical data and business processes. The chapter also discusses risk management approaches to sustain these business processes during a disaster.

Chapter 11 Topics

This chapter covers the following topics and concepts:

- What data classification policies are
- What data handling policies are
- Which business risks are related to information systems
- What business impact analysis (BIA) policies are
- What risk assessment policies are
- How business continuity plan (BCP) policies protect information
- How disaster recovery plan (DRP) policies protect information
- What best practices for risk management policies are
- What some case studies and examples of risk management policies are

Chapter 11 Goals

When you complete this chapter, you will be able to:

- Explain various data classification approaches
- Explain the difference between classified and unclassified data
- Describe common business classification techniques
- Understand the need for policies that govern data in transit and at rest
- Explain common business risks in a disaster
- Describe a BIA
- Describe a BCP
- Explain a DRP and its policies
- Describe the relationship between BIA, BCP, and DRP

Data Classification Policies

Data **classification** is all about labeling data. Labeling data enables people to find it quickly and handle it properly. You classify data independently of the form it takes. In other words, data stored in a computer should be classified the same way as data printed on a report.

There is a cost to classifying data. Classifying data takes time and can be a tedious process. This is because there are many data types and uses. It's important not to over-classify. A data classification approach must clearly and simply represent how you want the data to be handled.

The Need for Data Classification

You can classify data for different purposes depending on the need of the organization. For example, the military would have a very different classification need than the local grocery market. Both handle data, but handling requirements differ greatly. The more sensitive the data, the more important it is to handle the information properly.

An organization has several needs to classify data. The three most common needs are to:

- Protect information
- Retain information
- Recover information

Protecting Information

The need to protect information is often referred to as the "security classification." An organization has to protect data when its disclosure could cause damage.

Data classification drives what type of security you should use to protect the information. Data classification also helps define the authentication and authorization methods you should use to ensure the data does not fall into unauthorized hands.

Authentication is the process used to prove the identity of the person. **Authorization** is the process used to grant permission to the person. Both authentication and authorization control access to systems, applications, network, and data. When an individual is said to be an "authorized user," it means that he or she received formal approval to access the systems, applications, network, and data.

All organizations have some form of data that requires protection. Any organization that has employees has sensitive personal information, which by law must be protected.

Retaining Information

An organization must determine how long to retain information. It's not practical to retain data forever. When you purge and delete sensitive data, there's less of a target for a future breach. Therefore, organizations should retain only data that is needed to conduct business. Data retention policies define the methods of retaining data as well as the duration.

You need to retain data for two major reasons: legal obligation and needs of the business. All organizations have some legal requirements to keep records, such as financial and tax records. Generally such records are retained for seven years in the United States. There are also business reasons to keep records, such as customer information, contracts, and sales records. Table 11-1 depicts a sample retention classification scheme.

There are records which there is no legal or business reason to keep. Many organizations require that such records be deleted at some point. Deleting this information helps the company cut down on storage costs and protects the information from accidental disclosure.

TABLE 11-1 Data classification for retention of information.

DATA CLASS	CLASS DESCRIPTION	RETENTION PERIOD	EXAMPLES
Regulated	Records that are required to be kept by regulations	Seven years	Financial and tax records
Business	General business records needed to support operations	Five years	Customer records Vendor records
Temporary	Temporary records that are not mission-critical	One year	E-mails

NOTE

According to a legal memorandum by Ater Wynne LLP, each person in a corporate setting produces about 736 megabytes annually of electronic data. That equates to a stack of books 30 feet tall. Additionally, it's estimated that e-mail accounts for 80 percent of corporate communications in the United States.

Storage can be expensive for an organization. A corporate setting can have thousands of employees generating huge volumes of data. Retaining this data takes up valuable resources to back up, recover, monitor, protect, and classify. If you delete unneeded data, these costs are avoided.

Given the volume of data produced, it is inevitable that sensitive data will show up where it's not supposed to. A good example is e-mail. A service agent might try to help a customer by e-mail to resolve a payment problem. Despite the agent's good intentions, the agent might include the customer's personal financial information in the e-mail. Once that data is in the e-mail system, it's difficult to remove. The person receiving the e-mail may have designated others to view the mail. Backups of the desktop and mail system will also have copies of the personal information. Wherever that data resides or travels, the information must now be protected and handled appropriately.

You can reduce the likelihood of accidental disclosure by routinely deleting data that is no longer needed for legal or business reasons. Classifying what's important ensures that the right data is deleted. Without retention policies, vital records could be lost. The retention policy can use data classification to help define handling methods.

It's important to work with management in determining the retention policy. It's also important to work with legal staff. The legal obligations can change depending on the business context. Let's assume a service agent with a securities brokerage wrote an e-mail about a customer's stock trade. This type of e-mail correspondence must be retained by law. The Securities and Exchange Commission (SEC) Rule 17a-4 requires all customer correspondence to be retained for three years. This is to ensure a record is kept in case of an accusation of fraud or misrepresentation. The SEC rule also says the correspondence must be kept in a way that cannot be altered or overwritten. This means the retention policy must specify how the data is to be backed up. An example is a requirement that data should be kept on write-once optical drives. Regulations make data classification even more important in defining proper handling methods.

A retention policy can help protect a company during a law suit. The courts have held that no sanction will be applied to organizations operating in good faith. This is true even if they lost the records as a result of routine operations. "Good faith" is demonstrated through a retention policy that demonstrates how data is routinely classified, retained, and deleted.

Recovering Information

The need to recover information also drives the need for data classification. In a disaster, information that is mission-critical needs to be recovered quickly. Properly classifying data allows the more critical data to be identified. This data can then be handled with specific recovery requirements in mind. For example, an organization may choose to mirror critical data. This allows for recovery within seconds. In comparison, it can take hours to recover data from a tape backup. Table 11-2 depicts a sample recovery classification scheme.

TABLE 11-2 Data classification for recovery of information.

DATA CLASS	CLASS DESCRIPTION	RECOVERY PERIOD	EXAMPLES
Critical	Data that must be recovered immediately to avoid serious impact on the organization	30 minutes	Web site and e-commerce channels Customer records
Urgent	Data that can be recovered later with minimal impact on the organization	48 hours	E-mail backups
Non-Vital	Data not vital to the daily operations of the business	30 days	Historical records Archived contract files

There are various approaches, sometimes called "classification schemes," to classifying data. A good rule of thumb is to keep it simple! A dozen classes within each scheme for security, retention, and recovery would be confusing. Employees cannot remember elaborate classification schemes. It's difficult to train employees on the subtle differences among so many classes. A good rule is to use five or fewer classes. Some classification schemes use three classes. These three classes represent a lower and upper extreme combined with a practical middle ground. It's also good to keep the class names short, concise, and memorable. Some classification requirements are influenced by specific legal requirements. In other cases, classification requirements will be driven by what the business is willing to pay for. For example, Table 11-2 indicates a recovery time of less than 30 minutes for critical data. This sample recovery scheme may not be appropriate for all organizations. For example, the scheme might be too expensive for an elementary school to implement. A Wall Street brokerage firm might find 30 minutes inadequate.

Military Classification Schemes

A security data classification reflects the criticality and sensitivity of the information. "Criticality" refers to how important the information is to achieving the organization's mission. "Sensitivity" refers to the impact associated with unauthorized disclosure. A specific piece of data can be high on one scale but low on the other. The higher of the two scales typically drives the data classification. As data becomes more important, generally it requires stronger controls. The U.S. military classification scheme is used by a number of federal agencies.

The U.S. military classification scheme is defined in National Security Information document EO 12356. There are three classification levels:

- **Top Secret** data, the unauthorized disclosure of which would reasonably be expected to cause grave damage to the national security
- **Secret** data, the unauthorized disclosure of which would reasonably be expected to cause serious damage to the national security
- **Confidential** data, the unauthorized disclosure of which would reasonably be expected to cause damage to the national security

Any military data that is considered "classified" must use one of these three classification levels. There is also unclassified data that is handled by government agencies. This type of data has two classification levels:

- **Sensitive but unclassified** is confidential data not subject to release under the Freedom of Information Act
- **Unclassified** is data available to the public

Sensitive but unclassified is sometimes called "SBU." It's also sometimes called "For official use only" (FOUO) in the United States. The term FOUO is used primarily within the U.S. Department of Defense (DoD). Some examples of SBU data are Internal Revenue Service tax returns, Social Security numbers, and law enforcement records.

The Information Security Oversight Office (ISOO) oversees the U.S. government's classification program. The ISOO produces an annual report to the president summarizing the classification program from the prior year. The report outlines what data has been classified and declassified each year. The 2009 report stated that of all the classified data, 2 percent was Top Secret, 77 percent was Secret, and 21 percent was Confidential.

Declassifying data is very important. It's not practical to keep data classified forever. First, it's better to focus limited resources on protecting a smaller amount of the most important data. Second, in democracies, we expect the government to be transparent. Unless there's a compelling reason to keep a secret, the expectation is the information will be released to the public.

The government routinely declassifies data. **Declassification** is a term that means to change the classification to "unclassified." The declassification of data is handled in one of three programs run by the ISOO:

- **Automatic declassification** automatically removes the classification after 25 years.
- **Systematic declassification** reviews those records exempted from automatic declassification.
- **Mandatory declassification** reviews specific records when requested.

These three programs declassified 28.8 million pages of information in 2009. Figure 11-1 is an excerpt from the ISOO "Information Security Oversight Report 2009" report. As you can see, the government is protecting more and more data. The amount could become overwhelming unless there are policies to reduce the amount of data the government protects.

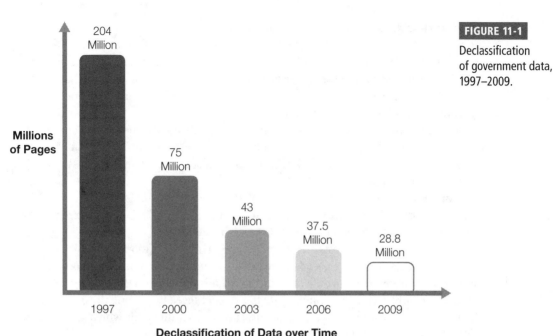

FIGURE 11-1

Declassification of government data, 1997–2009.

Declassification of Data over Time

Business Classification Schemes

The private sector, like the military, uses data classification to reflect the importance of the information. Unlike the government, there is no one data classification scheme. There is no one right approach to classification of data. Also like the military, data classification in business drives security and how the data will be handled.

Although there is no mandatory data classification scheme, there are norms for private industry. The following four classifications are often used:

- Highly sensitive
- Sensitive
- Internal
- Public

Highly sensitive classification refers to data that is mission-critical. You use criticality and sensitivity to determine what data is mission-critical. This classification is also used to protect highly regulated data. This could include Social Security numbers and financial records. If this information is breached, it could represent considerable liability to the organization. Mission-critical data is information vital for the organization to achieve its core business. As such, an unauthorized breach creates substantial risk to the enterprise.

Access to highly sensitive data is limited. Organizations often apply enhanced security and monitoring. Monitoring can include detailed logging of when records are accessed. Additional security controls may be applied, such as encryption.

Sensitive classification refers to data that is important to the business but not vital to its mission. If information is breached, it could represent significant financial loss. However, the breach of the information would not cause critical damage to the organization. This data might include client lists, vendor information, and network diagrams.

Access to sensitive data is restricted and monitored. The monitoring may not be as rigorous as with highly sensitive data.

The key difference between highly sensitive and sensitive is the magnitude of the impact. Unauthorized exposure of highly sensitive data may put the business at risk. Unauthorized exposure of sensitive data may result in substantial financial loss, but the business will survive.

Internal classification refers to data not related to the core business. The data could be routine communications within the organization. The impact of unauthorized access to internal data is a disruption of operations and financial loss.

Access to internal data is restricted to employees. The information is widely available for them, but the data is not released to the public or individuals outside the company.

Public classification refers to data that has no negative impact on the business when released to the public. Access to public data is often achieved by placing the data on a public Web site or through press releases. The number of individuals who are permitted to make data public is limited.

Many laws and regulations require you to know where your data is. These laws require you to protect the data commensurate to the risk to your business. Data classification is an effective way of determining risk. The organization is at greater risk when mission-critical data is breached. By classifying the data, you are able to find it quickly and define proper controls.

Developing a Customized Classification Scheme

You can often create a customized classification scheme by altering an existing one. Federal agencies cannot customize a scheme. This is because their classification schemes are mandated by law. Many security frameworks provide guidance and requirements to develop a classification. Some sources of guidance and requirements include the ISO, Control Objectives for Information and related Technology (COBIT), and Payment Card Industry Data Security Standard (PCI DSS).

Sometimes customizing a classification scheme is minor. This might include modifying the label but not changing the underlying definition. For example, the "highly sensitive" classification could equate to private, restricted, or mission-critical. It's not the name that matters but the definition. Classification names can vary depending on the organization and the perspective of the creator. "Private" classification in one organization could mean "highly sensitive" in another. In still another it might mean "sensitive."

When developing a customized data classification scheme, keep to the basics. You should consider the following general guidelines:

1. Determine the number of classification levels.
2. Define each classification level.
3. Name each classification level.
4. Align the classification to specific handling requirements.
5. Define the audit and reporting requirements.

You determine the number of classification levels by looking at how much you want to separate the data. One approach is to separate the data by aligning it to critical business processes. This helps you understand the business to better protect the assets. For example, a power plant may want to isolate Supervisory Control and Data Acquisition (SCADA) systems. SCADA data helps run the facility. Special security and controls may be placed on these systems and data. This can be achieved by classifying the SCADA data differently than other types of data.

The definition of each classification level depends on how you want to express the impact of a breach. Federal agencies determine impact based on confidentiality, integrity, and availability. They assign a rating of low, moderate, or high impact to each of these. By applying a formula they can determine an impact. Organizations outside the government have adopted similar approaches. Table 11-3 depicts the basic impact matrix described in National Institute of Standards and Technology (NIST) Federal Information Processing Standard (FIPS) 199.

The FIPS-199 publication uses phrases such as "limited adverse effect" to denote low impact. For moderate and high impact, it uses "serious adverse effect" and "severe or catastrophic adverse effect."

In the business world, impact definitions closely align with measured business results. For example, low risks can be defined as causing "operations disruptions and minimal financial loss." An organization understands these terms because a financial scale can be used. For example, a low impact may result when $1 to $20,000 is at risk. A moderate impact might be defined as $20,000 to $500,000. A high-impact risk might be defined as $500,000 and above. The exact amounts vary depending on the size of the organization and its risk tolerance. Applying specific dollar amounts to impacts makes the definitions clearer.

TABLE 11-3 Data classification for security of information.

SECURITY OBJECTIVE	POTENTIAL IMPACT		
	LOW	MODERATE	HIGH
Confidentiality			
Integrity			
Availability			

The name of each classification level is usually taken from the definition itself. The important point is to select a name that resonates within the organization. You may also consider using a name that peer organizations adopt. This can help facilitate the exchange of approaches within the industry. The name can reflect leadership's view of risk, such as classifying data as "proprietary" versus "sensitive."

To align the classification to specific handling requirements is a critical step. Once you determine the classification level, you must apply the appropriate security control requirements. Consider combining the levels where there's little to no difference in security requirements.

Audit and reporting requirements depend on industry and regulatory requirements. Many organizations are subject to privacy law disclosures. You should consider these reporting requirements when classifying data. For example, sensitive data for audit and reporting requirements can be assigned a special classification. This classification can include additional logging and monitoring capability.

Classifying Your Data

You need to consider two primary issues when classifying data. One issue is data ownership. The other issue is security controls. These two issues help you drive maximum value from the data classification effort.

The business is accountable to ensure data is protected. The business also defines handling requirements. IT is the custodian of the data. It's up to the business to ensure adequate controls are funded and they meet regulatory requirements. The COBIT framework recommends that a data owner be assigned. This person would be accountable for defining all data handling requirements with the business. The data owner determines the level of protection and how the data is stored and accessed. Ultimately, the data owner must strike a balance between protection and usability. The data owner must consider both the business requirements and regulatory requirements.

The position of the data owner should be senior enough to be accountable. The data owner has a vested interest in making sure the data is accurate and properly secure. The data owner needs to understand the importance and value of the information to the business. He or she also needs to understand the ramifications that inaccurate data or unauthorized access has on the organization.

The data owner guides the IT department in defining controls and handling processes. The IT department designs, builds, and implements these controls. For example, if cardholder data is being collected, the data owner should be aware of PCI DSS standards. The IT department would advise the data owner on the technology requirements. Responsibility stays with the data owner to fund the technology. The duties and responsibilities of the data owner should be outlined in the security controls, or in security policies.

TABLE 11-4 Data classification and security controls.

DATA CLASSIFICATION	SECURITY CONTROLS		
	AUTHENTICATION	MONITORING	LOGGING
Highly sensitive	Two factors	Real-time alerts	Detailed logs
Sensitive	ID/password	Daily log review	Support monitoring and for forensic use
Internal	ID/password	None	For forensic use
Public	None	None	Log when data is updated

Determining the security controls for each classification level is a core objective of data classification. It would make no sense to identify data as "highly sensitive" or "Top Secret," and then allow broad access. The data owner and IT department determine what controls are appropriate. The following is a sampling of the security controls to be considered:

- Authentication method
- Encryption
- Monitoring
- Logging

It's up to the business to ensure adequate controls are funded and they meet regulatory requirements.

It's important not to treat security controls as a "wish list" of technologies. For example, encryption is not necessary for all data. Encryption can be challenging and expensive. Be sure that all the technologies within the policies have a realistic way of being implemented. Otherwise, the security policies are viewed as unrealistic and may even be ignored. Table 11-4 depicts a simple approach to linking data classifications to security controls.

Data Handling Policies

One of the difficult exercises when defining access requirements is understanding exactly who has a clear need to use the information. It's important that data handling policies assign responsibility for how the data is to be used. For example, data handling policies should limit what data is allowed to be printed. Another data handling concern is protecting data when it's moved. The concern is that the data gets used in a way that is no longer protected.

As with data classification, the data owner must strike a balance between protection and usability. The data owner must consider both the business and regulatory requirements.

The Need for Policy Governing Data at Rest and in Transit

A discussion on how best to protect data at rest and in transit inevitably leads to the subject of encryption. There certainly is more to protecting data than just encrypting it. There's an array of factors that must be considered, such as authentication, authorization, logging, and monitoring. However, the one topic that gets much attention is encryption. That's due in part to the emergence of state privacy laws. The majority of states today have privacy laws that fall under two types of encryption requirements:

- Laws that require private data to be encrypted
- Laws that require notification of breaches when private data is not encrypted

> **NOTE**
>
> The term "data at rest" refers to data that is in storage. This includes data on a server, laptop, CD, DVD, or universal serial bus (USB) thumb drive. Any data that is stored is considered data at rest. The term "data in transit" refers to data that is traversing the network. That includes data on a private network, the Internet, and wireless networks. If the data is moving over any type of network, the data is in transit.

Both requirements are driving businesses to adopt encryption. There are differences among state laws as to the level of encryption that's required. For example, the California privacy law requires notification when private information that has not been encrypted is breached. The Massachusetts privacy law requires encryption of data, at rest or in transit, when it leaves the confines of a company's network. Nevada privacy law mandates the use of PCI DSS, which requires cardholder data to be encrypted both inside and outside the company's network.

Regardless of your opinion about whether encryption is a good idea, encryption is a mandate for many organizations. You need to ensure that IT security policies addressing where and how encryption will be used are well defined within those policies.

Security policies need to be clear about when you should use encryption. The policies should also state the level of encryption that is acceptable. Sometimes when people discuss encrypting data within the network, they raise passionate arguments about the value of the protection obtained by encrypting data. Some argue there's little value because absent stealing the physical hard drive, the data is automatically decrypted. Others argue that it's another layer of control preventing access because the decryption process is controlled. Both are right. Sometimes the data is automatically decrypted and other times it is not.

Figure 11-2 illustrates both points of view. There are two scenarios presented. In both scenarios, a hacker breaches the environment. In scenario #1, a breach of the application leads to unencrypted data being exposed. In this case, encryption was of no value in protecting the information. In scenario #2, a breach of the operating system leads to a database file being stolen. In this case, the data remained encrypted, which significantly helped prevent the data from being exposed. Encryption of data within the network can offer valuable protection depending on the type of breach. The key factor is whether the encryption key becomes exposed in the process.

Let's examine how this works in more detail. In scenario #1, a breach of the application allows the hacker to retrieve unencrypted data. The critical point here is that the application and/or database server have access to the encryption key. In this example, the database is decrypting the data. Alternatively, it could be the application that is decrypting the data. Either way, you are in essence asking the application to get the information and decrypt it for you. However, in scenario #2, the hacker has breached the operating system (OS), bypassing the application and database server. In this scenario, the hacker only has access to the file system. In other words, the hacker can retrieve the database files but they remain encrypted. Thus, no data has been breached.

Encrypting data within the network does protect against many attacks but does not protect against a breach of the application. What makes scenario #2 a viable solution is that the key management layer is outside the application and database layer. Without the encryption key the data is unreadable. It would not make sense to encrypt the data on the server and leave the encryption key on the same server. That's like leaving your car key in the ignition of your car. For encryption to be effective, security policies must establish core requirements and standards, such as:

- Encryption keys must be separated from encrypted data.
- Encryption keys must be retrieved through a secure process.
- Administrator rights at the OS layer do not give access to the database.

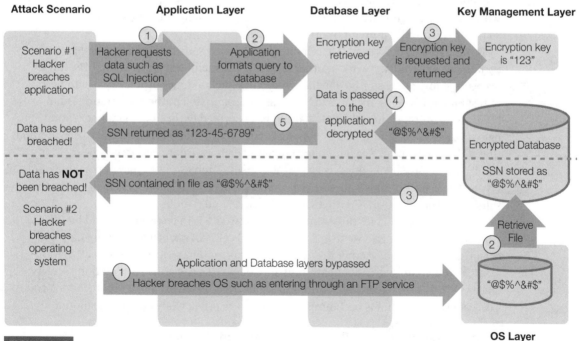

FIGURE 11-2

Database encryption attack scenarios.

What's generally accepted as best practice is that whenever sensitive data leaves the confines of the organization's private network, the information should be encrypted. This is not consistently applied within many organizations. For example, an organization encrypts all laptop hard drives. However, the organization may fail to encrypt e-mail, USB, or CD/DVD drives. In this case, it's common to deploy a patchwork of encryption solutions. Many organizations fail to comply completely with encryption requirements. The use of the term "best practice" in this context recognizes that the level of success among organizations varies. This lack of full compliance to implement encryption is due to:

- Confusion over the new laws
- Cost to comply
- Lack of a standardized approach among vendor products

The IT industry is quickly adapting. New vendor products are beginning to offer encryption solutions. Today the encryption of mobile hard drives and encryption over the Internet are commonplace. For example, it's common in many organizations to encrypt the hard drive of mobile devices, such as laptops and smartphones. This protects the sensitive information contained inside the device. If the device is lost or stolen, the information cannot be read. Also, encryption over the Internet is commonplace. For example, employees routinely connect to an office through virtual private network (VPN) solutions that encrypt all the traffic between the employees and the private network. Organizations with consumers who buy online routinely encrypt the consumers' Web site sessions so they can enter their credit information safely.

Beyond mobile devices and traversing the Internet, sensitive information leaves the confines of a private network in other forms. These include backup tapes, CDs, thumb drives, and any other storage media. Encrypting backup tapes protects the data both at rest and as it's being transported. If a tape is lost or stolen, the information is not breached. This is because the data cannot be decrypted without the key. Encrypting backup tapes is commonplace in industries such as financial services. Also, keep in mind that not all backups are well managed through elaborate data center processes. Many small offices make backups on very portable media such as mini tapes or portable hard drives. These backups also need to be protected. There's a lack of consensus on best solutions to protect CD/DVD drives, thumb drives, and e-mail.

The IT security policies must state clearly how data is to be protected and handled. An organization can choose to lock out CD/DVDs or USB ports from writing data. An organization can also attempt to encrypt any information written to the drives. Both solutions have complexity, benefits, and drawbacks. It's the chief information security officer's (CISO's) role to bring the organization to a consensus. Some organizations choose to accept the risk. That is becoming harder to do as privacy laws mandate solutions.

Policies, Standards, and Procedures Covering the Data Life Cycle

Data has a life cycle like any IT asset. It's created, accessed, and eventually destroyed. Between these states it changes form. It is transmitted, stored, and physically moved.

Security policies, standards, and procedures establish different requirements on the data depending on the life-cycle state. The main objective is to ensure that data is protected in all its forms. It should be protected on all media and during all phases of its life cycle. The protection needs to extend to all processing environments. These environments collectively refer to all applications, systems, and networks.

Policies state that users of information are personally responsible for complying with policies, standards, and procedures. All users are held accountable for the accuracy, integrity, and confidentiality of the information they access. Policies must be clear as to the use and handling of data. For discussion purposes, this section outlines some of the policy considerations for data handling at different points:

- **Creation**—During creation, data must be classified. That could be simply placing the data within a common storage area. For example, a human resources (HR) system creates information in the HR database. All information in that database can be assigned a common data classification. Security policies then govern data owner, custodians, and accountabilities. Security procedures govern how access is granted to that data.

- **Access**—Access to data is governed by security policies. These policies provide special guidance on separation of duties (SOD). It's important that procedures check SOD requirements before granting access. For example, the ability to create and approve a wire transfer of large sums out of a bank typically requires two or more people. The SOD would have one person create the wire and one person approve it. In this case, the procedure to grant authority to approve wires must also include a check to verify that the same person does not have the authority to create a wire. If the person had both authorities, that person could create and approve a large sum of money to himself or herself.

- **Use**—Use of data includes protecting and labeling information properly after its access. The data must be properly labeled and safeguarded according to its classification. For example, if highly sensitive data is used in a printed report, the report must be labeled "highly sensitive." Typically, labeling a report "highly sensitive" means there will be data handling issues related to storage.

- **Transmission**—Data must be transmitted in accordance with policies and standards. The organization may have procedures and processes for transmitting data. All users must follow these procedures. This ensures that the data is adequately protected using approved technology, such as encryption.

- **Storage**—Storage devices of data must be approved. This means that access to a device must be secured and properly controlled. For example, let's say mobile devices are encrypted. Once a device is approved and configured, access can be granted through normal procedures. Storage handling also relates to physical documents. "Highly sensitive" documents, for example, need to be locked up when not in use. They should be shared with those individuals authorized to view such material.

- **Physical transport**—Transport of data must be approved. This ensures that what leaves the confines of the private network is protected and tracked. The organization has an obligation to know where its data is. Also, it needs to know that data is properly protected. When possible, the data should be encrypted during transport. In the event of data media being lost or stolen, the data will then be protected. Many organizations use preapproved transport companies for handling data. These services provide the tracking and notification of arrival needed to meet the companies' obligations.

- **Destruction**—Destruction of data is sometimes called "disposal." When an asset reaches its end of life, it must be destroyed in a controlled procedure. The standards that govern its destruction make sure that the data cannot be reconstructed. This may require physical media to be placed in a disposal bin. These bins are specially designed to allow items to be deposited but not removed. The items are collected and the contents shredded. All users are required to follow procedures that have been approved for the destruction of physical media and electronic data.

IT security policies, standards, and procedures must outline the clear requirements at each stage of the data's life cycle. The policies must be clear on the responsibilities of the user to follow them. They also need to outline the consequences of noncompliance and purposely bypassing these controls.

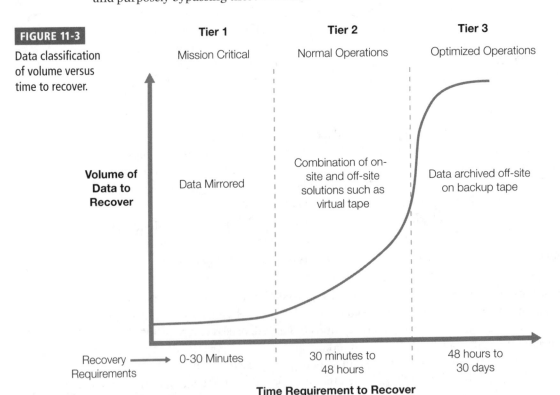

FIGURE 11-3

Data classification of volume versus time to recover.

Identify Business Risks Related to Information Systems

Chapter 8 discussed business risks in the context of an IT policies framework. This section expands the discussion into how you can reduce these risks through effective data classification.

No matter the size of your organization, understanding data is vital to its success. It's a simple fact that good decisions are more likely to come from good data. Data classification lets you understand how data relates to the business. Data classification is the foundation required for data quality. A well-defined data classification approach helps achieve good data quality. This is because data classification enables you to stratify data by usage and type. Understanding your data allows you to reduce risks and minimize costs.

Types of Risk

Much IT risk is operational risk. Operational risk is a broad category. It includes any event that disrupts the activities the organization undertakes daily. In technology terms, it's an interruption of the technology that affects the business process. It could be a coding error, slow network, system outage, or security breach. Data classification helps focus resources on those assets needed to recover the business. For example, data classification identifies what data is critical to resuming minimal operations. Figure 11-3 illustrates that point, with Tier 1 representing mission-critical applications. With mission-critical applications, data should be mirrored so it can be recovered quickly.

Notice the transition between Tier 1 and Tier 2. This is represented by the dotted line cutting across the curved line. In this case, only a small percentage of data needs to be recovered for minimum operations. Conversely, for optimized operations, a significant amount of data needs to be recovered. This is represented by the path of the curved line in Tier 3. However, this large amount of data is not as vital in the short term. Data classification allows you to stratify this data so the mission-critical data can be found quickly and recovered.

Physical, environmental, and technical hazards can disrupt IT operations. A physical hazard can be any physical threat, such as a fire within the data center. An environmental hazard can be an environmental event, such as a storm or earthquake. A technical hazard is a general category that covers other types of hazards. Data classification helps plan for many hazards. Such hazards might necessitate selecting a mirroring solution that copies mission-critical data across two data centers in two different locations.

Financial risk is the potential impact when the business fails to meet its financial obligations. Financial risk is often driven by a lack of adequate liquidity and credit for the business to meet its obligations. Financial decisions depend on financial data being accurate and available. Data classification builds processes that ensure the integrity of the information. When data is properly classified, you can identify financial information clearly. In addition, you can apply appropriate protection and handling methods.

Strategic risks may change how the organization operates. Some examples are mergers and acquisitions, a change in the industry, or a change in the customer. Understanding the sensitivity and criticality of your data brings you closer to understanding your customer and products. Stratifying your data through classification helps you understand what your core business truly is and what it is not.

The key take-away is recognizing that the process of data classification is more than a label or tag. It's a review of how data drives your business. The benefit of data classification is identification of critical information assets and properly protecting those assets. The residual benefit is that you will understand your business and customers better.

Development and Need for Policies Based on Risk Management

Establishing a new risk-based management approach can be a daunting challenge. The objective of a risk-based approach is to focus on the greatest threats to an organization. IT security policies that are risk-based will focus on the greatest threats to business processes and promote a risk-aware culture. Policies, processes, and controls have more value when they reduce real business risk.

Compliance is more than adhering to laws and regulations. Regulators also want an organization to demonstrate that it can systematically identify and reduce risk. Policies based on risk management principles can achieve this. Security policies steer the organization within regulatory boundaries. Policies also need to reflect the organization's risk culture, tolerance, appetite, and values. For example, the Health Insurance Portability and Accountability Act (HIPAA) requires a risk management and analysis approach. This promotes a thorough understanding of the risks. This understanding leads to the selection of appropriate safeguards. These safeguards are based on the level of risks faced by the organization.

Developing tools to make mathematical calculations of these factors provides a means of assessing the risk in an objective fashion. Table 11-4 is a simple example of this approach. Tools can inform the organization's leadership of trends and emerging risks. But in the end they are only tools. There is no substitute for common sense. As much as they enlighten us, they can also cloud our judgment when they are followed blindly. An experienced leader knows to dig deeper when a model is saying something that doesn't make sense.

The use of security policies based on sound risk management will help to educate the organization on tradeoffs that are implicit in the risk-reduction decisions. The following are some benefits of a risk management approach to security policies. Such an approach:

- Identifies possible costs and benefits of decisions
- Considers actions that may not be apparent to the leaders and forces alternative thought
- Provides analytic rigor to ensure an objective consideration of risk

Risk management that is rigorous and well executed helps leaders make choices that reduce risk over the long term. This is critically important. Reducing risks is not a one-time activity.

Risk management is a continuous dialogue. As time passes, other pressing needs compete for resources, and support for the risk reduction effort wavers. An effective risk management system explains the risks in the context of the business. It justifies its priority and funding.

Risk management is a process of governance. It's also a continuous improvement model. Figure 11-4 depicts a simple continuous improvement model for risk management. The following steps are cycled through each time a new risk is discovered:

1. Prioritize the risk; align the risk to strategic objectives.

2. Identify an appropriate risk response; sometimes this may require adjusting policies.

3. Monitor the effectiveness of the response and gauge the reduction in risk.

4. Identify residual and new risks whereby the cause of the risk is determined.

5. Assess risk to measure the impact to the organization.

This risk management continuous improvement model can be used to start a risk management program. In a startup you would begin by prioritizing all known risks. This means aligning the risks to strategic objectives. This process may cause a change in the risk management programs or policies themselves. This is vital to ensure the program drives value into the business.

Controlling risk to the business extends beyond daily operations. It is important that you understand risks that can affect how to recover and sustain your business.

FIGURE 11-4

Risk management continuous improvement model.

Business Impact Analysis (BIA) Policies

A **business impact analysis (BIA)** is the first step in building a business continuity plan (BCP). The purpose is to determine the impact to an organization in the event that key processes and technology are not available. You use the BIA to develop business continuity plans to minimize losses. The BIA is based on multiple scenarios. Each scenario assumes a worst-case situation, such as the entire infrastructure has been destroyed. The main intent of a BIA is to identify what assets are required for the business to recover and continue doing business. These assets include critical resources, systems, facilities, personnel, and records. Additionally, the BIA identifies recovery times.

Once the data is collected, you need to perform an analysis. Compile all requirements, dependencies, and impacts. Issue a final report with recommendations of recovery strategies. This will allow the business to determine what recovery strategies and solutions it will implement.

Component Priority

Use the BIA to identify adverse impacts to the organization caused by a disaster. This process identifies key components. A component can be a function or process. How detailed the component definition is depends on the organization. It must be of sufficient detail that the impact to the business is clear and a recovery strategy can be selected.

The source for this information is the business. A BIA cannot be conducted in isolation. It is the business that must establish the priority of components. This phase of the BIA has the following objectives:

- Identify all business functions and processes within the business.
- Define each BIA component.
- Determine the financial and service impact if the component was not available.
- Establish recovery time frames for each component.

Component Reliance

One of the most important parts of the BIA is to determine dependencies. This includes dependency on other BIA components. The BIA must also identify specific resources, such as technology and facilities. Other dependencies may include specific skills in short supply. The key objective of this phase of the BIA is to:

- Identify dependencies, such as other BIA components.
- Identify resources required to recover each component.
- Identify human assets needed to recover.

Impact Report

Once you complete the assessment, compile the results. Formulate recommendations. Then the business can make decisions. The BIA impact report is not just issued. You should develop it as a collaborative effort among key stakeholders. These stakeholders include executive leadership, risk teams, IT, and the business. The process of producing the report creates the consensus. Most importantly, the collaboration process builds the political will to implement the BIA recommendations.

The key objective of this phase of the BIA is to:

- Validate findings of the BIA report.
- Create consensus for its findings and recommendations.
- Provide a foundation for other assessments.
- Start educating individuals who are key to recovery.

The BIA final report is an essential component of an organization's business continuity planning. It sets the organization's priorities for assessments and for funding IT resiliency efforts. Resiliency is a term used in IT to indicate how quickly the IT infrastructure can recover.

Development and Need for Policies Based on BIA

The BIA describes the mission-critical functions and processes. This report leads to further assessments that identify threats and vulnerabilities. You typically produce a BIA annually. Next, you compare the findings to security policies. This comparison identifies gaps that may be opportunities to improve policies.

As a business changes over time, the BIA is an excellent way to understand the business. This top-priority list of business processes helps focus security efforts to protect the business' most vital assets.

Risk Assessment Policies

A risk assessment is one of the most important activities that an organization performs. A risk assessment defines threats and vulnerabilities and determines control recommendations. It allows the organization to make informed decisions to invest in risk reduction. Risk-based decisions are the basis of most IT security policies.

Risk Exposure

A risk exposure is the impact to the organization when an event occurs. There are several ways to calculate risk exposure. Ideally, you want to quantify it within business terms, such as putting a dollar value on the losses. A generally accepted formula can be used to calculate exposure, as follows:

Risk exposure = Likelihood the event will occur × Impact if the event occurs

For example, if there's a 50-percent chance that a $2 million loss may occur, the risk exposure would be $1 million (.5 × $2 million = $1 million). This calculation, plus other assessments, can lead to understanding the total risk exposure of a business unit.

You can use different analytical methods to determine likelihood and impact. These methods fall into two types: quantitative and qualitative. Quantitative methods involve using numerical measurements to determine risks. Measurements may include a range of measurements, such as asset value and frequency of the threat. A shortcoming of quantitative methods is a lack of reliable data. This can be overcome by reaching a consensus on the use of industry benchmarks.

Qualitative analysis involves professional judgment. This means making a well-educated guess, so to speak. Qualitative techniques may include questionnaires, interviews, and working groups. Qualitative analysis can be used to adjust measurement created through quantitative methods.

These are very powerful tools that allow you to have an engaged conversation on risk with the business. When presented with the risk exposure, the business can accept the risk or fund its mitigation. It's important that you discuss with the business any assumptions made in determining the likelihood or impact. This serves two purposes. It validates your assumption. It also builds credibility for the analysis. This avoids the situation where the analysis is discarded as unrealistic.

Prioritization of Risk, Threat, and Vulnerabilities

When you combine the risk exposure and BIA you can see the direct impact on the business. This view of risk allows you to prioritize the risks. A risk management program creates a balance. The balance is between reducing the most likely events and mitigating risks with the greatest impact. Controls addressing one risk can impact other risks.

Security policies and controls can reduce reputational, operational, legal, and strategic risk. This is accomplished by limiting vulnerabilities and reducing breaches, which builds consumer confidence.

Risk Management Strategies

Once you identify a risk you choose a strategy for managing it. There are four generally accepted risk management strategies, as follows:

- **Risk avoidance**—Not engaging in certain activities that can incur risk
- **Risk acceptance**—Accepting the risk involved in certain activities and addressing any consequences that result
- **Risk transference**—Sharing the risk with an outside party
- **Risk mitigation**—Reducing or eliminating the risk by applying controls

Risk avoidance is primarily a business decision. You need to look at the risks and benefits to determine how important they are to the viability of the business. Government organizations may not have that option. A local police department, for example, cannot choose to stop policing because of the potential risks. An example of risk avoidance would be if a company moves its data center from Florida to Iowa to avoid the risk of hurricanes.

Risk acceptance is either a business or technology decision. The business needs to know about risks that impact its operations. If the business does not think it is feasible or cost-effective to manage the risk in other ways, it must choose to accept the risk. There are a host of daily technology risks that are accepted by the IT department.

Hopefully, these risks have a low probability of impacting the business. From a practical standpoint, not all risks can be formally accepted by the business. The key is to have a process by which risks are assessed and rated. This rating can be used to determine who has the authority to accept each risk.

Risk transference is taking the consequences of a risk and moving the responsibility to someone else. The most common type of risk transference is the purchase of insurance. For example, you might purchase data breach insurance that would pay your expenses in the event of a data breach. Transferring a risk does not reduce the likelihood that a risk will occur. It removes the financial consequences of that risk.

There is no one list of mitigation strategies. The mitigation strategy depends on the risks, threats, and vulnerabilities facing the organization. A grocery market protecting customer credit cards has a different set of threats than a nuclear power plant. Their mitigation strategies will also differ.

However, all mitigation strategies have a common objective. This objective is prevention. The prevention of risks is less costly than dealing with their aftermath. To be effective, you must have a process in place to identify risks before they threaten the business. Risk management policies promote a series of efforts that allow an organization to be always self-aware of risks. The following is a sampling of those efforts:

- Threat and vulnerability assessments
- Penetration testing
- Monitoring of systems, applications, and networks
- Monitoring of vendor alerts on vulnerabilities
- Active patch management
- Effective vendor management and oversight
- Aggressive risk and security awareness

These methods reduce risk. They also provide a source of new information about the environment. This information can be used to design better solutions and understand limits of the existing environment. You can measure the impact of these effects in reduced risk to data integrity, confidentiality, and availability.

Vulnerability Assessments

Vulnerability assessments are a set of tools used to identify and understand risks to a system, application, or network device. "Vulnerabilities" is a term that identifies weaknesses in the IT infrastructure, or control gaps. If these weaknesses or control gaps are exploited, it could result in an unauthorized access to data.

There are a number of tools and techniques to perform vulnerability assessments. Here are a few examples:

- A penetration test on a firewall
- A scan of the source code of an application
- A scan of an operating system's open ports

It's important to understand that these are tools, not assessments. They are valuable tools identifying potential weaknesses. However, the assessment comes from the analysis of the results. The assessment must address the vulnerability. It must also address the impact to the business and cost of remediation.

Security policies define when and how to perform a vulnerability assessment. The following are typical steps to be followed:

1. Scope the assessment.
2. Identify dependencies.
3. Perform automated testing.
4. Analyze and generate reports.
5. Assign a rating.

You need to scope the assessment and understand the environment prior to any assessment work. This work involves both technical and business aspects. You need to understand what business processes are being used on the internal networks, plus what processes are being used externally through the firewall. Based on this information you can assess the security policies, standards, and procedures. This should provide a comprehensive baseline to compare the assessment results again.

A comprehensive vulnerability assessment looks at the processes end-to-end. This is more effective than just looking at processes on an isolated component. For example, assume your organization has a network of car dealerships across the state. Also assume there is a VPN network available to cross-check inventory and delivery of new cars. You conduct a vulnerability assessment. The assessment finds a control weakness that could prevent a car dealership from receiving new cars. That is a much more meaningful conclusion than, "XYZ server has open ports."

Next, you identify dependent processes and technology that support each primary process. For example, remote access from home may be dependent on the **security token**. A security token is either a hardware device or software code that generates a "token" at logon. A token is usually represented as a series of numbers. A security token is extremely difficult and some say impossible to replicate. When assigned to an individual as part a required logon, the token provides assurance as to who is accessing the network. The home environment and the security token each create a potential vulnerability. The home and token both need to be discussed beyond the firewall.

It is important to understand how information is used. For example, the assessment should address employee access, use, and dissemination of information. Network and application diagrams are good sources of information.

The use of automated testing tools is best practice. They can scan a large volume of vulnerabilities within seconds. The key take-away is that the results must be examined and put into the context of the process and risk.

Automated testing tools call for you to rank threats in order of greatest risk. Classifying risks allows the organization to apply consistent protection across its asset base.

During analysis and reporting, you bring the data together and determine the business impact. Using the BIA results helps align risks to the business. For example, if the assessment includes a process that the business has already declared mission-critical, then the assessment can reflect that fact. This approach helps you assess vulnerabilities that deserve priority attention.

With the vulnerability analysis completed, it's time to assign a rating. A vulnerability assessment rating describes the vulnerability in relation to its potential impact on the organization. The rating typically follows the same path as any risk rating adopted with other risk teams. You typically calculate the exposure, as discussed earlier in the section entitled "Risk Exposure." Based on the risk exposure you assign a value. Then, using a scale, you can assign a rating such as low, moderate, or high, as discussed in Table 11-4.

You do not have to apply a report rating. You could rate the report based on risk exposure. More organizations tend to use the low, moderate, and high ratings. The feeling is that these ratings can more accurately reflect risk by applying professional judgment.

Vulnerability Windows

Vulnerabilities are weaknesses in a system that could result in unauthorized access to data. All software has some vulnerability. The goal is to produce code with the lowest number of vulnerabilities possible. That means designing code well and reducing defect rates. Equally important is closing vulnerabilities quickly once they are discovered. For commercial software, closing vulnerabilities often comes in the form of the vendor issuing a patch or an update release.

At some point vulnerabilities become known. This is called zero day. From that point to the point where a security fix can be distributed is the vulnerability window. For example, assume a new virus is found on a desktop. Your virus scanner and other preventative measures did not detect and prevent the virus. You discovered this vulnerability on March 1. You notified the vendor of the vulnerability on March 2. The vendor issued a new signature file to detect and prevent the virus on March 15. On the same day, you upgraded all the virus scanners with the new signature file. In this example you have a vulnerability window from March 1 to March 15. The zero day is March 1, which is the day the vulnerability became known.

Vulnerability can last for years when the distributed fix does not fix the root cause. When a vulnerability is exposed through a specific type of attack, you create a security fix. Later, however, you may discover that a different type of attack exploited the same vulnerability. It turns out that the original fix did not address the root cause of the vulnerability. The security fix of the first attack only cut off the original avenue of attack. This avenue of attack is also known as an "attack vector." The fix did not resolve the root cause of the vulnerability.

Reducing the vulnerability window is important for an organization. It reduces the possibility of unauthorized data access and disclosure of information. That means working quickly with vendors and in-house development teams to identify fixes.

Patch Management

The objective of a patch management program is to quickly secure against known vulnerabilities. Patches are produced by the vendors of systems, applications, and network devices. The objective to patch quickly seems straightforward. However, implementing patches can be challenging. For a large organization with a diverse set of technologies, there may be a continual flood of vendor patches. The dilemma is that failing to apply the patch leaves a security vulnerability that a hacker can exploit. Applying every patch that comes your way may lead to incompatibilities and outages.

Security policies outline the requirements for patch management. These includes defining how patches should be implemented. The security policies also define how the patches should be tracked.

The key to success in patch management is to have a consistent approach to applying patches. This approach includes:

- Vetting
- Prioritization
- Implementation
- Post-implementation assessment

Vetting the patch is important to understanding the impact to your environment. Not all patches will apply to your environment. You must determine what security issues and software updates are relevant. An organization needs a point person or team responsible for tracking a patch from receipt to implementation. An asset management system helps inventory all system, applications, and network devices. This is used to track what assets have been patched.

Each patch needs to be tested to ensure its authenticity. It also needs to be checked as to whether it is compatible with the organization's applications. Regardless of how well you tested the patch, systems may encounter an incompatibility. When that occurs, you will need to work with the vendor to resolve the issue. You could also find an alternative way to mitigate the vulnerability.

You need to determine the priority of the patch before you implement it. Security policies should provide guidance on how long any security vulnerability can go without being mitigated. The patch team should have clear guidance about how quickly critical patches must be applied. Critical patches are those that mitigate a risk that is actively spreading within the company. Generally, critical patches are applied within hours or days.

Once you assess the priority, you can schedule the patch. You typically schedule patches monthly or quarterly. You make all patches viewable, such as on a Microsoft SharePoint site, by key stakeholders. These stakeholders could be systems, application, and network administrators. This gives them the ability to review and comment on patch deployment. Security policies should identify the notification period before patches are applied.

> ▶ **TIP**
>
> The implementation should include a back-out plan, in the event the patch creates major problems. It's not unusual to test patches on small populations of users before it becomes more widely distributed.

At this stage the patch process is most visible to the organization. You need to assess the security of the patch management application itself periodically. By its nature, the patch management application needs elevated rights. The patch may need to be applied to every system, application, and network device. A breach of the patch management application can be devastating to an organization.

These patch management tools also provide a vital task of discovery. These tools can examine any device on the network and determine its patch level. Some of these tools are used for dual purposes, such as patch and asset management.

Perform a post-implementation assessment to ensure that the patch is working as designed. Patches can have unintended consequences. Problems with patches need to be tracked and the patch backed out, if necessary.

Business Continuity Planning (BCP) Policies

A **business continuity plan (BCP)** policy creates a plan to continue business after a disaster. BCP policies establish the requirement to create and maintain the plan. The BCP policies give guidance for building a plan. These include elements such as key assumptions, accountabilities, and frequency of testing.

BCP policies must clearly define responsibilities for creating and maintaining a BCP plan. The BCP plan identifies responsibilities for its execution. The plan needs to cover the support structure. The support structure includes things like facilities, personnel, equipment, software, data files, vital records, and contractor and service provider relationships. When you must have minimum downtimes of minutes, the level of precision of the BCP planning and documentation must be high. There's no room in BCP planning for individuals to start asking, "What does this mean?"

> **NOTE**
>
> A BCP is about recovering the business, which includes technology components. A disaster recovery plan, which you'll learn about later in this chapter, is exclusively about recovering the technology.

A vulnerability assessment is similar to a risk assessment. It can identify control weaknesses that need to be considered in a BCP plan. The BCP policies and procedures include a review of existing risk assessments. This review determines control weaknesses that could affect recovery of the business. For example, let's assume a key component of your BCP plan is depending heavily on a strategic vendor relationship. This could include executing your mission-critical application from the vendor's facilities for a period of time. A recent vendor risk assessment has identified serious control weaknesses based on poor physical security at their facilities. Well-defined BCP policies would require a gap analysis along with the risk assessment. This approach allows you to assess the vendor weaknesses as part of the BCP planning process. In this example, you may choose to continue this strategic relationship but consider how to mitigate the vendor physical security risk.

As previously mentioned, the BIA is the initial step in the business continuity planning process. The purpose of a BIA is to identify the company's critical processes and assess the impact of a disruptive event. The desired results of the BIA include:

- A list of critical processes and dependencies
- A work flow of processes that include human requirements to recover key assets
- An analysis of legal and regulatory requirements
- A list of critical vendors and support agreements
- An estimate of the maximum allowable downtime

The BIA is the foundation upon which a BCP is developed. The individuals accountable for the BCP should be key stakeholders in the BIA process. These include the auditors who need to assess the adequacy of the planning process. Poor quality results in the BIA will lead to poor quality BCP planning.

Dealing with Loss of Systems, Applications, or Data Availability

The list of critical systems, applications, and user access requirements comes from the BIA. The BIA also includes maximum downtime. This drives the selection of recovery methods and techniques. As the recovery window is shortened, there needs to be more reliance on technology. People can only react so fast.

Speed of reaction can be a problem if a disaster strikes while individuals are most distracted, such as during a long holiday weekend. Key staff may be away for the holidays and out of communication. In that case, you should rely more heavily on automation and well-documented plans that others can execute. In the case of a long holiday weekend, it may take hours to connect with key personnel with a reasonable understanding of the event. At worst, it may take days.

Coping with the loss of systems and technology requires effective planning. It also requires coordination, often with a greater reliance on manual processes. These manual processes need to be well defined. The BCP policies require the same level of care for the information. Assume a clinic faces a disaster. It chooses to capture information by hand. The information captured needs the same level of care as if the information were entered into a computer. The information may be covered by HIPAA and requires the same diligence on security and handling. The BCP plan would detail the access controls needed to protect the information. These controls might include securely storing and transporting the information.

> **NOTE**
>
> An organization that has a BCP has a COOP. The terms may be different but the core objectives are the same. For an organization, the objective is to ensure mission-critical services are provided. The objective is also to minimize financial losses.

Continuity of Operations Plan (COOP)

The **continuity of operations plan (COOP)** provides the detailed procedures and processes needed to coordinate operations during a disaster. The COOP ensures the capabilities exist to continue minimum operations. Federal, state, and local governments have COOPs in place to handle disasters. As an example, during hurricane season the state of Florida creates a central operations center that includes agencies across the state. When a hurricane strikes, the operation center coordinates relief efforts. It also becomes a liaison to the federal government. This united effort ensures essential services are provided to minimize loss of life and damage from the storm.

The central operations center for an organization might be a conference room, hotel facility, or alternate site. The participants in the central operation center would be business and technology leaders across the organization. Joint decisions, prioritization, and coordinated efforts target the restoration of minimal business services. They also aim to reduce financial losses.

One department or government agency needs to be designated by policy as the COOP planning agent. The planning agent's role is to put together the COOP plan. This includes arranging for the support infrastructure and facilitating its execution. The plan also includes keeping contacts and agreements in place to support the COOP efforts. These contacts and agreements might cover things like special facilities for the central operations center, housing for the participants, communications, and transportation for keep participants to the special facilities.

The Federal Emergency Management Agency (FEMA) serves as the federal government's COOP planning agent. FEMA coordinates efforts in case of a national disaster. In private organizations, the IT department often serves as the COOP planning agent. This is because technology pays a significant role in the recovery of a business.

Response and Recovery Time Objectives (RTO) Policies Based on the BIA

The **recovery time objective (RTO)** is how quickly a business process should be recovered. It's important to understand that the RTO relates to the business process. It does not relate to the dependent components, such as the technology. The RTO is the measurement of how quickly individual business processes can be recovered.

The RTO is a natural extension of the BIA. It identifies the maximum allowed downtime for a business process. The maximum allowed downtime is based on the business tolerance for loss. This in turn becomes the RTO. That is why the BCP planner is part of the BIA process. The BCP planner understands the capabilities of the organization to recover from a disaster. An unrealistic RTO set by the business can be caught by the BCP planner during the BIA process. For example, the business may state it requires near real-time recovery of its applications in the event of a disaster. There are few organizations that could achieve that goal. The BCP planner facilitates a candid discussion on the cost of recovery and capabilities of the organization. The BCP planner can also push requirements that increase costs.

 NOTE

The BIA becomes the requirements document for the BCP and RTO. You rarely change the BIA requirements during the BCP process.

The RTO policies often include a discussion of **recovery point objectives (RPOs)**. The RPO is the maximum acceptable level of data loss from the point of the disaster. The RTO and RPO may not be the same value. Let's assume that an organization has a maximum RTO of two days. The same organization can also have a RPO of one week. This is to say, the business can afford a loss of a week's worth of data. This can be acceptable if the business can take the restored data from a week before and reconstruct the lost data from there. An example is financial data that is based on calculations that can be rerun.

The RPO can be shorter than the RTO. In that case, the business is saying the business process can be down longer. However, when the business resumes it needs the data from an earlier point such as the point of outage. It's important to understand that the RPO relates to the data, not to a single RTO.

When you look at the RTO and RPO, the requirements to successfully recover a business emerge. It is these requirements that drive selection of recovery technology and design of the BCP.

Disaster Recovery Plan (DRP) Policies

The **disaster recovery plan (DRP)** is the policies and documentation needed for an organization to recover its IT assets after a disaster. These includes software, data, and hardware. The DRP policies and resulting plan address all aspects of recovering an IT environment. They consider people, processes, and technology.

In many cases, there are laws and regulations outlining the requirements for a DRP. When developing a DRP, it's important to work with the legal department to ensure requirements are being met. For example, the Occupational Safety and Health Administration (OSHA) requires organizations with 10 employees or more to have a DRP. The law in part is meant to protect employees' health and safety during a disaster.

Disaster Declaration Policy

The disaster declaration policy outlines the process by which a BCP and/or DRP is activated. It's not unusual to have an IT disruption event that is localized in the technology infrastructure. If such an event causes major business outages, the BCP plan would be activated. Localized technology outages often impact the business. They may not rise to the level of a disaster. Still, in those cases, the DRP portion of the BCP plan would be activated. It's important to note that technology outages occur often. A server goes down or a file critical file is deleted. This can disable a vital application in a smaller organization. In a large organization, many of these events occur each month. They are considered routine and would not trigger a DRP.

The disaster declaration policy defines the roles and responsibilities for assessing and declaring a disaster. Once a DRP is activated, a number of processes and capabilities are launched. You can handle many of these activities, such as notification to staff, through automated systems. The activation of a DRP for a large, complex organization costs thousands of dollars. In this case, who can declare a disaster is tightly controlled. Once the plans are activated, you want the process to be as automatic as possible. It should be second nature for those involved.

Once a disaster is declared it's very hard to stop its early ramp-up stages. These might include notifying key leaders and staging recovery capability. The process to declare the disaster is contained in the disaster declaration policy. The following is a sampling of activations also included in this plan:

- Emergency notification of personnel, stakeholders, and strategic vendors
- Alternative site activation
- Activation of the emergency control center
- Transport and housing arrangements
- Release of pre-positioned assets

Many of these activities will overlap with BCP activities. The difference is that they focus on the recovery of the IT infrastructure as opposed to the business.

Assessment of the Severity of the Disaster and Potential Downtime

Disasters are not all alike. There's a difference between losing your entire data center to a flood and having a contained fire disable a few dozen servers. Both would activate a DRP. In the case of the fire, however, once the smoke clears and all the safety checks are performed, the disaster would be contained.

Assessment of the severity occurs throughout the life of a disaster. It starts with the disaster declaration and is continually updated. You forward the information to the emergency control center. Here it's included in the decision-making process. Performing this continued assessment off the potential downtime is important. It ensures the right resources are being allocated to the problem. There are many critical business decisions during a disaster that rely on the assessment of the severity of the problem. Here's a small sampling:

- Allocation of resources
- Notification to customers
- Assessment of financial losses and costs

Allocation of resources gets the right people to focus on the right problem. Consider a major outage of a vital vendor application. Your IT team estimates the outage for an hour or so. Then you reassess and estimate the potential downtime to be several days. The leadership in the emergency control center may be more patient in the first case. In the second case, the leadership may be on the phone with the vendor and begin flying in additional resources.

Having realistic estimates of downtime is important for customer relations. Overly optimistic recovery estimates often lead to loss of credibility. Airport travelers may be told they face a flight delay of 20 minutes. The plane, however, finally leaves three hours later. This can cause a big public relations problem.

The best professional judgment on potential downtime is expected in a DRP. Unrealistic estimates can over-complicate and undermine the recovery process. It's important that a complete history and basis for the estimates is kept throughout the recovery process. You can use this information in post-disaster assessments to improve the process.

Assessments during a disaster are needed to determine financial losses and costs. An extended outage will require the infusion of capital to sustain an organization throughout the disaster. The amount of capital required will depend on the duration of the outage. Borrowing money can be expensive. Accurately estimating potential downtime is important to controlling those costs.

Dealing with Natural Disasters, Man-Made Disasters, and Catastrophic Loss

Certain regions often face natural disasters, such as hurricanes, tornadoes, earthquakes, severe snowstorms, and volcanic eruptions. Expected natural disasters can be incorporated into the BCP and DRP planning process. Companies in a region often share planning efforts to cope with potential natural disasters. In this case, local officials often pull organizations together to coordinate planning efforts. A natural disaster, by definition, affects more than one organization. Coordinating efforts at a regional level is more efficient.

Man-made disasters are much harder to plan for. These might include plane crashes, train derailments, nuclear power plant problems, power failures, chemical spills, and gas line explosions. These types of disasters may not be spelled out explicitly in the plan. However, recovery plans are expected to deal with such disasters.

Whether disasters are natural or man-made, dealing with them effectively is based on capability. Your plans may outline a way to recover if you lose a data center. If so, then you have the capability to manage through certain types of disasters. In the end, it doesn't matter if the data center was disabled by a flood or a gas line explosion. In both cases, the capability to recover the data center in a new location allows the business to resume.

A well-defined DRP deals with a wide variety of disasters. It can include, for example, real-time recovery of files through mirroring. It can also include redundant communications capabilities obtained through multiple service providers.

Disaster Recovery Procedures for Mission-Critical System, Application, or Data Functionality and Recovery

Business relies on an end-to-end process working. From a technology perspective this means that the system, application, and data must all be in place and working. If any one of these components is not recovered or is out of alignment, the process fails. Disaster recovery policies define what to back up, how often, and how to recover data during a disaster. There are unique requirements for backup and recovery for systems, applications, and data.

Systems and applications in some ways are easier to recover. They change less frequently and often rely on software from vendors. Having multiple sources to recover systems and application makes recovery easier. The customization for systems and applications is a different story. These customization settings are commonly referred to as "configuration." They must also be captured and available during a recovery.

The configuration for operating systems and databases includes security controls. The DRP needs to ensure these controls are not disabled during a disaster. A subset of the DRP is a security plan that outlines how security controls will be monitored and maintained during a disaster. The plan may restrict access to key staff to improve performance and stability. Approval for access may have to go through the emergency control center. It may require CISO approval. The key point is that security planning and execution during a disaster is an important consideration when building a DRP.

Recovery of mission-critical data can be more challenging than recovery of systems and applications. The value of data is often time-dependent. Data backups taken at the point of the disaster are typically more valuable than data backups from the prior month. The BIA process and data classification effort identifies the data that must be recovered. The amount of mission-critical data depends on the organization and industry. Mission-critical data should represent a small portion of the total population, such as less than 15 percent. When the percentage is exceedingly small or large, it's a flag to challenge that percentage. The challenge may reveal weaknesses in the current controls, such as the way backups are taken. Backups should be able to isolate mission-critical data. It's not uncommon for an error in the backup process to cause you to have to restore large volumes of data so the mission-critical data is restored. This can cause unnecessary delays.

RTO Policies Based on Disaster Scenario

RTO varies depending on the disaster scenario. The type of disaster drives the business timeline and customer urgency. This is especially true for natural disasters, in which customer priorities dramatically shift to the short-term. Those businesses that are considered non-essential will have less pressure to resume operations quickly.

Let's assume a hurricane is cutting across Florida. You work for a chain of movie theaters. It's unlikely local residents are thinking of going out to see a movie. The movie theater's ticket system is probably down, along with many business systems in the area. In this scenario, the focus would shift to the safety of the theater workers. During the aftermath, theater operations could resume with a manual ticket process. Customers would be more understanding, given the nature of the disaster.

Conversely, there is more competitive pressure on an organization that experiences a disaster that's limited to the organization. There will be a different kind of pressure to retain customers and reduce financial losses. In this scenario, customer priorities and expectations will not change. They will expect business as usual. The organization may feel pressure from regulators, depending on the industry. For example, banks that have closed their doors for more than a limited number of consecutive days must explain the action to regulators.

Although all scenarios cannot be detailed or anticipated, they can be divided into categories that help plan RTOs. The categories should consider probability and impact. They are generally divided between natural and man-made disasters, based on regional history.

Best Practices for Risk Management Policies

Risk management policies provide the framework for assessing risk across data classification and BCP activities. The resulting risk assessment looks at how risk is managed end to end. This means that the risk assessment can examine how data classification affects data handling and the BIA process. It can also identify control gaps between the BIA and BCP processes.

Risk management policies identify the criteria and content of assessments. Risk management requirements may vary by industry and regulatory standards. For example, NIST 800-34 outlines a specific approach to continuity planning. This approach would be incorporated in the following disaster plans in the risk management policies for assessment:

- **Business continuity plan (BCP)**—Plan to sustain essential business operations for the duration of the disaster
- **Business recovery (or resumption) plan (BRP)**—Plan to recover business operations immediately following a disaster
- **Continuity of operations plan (COOP)**—Plan to support strategic functions for the duration of the disaster
- **Continuity of support plan/IT contingency plan**—Plan to recover major systems and applications
- **Crisis communications plan**—Plan for communicating information to personnel and the public
- **Cyberincident response plan**—Plan to detect and respond to cyberincidents
- **Disaster recovery plan (DRP)**—Plan to recover facility at an alternate site
- **Occupant emergency plan (OEP)**—Plan to minimize loss of life or injury and protect property from a physical threat

The take-away is that there is no one common approach to defining risk and controls within an organization. Some organizations may adopt the NIST 800-34. Others may use ISO. Many of the same elements are there but repackaged in a different form. Regardless of what the plan is called, it's important that the risk management policies promote a thorough understanding of the business. They should include a definition of its risks and the ability to recover in the event of a disaster.

Case Studies and Examples of Risk Management Policies

The following case studies and examples examine the implementation of several risk-management-related policies. The case studies focus on the risks and policies outlined in this chapter. Risk management policies represent a broad category of risks. These case studies and examples focus on a single policy group, such as disaster recovery, and represent successful implementations.

Private Sector Case Example

On December 27, 2006, Microsoft learned of a vulnerability in the Windows operating system. It was a Windows Meta File (WMF) vulnerability that allowed code to be executed on an infected machine without the machine user's knowledge. Microsoft immediately started working on a patch. Microsoft had planned to release the patch in January as part of its regular monthly security updates. After receiving feedback from the security community, the company released the patch on January 5, 2007. This was 10 days after the vulnerability was discovered.

That 10-day period is an example of a vulnerability window. It was the time in which no vendor solution was available to mitigate the risk.

This is an example of patch management policy working. It is a fair assumption that individuals responsible for patch management at organizations were monitoring events.

Once the vulnerability was known, they reached out to their vendor, Microsoft. The monitoring of such an emerging industry threat would be part of a well-defined patch management policy.

Public Sector Case Example

The University of Texas posted a data classification standard on its Web site. The standard classified data as Category I, II, and III. Category I was defined as data that is protected by law or university regulations. Some of the examples cited were HIPAA, the Sarbanes-Oxley (SOX) Act, and the Gramm-Leach-Bliley Act (GLBA). Category II was defined as other data needing to be protected. Examples cited were e-mail, date of birth, and salary. Category III was defined as data having no requirements for confidentiality, integrity, and availability. These three requirements defined the categories to which the university's data was assigned. The university cited security policies as the authority for the standard.

This is an example of a customized data classification scheme. The university tailored the scheme based on a review of critical data. The university determined that three classification levels were sufficient to meet regulatory requirements. In this case, the university called the data classification a standard. It could as easily have been labeled a policy. In either case, it clearly defined classification levels. It defined roles and responsibilities. It also defined scenarios, such as handling data on a professor's blog. It was a good example of how data assessment and regulatory compliance can come together to create a data classification standard.

Critical Infrastructure Case Study

An electric company serving over 170,000 consumers in metro Atlanta counties had business concerns. These concerns were related to the reliability of the local area network (LAN)/wide area network (WAN). To improve customer support, the company began to address its WAN failure. They created a solution that leveraged two different Internet service providers (ISPs). They also implemented a mirrored server in a disaster recovery site. The implementation was successful in improving customer support and providing a total failover solution.

This case study is a good example of risk assessments being leveraged in the BCP planning process. It's clear from the case study that there was a customer support issue related to the ISP. At some point there was an assessment that uncovered the ISP connection as a weakness. That assessment was also fed into the BCP planning process. As a result, the company found a solution that leverages two ISPs for redundancy. This provided failover disaster recovery capability while solving the redundancy problem. Leveraging risk assessments should be part of the BCP policies.

The case study is also an example of BIA. The company mirrored mission-critical data in a recovery site. To achieve this, the company had to have determined that those business processes were most critical. Additionally, the case study made a point of the failover capability. This addresses the RTO component that comes from a BIA. The business determined its critical system and felt its recovery time needed to be real-time through mirrored servers.

CHAPTER SUMMARY

We learned in this chapter how you can use data classification to identify critical data and protect it. The chapter reviewed military and business classification schemes. The chapter examined how these schemes apply to data handling policies. It examined the need to have policies govern data at rest and in transit. The chapter also discussed how data classification helps reduce business risks.

We expanded our discussion to business continuity planning. The chapter discussed key components of the BCP planning process and the importance of BIA in that process. The chapter also reviewed key plans that support an organization during a disaster, such as BCPs, COOPs, DRPs. Finally, the chapter looked at best practices for risk management policies.

KEY CONCEPTS AND TERMS

Authorization	Declassification	Secret
Automatic declassification	Disaster recovery plan (DRP)	Security token
Business continuity plan (BCP)	Highly sensitive classification	Sensitive but unclassified
Business impact analysis (BIA)	Internal classification	Sensitive classification
Classification	Mandatory declassification	Systematic declassification
Confidential	Public classification	Top Secret
Continuity of operation plan (COOP)	Recovery time objective (RTO)	Unclassified
	Recovery point objectives (RPOs)	

CHAPTER 11 ASSESSMENT

1. Which of the following is not a common need for most organizations to classify data?

   A. Protect information
   B. Retain information
   C. Sell information
   D. Recover information

2. Authorization is the process used to prove the identity of the person accessing systems, applications, and data.

   A. True
   B. False

3. You need to retain data for what major reasons?

   A. Legal obligation
   B. Needs of the business
   C. For recovery
   D. A and B
   E. All of the above

4. What qualities should the data owner possess?

   A. Is in a senior position within the business
   B. Understands the data operations of the business
   C. Understands the importance and value of the information to the business
   D. Understand the ramifications of inaccurate data or unauthorized access
   E. All of the above

5. In all businesses you will always have data that needs to be protected.

   A. True
   B. False

6. Risk exposure is best-guess professional judgment using a qualitative technique.

   A. True
   B. False

7. The lowest federal government data classification rating for classified material is _____.

8. Federal agencies can customize their own data classification scheme.

   A. True
   B. False

9. A BIA identifies which of the following?

   A. Critical business processes
   B. Minimum downtime
   C. Process dependencies
   D. All of the above

10. A BIA is not required when creating a BCP.

    A. True
    B. False

11. What does RTO stand for?

    A. Restoration team objectives
    B. Recovery timeline owner
    C. Restoration time objective
    D. Recovery time objective

12. A man-made disaster is easier to plan for than a natural disaster.

    A. True
    B. False

13. Data in transit refers to what type of data?

    A. Data backup tapes being moved to a recovery facility
    B. Data on your USB drive
    C. Data traversing a network
    D. Data being stored for later transmission

14. Encryption protects data at rest from all type of breaches.

    A. True
    B. False

Incident Response Team (IRT) Policies

N O MATTER HOW WELL YOUR DATA is protected, eventually there will be an unauthorized breach of security. It could be the result of a human error. It could be the result of a configuration error. It could be the result of an operating system vulnerability or a host of problems outside your control. No information security program is perfect. What is certain is that at some point, most organizations will have to respond to a security incident. The speed and effectiveness of the response will limit the damage and reduce any losses. When an incident occurs, an organization needs to respond quickly through a well-thought-out process. An effective response can control the costs and consequences resulting from the incident.

Well-prepared organizations create an incident response team (IRT). This team and its supporting policies ensure that an incident is quickly identified and contained. It's also the IRT's responsibility to perform a careful analysis of the cause of the incident. Understanding the nature of an incident can help prevent future attacks. An IRT is the first responder to major security incidents within an organization. It's not unusual for an attack to be active when the team responds. To ensure the IRT members are effective at what they do, the organization needs to provide the policies, tools, and training necessary for their success.

In this chapter, we define an incident and related policies. We discuss how to create an IRT. We discuss various roles and responsibilities within an IRT. We examine key activities that are performed during an incident. We also discuss specific policies and procedures ranging from reporting and containing to analyzing an incident. Finally, the chapter reviews best practices and explores several case studies.

Chapter 12 Topics

This chapter covers the following topics and concepts:

- What an incident response policy is
- How to classify incidents
- What a response team charter is
- Who makes up an incident response team (IRT)
- Who is responsible for actions during an incident
- Which procedures must be followed to respond to an incident
- What best practices to follow for incident response policies
- What some case studies and examples of incident response policies are

Chapter 12 Goals

When you complete this chapter, you will be able to:

- Explain the purpose of an incident response policy
- Define what an incident is
- Explain various incident classification methods
- Understand key components of an IRT charter
- Describe IRT member roles and responsibilities
- Understand major procedures for responding to an incident
- Explain best practices for incident response
- Apply knowledge learned in case studies to real-world issues

Incident Response Policy

An **incident response team (IRT)** is a specialized group of people whose purpose is to respond to major incidents. The IRT is typically a cross-functional team. This means the people on the team have different skills. They are pulled together in a coordinated effort. In many organizations, the IRT is formed to respond to major incidents only. Minor incidents are often managed as part of normal operations. When the team is called together, the IRT is said to be "activated."

It would not be practical to activate the IRT for minor incidents. Policy infractions, for example, are handled by an individual's manager. Let's say an employee shares his or her password with a second employee. This might occur when that second employee has been approved but is waiting for access to be granted. An incident report may be required in this case but the IRT would not be activated.

The incident response policy must be clear and concise to prevent ambiguity in the response process. The policy must define what an incident is versus an infraction. The policy must define the criteria for activating the IRT. There should be a centralized incident notification process so that appropriate individuals are aware of incidents. These individuals can then make a determination whether to declare a disaster. Most important, the policy and related processes must enable the IRT to respond to incidents quickly. From the point an incident is detected to the point the IRT is activated, as little time should pass as possible. Organizations cannot afford to be slow to respond to an active attack.

There are many types of security incidents. When to declare an incident and activate an IRT depends on the organization's policy. For the purposes of this chapter, our discussion focuses on major information security breaches. Major breaches can include incidents such as systems breached from the outside, internal fraud, or a denial of service attack.

What Is an Incident?

An **incident** is any event that violates an organization's security policies. An incident may disrupt normal operations of an application, system, or network. An incident may result in a reduction in the quality of service. An incident may also result in unauthorized access to or modification of data.

Examples of security incidents include:

- Unauthorized access to any computer system
- Deliberately causing a server to crash
- Copying customer information from a database
- Unauthorized use of computer systems for gaming

It is important that a formal incident definition is included in the incident response policy. This definition is then used to support processes for declaring an incident and activating the IRT.

Incident Classification

The classification of incidents is part of the security policy. The classification approach can be documented as an incident response policy or a standard. By definition, if you have an incident, a weakness in your security has been exploited. By classifying the incident you can better understand the threat and the weakness. Knowing the type of attack can help you determine how to respond to stop the damage. It can also help you analyze the control weaknesses in your environment. This helps reduce the risk of future attacks. There's no one standard approach to follow in classifying incidents. However, an industry often adopts similar approaches among companies. The key point is to select an approach that meets your legal and regulatory obligations. This should be an approach that provides sufficient detail to analyze an incident. This analysis will help you improve weaknesses that lead to incidents.

As an example, Visa requires its merchants to report security incidents involving cardholder data. This report should be issued whenever a breach is detected that violates the Payment Card Industry Data Security Standard (PCI DSS). Visa classifies incidents into the following categories:

- **Malicious code attacks**—A **malicious code attack** is defined as code, such as viruses, worms, Trojan horses, and scripts, used to gain access to systems, applications, and data.
- **Denial of service (DoS)**—A DoS attack is an incident that causes networks and/or computers to cease operating effectively.
- **Unauthorized access/theft**—This refers to unauthorized use of credentials or breaching of security to gain access.
- **Network reconnaissance probe**—This is a software tool that runs a series of network commands to determine security weaknesses.

Another example is the federal government. Under the Federal Information Security Management Act (FISMA), the government uses the National Institute of Standards and Technology (NIST) Special Publication 800-61. This publication classifies incidents into the following events on a system or network:

- **Malicious code**—Code that rapidly infects other machines
- **Denial of service**—An attacker crafting packets to cause networks and/or computers to crash
- **Unauthorized access**—An exploit to gain access
- **Inappropriate usage**—Unacceptable use of the computer, such as copying illegal software or inappropriate statements in e-mail

In both the Visa and FISMA approaches, incidents are classified within categories that help assess the threat level. It's not uncommon to find similarity among many incident classification approaches. They all share the goal of providing a common language to describe security incidents.

The incident classification is also used to assess the severity of the incident. That is, is an incident minor or major? Based on this severity you determine whether the IRT should be activated. What is considered a major incident versus a minor one depends on the organization's view of risk. Major incidents are generally viewed as incidents that have significant impact on the organization. The impact can be measured in several ways. It might be financial. It may be measured with regard to disruption of service or legal liability. From a practical standpoint, many major incidents are easier than minor incidents to identify. They might cause effects such as a significant number of users unable to process transactions or unauthorized access to millions of customers' personal data. Any incident related to the protection of human life is considered a major incident. What is considered a minor incident depends on how much risk the organization is willing to accept.

> **FYI**
>
> Incidents can turn into court cases. It's important that the actions of the IRT be clear and show reasonable due care. **Due care** refers to the effort made to avoid harm to another party. It's a legal term that essentially refers to the level of care that a person would reasonably be expected to exercise under particular circumstances. All documents produced during an incident should be written in a straightforward, professional manner.

The Response Team Charter

Typically, organizations require a charter before an IRT can be formed. A charter is an organizational document that outlines the mission, goals, and authority of a team or committee. It's important that legal review the IRT charter for any language that might create a liability. Always assume an outside party may eventually view the charter.

The first step in writing a charter is to determine the type of IRT model to adopt. This part of the charter determines the authority, approach, and deliverable of the IRT. There several types of IRT models:

- **IRT provides on-site response**—The IRT has full authority to contain the breach.
- **IRT acts in a support role**—The IRT provides technical assistance to local teams on how to contain the breach.
- **IRT acts in a coordination role**—The IRT coordinates among several local teams on how to contain the breach.

Many IRTs provide on-site response. In this case, the IRT is given complete authority to contain the threat. This typically means an IRT member is on-site with hands on the keyboard providing technical response. This IRT model requires its members to have full authority to direct local resources. The IRT members make key decisions in consultation with upper management. The IRT members may be required to have a specific local expert execute a task. However, the expert executes the task under the direction of the IRT member.

When the IRT is in a support role, its members become a resource for the local team. The local team has the responsibility to respond to an incident leveraging the IRT skills. This model is useful in limited circumstances where the local site team has appropriate skills to respond to an incident. This model may also be viable when the application or system is very specialized. In this case, the local team is better equipped to deal with the incident.

When the central IRT is in a coordination role, it becomes a facilitator among parties involved in the incident response. This model is useful when the response covers multiple geographical regions. In that case you might have to coordinate with IRTs in each location. In this model, the central IRT functions as the lead to facilitate the immediate response. The central IRT also coordinates the root cause analysis.

Once you determine the type of IRT model you'll use, you need to construct the actual charter. This includes setting specific goals. The goals must be simple and realistic. Overly ambitious goals create both a credibility and execution problem. It's important during an incident that the team focuses on specific achievable goals. These goals can include response times to incidents and level of cost containment. These goals will be used to create policies and processes and influence the selection of tools. For example, if the charter requires an on-site response in 30 minutes or less, the goal will drive a certain staffing level.

The structure of the charter document itself is simple and concise. A typical charter includes the following sections:

- **Executive summary**—Provides background of incident response and the importance it has to the organization. This section defines why the IRT exists and the type of incidents it handles.

- **Mission statement**—Defines the overall goals of the IRT. It also describes what the IRT is responsible for achieving. The mission statement is used to gauge the effectiveness of the IRT.

- **Incident declaration**—Defines an incident. It also describes how an incident is declared. This section becomes the basis for creating a process to activate the IRT team.

- **Organizational structure**—Documents how the IRT is aligned within the organization. It also indicates how the members are managed during an incident.

- **Role and responsibilities**—Describes the purpose and types of activities for each IRT member. This is important in the selection of the right team members. It's essential to remember that you need to fill these roles with capable individuals.

- **Information flow**—Defines how information will be disseminated. It establishes the central team responsible for collecting, analyzing, and communicating incident information to the upper levels of management. This insures the IRT is accountable for being the central point of contact.

- **Methods**—Defines the manner in which the goals will be achieved. This may include a list of services the IRT team will provide.

- **Authority and reporting**—Describes what authority the team has. This section defines the source of the IRT's authority. For example, the authority can be assigned by upper management in response to specific regulatory requirements.

A charter would not contain a detailed line budget. Funding should be included in the department budget as an annual expense. This avoids having to rewrite the charter every time there are changes in the budget.

Incident Response Team Members

The IRT members typically represent a cross-functional team. These team members are from several departments and bring together multiple disciplines. Being part of this designated team allows members to coordinate their efforts. They can also train together on how to respond to an incident. The team can offer a centralized, full-time service depending on the size of the organization and volume of incidents.

The IRT is comprised of a core team supplemented with specialties, when needed. These specialties are brought in based on the type of incident. Usually, full-time IRT departments exist to support very large organizations and the government.

Most organizations activate the IRT when a major incident occurs. In this case, the management of the process comes out of the information security team. Members outside the security team have normal job responsibilities. In the event of an incident, the team is pulled together to deal with the immediate threat. Once the threat is stopped, the team's mission shifts to incident analysis. This analysis determines the cause of the incident and formulates recommendations. Once the final report on the incident is issued the team is disbanded.

The IRT usually includes members of the information security team along with representatives from other functional areas. Common IRT members include:

- **Information technology subject matter experts (SMEs)**—The **information technology subject matter experts** have intimate knowledge of the systems and configurations. These individuals are typically developers and system and network administrators. They have the technical skills to make critical recommendation on how to stop an attack. The SMEs chosen for each incident response effort will vary depending upon the type of incident and affected system(s).

- **Information security representative**—The **information security representative** provides risk management and analytical skills. He or she may also have specialized forensic skills needed to collect and analyze evidence.

- **Human resources (HR) representative**—The **human resources representative** provides skills on how to deal with employees. Breaches do not always come from outside attackers. When internal employees are involved, the HR representative can advise the team on proper methods of communicating and dealing with the employees. They are experts on HR policies and disciplinary proceedings or employee counseling.

- **Legal representative**—The **legal representative** has an understanding of laws and regulatory compliance. This person can be a valuable advisor in ensuring compliance. His or her work will involve reviewing the incident response plans, policies, and procedures. During an incident the legal representative can help facilitate communication with law enforcement. This person can examine the ramifications of decisions. The representative can also provide expert guidance on legal issues, such as the notification of employees or customers affected by a breach.

> **NOTE**
>
> Many organizations choose to route all communication with law enforcement agencies through their legal counsel. If an incident involving criminal conduct is mishandled, the organization can conceivably be liable. It's important that all action be documented. This will help the company be seen as acting in good faith.

Legal representatives can also advise IRT members how to conduct themselves to preserve attorney-client privilege. When investigations are conducted by a legal representative as part of his or her duties to an organization, the communication is considered confidential and not subject to certain disclosure.

- **Public relations (PR) representative**—The **public relations representative** can advise on how to communicate with the public and customers who might be impacted by the incident. This is valuable to ensure that accurate information gets out and damaging misconceptions are prevented.

- **Business continuity representative**—The **business continuity representative** understands the organization's capability to restore the system, application, network, or data. This individual also has access to call lists needed to contact anyone in the organization during off hours.

- **Data owner**—The data owner understands the data and the business. As data owner, he or she understands how the data should be handled. The data owner understands the control environment. Because data owners are business leaders they also understand the data's impact to the business.

- **Management**— Management plays a key decision-making role. Management approves the response policy, charter, budget, and staffing. Management also makes the decision to turn to law enforcement and outside agencies. Ultimately, management is held accountable for the outcome of the incident response effort.

"Emergency services" is a broad category related to any outside agency. These agencies might include police, fire, and state and federal law enforcement. They bring government authority. They can also be useful in tracking down the identity of the hacker. It is rare that emergency services are part of the IRT core team. However, it does occur when the sensitivity of the breach requires specialized support. This can happen when there is a breach of a government or financial services firm that requires law enforcement support. More often, emergency services are simply coordinated through the IRT. As can be seen from this list, the IRT team has a vast array of skills available. You can add additional members as needed to deal with an incident. The team's effectiveness will be determined by how quickly a coordinated and focused effort can be deployed.

Responsibilities During an Incident

The IRT is the single point of contact during an incident. It provides management with information as to what has occurred and what actions are being taken. It serves as the repository for all related incident information. Keeping a repository is an important team function to determine the root cause of the incident.

During an incident a core team is formed to respond to the threat. Figure 12-1 depicts a typical IRT core team. Notice that upper management is not considered part of the core team. Instead, upper management is a consumer of the results of the core IRT. Upper management is a critical decision-maker in responding to an incident.

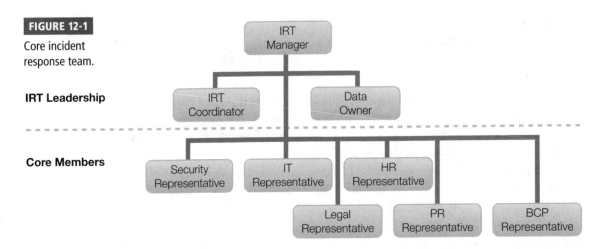

FIGURE 12-1

Core incident response team.

Users on the Front Line

It's the responsibility of all users in an organization to support the efforts of the IRT. When the IRT responds to an incident, time is of the essence. It's important that the users on the front line provide quick response to requests for information. Such requests may include preserving evidence. The users may be requested to document events and assist in gathering evidence.

The users on the front line also play an important role in detecting an incident. You increase the likelihood that incidents are detected early when an alert user reports suspicious activity.

System Administrators

The system administrator may be a core member of the IRT team. System administrators help analyze the threat and recommend immediate response. These individuals know the technology and technical infrastructure. They know how it's been customized. They are in a good position to assist with the response.

System administrators have the authority to make critical changes to repel an attack. The term system administrator can mean system, application, and network administrator. These individuals have the skills to identity anomalies to configuration and ability to respond. For example, they can disconnect devices from the network.

System administrators would also be critical to recovery of the environment. Administrators typically perform reconstruction. This is an important task that often needs to be performed to resume operations.

Information Security Personnel

The information security team has several roles during an incident. Team members may be the first to recognize the security breach. This is because the security team monitors the environment for signs of security breaches, such as intrusion detection alerts.

In addition, information security staff members understand the layers of security. They understand the points of potential breach.

The incident response process is typically designed and managed by information security personnel. Security personal are either directly or indirectly involved in most IRT activities. These activities include:

- Discovery
- IRT activation
- Containment
- Analysis and threat response
- Incident classification
- Forensics
- Clean-up and recovery
- Post-event activities

The information security team often provides management and oversight of an incident response. They are facilitators and subject matter experts on security and risk. As such, they may or may not be the individuals tasked with performing the activities listed above. In some organizations, these functions are performed by information security personnel. The security team is often responsible only for ensuring the activity occurs. For example, forensic investigations demand a highly specialized skill set. They require significant training and special tools. Forensic investigations can include the basic review of a desktop for inappropriate content. They can also involve a much deeper review of databases, firewalls, and network devices. Many organizations do not have the skills and tools to do a forensic review. Some organizations have only basic capabilities. Information security personnel often arrange for a forensic review through an outside firm.

Security personnel also ensure reviews are conducted after an incident to ensure lessons are learned and adopted. The role information security personnel most often perform is writing the final incident report to management. This role makes sense because in their oversight role they see all the issues. They track the timeline of the event. They can see the big picture and combine all the incident issues into a single document.

Management

Management provides authority and support for the IRT's efforts. When parts of the organization are not supporting or reacting quickly enough, it is management's responsibility to remove barriers.

Management also makes key decisions on how to resolve the incident. It's important to remember that the IRT recommends and management approves. If a purely technical decision needs to be made, the IRT operates independently. But a decision that significantly affects the business should be escalated to management, if possible. Management should empower the IRT with sufficient authority to take drastic action quickly when time is critical.

One of the early decisions during an active incident is whether to "pursue" or "protect." In other words, does the organization want to allow the breach to continue for a period of time? This might be done so the attacker's identity can be traced and evidence of activity gathered. Such evidence would be important to successful prosecution of the attacker. Alternatively, the organization can choose to immediately stop the attack. This approach to "protect" the network means the business could recover more quickly, but the attacker might not be caught and might try again.

The determination to "pursue" or "protect" is a business decision that management must make. This decision affects the response to the attack. Management must make other decisions during an incident, such as approving additional resources.

Support Services

This is a broad category that refers to any team that supports the organization's IT and business processes. The help desk, for example, would be a support services team.

During an incident the help desk may be in direct contact with customers who are being impacted by the attack. The help desk, at that point, becomes a channel of information on the incident. It's vital that the help desk provide a script of key talking points during an incident. Such a script can be very short and only refer questions to another area. Or the script can give more detail with the intent of keeping the public informed. These scripts should be developed and distributed by the PR department.

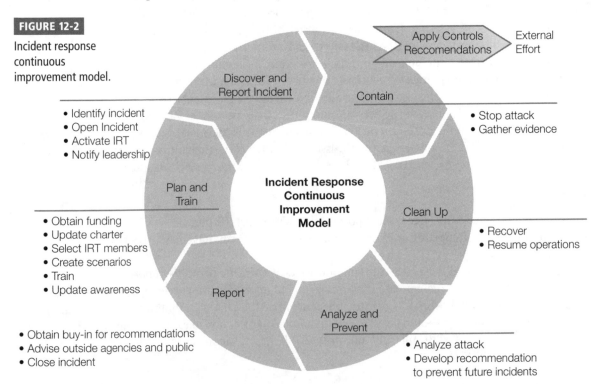

FIGURE 12-2

Incident response continuous improvement model.

Discover and Report Incident
- Identify incident
- Open Incident
- Activate IRT
- Notify leadership

Apply Controls Reccomendations — External Effort

Contain
- Stop attack
- Gather evidence

Plan and Train
- Obtain funding
- Update charter
- Select IRT members
- Create scenarios
- Train
- Update awareness

Incident Response Continuous Improvement Model

Clean Up
- Recover
- Resume operations

Report
- Obtain buy-in for recommendations
- Advise outside agencies and public
- Close incident

Analyze and Prevent
- Analyze attack
- Develop recommendation to prevent future incidents

Other Key Roles

The **IRT manager** is the team lead. This individual makes all the final calls on how to respond to an incident. He or she is the interface with management. The IRT manager must be proactive in letting management know the status of the incident and what steps are being taken. The IRT manager makes clear what decisions management needs to make. This person also advises management of the ramifications of not making a decision.

The **IRT coordinator** role is to keep track of all the activity during an incident. This person acts as the official scribe of the team. All activity flows through the IRT coordinator, who maintains the official records of the team. It's a critical position because what is recorded becomes the basis for the reconstruction of the event to determine a long-term response.

Procedures for Incident Response

There are a number of key steps necessary to effectively handle an incident. These steps are outlined in the incident response procedures.

Figure 12-2 depicts the basic steps of an incident response procedure. Notice the model is built as a continuous improvement model. This means that as lessons are learned from incidents they are used to improve the incident response program itself. Notice that the controls in place before the incident are improved by people outside the IRT. Implementation of control recommendations is typically not handled by the IRT members. Each of the steps in Figure 12-2 is discussed in this section of the chapter. The important takeaway is that incident response is not a one-time process. It takes significant time and effort to create and support an IRT. The organization's commitment and appropriate delegation of authority is essential to responding to incidents quickly and effectively.

Discovering an Incident

Discovering an incident quickly is a complex undertaking. It requires a solid understanding of normal operations. It also requires continuous monitoring for anomalies. It requires that alert employees report unusual events that can be indicators of an incident. An enterprise awareness effort must teach employees how to report suspicious activity.

The signs of an incident can be obvious or subtle. The number of possible signs is enormous. The following is a small sampling:

- Suspicious activity of a coworker is noticed, and accounts within the department's control do not balance.
- An intrusion detection sensor alerts that a buffer overflow occurred.
- The antivirus software alerts infection across multiple machines.
- Users complain of slow access.
- The system administrator sees a filename with unusual characters.
- The system administrator sees an unknown local account on a server.
- The logs on a server are found to have been deleted.
- Logs indicate multiple failed logon attempts.

These signs do not necessarily mean that an incident has occurred. However, each needs to be investigated to make sure there has been no breach. Some incidents are easy to detect. On the other hand, small, unexplained signs may only hint that an incident has occurred. Such a small sign might be a configuration file that has been changed. A well-trained and capable staff is necessary to evaluate the signs of an incident.

Reporting an Incident

It's important to establish clear procedures for reporting incidents. This includes methods of collecting, analyzing, and reporting data. When you receive a report of an incident, classify it. This process is often called "triage." Triage is an essential part of the incident response process. The triage process creates an immediate snapshot of the current situation. This is used to assess the severity of the threat. When the incident reaches a certain severity, the IRT is activated. This is the official declaration of an incident.

It's important to note that many security incidents are isolated occurrences, such as computer viruses. These are easily handled with well-established procedures. When an incident is reported, the triage process must be staffed with well-trained individuals who can classify the incident and its severity. A sample severity classification is as follows:

- **Severity 4**—A small number of system probes or scans detected. Or an isolated instance of a virus. Event handled by automated controls. No unauthorized activity detected.

- **Severity 3**—Significant numbers of system probes or scans detected. Or widespread virus activity detected. Event requires manual intervention. No unauthorized activity detected.

- **Severity 2**—A DoS attack detected, with limited impact disruption on operations. Automated controls failed to prevent the event. No unauthorized activity detected.

- **Severity 1**—A successful penetration or DoS attack detected with significant disruption of operations. Or unauthorized activity detected.

There's no one standard approach to assessing the severity of a reported incident. You may choose to allow the existing procedures to handle severity 3 and 4. The IRT may be activated to handle severity 1 and 2. You want to have a clear definition of terms. Severity 1 uses the term "significant interruption of operations." That definition might vary among organizations. You do not want to interpret definitions so strictly that the definitions lose common sense. For example, consider a breach of the scheduling system for lawn care at a major organization. Yes, it's a successful penetration. However, it is doubtful it would trigger a severity 1. Although it may seem like a silly example, that's the problem you have with acting on pure definitions. Definitions cannot cover every situation. The best practice is to use professional judgment in assigning severity classifications. Definitions should provide guidance but not prescriptive rules.

A severity classification alone is not used in determining a response. You should also consider the incident classification to understand the nature of the attack. For example, there is a substantial difference between a server being down due to a denial of service and an unauthorized access to your credit database containing millions of customer records.

A senior leader in the information security team is typically called to make the formal declaration decision. This person is the chief information security officer or a delegate. His or her responsibility is to ensure the analysis is sound and appropriate to declare an event. Once an incident is formally declared, the IRT response timeline starts. Triage captures all the actions taken to that point. The process activates the IRT plan and also notifies upper management. The documentation includes what the basis for the severity was.

> **NOTE**
>
> During the early stage of an attack, you don't know what the final impact and damage to the organization will be. During triage, the focus is to understand the nature of the attack and containment. Severity and incident classifications can help you to quickly come to a decision on how to contain the threat.

Containing and Minimizing the Damage

There are several quick actions you can take to contain the incident. This might include blocking the Internet Protocol (IP) from which the attack is being launched. It also might include disabling the affected user ID or removing the affected server from the network.

Before a response can be formulated, a decision needs to be made. This involves whether to immediately pursue the attacker or protect the organization. You will obviously not know the type of incident in advance. Therefore, you may find that getting pre-approval from management to take action is difficult to impossible. A decision on what action to take should come from management. However, management needs to understand the damage that will occur by allowing the attacker to continue. Having a protocol with management can establish priorities and expedite a decision. Management should understand in advance the type of decision they will be asked to make. They should also understand the range of implications involved.

Allowing an attacker to continue provides you an opportunity to gather evidence on the attack. It also provides an opportunity to work with law enforcement to determine the attacker's identity. However, many organizations are not equipped to perform such analysis. Also, the legal department will need to be consulted, because allowing a breach could have legal consequences. The most common response is to stop the attack as quickly as possible.

FYI

FISMA requires federal agencies to report major incidents to the United States Computer Emergency Readiness Team (US-CERT). This is a government organization that assists agencies in handling incidents. Private companies may also be required to report incidents, such as banks notifying regulators. Additionally, many states have privacy laws. These require breaches of personal information to be reported to the state and consumers.

The IRT will work to classify the attack. It will also work to determine the best means to stop it. You should document each step of the decision-making process.

It's important to have a set of responses prepared in advance. The initial analysis provides the picture of the threat to prioritize a sequence of pre-rehearsed steps. This could range from taking the server offline to blocking outside IP addresses. These predetermined responses should be well documented. Documentation should include what level of authority is needed to execute. For example, management may grant the IRT permission to block overseas IP addresses. Blocking domestic IP addresses, however, may need management approval. In that case, management should be alerted early when domestic IP addresses are involved. Such an alert would advise management of the situation and ensure someone is available to make a quick decision.

An important part of containment is evidence-gathering. Parts of the IRT team will be focused on stopping the attack while others take snapshots of logs, configuration, and other evidence. Remember, a successful breach is a crime scene. If there's a chance you can prosecute the attacker, it's important to gather as much evidence as possible. You should also disturb the environment as little as possible. This is very difficult when you're trying to stop an attack. However, it's important to be aware of the need to collect evidence.

Cleaning Up After the Incident

A core mission of the IRT is to ensure efficient recovery of the operations. Recovery includes ensuring the vulnerabilities that permitted the incident have been mitigated.

The recovery phase begins once the threat has been contained. You can implement an effective recovery strategy together with the business continuity plan (BCP) representative. This may require restoring servers and rebuilding operating systems from scratch. The next step would then be to test the affected machines and data. The testing should include looking for any signs of the original incident, such as virus or malware. Once you test the servers and systems, you can certify them to be put back into production.

During the containment phase, you have little time to gather evidence. You have more time in the clean-up phase. However, management may pressure you to resume operations. Image the damaged computer(s), if possible, for further analysis after operations have resumed. That way you know the exact state prior to recovery. There are forensic tools that can perform this function quickly and effectively.

If your organization is successfully attacked, it may be attacked again. It's important that the security controls are hardened to withstand another attack. It is often a good idea to install additional monitoring after systems are brought back online. You can use the additional monitoring to validate that the systems have been hardened. You can also use additional monitoring to change how management approaches future attempts to breach the same systems.

Documenting the Incident and Actions

As a focal point for the enterprise, the IRT can gather information across the organization. The IRT assesses the information gathered during and after the incident to gain insights into the threat. It's important that all status reports be issued through the IRT manager. Status reports are internal communications between the IRT and management. However, you should assume that others may end up viewing them. They might even end up in a court of law. You should avoid speculation in these reports. The reports should stay with the basic facts. These include what you know and what you are doing about it.

You should start incident analysis immediately upon declaring an incident. Quickly determine the type of threat. Then determine the scope of the incident and the extent of damage. This will allow you to determine the best response. During this analysis you are collecting information to contain the incident. You are also collecting it for the future forensic analysis.

Collecting forensic evidence is an important part of the IRT's responsibility. This means collecting and preserving information that can be used to reconstruct events. Analysis depends on gathering as much information as possible about the following:

- What led up to the event
- What happened during the event
- How effective the response was

There are specific tools and techniques used to collect forensic evidence. It's important that a trained specialist collects the information. This is because the evidence may end up being used in a court of law. The gathering of information must follow strict rules that the court finds acceptable.

Part of these rules involves a "chain of custody." It's not only important that the information be gathered a certain way. It's also important that the information be stored securely after it's collected. **Chain of custody** is a legal term referring to how evidence is documented and protected. Evidence must be documented and protected from the time it's obtained to the time it's presented at court.

There is a basic approach to proving that digital evidence has not been tampered with. It is to take a bit image of machines and calculate a hash value. The hash value is obtained by running a special algorithm. This algorithm generates a mathematical value based on the exact content of the bit image of the machine. The hash value is essentially a fingerprint of the image. When the image is submitted to the court, another hash value is taken. When the two digital fingerprints match, it proves the image was not tampered with. If one bit of data on the bit image copy is altered in any way, the hash value would change.

> **TIP**
>
> Strongly consider using a well-known forensic tool software package when gathering evidence to be submitted to a court. Examples of such tools are ProDiscover by Technology Pathways or EnCase Forensic by Guidance Software.

The IRT coordinator should maintain an evidence log. All evidence associated with the investigation should be logged in and locked up. If any evidence needs to be examined, it's logged out and then logged back in. Where possible, once evidence is logged in, only copies should be logged out for further review. It is important to maintain a chain of custody to be sure the material is not altered or tampered with.

Analyzing the Incident and Response

The goal of the analysis is straightforward. It is to identify the weakness in your control. Knowing the weakness allows you to continuously improve your security. It helps prevent the incident from occurring again. As you examine your control, you may find other weaknesses unrelated to the incident. Ideally, you want to be able to identify the following:

- The attacker
- The tool used to attack
- The vulnerability that was exploited
- The result of the attack
- The control recommendation that would prevent such an attack from occurring again

Each incident is different and may require a different set of techniques to arrive at these answers. There are some steps you can take to help the analysis:

- **Update your network diagram and inventory**—Be sure to have a current network diagram and inventory of devices available
- **Profile your network**—Map the network traffic by time of day and keep trending information
- **Understand business processes**—Understand normal behavior within the network and business
- **Keep all clocks synchronized**—Be sure the logs all have a synchronized time stamp
- **Correlate central logs**—Be sure logs are centrally captured and easily accessible
- **Create a knowledge base of threats**—Create and maintain a library of threat scenarios

This information can help expedite an incident analysis. Understanding the environment makes it easier to detect suspicious activity. As you become more familiar with the business processes, you can consider new threat scenarios.

The key point is to use these incident analyses to be proactive in defending against threats. The reports examine how to close a security weakness. The reports also examine why the security weaknesses were not originally considered and closed. Reports improve the risk assessment process as much as they help close a specific vulnerability.

Creating Mitigation to Prevent Future Incidents

Part of the analysis is to trace the origin of the attack. This is important for preventing future incidents. This activity involves finding out how hackers entered the application, systems, or network. The analysis should create a storyboard and timeline of events. The storyboard is a complete picture of the incident. This includes actions taken by the hacker, employees, and IRT team.

The IRT may engage outside help in determining the hacker's identity. This outside help may include consulting firms that specialize in forensic investigations. It may also include various law enforcement agencies. These outside resources have established contacts with

Internet service providers (ISPs). They have the ability to track down online users. Although the exact identity of the hacker may not always be determined, these firms can often identify the point of origin. In other words, you may never know the hacker's real name. However, there's a good chance you will know the country and city of origin. These firms can also provide a profile of the attacker. Such a profile might include the attacker's level of skill and potential motive. The attacker might be a high school student. It might also be a foreign government. This information could be valuable to know in determining a response.

> **WARNING**
>
> Engaging outside government agencies has legal implications. The determination on when and how to engage these agencies must be made by management and the legal department.

It is vital that an organization learn from incidents to improve its controls. Sometimes that may mean changing its policies and procedures. Other times it may mean improving security awareness to reduce human error. It can also mean making changes in your security configuration standards.

A final IRT incident report should be published for executive management. This report will bring everyone up to date on the risk that was exploited. It will also show how it was mitigated. The report should answer the following:

- How the incident was started
- Which vulnerabilities were exploited
- How the incident was detected
- How effective the response was
- What long-term solutions are recommended

After a major incident, you should hold a lessons-learned meeting with key stakeholders. This meeting will review key points in the IRT incident report. A lessons-learned meeting should also be held periodically for minor incidents. You can use an annual trending report as an effective measure of progress in reducing risk.

The lessons learned should include how to improve the incident response process. These lessons can be used to help training. They can also help improve IRT skills. Skills can be improved using methods such as additional training. They can also be improved through testing using new scenarios built from the lessons learned.

Handling the Media and What to Disclose

The PR department will play an important role in communicating the incident to the media and impacted parties. The PR department can correct misinformation that could damage the company's reputation. The decision to release information to the public is often handled through a press release.

The PR department is also a point of contact for press inquires. If a reporter contacts the PR department, it's important the PR department has the latest information on the incident. How much information to release is a decision for management. It is the role of the IRT management to ensure the PR representative has the core facts. It's then up to management and the PR department to work out the type of disclosure that's appropriate for the situation.

Notification may be required that will impact consumers. Many privacy laws require consumers to be notified if their personal information has been breached. Once again, the PR department will work with management and legal to determine what needs to be disclosed to stay in compliance.

Best Practices for Incident Response Policies

Incident response policies recognize that an organization needs to build strong external relationships. The policies need to identify which role is responsible for maintaining these relationships. For example, the legal department often maintains relationships with outside law firms.

The IRT may wish to establish a formal contractual arrangement with consulting firms that specialize in incident response. These firms can provide a depth of knowledge on specific attacks. Such knowledge may not be available within the organization. Because consulting firms respond to multiple incidents across many customers, they are able to respond to incidents rapidly.

Incident response policies and capabilities need to be tested. Testing can also act as training for the IRT. Training ensures the staff has the required skill set to respond quickly to an incident. Ideally, the test should not be announced, so the activation process can also be tested.

The effectiveness of the IRT and its related policies needs to be measured. This is to ensure that the IRT is achieving its stated goals. The measurement should be published annually with a comparison to prior years. The measurements should include the goals in the IRT charter, plus additional analytics to indicate the reduction of risk to the organization. This might include:

- Number of incidents
- Number of repeat incidents
- Time to contain per incident
- Financial impact to the organization

Case Studies and Examples of Incident Response Policies

The case studies in this chapter examine various organizations that have formal incident response teams established by policies. The case studies examine how effective these teams were during a security breach.

Private Sector Case Study

An online forensic case study was published about a multi-billion dollar publicly traded company. The company is a leader in the IT infrastructure market. The company was not named in the article.

The problem: The company's servers had been compromised to be the jumping-off point to attack a host of other companies.

The company was notified by another company of what was being attacked. The company's administrator activated an IRT to assess the threat. The administrators were unable to find that a breach had occurred. They called in a consulting firm named Riptech, which specialized in intrusions and forensic analysis. Riptech discovered that a server had been compromised. The firm wanted to monitor the intruder's activities. However, Riptech was advised by in-house counsel that the company was not comfortable allowing the breach to continue. Riptech managed to trace the attack to a North Dakota high school.

This case study illustrated weaknesses in the company's incident response policies and plans. It did point to the skills and tools available to the company. In addition, information response policies were clear on the role and skill requirements to form an IRT. The team did appear to be cross-functional, as the legal department was clearly engaged. Also, the IRT was activated quickly. However, the administrators were unable to find the breach.

The incident was a good example of working with legal specialists to determine the appropriate response. Although Riptech preferred to track down the attacker, the company's legal counsel was concerned over the potential liability of permitting a breach. The decision was to protect the organization and stop the intrusion.

The case study illustrated how forensic tools are used to gather evidence. A bitmap copy of the infected systems was made prior to the system's being restored. This preserved the affected server. The image could then be used as evidence or for further analysis of the incident.

The case study also illustrated the public relations approach that was taken. Because there was no breach of data, the company decided not to publicly acknowledge the attack. The article indicated the concern was public perception. The organization did not want it known that a teenager was able to breach its system.

The final incident report issued by Riptech outlined a series of control weaknesses that allowed the breach. The consulting firm helped the company restore its system and mitigate the threat in the future.

Public Sector Case Study

Georgia Tech is a university that enrolls over 16,500 students and employs 700 faculty members. The school has an active information security program. It also has a well-defined incident response policy. On March 14, 2003, an intrusion detection sensor indicated a possible compromise on a server. The server contained a ticketing system for a performing arts theater. The ticketing system contained credit card numbers and personal information for 57,000 patrons.

In accordance with the incident response plan, an IRT was activated. Georgia Tech's team is called an executive response team. It consists of top leaders and staff across the organization. Members include representatives of technology, public relations, and the administration. The forensic analysis indicated the server was not placed behind a firewall. It did not have current security controls. The forensic analysis was not conclusive whether the credit card information was compromised. However, the server had clearly been breached.

The IRT team took the following action:

- Notified law enforcement
- Notified cardholders, banks, and credit card companies of the potential breach of information
  - Implemented a new ticket system with the appropriate controls

As a result of this incident, Visa threatened to revoke the university's right to process credit cards. The university worked with Visa to bring its systems into compliance with PCI DSS and was allowed to continue processing transactions.

Although such a breach is unfortunate, this case study is an example of an effective incident response policy. Top management was engaged immediately. The team had a plan and executed it effectively. The threat was quickly contained by the technology team. Although there was no direct evidence the credit card information was compromised, the team took a conservative approach. It assumed the database containing the credit cards was breached. This is an indication that the team reflected the value of the organization in its decision making. The public relations department helped facilitate communications. The business moved quickly to implement a new ticketing system.

Critical Infrastructure Case Study

A case study was published by the Carnegie Mellon CERT program. It described how one of the largest banks in the country started an IRT. The case study concealed the bank's name, referring to it as AFI. The case study described the process that AFI went through to create the team and related policies.

The need for an IRT was clear to the security manager. He had observed security incidents being handled inconsistently. This was a problem because the bank was governed by certain regulations. The approach was to involve several of the risk groups and key stakeholders. The effort was jump-started by using best practices. It took several years to deploy globally. This was because of the size and complexity of the organization. The effort was initially understaffed. The effort that would be required was underestimated. Requirements were not clearly understood.

This case study is a good example of how regulated industries are required to have effective information response policies. This is also an example of an IRT that is filled with appropriately skilled individuals. There was no indication in the case study that an external firm was engaged to assist the company. It would be a best practice to engage an outside firm to help plan such an effort when internal skills are not available.

CHAPTER SUMMARY

You learned in this chapter what incident response policies are needed to respond effectively to security breaches. It's important that policies define what an incident is. They should also state clearly how to classify an event. You also learned how to build a team charter. The chapter examined the difference between on-site response teams and teams that facilitate responses. The chapter discussed key roles and responsibilities within the team during an incident.

The chapter also examined typical procedures you should follow during an incident. We examined key decisions that are needed at each step in responding to an incident. This includes containing the incident and gathering evidence. We also discussed best practices and the importance of using outside firms to supplement an organization's skill sets. Finally, the chapter explored how these principles are applied in the real world. Implementing well-defined incident response policies takes significant time and effort. However, the value in containing threats and limiting damage to an organization outweighs the costs.

KEY CONCEPTS AND TERMS

Business continuity
   representative
Chain of custody
Due care
Human resources representative
Incident

Incident response team (IRT)
Information security
   representative
Information technology subject
   matter experts
IRT coordinator

IRT manager
Legal representative
Malicious code attack
Network reconnaissance probe
Public relations representative

CHAPTER 12 ASSESSMENT

1. All incidents regardless of how small should be handled by an incident response team.

   A. True
   B. False

2. Which of the following should not be in an information response team charter?

   A. Mission
   B. Organizational structure
   C. Detailed line budget
   D. Roles and responsibilities

3. Which of the following IRT members should be consulted before communicating to the public about an incident?

   A. Management
   B. Public relations
   C. IRT manager
   D. All of the above

4. As defined by this chapter, what is *not* a step in responding to an incident?

   A. Discovering an incident
   B. Reporting an incident
   C. Containing an incident
   D. Creating a budget to compare options
   E. Analyzing an incident response

5. A method outlined in this chapter to determine if an incident is major or minor is to classify an incident with a _____ rating.

6. When containing an incident, you should always apply a long-term preventive solution.

   A. True
   B. False

7. The IRT starts recording events once an _____.

8. During the containment step, you should also gather as much evidence as reasonably possible about the incident.

   A. True
   B. False

9. To clean up after an incident, you should always wipe the affected machine clean and rebuild it from scratch.

   A. True
   B. False

10. What value does a forensic tool bring?

    A. Gathers evidence
    B. Helps evidence to be accepted by the court
    C. Can take a bit image of a machine
    D. All of the above

11. How important is it to identify the attacker before issuing a final IRT report?

    A. Critically important; do not issue the report without it
    B. Moderately important; nice to have but issue the report if not available
    C. Not important; focus on the incident and do not include identity of attacker even if you have it
    D. Important, but allow law enforcement to brief management about attacker's identity

12. When analyzing an incident, you must try to determine which of the following?

    A. The tool used to attack
    B. The vulnerability that was exploited
    C. The result of the attack
    D. All of the above

13. Which IRT member is responsible for handling the media?

14. It is a best practice to test the IRT capability at least once a year.

    A. True
    B. False

15. A federal agency is not required by law to report a security incident.

    A. True
    B. False

PART THREE

Implementing and Maintaining an IT Security Policy Framework

IT Security Policy Implementations

I T SECURITY POLICIES are the foundation upon which you build good security habits. They are a useful tool for creating a culture that protects information. Users can turn to policies for guidance in their daily work.

To be effective, everyone must follow the policies. A security policy implementation needs user acceptance to be successful. You can gain user acceptance, in part, through effectively communicating policies that are also easy to understand. A security awareness program, in addition to other methods, helps users understand policies and why they're important. The implementation of security policies also requires management support. Thorough planning allows you to overcome challenges and gain management support.

In this chapter, we explore the major issues encountered while implementing security policies. We discuss how to overcome challenges, part of which includes creating a communications plan. The chapter also examines best practices for security awareness and distribution of policy material. Finally, the chapter presents several case studies that reinforce important topics and concepts.

Chapter 13 Topics

This chapter covers the following topics and concepts:

- Which issues you'll face when implementing IT security policies
- How to develop and implement a security awareness policy
- How to educate employees through proper dissemination of information
- How to overcome technical hindrances
- How to overcome nontechnical hindrances
- Which best practices to follow when implementing IT security policies
- What some case studies and examples of successful IT security policy implementations are

Chapter 13 Goals

When you complete this chapter, you will be able to:

- Identify key organizational and cultural issues in implementing policies
- Describe why executive support is so important
- Define what a communications plan is
- Explain the importance of a communications plan
- Explain the different between awareness and training of security policies
- Describe examples of policy training
- Describe what a brown bag session is and its benefits
- Explain techniques for overcoming objections
- Describe different ways to disseminate policy material
- Explain the technical and nontechnical barriers to implementing IT security policies
- Use case studies of successful IT security policy implementations as examples for your organization

Implementation Issues for IT Security Policies

Business and IT are often overworked and overcommitted. Information security is sometimes seen as an additional layer of complexity. Some people perceive security policies as a roadblock to the delivery of services. These perceptions of security policies are inaccurate. Security policies can enable organizations to expand by creating reliable controls that protect vital systems and applications.

Implementation is as much about changing attitudes as it is about implementing controls. Overcoming perceptions and changing culture are goals of security policies. In other words, it is about implementing in a way that wins hearts and minds. You achieve this by having a clear and concise plan. You need to be transparent about what risks security policies can and cannot reduce. Most importantly, security policies need to be viewed as a useful tool.

Changing an organization's culture and users' perceptions is not a one-time event. Simply releasing security policies does not change attitudes. Security is a tough sell because the benefits are not always obvious. Cultural change comes from having a clear value message that is demonstrated daily. It also requires collaboration and an understanding of the business. Culture is changed in small increments. That's why you need a well-planned step-by-step approach to implementing policies. Three common messages for defining the need for policies are:

- Personal accountability
- Directive and enforcement
- Being a valuable tool

You might hear the phrase "selling security" in relation to policy implementation. How do you sell security? A classic technique is to discuss personal accountability and the consequences of not implementing policy. The consequences can range from loss of data to lack of regulatory compliance. This message can resonate with executives, especially those who operate in a regulated industry. In highly regulated companies, executives can be held personally accountable for failure to implement effective controls. The Sarbanes-Oxley Act is an example of this type of regulation. Although this technique has had some success, it can go only so far because the consequences may not seem real. The more abstract the perceived argument as to why information security is important, the less convincing it becomes.

Another technique for implementing security policies is through management directive and enforcement. Management can require policies to be implemented. Management sets the tone within an organization through how it enforces its policies. Inevitably, someone will fail to follow policy. The level of tolerance and how aggressively policies are enforced sets the tone. It also shapes whether policies are perceived as important.

The third technique is to position policies as a valuable tool. This is accomplished when management and users have clearly defined responsibilities to manage risk. You can show how security policies can be used as a valuable tool to help them meet those responsibilities. When security policies provide measureable evidence that they achieved their goals, the policies will be embraced. The challenge is finding responsibilities in which policies can directly influence the outcome. The more measureable the responsibilities, the more value the security policies become as a tool. For example, a role that is responsible for reducing fraud may rely on strong authentication policies to reduce the likelihood of a customer account being compromised. This might translate into requiring two-factor authentication to access a bank account online. The implementation of these policies can help the online banking manager achieve his or her goals of reducing online fraud.

For management, security policies are valuable for managing risk. The policies define clear mandates from many regulators on how risk should be controlled. IT security policies can help management identify risk, assign priority, and show, over time, how risk is controlled. This is an extremely valuable tool for management. This is an example of how to build value that solves a real problem for management. For example, a company wanting to offer services to the government may have to prove it is compliant with the Federal Information Security Management Act (FISMA). In that case, implementing National Institute of Standards and Technology (NIST) standards clearly demonstrates to regulators how risks are controlled in accordance with FISMA requirements.

In the real world, you will use all three techniques to implement policies. These techniques help you define value and overcome objections. However, the third technique of using policies as a valued tool is more likely to change attitudes over the long term. As policies are perceived as solving real business problems, management and users are more likely to embrace the policies. This is the first step towards building a risk-aware culture.

Organizational Challenges

Organizational challenges depend on the culture and industry. For example, the financial services industry puts significant resources into implementing security policies. In these organizations, the focus is on how to implement security policies to meet compliance. Other organizations that are less regulated may question whether they should implement security policies. Understanding and overcoming these objections is an important part of obtaining buy-in. The following is a list of organizational challenges you might face when implementing security policies:

- Accountability
- Lack of budget
- Lack of priority
- Tight schedules

> **NOTE**
>
> Policies are, by definition, organizational directives. Assigning specific tasks and responsibilities during implementation is important. This becomes even more important when dealing with large, complex organizations. An implementation plan must have clear accountabilities defined from the leadership level to the IT security team.

The ultimate accountability for protecting information is with management. Thus, management has a key role to play in implementing the right policies. Implementations require management to be accountable for their success. A challenge is when leaders perceive policy implementation as an IT function. Leaders need to support the implementation and provide the right message to all teams.

Another organizational challenge is a lack of budget. Implementing security policies across the enterprise requires resources and funding. It may be a challenge to obtain funding without management support. The implementation of policies is more than sending out e-mails and posting a policy on a server. It takes time and funding to create training collateral, brief departments, train users, and hold town hall meetings. A **town hall meeting** is a gathering of teams to make announcements and discuss topics. These types of efforts take time and funding on both the IT and business side. It's even more challenging when the business is asked to allocate funds from its own budget. Competing for limited funds is always a challenge in an organization.

Information security has to compete for organizational priority. It's no different than any other activity. An organization faces many conflicting priorities. An organization may be facing business challenges that drive its priorities. For example, a priority may be to expand customer services. An organization may need to reduce defects in its product line. The key point is that organizations have limited resources. Often, there are more priorities than resources available.

The challenge is to avoid security policies becoming low-priority items. For the implementation of security policies to be effective, it must be taken as a serious organization commitment. In part, you accomplish this by avoiding direct conflicts with other priorities. You should time the implementation of security policies so it doesn't conflict with other events. For example, assume you know over the next three months that a new product will be released. You may want to hold off implementing major security policies until after the product launch. Companies in this situation may not have the bandwidth to deal effectively with both efforts.

13

IT Security Policy
Implementations

You don't always have the luxury of waiting to implement policies. You may be under a regulatory requirement to meet specific timelines. When you do have flexibility, plan the timing of the implementation to ensure the organization can properly focus on the effort. Even in the best of circumstances, you often face tight implementation schedules. Once an organization has agreed on the content of security policies, the tendency is to implement them quickly. The organization can then move on to other priorities. Tight schedules may also be a byproduct of how well you communicated the benefits. For example, an organization that is facing significant audit findings may view the implementation of security policies as an important step in controlling those risks. This results in significant pressure to implement quickly. It's important that an implementation plan recognizes the time and effort required to reach and train everyone involved in the changes.

Organizational and Cultural Change

For policies to prevent security breaches, they must be practiced by everyone. This requires that everyone in the organization be accountable for implementing security policies. This is a cultural change for any organization that views security policies as an abstract concept or an additional layer of complexity. Security policies that hold everyone in the organization accountable help promote a cultural change.

To promote a cultural change, the goal should be to make security policies:

- A routine part of the daily interaction
- Supported by organizational committees
- Instinctively reactive

These goals are measureable indicators of a shift in organizational thinking. Security policies cannot outline every potential situation. You cannot expect people to memorize volumes of material. Information overload is a real concern when implementing security policies. When information security policies are large, complex documents, they become hard to understand. They are also hard to teach. Security policies need to include core concepts that can be applied to a wide range of situations. In this way, the security policies' tenets can be easily recalled. The advantage of core values is that they can be applied to unexpected situations.

You can measure routine daily interaction to see if policies are being used. For example, you can review business deployment plans. Usually it becomes obvious if security policies were clearly considered. When security is considered as an afterthought or a **bolt-on** set of requirements, cultural change has not occurred. You can also gauge the level of interaction based on the number of requests from the business to interpret security policies. When information security is at the forefront of everyone's mind, the business often asks for clarification on policy details when implementing new processes. The natural source for this interpretation is the IT security team. If the volume of requests for interpretation is low, it's a good indicator that active conversations on security risks are not occurring. When you have a large number of initiatives, you should expect lots of questions on policies.

You can measure committee support by the conversations that occur between members. A quick indicator is to look at the minutes of committee meetings, such as the operational risk committee, audit committee, and others. They should all be dedicating time to discussing information security and policies. These committees should be discussing enforcement. They will want to know how to manage overall risk to the organization. If these committees spend little or no time on these topics, it's a good indicator they have delegated the conversation to lower ranks. A risk-aware culture has senior management equally engaged in these discussions. The chief information security officer (CISO) can help overcome organizational apathy toward security policies by attending key committee meetings. The CISO can promote candid discussions on policies and risks.

 NOTE

You'll see over time how engaged discussions result in leaders becoming more security aware. These leaders also take that message back to their individual teams. Both of these actions are essential in promoting the need for security policies.

A culture shift occurs when users instinctively react to situations consistent with the core values of the security policies. This personal accountability can help promote security thinking across a broad range of situations. It could be as simple as asking a stranger in the office for their identification. It could be questioning the need for access even though a procedure allows it. This can be measured in several ways. An organization with a high number of security policy exceptions might not appreciate the importance of security.

Organizational and Individual Acceptance

Collectively, user behavior defines the organization's acceptance of security policies. When security policies are widely accepted they become part of the culture. That tends to reduce risk, resulting in a lower number of security incidents. The converse is also true. When security policies are not widely accepted, there's an increase in security incidents. It's important that users embrace security policies to ensure the policies are used and effective.

One report from the SANS Institute states that the "vast majority of security breaches originate from human actions."[1] The report indicates several reasons, such as:

- Poor training and security awareness
- Poor motivation
- Deliberate acts
- Poor management and user decisions

Users are more likely to accept what they understand. Security awareness is the first step in getting people to think about security. Security awareness gives you an opportunity to explain the value of security policies. When security policies help users do their work, users consider the polices to be valuable. Consequently, the goal of the security awareness program should be to gain support as well as to teach material. You need to tailor training to the users. For example, the type of training senior leaders receive would be different from individual user training.

> **FYI**
>
> Deliberate acts and malicious behavior of insiders are hard to control. Strong enforcement of policies can potentially lower the number of occurrences. Seeing others caught and disciplined can be a deterrent. Employees can be trained to identify and report suspicious activity. Segregation of duties can also reduce deliberate acts and malicious behavior. In the end, there needs to be diligent controls focused on the insider threat in additional to those reducing external risks.

Motivation is a broader topic. How individuals are motivated varies by person. One clear motivation is self-interest. A powerful motivator is when management rigorously enforces security policies. This can be demonstrated by how management holds users accountable for not following policies. Users need to know that management is serious about implementing security policies. This clear message of rewards and discipline is important in motivating users.

Poor decisions can lead to security incidents, even when individuals are trained. Poor decisions can occur anywhere within the organization. A user can fall prey to social engineering pretexts. A user can fail to report a control weakness. Management can fail to act when a report is received. Risk experts can fail to assess the extent of the vulnerability. Senior leaders can fail to fund the mitigation. Regardless of the failure, there's a danger that polices are perceived as ineffective when security incidents rise.

The key point is that effective security policy implementation depends on acceptance. Acceptance depends on the individuals who perceive value in the policy. Ultimate acceptance depends on the value being demonstrated by lowered risk to the organization.

Security Awareness Policy Implementations

The primary objective of a security awareness program is to educate users. This includes teaching them about policies. It also includes teaching core security concepts. Effective security awareness helps drive acceptance. When users understand policies, they can be held accountable for using the policies. This promotes a long-term security culture shift. With so much at stake, it's important to have a well-thought-out approach to education.

Typically, an organization offers security awareness training. This is broken down into two components:

- **Awareness**—The objective is to raise understanding of the importance and value of security policies.
- **Training**—The goal is to provide the skills needed to comply with security policies.

Awareness should be an ongoing effort that reinforces key concepts. The awareness component is important because it sets the tone and goals for security policy implementation. By setting realistic goals, you build credibility for the policies. It also promotes candid conversations. Security awareness is, in part, about effective marketing and messaging.

The training component is more straightforward than delivering awareness. In security training, you review security policies in detail. You discuss how the policies apply to individual roles. You set expectations on behavior. Security training focuses on mechanics—what is expected to be done and when. Often in security policy training you will discuss the supporting processes. For example, you might discuss restricting security administrator accounts. This can lead to a discussion on how to grant rights.

Development of an Organization-Wide Security Awareness Policy

Effective security awareness training has to reach everyone in the organization. This includes anyone with access to data such as employees, contractors, and vendors. The form of security awareness training may vary depending on the type of user. For example, security awareness training for a vendor might be handled by its parent company. The contract with the vendor should specify the type of awareness training the client requires. Typically, the vendor is responsible for training its employees. This is different from contractors. Contractors usually go through the same type of training as regular employees. In this case, the organization is responsible for security awareness training. However, contractor training may be condensed. If a contractor will be on-site for a short time—three weeks, for example—it does not make sense to require weeks of security awareness training.

> **NOTE**
>
> All users must receive some type of security awareness training. A security awareness policy should outline the training requirements. The policy should define how such training will be delivered.

13

IT Security Policy Implementations

The security awareness policy ensures that education reaches everyone. For example, the policy might require that all users receive security awareness training before being granted access to data. This might include complete basic security awareness training during orientation. This ensures newly hired individuals receive training before handling sensitive information.

The security awareness policy typically beaks down the frequency and type of training required. Awareness training is conducted at least annually. A security awareness training policy may require the following types of training:

- **New employee and contractor**—At time of hire before access to data is granted
- **Promotion**—As individuals are promoted into significantly different roles
- **All users**—Annual refresher training
- **Post-incident**—After major security incidents when lack of education was noted
- **Vendor**—As defined in the contract

It's important that you know your audience. You should tailor training that resonates with them. For example, humor is often cited as an effective tool in awareness training. Humor can capture an individual's attention. It can also elicit cooperation and make the topic fun. Although that may be appropriate in larger audiences, it may not be the best choice when training executives. As a general rule, you want to tailor your approach based on:

- **Job level**—The higher in the organization, the more strategic the training needs to be.
- **Level of awareness**—Some users need more training on basic security concepts.
- **Technical skill level**—Individuals who are technically savvy may be able to understand threats more easily.

> **TIP**
>
> Best practices and standards often include information on how to create a security awareness training policy. Following this guidance can ensure you meet regulatory requirements. For example, FISMA security awareness compliance is based on NIST Special Publications 800-16 and 800-50.

The security awareness policy determines the type of awareness training that's provided. The policy also defines the audience that receives the training. For example, the policy could require senior management to receive strategic security and policy training. Middle management is required to take policy and basic security training. Training should focus on individual roles and responsibilities. Middle management needs to understand basic security concepts and risks they may encounter running daily operations. Senior management is less likely to encounter those risks when they focus on strategic issues in running the organization. Basic security training might include concepts on how to implement encryption methods. This is a real issue that middle management may face. Senior management would have little interest or bandwidth to deal with basic security issues. The scope of security awareness training is not one size fits all.

> **NOTE**
>
> The security awareness policy needs to require specific training across the organization. This ensures expectations are set consistently. The message and type of training can vary by role.

One approach to security policy awareness training is to define the user population and types of security awareness training offerings. This allows you to require specific training to address individual needs. Table 13-1 is a simple example of this concept. Notice there are four basic user types defined. The security awareness policy would define each of these user types to ensure individuals in these roles can be quickly enrolled in training. The columns represent the type of training offered. The type and level of training would vary depending on the organization's needs. Notice the emphasis on reporting suspicious activity. This is reflected by the fact that all users are required to receive this type of training.

In many organizations, this type of training is tracked through an online course registration tool. The application allows an individual to enroll in available training sessions. The application can also automatically assign required courses to individuals. The application can track attendance as well. Online course registration tools help enforce the security awareness policy. These tools can also show evidence of enforcing the security awareness policy.

TABLE 13-1 Simple security policy awareness requirements.

TYPES OF USERS	SECURITY BASIC REQUIREMENTS	LEGAL AND REGULATORY REQUIREMENTS	DETAIL POLICY REVIEW	LOGGING AND MONITORING POLICIES	SUSPICIOUS ACTIVITY REPORTING
Senior management	X	X			X
Middle management	X	X	X		X
End users	X				X
IT custodian	X		X	X	X

Conducting Security Awareness Training Sessions

The goal of formal security awareness training is to build knowledge and skills to help workers perform their roles in a way that protects assets and complies with policies. Security awareness training is not just about echoing back the trained material. The measure of success is how effectively the workers apply their training on the job.

Today there are two main ways of formally delivering security awareness training: in the classroom and through **computer-based training (CBT)**. Both methods are widely used and both have strengths and weaknesses. Large organizations often use a combination of methods. There are also a host of informational methods. They can be as simple as a manager e-mailing a policy to the team asking everyone to read the material. Information dissemination methods are discussed later in this chapter.

In the classroom setting, a trained instructor usually conducts security awareness training. The advantage of having an instructor deliver the training is flexibility. Let's assume some training materials were developed under the assumption that the audience has a certain technical skill set. If a session is delivered and the audience doesn't have the necessary background, an experienced instructor can adjust the delivery accordingly. Benefits of the classroom setting are the ability to answer questions and connect with the audience.

13

IT Security Policy
Implementations

FYI

A classroom session can be a positive experience where individuals exchange ideas and make a personal connection with other students and the instructor. Another significant benefit is that the instructor can gauge the audience's acceptance of the material. Through questions and discussions, an instructor can determine how well the message is truly understood. Based on this feedback, the instructor can adjust the training to be more effective.

> **NOTE**
>
> Simply knowing the subject material doesn't mean you are able to teach the material. It's important that the core message doesn't change as the material is adjusted to fit the audience. Delivering a consistent message is important.

There are also drawbacks to a classroom setting. The first is cost. Classroom sessions can be expensive based on facility and travel costs. You need to find a suitable classroom and arrange everyone's attendance. Conference rooms can be effective but are sometimes a poor choice depending on class size and number of interruptions. It's not uncommon for individuals to be pulled out of training sessions held within the office setting. Alternatively, arranging for a conference room at a local hotel or alternative location often comes with a price tag. Attendance could mean flying individuals to a training location or flying an instructor to remote offices. Another problem is the skill set of the instructor. Experienced instructors are typically in short supply. It takes a specific skill set to facilitate a training session.

The CBT approach is a lower-cost alternative to classroom training. You can teach an unlimited number of workers a set of messages in a consistent fashion. Online courses also allow workers to take courses at their convenience. This can include taking a course at night or on weekends, away from the pressures and distractions of the office. Online courses offer quizzes throughout each session to automatically score competency. An online training tool can also require review of material the attendee found challenging. CBT offers statistical tracking of who takes courses and what part of the material individuals are struggling with.

> **NOTE**
>
> Many organizations use a combination of approaches, offering classroom and CBT training.

The CBT approach has drawbacks compared to classroom sessions. It can only measure what individuals know about the material. Unlike an instructor, it cannot measure how well the material is being accepted. A strength and weakness of CBT is the consistent format in which it's presented. The message in the material is consistently delivered. However, there's usually no opportunity to tailor the message to a specific audience. Finally, the CBT is impersonal. Unlike the classroom, there's little opportunity to connect with others in the organization.

The effectiveness of security awareness programs varies. John Leyden, a reporter with *The Register*, reported in December 2005 on a McAfee study that surveyed typical office workers. The results indicated the following:

- 21 percent of workers let family and friends use company machines to access the Internet
- 51 percent connected their own devices to their work PC
- 60 percent admitted to storing personal content on their work PC
- 10 percent admitted to downloading content at work they shouldn't
- 62 percent admitted they have a very limited knowledge of IT security
- 51 percent had no idea how to update antivirus protection

The exact percentages are not important to this discussion. The overall results indicate that the effectiveness of some security awareness programs is weak. Simply delivering security awareness is not a measure of success. Having that knowledge used is the goal of training.

It's important that as much feedback is provided to the program as possible. This feedback should focus on how well the material is being accepted beyond what knowledge was conveyed. In other words, it's more important to know the attendee is using the knowledge than simply memorizing the material. Some suggested ways of getting feedback include:

- Anonymous surveys after the session
- Focus groups
- Interviews of attendees
- Exit interviews of individuals leaving the company
- Monitoring compliance through incident reports

Executive Management Sponsorship

Without **executive management sponsorship**, users will be less likely to eagerly participate in awareness training. Training takes time away from an individual's regular job. Many organizations are understaffed and overcommitted. Training may not be seen as valuable or urgent. Executive management sponsorship changes that perception.

You should expect funding with a defined budget. Creating and buying training materials are start-up costs. These costs may not be in the current budget. Additionally, you should expect a formal communication from management supporting the program. This communication can be a simple e-mail that emphasizes the importance of team participation. This tone at the top is important to overcome common objections, such as, "I'm too busy right now."

> **NOTE**
>
> You should expect some level of participation by executives during training. An executive may simply stop by to kick off a session. A few opening remarks in a training session send a powerful message throughout the organization. Also, videotaping a message from a senior leader is an effective technique. This avoids the problem of scheduling his or her time for multiple training sessions.

Gathering support should not be limited to a single executive. A security awareness program spans the enterprise. This means you should seek multiple executive supporters. Remember, awareness is ongoing and extends well beyond the classroom. For example, partnering with corporate communications or marketing allows the security message to be included in company newsletters and bulletins. The IT security team provides the content, whereas the communication and marketing department professionally packages the message. Executive sponsorship in those areas can extend the reach of the message. These executives can advise the IT security team on how best to market through existing communication channels.

Human Resources (HR) Ownership of New Employee Orientation

Access to new employees can often be achieved through the HR department. The HR department usually manages the onboarding of new employees. HR usually has an array of employment documents to be completed by new employees, from benefits forms to ID badge acknowledgments. They also provide a series of training sessions to help new employees ease into the organization's culture.

 TIP

The security awareness training that all employees must take should be delivered during new employee orientation. Additional training can be handled after the employee is on the job.

Most organizations add security awareness training to the list of items the HR department provides to new employees. It's cost efficient because it simply adds material to new employee training conducted by HR. You don't have to pull new employees offline into a separate training session. It's also practical from a timing perspective. You don't want new employees to access sensitive data until they received training. You want to get to the employees as early as possible. By adding this to new employee training, you minimize any delays in granting their access.

NOTE

The AUP is a document that clearly defines a core set of user responsibilities and expectations. It also discusses the consequences of failing to comply. The document is meant to be enforceable. A violation of the policy could lead to disciplinary action, including termination. As result, the AUP language is precise.

Review of Acceptable Use Policies (AUPs)

A core topic in security awareness training is reviewing the acceptable use policy (AUP). It's not uncommon to require employees to sign the AUP. This acknowledges they have received and read the policy. The AUP clearly defines what's considered acceptable and unacceptable use of technology. The AUP, for example, specifies that the organization's computers should be used for business purposes only. It may also exclude specific types of usage such as gambling or accessing offensive material. The AUP also defines personal responsibilities, such as protecting an individual's password.

One of the more critical training points in an AUP is to prohibit sharing of an individual's ID and password. Sharing such information can place sensitive data at risk from unauthorized access. It also undermines the concept of nonrepudiation. Let's assume a supervisor asked a user to share his or her password. This is a violation of the AUP by both the employee and the supervisor. In the real world, if the employee promptly reported the violation, no action would be taken against him or her. Although it may be a violation by the employee, the supervisor is the source of the breach. It's not always reasonable to expect an employee to stand up against a supervisor, manager, or executive. However, failure to report the violation might be considered significant cause to discipline the employee. In either case, the supervisor should be disciplined for requiring the employee to provide that information. The level of discipline depends on the organization. If the violation leads to a fraud or security breach, there's a strong case to be made for terminating the supervisor.

As discussed in Chapter 9, the AUP does more than protect passwords. It also addresses other high risk behaviors, which should be included in security training:

- Handling and sharing of sensitive customer information
- Transmission of information outside the company
- Handing of company intellectual property

Information Dissemination— How to Educate Employees

> **NOTE**
>
> Security awareness is more than just formal training. It's reinforcing the message and keeping information security in everyone's mind. The policies themselves are good resources for individuals.

There are two ways of educating users—formal and informal. Formal methods are those that communicate policies in a formal training environment, such as a classroom or CBT. The advantage of formal training is that you know who's taking the training, and you can measure to some extent its effectiveness.

Remember, people learn in different ways. It's a good idea to select multiple methods to disseminate security policy messages and materials. Because people learn differently, this increases your odds of reaching everyone. For example, those that find computer-based training less appealing may find a department newsletter more relevant to their job.

It's also important to understand the culture and the audience in the organization. If an organization has many remote offices, face-to-face presentations of the material will be less practical. In addition, some organizations distribute too many newsletters. Some users simply stop reading newsletters due to the volume. As a consequence, newsletters may not be the best choice for communicating critical information. The following is a list of potential ways to disseminate security policy information:

- Telephone town hall meetings
- E-mails
- Newsletters
- The intranet
- Posters
- Face-to-face presentations
- Giveaways such as pins, mugs, sticky notes, and so on
- Contests that includes giveaways

Any communication method that keeps the security message "alive" is effective. You are usually limited by time and money. However, communicating the policy message does not have to be expensive. It's only limited by imagination. You could sponsor a security policy awareness contest. It might be as simple as asking individuals to answer security policy trivia questions online. The winner gets a basket of goods worth less than $20. For a little expense, you can apply creative ideas to engage employees and reinforce key messages.

To successfully disseminate security policy messages, you need a communications plan. A **communications plan** outlines what information is to be shared. A communications plan defines the message, the people, and the method of delivery. By laying out an entire communications plan, you can quickly assess if the right message is reaching everyone.

When developing a communications plan, you should ask yourself the following key questions:

- **Who communicates**—Are the right people delivering the message to build credibility for the effort?
- **What is the target audience**—Is everyone receiving the appropriate message?
- **What is communicated**—Is the right message being delivered?
- **How is it communicated**—Are we delivering the message in the most efficient manner?
- **When is it communicated**—Is the communication well timed?
- **What collateral is used**— Is the message being consistently delivered?
- **What objective is achieved**—Are specific goals being achieved?

Table 13-2 depicts a simple communications plan that has two events. Both events are to be communicated by senior management. The first communication event prepares middle management for the announcement to staff. One can anticipate questions during a policy launch. Leadership needs to be well prepared to answer questions from staff, which makes the policy rollout more effective. The second communication event is the actual kick-off of the security awareness effort.

A communications plan can help rationalize the implementation strategy. For example, your strategy may call for everyone to receive at least three communications during the first six months of the security awareness program. If that's the case, by scanning the Target Audience column in the communications plan, you can quickly determine if the goal is being achieved.

TABLE 13-2 Simple communications plan.

WHO COMMUNICATES	TARGET AUDIENCE	WHAT	HOW	WHEN	COLLATERAL	OBJECTIVE
Senior management	Middle management	Key messages to be conveyed to staff	Leadership staff meeting	Before xx/xx/xx	Management talking points	Ensure key leaders have talking points to answer staff questions after kick-off e-mail
Senior management	All employees	Security awareness program announcement	E-mail broadcast	xx/xx/xx	Kick-off e-mail	Program kick-off

Hard Copy Dissemination

Sending out hard copies of policies is rarely done today. The challenge in sending out volumes of paper is the cost and accuracy of the material. All of the security policies, standards, processes, and guidelines in an enterprise can be thousands of pages long. That doesn't include the supporting materials such as executive summaries, slide decks, and spreadsheets. Consequently, it's not practical to disseminate the material in print form. Printing costs would be high, and it would take time, money, and effort to disseminate. In addition, as soon as changes to the material are made, the printed material is out of date.

You should, however, retain a master hard copy. Some organizations require physical signatures and committee approvals before policies can be released. In this case, a limited set of master copies is kept to retain the approver's signature and any required stamps to make the document officially approved for release. You should keep master copies in a safe place.

You may decide to distribute supporting collateral in hard-copy format. Perhaps you have a brochure or a chart that depicts the relationship between all the security policies. You may find the need to create a quick-start guide, such as for policies related to filing suspicious activity reports. Although the documentation can quickly become out of date, the benefit of releasing a limited number of materials often outweighs the risk. Material that helps an organization navigate through thousands of pages of security material can be a significant benefit.

Some non-policy security materials are good candidates for non-electronic distribution. Such material includes brochures, posters, sticky note, and mugs. This type of material reinforces key security messages. As a result, the material rarely goes out of date.

 TIP

Selecting which material is a candidate for hard copy publishing depends varies by organization. The general rule of thumb is to keep it to a small amount of material with a limited distribution.

TIP

Regardless of form, include your communication channels in your communications plan.

Posting Policies on the Intranet

The best method for communicating security policies is through a document-handling server such as an intranet. These servers offer multiple benefits, such as:

- Low cost to disseminate material
- Policies are kept current
- Policies are searchable
- Changes to policies can be highlighted
- Supporting material can be linked to

Many organizations already have an intranet deployed. Consequently, the incremental costs for housing security policies are minimal. Centralized security policy management helps you keep policies current.

13

IT Security Policy Implementations

A significant advantage of electronic versus hard copies is the ability to search for documents. Anyone who has browsed the Internet is familiar with search engines. You can enter key phrases and get a list of related documents. The same technology applies to an intranet. Your internal policies can be quickly searched for key phrases. In seconds, thousands of pages can be searched. For example, assume a business has decided to work with a vendor to process sensitive information. A quick search of policies using the keyword "vendor" may return a half-dozen documents. The topics may range from the need for a vendor assessment to secure connection requirements.

Another powerful tool of document-handling servers is the ability to track changes. When a modified policy is released, it's helpful to know the exact wording that was changed. Policies often include a high-level explanation of the changes but few details. Having the ability to view the actual word-level changes in the policy is a powerful tool. This allows you to better assess the impact of the change on your existing controls.

Another significant benefit is the ability to link policies to supporting materials. The supporting materials can be executive summaries, slide decks, or a wide array of educational material. You can link any supporting material that makes it easier to understand the policy. For example, suppose you are reading a security policy on database logging but you don't quite understand the material. You notice a slide deck linked to the policy. After clicking on it, you are presented with a tutorial created by the database administrator explaining how the policy is to be applied.

Using E-mail

Although the level of sophistication varies between organizations on how policies are disseminated, most organizations still rely on e-mail. Organizations depend on e-mail to approve policies and keep management informed on implementation activities.

E-mail also plays a central role in most communications plans. E-mail allows you to notify a large population of users of major events. It also allows you to track everyone who has read the notification. This is a good tool for ensuring that individuals are properly notified of policy releases. E-mail also allows you to send out surveys and follow up on how well the implementation is being perceived.

Brown Bag Lunch and Learning Sessions

A brown bag session is a training event. An expert on a topic is invited to share his or her thoughts, ideas, and experiences. The term "brown bag" came about because sessions were usually held over lunch time, and everyone brought their own lunch in a brown bag. The term brown bag is more widely used today. These sessions may or may not be held over lunch. Lunch may even be catered. As a broad term, brown bag can be applied to a wide variety of less formal training situations.

The core concept of a brown bag usually applies to a small group of people that has access to one or more experts. Participants ask the experts questions. The experts guide the conversation. There may or may not be a formal presentations. The key idea is that the sessions are less scripted than a formal classroom setting.

How successful these sessions are depends on the expert. A brown bag session provides an opportunity to persuade and influence both the experts and the attendees. Regardless of your position on a topic, a brown bag session is a good opportunity to create a personal connection.

Brown bag sessions can also be divided by type of security policy. For example, a new policy on e-mail acceptable use might be of particular concern to customer service. A security team member might be the selected expert to help explain why the new policy has been implemented and talk through how e-mail communication to customers might change.

 TIP

Brown bag sessions are good opportunities for senior leaders to convey expectations related to information security policies. This is especially true for the CISO. It provides a non-threatening forum for the CISO to connect to various levels within the organization.

Overcoming Technical Hindrances

The effectiveness of a security policy implementation is closely tied to technology controls. You can have the best policies, but if they cannot be implemented, they're useless. This section outlines several common technology challenges that can hinder the implementation of security policies.

Distributed Infrastructure

Security policies are enterprise-wide. As such, they rely on a centralized view and control of risks. You design a central set of policies and apply them across the enterprise. However, today's technology is highly decentralized. Smart devices are mobile. Users' laptops and desktops have tremendous computing power. Remote offices have servers and complex data closets supporting local networks. These are just a few examples.

For many organizations, the amount of technology outside the data center is significant. How do you implement centralized security policies in a decentralized environment? It's challenging. You first look at the administration of the distributed infrastructure.

Fortunately, while many technologies are distributed, many administration tools are centralized. Centralized administration tools allow for policies to be centrally distributed. A classic example is malware protection. Most organizations use a central malware management tool that keeps malware scanners up to date. This typically occurs when the desktop or laptop is connected to the network. An agent on the devices communicates with the central server and downloads the latest updates.

 NOTE

You'll learn more about centralized administration tools in Chapter 15.

A distributed infrastructure is typically managed through an agent or agent-less central tool. An agent is a piece of code that sits on the distributed device. As in the case of the virus scan, the agent software periodically reports back to the central management tool. An agent typically has multiple functions. The most common function is to report the state of the device back to the central server. It also receives commands and updates. In the case of the malware scan, the agent would report any malware detected and to receive updates to the scanner.

An agent-less central management tool has the ability and authority to reach out and connect to distributed devices. Unlike the malware example where the agent software pulls the updates onto the device, the agent-less software is centrally housed and pushes the changes to the device. Agent-less management products use standard interfaces within the operating system or devices. They then authenticate to those interfaces, which grants them rights to perform their function. For example, Intelligent Platform Management Interface (IPMI) can be used as an agent-less interface to Dell's OpenManage IT Assistant tool. This tool can be used to monitor and maintain a server's performance.

An current inventory is key to implementing in a highly distributed infrastructure. You need to know how many devices are on the network. You also need to know which devices adhere to security policies. Many organizations use discovery and inventory tools to capture and track this information. These tools track devices connecting and disconnecting from the network. They can also capture key security control information.

The combination of a good inventory and configuration information allows you to implement security policies in a distributed infrastructure. This is because you can assess the population of network devices and compare compliance to security policies. For example, a typical policy might state that all desktops are required to have updated virus protection. The inventory might indicate 2,000 desktops. The central malware management tool might indicate that 1,800 desktops have updated malware protection. You can now assess the effectiveness of the security policy implementation. Approximately 90 percent of your desktops comply with the policy.

Outdated Technology

Outdated technology makes implementing best practices difficult. Outdated technology generally does not adhere to current best practices. When that occurs, you must decide how to address the lack of security controls within policies. You have three basic choices:

- Write security policies to best practices and issue a policy waiver for outdated technology that inherently cannot comply.
- Write security policies to the lowest, most common security standard the technology can support.
- Write different sets of policies for outdated technologies.

None of these are good choices. The least objectionable choice is the first option. The technology that is not outdated will conform to policies. The technology that cannot conform is typically granted a waiver with additional hardening to mitigate any risk that can be reduced. Waivers provide transparency on the risks the business is accepting.

The ideal solution is to replace all outdated technology. However, that's not always an option, especially in a declining economy when many organizations are cutting costs.

It's sometimes less expensive to replace technology than to upgrade its security. Figure 13-1 illustrates that point. Assume you had outdated technology in your network. One response would be to improve segmentation controls to compensate. If you had outdated technology in the segment's network controls, you would place more reliance on operation system controls. If your operating system technology was outdated,

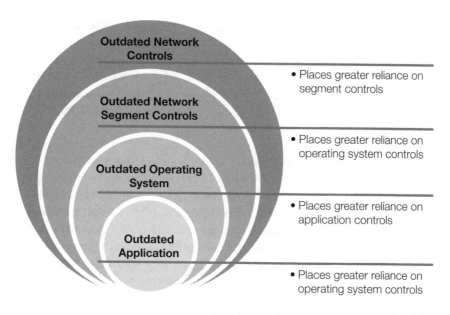

- Places greater reliance on segment controls

- Places greater reliance on operating system controls

- Places greater reliance on application controls

- Places greater reliance on operating system controls

you would place greater reliance on application controls. Any combination of the enhanced controls might mitigate some of the risk of outdated technology. All these additional layers of controls would increase costs to the organization.

In the end, outdated technology creates security vulnerabilities. Vendors usually do not support outdated technology, so new security vulnerabilities will not be patched. Even adding additional layers of security can only go so far. There's significant risk to having outdated operating systems. Once the operating system is breached, it's likely the application will be breached.

Lack of Standardization Throughout the IT Infrastructure

Another technical challenge is the lack of standardization within the infrastructure. This can come in two forms. It could be a lack of consistency with configurations. It could also be due to a diverse population of technologies deployed.

The lack of a consistent configuration occurs against a population of similar technologies. This can occur in a distributed environment when you have multiple lines of business. Each line of business has its own technologists applying different standards to similar technology. Let's assume you have a company that has physical stores and an online presence. Both lines of business have an inventory application that the public cannot access. The application may be on the same operating system and perform the same basic functions. Yet the configuration may look completely different if the application is maintained by two different groups of administrators.

This diversity in security approaches can be overcome in time. It may create delays in the implementation of the security policies. Both administration groups need to agree on a common approach to security. The implementation of the policies needs a transition plan so both types of configurations can migrate to the new policy in an orderly fashion.

When you have a diverse number of technologies deployed, security policies need to be more generic. The policies need to ensure as much of the technology as possible can comply. That means that if one set of technologies has a weakness, the policy may choose to apply the weaker standard across the broadest set of technologies. Security policies often consider minimum standards. So, while one set of technologies has a weakness, the remaining technologies can add security beyond what's called for in the policies. The problem is that policies are mandatory. By removing a security requirement from policy, there's no certainty that additional controls will ever be applied.

Consequently, having a diverse population of technologies creates a set of tradeoffs. You want security policies to be as inclusive of the technology within the organization as possible. That may mean lowering some of the security standards at times. One option is to publish a security policy with an effective date that's in the future. This gives the organization time to upgrade technology and configurations over time. Whatever approach is selected, it's important that security policies are realistic in their expectations. Security policies should not be a theoretical exercise or an ideal state. They should reflect realistic expectations on how the organization needs to control risks.

Overcoming Nontechnical Hindrances

It's not just technical challenges that can delay security policies from being implemented. It's important to remember that success depends on how well the policies are accepted.

Distributed Environment

> **NOTE**
>
> Security policies reflect a core set of principles. When you have different views of risk, it becomes a challenge to agree on these core values. It also becomes a challenge to decide how the policies will be enforced.

Many organizations operate in a distributed environment. Organizations are typically divided by lines of business, product, or geography. In a distributed infrastructure, an organization is run by different individuals with different business objectives. Therefore, different parts of an organization can have different views of risk.

This diverse set of leaders can delay security policy implementation. The first challenge is to get senior leadership to agree on a common set of security policies. The second challenge is agreeing on a timeline of implementation.

User Types

A diverse set of views is not just reflected in leaders. There is also a diverse set of views in the organization's general population. As discussed in Chapter 5, there are many types of users in the workplace.

Remember, you often operate within an existing culture. This culture might not share the same principles stated in the security policies. Even in the best of circumstances, it takes time for security policies to change the culture. In the meantime, you need to recognize the type of culture and users that exist when security policies are being implemented.

This sometimes means working in the culture that thinks of information security as an afterthought. The type of users that operate in this environment may do the minimum to get by. You have to educate these users on security policies and help them shed bad habits. Security awareness that targets specific habits can help. It's important that these users and habits are identified early. Plan specific communication events that focus on awareness training to change existing habits.

Some users think information security is a technology problem, not their problem. They might not object to the rollout of new policies, but they might undermine the effectiveness of policies by doing the bare minimum. This type of user attitude can best be managed through effective leadership. When a user knows that his or her job responsibility includes implementation of security policies, such attitudes begin to change.

Lack of Executive Management Support

Executive management support is critical in overcoming hindrances. A lack of support makes implementing security policies impossible. It takes a strong partnership between management and the IT security team to implement security policies.

Consequently, it's vitally important to gather support for the security program. One method of gaining support is to listen to the executives' needs. If executives, for example, are particularly concerned about regulatory compliance, be sure the policies address compliance thoroughly. The more you can convey that security policies solve real problems for executives, the more likely they will provide support.

When dealing with executive management, define expectations clearly. Executives generally have little time to create specific strategies. They expect well-defined security approaches and recommendations. You might need their input on key, undecided issues. However, executives expect you to do your homework. You should have already spoken to their staffs and worked out most of the details. By the time a CISO is in front of an executive to talk about implementing security policies, it should be a short conversation. The conversation should focus on "this is our recommended approach" and "this is what I need." The executive will want to know the following, at a minimum:

- Level of commitment
- How the policies impact the current environment
- What risks the effort will address
- How success will be measured

Also, be sure to communicate major successes and setbacks throughout the implementation. Keep the lines of communication open with executives. Executives want to avoid surprises. If something is not going well, they prefer to hear it from you first. They will also use success as a barometer for future requests.

Best Practices for IT Security Policy Implementations

Effective communication is one of the most important best practices to consider. A communications plan is vital. Such a plan needs to consider all communication channels.

It's critical to obtain executive support early on. Without management support, the implementation of security policies is impossible. This support should include obtaining a realistic budget and timeline for policy implementation. Visible executive support helps users accept new policies.

Keep expectations realistic. Credibility is built on delivering real solutions. For example, protecting against malicious insiders is difficult at best. Clearly communicate the expected results of the investment in security policies. When implementing security policies, executives want to know what value their investment brought.

Keep the security policies flexible. A security best practice today might be considered obsolete tomorrow. Allow for some elasticity in your policies. Take into account that the business changes over time. Also consider new technologies that are introduced, and new threats that are discovered. Security policies should not be so rigid that they cannot change when the need arises.

Be sure to follow up on the implementation. It is common for security policies to be declared a success once they are released but enthusiasm soon fades. Keep the message and interest alive. The effectiveness of the implementation should be judged in part by how well the policies are accepted and how well they reduce risk.

Case Studies and Examples of Successful IT Security Policy Implementations

The case studies in this section discuss various issues with implementing security policies. They all highlight the importance of having security policies. However, they also highlight challenges and issues.

Private Sector Case Study

A case study describing the implementation of a targeted security awareness program at Northrop Grumman Corporation was presented to the 13th Colloquium for Information Systems Security Education conference in June 2009. The case study was entitled "Using Security Awareness to Combat the Advanced Persistent Threat." The case study detailed the need, challenges, and steps taken to successfully implement a security awareness program.

The case study noted that the company is a global leader in providing technology products to private companies and governments. The company has 120,000 employees worldwide. The company is the nation's second largest defense contractor. As such, the company is a target for what it terms a "persistent threat." The company defines this persistent threat as well-funded entities attempting to penetrate its infrastructure. The company also identifies its senior leaders and administrators as prime targets.

Although the company has extensive technology controls, it also recognized the need to focus on the "human factor" to protect its systems, applications, network, and data. The security awareness program was designed to address many of these human issues.

The company developed its security awareness program around the concept of a "campaign." Some of the key steps the company took included:

- **Obtaining leadership sponsorship**—The study emphasized that buy-in included both funding and participation of senior leaders.
- **Creating policy and strategy**—The company aligned the awareness training with security policies and targeted training based on geographical needs.
- **Assembling a campaign team**—The company formed a team to manage the awareness campaign. This included identifying roles and responsibilities such as a formal approach to approving and disseminating awareness material.
- **Performing a needs assessment**—A needs assessment was used to identify individual training needs, including those for management and administrators.
- **Developing a communications plan**—The company developed a detailed communications plan.
- **Branding the campaign**—The company used an advertising approach with short "one-line" education taglines that could be reused in various materials.
- **Identifying information sources**—The company identified subject matter experts that can be used in various training events.

The detailed communications plan included the following communication channels:

- **Intranet Web site**—An intranet Web site was developed to provide access to awareness material, answer questions, and convey the latest awareness message.
- **Monthly communications**—A monthly one-page awareness newsletter was sent out to reinforce the awareness message.
- **Audio vignette**—A five-minute multimedia message was created to introduce key concepts about what a "persistent threat is" and how to defend against it.
- **Audio message from the vice president and CISO**—An audio message from senior management was created to elevate the importance of the topic and of training.
- **Management briefing**—Canned slide decks of awareness materials were developed for management to use when delivering the awareness message.
- **Incorporation into existing communications and training events**—Key messages were incorporated into existing awareness training for new employees, administrators, and management.

The study illustrates how to build a structured approach to security awareness. This includes the need for executive participation. Notice that executive involvement included participation in the form of a personal audio message.

Another important part of the campaign's success was the needs assessment. This helped target specific training needs for different types of users. In this case, particular emphasis was given to management and administrators. There was also a training component geared toward everyone in the company.

A communications plan was a critical part of the campaign's success. Management recognized that everyone learns differently. As a result, they used multiple communications methods, including the intranet, newsletters, and multimedia. The study indicated that management was sensitive about information overload. They tailored their messages in short bursts that reinforced a common message such as one-page newsletters and five-minute audio messages.

Public Sector Case Study

In December 2009, the United States House of Representatives accepted five new IT security policy recommendations. The new policies were a result of a security review. The security review was requested because of a data leak incident. Some confidential information was leaked when a junior staffer used an unsecure network.

The security policy changes required mobile devices containing sensitive information to be encrypted. They also required security awareness training and malware scanning of laptops. The increased scanning of laptops will occur whenever a device leaves or reenters the country.

This is a good example of a security breach driving a security policy change. Whenever a security breach is uncovered, a review of security policies should be conducted. The point of such a review is to determine if a reasonable policy change would have prevented the incident or mitigated the vulnerability.

This is also a good example of the importance of a security awareness program. In this case, the focus was not solely on the breach. The review took a broader view of risk. The Representatives recognized that preventing a security incident includes user education. This is also an indication of the importance placed on individuals being a critical component of the policies' success.

Critical Infrastructure Case Study

The U.S. Social Security Administration (SSA) published an analysis of its current and future technology state. The report detailed the enormous volume of data the SSA processes each day. In 2005, the workload approached 50 million transactions a day. The report also stated that the agency manages about 30 terabytes (or 1 trillion bytes) of data.

The report highlighted concerns about "outdated technology." The report mentioned the dependence on 20-year-old software language. Specific concerns highlighted the ability to implement various "privacy and security policies."

This is a good example of how outdated technology can hinder the implementation of security policies. An unintended consequence of having outdated technology is that your policies are either unrealistic or have been weakened. In either case, the policies would have a problem reflecting today's best practices.

CHAPTER SUMMARY

You learned in this chapter how organizational challenges can affect security policy implementation. You learned the importance of users' acceptance of policies. The goal is to have the policies become second nature to users over time. When users embrace security policies as part of their daily routines, you begin to see a cultural change. You learned about the importance of security awareness training. It ensures that everyone understands the policies. It also increases the chance policies will be used. You can hold users accountable if they understand the polices.

The chapter also examined how security policies are published and disseminated. You explored various communication methods. You learned the importance of a communications plan. It's used to coordinate a consistent message. Finally, the chapter examined how to overcome technical and non-technical hindrances. This included a discussion of best practices.

KEY CONCEPTS AND TERMS

Bolt-on
Communications plan
Computer-based training (CBT)
Executive management
  sponsorship
Town hall meeting

CHAPTER 13 ASSESSMENT

1. Which of the following indicate that the culture of an organization is adopting IT security policies?

   A. Security policies are part of routine daily interaction.
   B. Security policies are supported by organizational committees.
   C. Security policies' core values are demonstrated in workers' instinctive reactions to situations.
   D. All of the above

2. Effective security policies require that everyone in the organization be accountable for policy implementation.

   A. True
   B. False

3. A quick indicator of whether a risk committee has discussed security policies or if the topic has been delegated to lower levels is by looking at _____.

4. Deliberate acts and malicious behavior by employees are easy to control, especially when proper deterrents are installed.

   A. True
   B. False

5. Which of the following is not an organizational challenge when implementing security policies?

   A. Accountability
   B. Surplus of funding
   C. Lack of priority
   D. Tight schedules

6. Which type of plan is critical to ensuring security awareness reaches specific types of users?

   A. Rollout plan
   B. Media plan
   C. Executive project plan
   D. Communications plan

7. Why should a security policy implementation be flexible to allow for updates?

   A. Unknown threats will be discovered.
   B. New ways of teaching will be introduced.
   C. New technologies will be introduced.
   D. A and C
   E. All of the above

8. Which of the following is the least objectionable when dealing with policies in regards to outdated technology?

   A. Write security policies to best practices and issue a policy waiver for outdated technology that inherently cannot comply.
   B. Write security policies to the lowest, most common security standard the technology can support.
   C. Write different sets of policies for outdated technologies.
   D. All of the above

9. What is a strong indicator that awareness training is not effective?

   A. A firewall breach
   B. Sharing your password with a supervisor
   C. Sharing a laptop with a coworker
   D. A fire in the data center

10. Which of the following is a common cause of security breaches?

    A. Improved training and security awareness
    B. Increased employee motivation
    C. Outsourced processing to vendors
    D. Inadequate management and user decisions

11. Classroom training for security policy awareness is always the superior option to other alternatives, such as online training.

    A. True
    B. False

12. To get employees to comply and accept security policies, the organization must understand the employees' _____

13. A brown bag session is a formal training event with a tightly controlled agenda.

  A. True
  B. False

14. What is the best way to disseminate a new policy?

  A. Hardcopy
  B. Intranet
  C. Brown bag session
  D. All of the above

15. Without _____, implementation of IT security policies is impossible.

ENDNOTE

1. "Developing a Security–Awareness Culture – Improving Security Decision Making" (SANS, July 2004). *http://www.sans.org/reading_room/white-papers/awareness/developing-security-awareness-culture-improving-security-decision-making_1526* (accessed May 1, 2010).

13

IT Security Policy
Implementations

IT Security Policy Enforcement

T HE ENFORCEMENT OF IT SECURITY POLICY begins when the hard work of creating the policy and providing initial security awareness is done. All the effort put into creating the policy is of little value if it's not used. A compliance program is essential to ensure that policies deliver intended value. Compliance reviews and vulnerability assessments are two important components of a compliance program.

A compliance review determines if policies are being followed. The vulnerability assessment is used to measure the effectiveness of the policies. If everyone follows the policies then the number of vulnerabilities declines. If the number of vulnerabilities does not decline, the fault lies with either individuals or poorly designed polices. Vulnerability assessments need to be aligned with business goals. The level of enforcement needs to align to the level of risk.

NetApp, headquartered in Sunnyvale, California, took a survey in 2004. The results showed that 73 percent of workers used the Internet for personal use on the job. Of those individuals, 85 percent said there was little or no security threat. The exact percentage is less important than the issue of entitlement. These employees felt they had a right to use company technology regardless of stated IT policy. Enforcement of policies is necessary throughout each organization.

Policy compliance reviews and vulnerability assessments are the first steps to understanding how effective your policies are. You can use detective controls to identify situations when individuals have failed to follow policies. These tools can identify situations that require management action.

This chapter reviews the organizational and technical methods of enforcing security policies. It discusses the importance of executive support for the enforcement process. It discusses specific roles in the organization. The chapter also discusses legal considerations when enforcing security policies. It then ends by illustrating the points made through a discussion of best practices and case studies.

Chapter 14 Topics

This chapter covers the following topics and concepts:

- Who is responsible for IT security policy enforcement
- How an organization can structure support for policy enforcement
- What rights an organization has to monitor user actions
- How security policies balance local requirements and risk management
- What the difference is between laws and policies
- How policies can be enforced manually and automatically
- Who is legally accountable for IT security policies
- What role is best suited to enforce policies
- Which best practices are related to policy enforcement
- What some case studies and examples of successful IT security policy enforcement are

Chapter 14 Goals

When you complete this chapter, you will be able to:

- Describe the basic layers of controls within an organization to enforce policies
- Explain the role of executive management and middle management in enforcement
- Describe how monitoring can help policy enforcement
- Explain the difference between automated and manual policy enforcement
- Explain who is ultimately accountable for enforcement of security policies
- Describe legal implications when enforcing policies
- Describe best practices for enforcing policies

Organizational Support for IT Security Policy Enforcement

Abuse of a company's technology can leave it at risk. Failure to follow policies could lead to regulatory noncompliance. Failure to follow up and resolve issues can result in lawsuits. These situations can lead to more regulatory sanctions and expensive legal fees.

Enforcement of security policies needs to be ingrained in an organization. Many people must participate—enforcing policies is not a one-person role. Enforcement of policies is achieved through layers. This includes organizational committees enforcing policies and monitoring workers' actions. Each layer validates that security policies are being followed. The goal is to build awareness and enforcement throughout the organization over time. IT security policy compliance is everyone's role.

> **NOTE**
>
> The introduction of new policies forces change within the existing culture. It means stopping bad habits and introducing new ways of dealing with risk. Individuals tend to resist change. It's important that change be discussed well in advance of introducing new policies. Individuals must internalize and embrace policies for them to be effective.

An organization needs to decide what it wants to accomplish through policy enforcement. The organization can choose to focus on a limited number of areas such as access control, **data leakage** protection, and virus protection. Alternatively, the organization can use policies to enforce change in the culture. Certainly, enforcing security policies changes habits and thus the culture. However, it's important to remember that an organization matures into that state over time.

When introducing change, remember that it may create conflict. Security policies may conflict with how people naturally react. For example, you've been trained on social norms such as the simple act of opening the door for someone. You probably see these acts as being polite. Yet a security policy prohibits opening a door or allowing someone behind you to gain entry. You're expected to deny access to uncredentialed workers and perhaps even to a well-liked coworker. Policies may require you to deny access to senior executives. These seem like small issues, but they can create internal conflict and uneasiness in workers. These conflicts are inevitable. Workers who take a common-sense approach may have their thinking challenged. Nevertheless, part of enforcement is recognizing the conflicts and working with employees to overcome them.

> **NOTE**
>
> The goal setter in security is the chief information security officer (CISO). The CISO's key task is to build support for implementing security policies and programs within the executive ranks. The CISO's ability to build personal relationships with executives and gain their trust is the most effective tool for implementing security.

Executive Management Must Provide Sponsorship

Executive management today is pulled in many directions. It's a fast paced life. To be effective, executives need to be surrounded by employees with a strong sense of clarity, purpose, and action. Executive support does not mean getting the authority to flog people into submission. Effective leaders have the ability to encourage people to achieve the leaders' goals. They lead the organization in the right direction in order to achieve a specific goal. They use their values, knowledge, and skills to motivate and get others to excel. Effective executives persuade people to do the right thing for a better future.

Executive management support is not just about budgets and mandates. When you have executive management support you have powerful allies. Executives can overcome objections and persuade an organization to adopt policies. They can coach the chief information security officer (CISO) on how to avoid pitfalls.

Executive support is key to security policy enforcement. At some point in the enforcement process you need to change workers' behaviors. This can require disciplinary action. Even taking workers aside and coaching them runs the risk of negatively impacting a department. It is important that you lay the foundation for such discussions in advance. You accomplish this through the executive of the department. This executive can send a clear message that there's zero tolerance for ignoring security policies. The executive must be clear that violations of policies will be taken seriously. This type of message establishes a tone at the top.

TIP

Work with the people who report directly to executive management before presenting any proposal. Direct reports are often trusted advisers. Even if you have a good idea, the executives often defer decisions until they can discuss the issue with advisers. By presenting your proposal to the adviser first you avoid delays. Advisers can also be strong advocates for you with the executive.

It's important to remember that the employees look to executive management for direction. The executive leaders are expected to lead by example. This means they follow the same policies as employees. The act of exempting themselves devalues the policies' importance. Executive management needs to take an active interest in key performance indicators and show continued support. They should be visible in approving a deviation from policies only when necessary. This visibility sends a powerful message about the importance of security policies and risk management.

When an incident does occur, this preparation creates less of a chance of pushback. The executive is more likely to enforce policies to support direction and his or her personal credibility. Once executives put their own credibility behind policies, they are less likely to allow violations to occur.

Hierarchical Organizational Approach to Ensure Roles, Responsibilities, and Accountabilities Are Defined for Security Policy Implementation

The organization itself has a role in enforcing policies. This is typically handled through **gateway committees**. These committees review technology activity and often provide approvals before a project or activity can proceed to the next stage. This is why they are referred to as "gateways."

Some organizations combine different functions into one oversight board. Larger organizations often separate committee functions. The names of these committees depend on the organization. Regardless of how these committees are combined or divided, the membership should include senior leaders across the organization.

Don't get confused by committee names or the number of committees in an organization. The key is to understand how committees within an organization view risk and enforce policies. The following are committee roles and responsibilities found in most organizations:

TIP

Committees often have charters. These are formal documents that outline the mission and goals of the committee. These charters are valuable sources of information as to the function of the committee. Charters were discussed in Chapter 6 in relation to IT security policy frameworks. Incident response team charters were discussed in Chapter 12.

- **Project committee**—Approves project funding, phases, and base requirements
- **Architecture review committee**— Approves standard technologies and architectures
- **External connection committee**— Approves external data connections
- **Vendor governance committee**—Approves new vendors and oversight of existing vendors
- **Security compliance committee**—Approves controls for compliance such as Sarbanes-Oxley (SOX)
- **Operational risk committee**—Approves risk tolerance and oversight of risk exposure to the business

These committees have line of sight into all major projects and initiatives within the organization. Each committee looks at risk from a different perspective. However, they all play a role in enforcing security policies.

Project Committee

The **project committee** reviews project concepts, designs, and testing phases. It approves when a project can go into production. The number of phases requiring the committee's approval depends on the project life cycle (PLC). The intent is to identify project problems early to reduce costly mistakes. This external project review is an ideal time to examine any security policy issues.

This committee has the authority to stop a project that fails to adhere to policy. This is a powerful organizational enforcement mechanism. At a minimum, the committee asks the project team about any known security policy deviations. Additionally, representatives from the security team are members of the committee. They can ask focused security policy questions. For example, they may ask Payment Card Industry Data Security Standard (PCI DSS) compliance questions about a new online credit card processing system being deployed. The security or audit staff often performs an assessment of a project. That assessment would be submitted to the committee for resolution of any security policy issues.

Architecture Review Committee

The **architecture review committee** promotes standard use of technology and architecture. By creating architectural models to be followed, the organization can more rapidly deploy consistent technology solutions. These models usually have much of the security policies embedded in their design. Consequently, deploying standard sets of technology ensures highly reliable and compliant solutions.

This committee has the authority to stop a project that fails to adhere to these technology standards. The committee can enforce security policies. This is accomplished by deploying technology solutions that are compliant with security policies.

Additionally, the committee needs to resist adopting technology that deviates from the security policies. When noncompliant technology needs to be adopted, the risk must be accepted by the business. The committee presents the risk and technology recommendation to the business.

External Connection Committee

The **external connection committee** defines how data is transmitted outside the organization. This includes how data is received. This committee works closely with the vendor governance committee to make sure no external connections are approved to unauthorized parties. The focus of the committee is the security and reliability of these third-party connections. For organizations with little external connection, these responsibilities may be rolled into other committees such as the architectural review committee.

This committee enforces communication and encryption security requirements. No connections that violate these policies are approved.

Vendor Governance Committee

The **vendor governance committee** has both a business and a technology role. The business role is the oversight of the vendor relations. This role ensures that vendors deliver on commitments. In other words, this committee ensures if the vendor meets the service level agreement (SLA) in the contract. The committee also examines concerns about product quality.

The technical role of the committee is to ensure that the vendor complies with contracted policies. These contracted policies should be at least as restrictive as your own policies. For example, assume you identified a security policy requirement to log access to a file. This is to be compliant with a regulation. Just because that file is now transmitted to a vendor to be processed, the security policy requirement for logging doesn't cease to exist.

Vendor contract requirements must require a level of care for data equal to or better than the organization's. Vendor governance policies must require the organization put in place a way of ensuring such care is taken. It's not adequate to simply sign a contract. Accountability for that data remains with the organization. For example, under the Gramm-Leach-Bliley Act (GLBA), a bank is responsible for protecting an individual's personal financial records. The bank is still accountable if a vendor on the bank's behalf processes that data.

The bank must ensure the vendor has adequate controls in place. This can be accomplished by auditing the vendor. You can also ask the vendor to provide evidence of a recent audit. The contract itself, which is a promise by the vendor, is not considered evidence that the vendor is adequately handling the bank's data.

Security Compliance Committee

The **security compliance committee** typically has many roles. One of the key roles is to determine when policy violations occur. The security compliance committee reviews risk and vulnerability assessments. The committee often focuses on pervasive controls.

A "**pervasive control**" is a common control that is used across a significant population of systems, applications, and operations. For example, assume the same ID and password can be used across many systems and applications. That control would be considered pervasive in the environment. The security compliance committee role is to ensure those controls conform to the security policies. The committee may also be a gateway for projects to ensure that controls follow policies.

It is important that pervasive controls comply with security policies. These controls have significant impact on securing systems and applications. If there is a weakness in one of these controls, a weakness exists throughout the infrastructure. These controls are also critical to compliance testing. For example, many organizations rely on these controls for SOX compliance. When these controls do not work, organizations can find themselves out of compliance with key regulations.

Operational Risk Committee

The operational risk committee has both a business and a technology role. The committee's primary role is to manage risk to the business. It has an enforcement role for security policies. Security policies, by definition, control business risk. This means the committee is required to approve any deviations from security policies. The approval of a policy deviation is the way the business says it accepts the risk.

The operational risk committee views risk as an individual event and as a portfolio of risks. By looking at risk both ways, the committee can determine a risk tolerance for the organization. For example, the committee finds isolated instances of policy violation. Perhaps it's too expensive to replace outdated technology. These isolated instances may be acceptable risk individually. However, the combination of so many isolated cases may undermine a key compliance program. The committee needs to look at accepting risk both from the specific event and as part of a larger portfolio of risk.

The CISO or delegate is typically a committee member. He or she plays an important role by explaining the level of risks accepted by the committee on behalf of the business. Other members of this committee are typically business leaders. These leaders help enforce security policies within the business.

Organizations vary in size and management approach. As a result, the number of committees and their responsibilities can vary. Some organizations combine the functions of several of these committees. The key point is that these responsibilities need to be formally assigned to some committee within the organization.

Front-Line Managers and Supervisors Must Take Responsibility and Accept Accountability

Once policies are established, management must figure out how to implement them. This includes making the policies operational. For line management that means the following:

- Ensuring everyone on the front-line team is trained
- Taking on role as the go-to person for questions
- Applying the policies consistently
- Gathering metrics on the policy effectiveness
- Ensuring everyone follows the policy

Front-line managers and supervisors work with employees every day. They see what works and what does not. They need to work with their teams to make sure everyone understands the new policies. Managers ensure everyone has gone through awareness training. They also answer any outstanding questions. If they don't know the answers, they find out where to get the information. They are responsible for ensuring their team is ready to implement policies. They also ensure the policy rollout is on schedule within their team's responsibility.

Front-line managers and supervisors are directly accountable to ensure that employees are implementing the policies consistently. This oversight includes gathering metrics on how well the implementation is working. Sometimes policies have unintended consequences. These individuals need to document the situation when policies don't work out as designed. They are responsible for notifying management of issues and problems.

Inevitably something will go wrong. If someone fails to follow policy, managers are responsible for finding out why and resolving the problem. Sometimes that includes disciplining an employee. Other times, it is more a matter of finding out why the employee wasn't successful and overcoming the problem with coaching or additional training.

The result of these managers' and supervisors' efforts is enforced policies. These efforts ensure policies are implemented and are working properly.

Grass-Roots Employees

Employees react to the environment around them. It's rare that a worker comes to work with the intent not to follow a security policy. However, when employees see coworkers ignoring policies without consequences from managers and supervisors, they are more likely to do the same.

So the front-line employees have great influence over coworker actions. This peer pressure provides a grass-roots enforcement method. In close-knit teams, peer pressure can be a tremendous asset. Such pressure is most effective when employees know that infractions will bring scrutiny and lead to embarrassment in front of the group. The key is management's response to security policy violations. The peer pressure is more likely to be applied when the response of management is visible.

This peer pressure also works with rewards. When an individual or team is rewarded for complying with policies, there is peer pressure to emulate the behavior. A reward system can also build a change in attitude and behavior.

Employees are key to understanding how to align policies to business. They understand the level of risk for a particular business function. Based on that risk, appropriate enforcement can be applied from employees, front-line managers, and supervisors.

Policies evolve as the business evolves. The risk management process must have a feedback loop from employees to ensure that the policies still make sense for the business.

An Organization's Right to Monitor User Actions and Traffic

The prevailing legal view is that employers have the right to monitor workers' activities on company computers. This right is not absolute. In other words, it's important that an organization acts in accordance with its policies and the law. The policies must be clear and concise. This does not mean you need a policy that creates a right to monitor employees. That right is already written in law. The Electronic Communication Privacy Act (ECPA) gives employers the right to monitor employees in the ordinary course of business. These broad rights include monitoring telephone calls and computer usage such as e-mail. Having such a policy reduces an employee's argument that he or she perceived a right to privacy. It's always best that organizations put in writing their intent to monitor workers' activities on computers.

There are a number of good reasons to monitor workers' computer activities. The following is a list of some of those reasons:

- Maintaining a productive workforce
- Detecting when security policies are not being followed
- Maintaining security of sensitive data
- Ensuring quality and protecting organization's reputation
- Avoiding liability from pirated intellectual property such as software and music

Employers argue that because the computers are their property they have the right to any information contained. This is especially true when policy requires employee notification that computers are for company use only. All files contained in the computer potentially represent a record of the company's business.

Not only does productivity drop when workers spend many hours writing personal e-mails but there's also a danger of viruses or security breaches. The companies argue that they have a have right to inspect all files on the computer, even when the file is a personal e-mail sent from a work computer.

The acceptable use policy (AUP) typically includes statements regarding the employer's intent to monitor. Employees typically read and sign this document. Many of these documents state that the employee should not expect any right to privacy while using company computers.

However, the right is not absolute. Let's assume you are a worker planning on suing your company. You use a company laptop to sign on to a personal e-mail account to exchange messages with your attorney. It's not a company e-mail account, but rather a personal account such as Yahoo! or Gmail. After you leave the company and file your lawsuit, the company scans your laptop and finds portions of your communications. The company has a clear policy stating you have no right to privacy on company equipment. Did the company violate your privacy? Yes. Let's look at a specific court case to understand why.

The situation was reported in a *New York Post* article written in April 2010 and several online law articles such as the Sacramento Bankruptcy Lawyer blog. This was a case (*Marina Stengart v. Loving Care Agency, Inc.*) of Marina Stengart, a woman who worked for a health company from home. She had exchanged e-mails with an attorney regarding a possible lawsuit against her company. Ms. Stengart had used her employer-issued laptop computer to access her Web-based e-mail. After leaving the company, she turned in her laptop. Her former employer scanned her laptop and found her conversations with her attorney. In this case, the court held there was a reasonable expectation of privacy on behalf of Ms. Stengart.

This was a significant case because until that time it was assumed that with the right policy in place, an organization could monitor any activity on a company device. When the lines between a worker's personal and professional life blur, the court rulings become less clear. Organizations that allow the use of employee-owned devices may find themselves in the same situation. Some organizations, for example, allow personal smartphones to be used to send and received company e-mails. Even when these devices have the same encryption and other controls, it blurs the legal lines between work and personal life. Although this is done to reduce costs, it can quickly create legal entanglements.

There is little dispute that organizations can monitor employer-owned computers used during work hours through company accounts. There are typically three areas of monitoring employee actions:

- Internet
- E-mail
- Computers

Internet Use

Internet use is typically monitored for access to inappropriate sites such as those that contain pornographic or obscene material. Access is also monitored for unauthorized access to for-pay sites. Access to competitor sites or copyrighted material can be monitored. Uploading confidential material is a potential problem.

Most recently concerns have increased around social networking sites. These are sites that build online communities of people who share interests and information. The concern is that workers in these social communities begin exchanging information about the company. This information runs the gamut from entirely innocent remarks to negative commentary on the company all the way to divulging company secrets. The question for companies is how much of this activity should be monitored. Many organizations block these sites. This solves the problem of access while on the company network during work hours. The problem becomes more challenging when it comes to monitoring employee activity during off-hours.

Organizations do routinely monitor for any negative publicity on the social networking sites, blog spaces, and the Internet in general. If it's determined that an individual's public posting reflects negatively on the organization, then the employee will be asked to remove the posting. Usually that's as far as things will go for minor infractions.

Unless you have a highly sensitive job dealing with national secrets, most organizations are reluctant to monitor employee activity after hours. Employers do take action against employees who post extremely negative comments about the organization. This is what happened to a Web designer who lost her job after posting negative comments about her bosses. She also mentioned her company by name.

E-mail Use

E-mail use is typically monitored for viruses and malware. Companies also monitor e-mail for data leakage protection (DLP) and sensitive information. DLP monitoring may look for large files being e-mailed outside the organization. It can also scan e-mails for sensitive information such as account numbers and Social Security numbers. E-mail can also be monitored for abusive or threatening language.

Company e-mail accounts are difficult to permanently delete. It may be illegal to delete some e-mails and records that are part of a lawsuit. For example, e-mails are considered part of the public record in Massachusetts for state government agencies. These e-mails must be retained for two years. A Boston city official, under a corruption investigation in 2009, was found to be "double deleting" his e-mails each day. "Double deleting" means deleting e-mail from the inbox or sent box and then immediately deleting it from the trash bin. The attempt is to permanently delete the e-mail. Yet nearly 5,000 e-mails were still recovered. This is because e-mail can be recovered from multiple sources such as fragments on the user's computer, backups, proxy servers, and whoever receives the e-mail.

Every organization should have an e-mail policy. This builds on the AUP and talks specifically about the proper use of e-mails. The e-mail policy should require disclaimers and warn individuals that their e-mail is subject to monitoring. With these measures in place the courts have put few limits on organizations that act in good faith, such as a court case in 2001 of *Fraser v. Nationwide Mutual Insurance Company* (135 F. Supp. 2d 623 (E.D. Pa. 2001)). In this case, a worker e-mailed a competitor company with the objective of stealing customers. The court noted that "an employer can do anything with e-mail messages sent and received on company computers." The court went on to note that "as long as it has notified employees that they have no expectation of privacy," e-mail can be monitored at anytime without notice.

Computer Use

An employee's computer is also monitored for viruses and malware. It's typically monitored for pirated software and excessive use such as game playing. A user's computer is also monitored for unauthorized files that have been removed from secure servers. The extent of the monitoring depends on the concerns of the organization.

With the right policies, companies can protect themselves against these risks. There are a few restrictions on monitoring company equipment on a company network. The basic policies that should be in place to allow monitoring to be enforced are transparency and clarity. The basic steps are to make sure you have informed the workers that such monitoring can take place. Be clear through an AUP policy what the expected behavior is while using the organization's computers.

Compliance Law: Requirement or Risk Management?

Security policies by their nature attempt to comply with all regulatory requirements to be met by the organization. The word "attempt" is used to reflect the balance policies create. The policies must balance achievable goals, best practices, and interpretation of regulations. This balance requires compromise. That's why the legal department is a key stakeholder in creating security policies. The legal department ensures the security policies are defensible with regulators and in the courts.

The regulators look at first at the organization's policies. They assess if the policies are reasonable and conform to guidance. The regulators ensure core requirements are met regardless of whether the organization feels they are achievable. However, even regulators must interpret legal language, which may be different than your organization's interpretation.

For example, under GLBA, organizations must notify regulators promptly of any unauthorized access that breaches customer financial records. You need to figure out what constitutes an unauthorized access or breach. There are clear examples, such as an outside hacker. There are also gray areas. If a teller accesses an account out of curiosity, would that be a reportable breach under GLBA? It could be. Regulators provide threshold guidance. It's doubtful a bank would notify a regulator over one customer account accessed inappropriately by an internal employee. It's not uncommon for a threshold to be set at 1,000 or more records. That doesn't mean the breach of a single account isn't important. Thresholds are a practical way of assessing the magnitude of a breach. Even a single account breach can have significant impact. Let's assume that single account breach was the result of a pervasive control weakness. That single account breach is now of interest to a regulator.

TIP

Regulators use publicly published guidance documents. They use these documents to assess compliance. You can compare them to your security polices to ensure all requirements are met. Guidance documents also provide evidence to the regulator of conformance.

Regulatory guidance addresses most gray areas in the law. The key point is that organizations need to establish a risk management program that ensures security policies address legal requirements. The risk management program also ensures these policies are enforced. It is important to provide regulators with evidence that the security policies help manage risk as well as prevent breaches.

What Is Law and What Is Policy?

Organizations enforce policies and report on compliance. Organizations generally do not internally enforce laws. In other words, security policies are not a legal interpretation of the law. Security policies are interpretations of legal requirements that lead to compliance.

A **law** is any rule prescribed under the authority of a government entity. A regulatory agency may be granted the authority under the law to establish **regulations**. Regulations inherit their authority from the original law.

The distinction between laws, regulations, and security policies is as follows:

- Laws establish the legal thresholds
- Regulatory requirements establish what an organization has to do to meet the legal thresholds
- Security policies establish how the organization achieves the regulatory requirements

Let's look at an example in the security world that relates to the interpretation of information security regulations. For example, the GLBA law was intended to ensure the security and confidentiality of customer information. GLBA Section 501(b) requires that the board or its designated committee adequately oversee the financial institution's information security program. What does "adequately oversee" mean? The Federal Deposit Insurance Corporation (FDIC) issued a regulatory ruling that the organization's board must receive a formal report at least annually. Many organizations interpret that to be a formal report to audit committee by both the CISO and auditors. The point is that organizations can achieve regulatory compliance in different ways. Often you write policies to achieve regulatory requirements. Most of the time, you do not write policy to specific language of the law.

A violation of a policy is not necessarily a violation of law. However, it might be. Legal interpretation of statutes is a different skill set than policy interpretation. Often, the legal threshold to violate a law is high. It considers circumstance and intent. Only a court or regulatory body can determine if there are sufficient grounds for determining a violation of the law.

Although it is important to remain aware of the current laws and regulations, they should not be your sole driver. There are many risks to the business that are not addressed by laws and regulations. Regulations are written to address a specific area of concern that may have been a result of a public incident or class-action suit. Although ensuring adherence to regulations is a must, there's no substitute for common sense. The key point is that law always trumps policies with the regulators and the courts. Laws and regulation do not cover all risks.

What Security Controls Work to Enforce Protection of Privacy Data?

Organizations have the ability to accept risk. They can accept risks that could potentially impact the business. These organizations do not have the right to accept risk on behalf of the customer. In other words, they cannot put their customer at risk by mishandling their data.

The risk management approach used to assess and accept business risk cannot be applied equally to customer's personal data. Any organization that collects, stores, processes, and transmits personal information must be compliant with privacy laws.

These privacy laws establish specific controls. Privacy laws do vary from state to state. Some of common security controls include:

- Notification when a breach occurs
- Encrypting data when it leaves the organization's network
- Each user having a unique identity when accessing the data
- Granting access for business purposes only
- Destroying data when no longer needed
- Having appropriate policies and security awareness in place

It is important to find out what privacy laws exist when you are doing business. Based on these laws you can determine a common set of core controls. These common controls need to be in the security policies.

What Automated Security Controls Can Be Implemented Through Policy?

Policy enforcement can be accomplished through automated or manual controls. The time and effort involved in manual policy management can make automated tools an attractive option. Automated controls are cost efficient for large volumes of work that need to be performed consistently.

An automated control is configured into a device to enforce a security policy. Here's a short list of several common automated controls:

- Authentication methods
- Authorization methods
- Data encryption
- Logging events
- Data segmentation
- Network segmentation

The number of automated controls is limited only by the technology's capability. Continued improvement in technology allows for more automation. The biggest challenge isn't the automation but the deployment.

Consider an example where a policy says that a user must change his or her password every 30 days. A central authentication server exists within the environment. The challenge is how to configure every device to use the authentication server. The IT environment can have thousands of devices. Each may have to be configured. Once configured, these devices have to be monitored to ensure the configuration is not changed. As new devices are added, the same configuration has to be applied to every device from servers to smartphones. The configuration of an automated control may be simple. Applying it consistently becomes the major challenge. The problem gets more complicated as the number of automated controls increase. The diversity of the technology in the environment can make supporting the automated controls more complex. Consequently, automation is the practical solution to implement this security policy.

Many commercial products come with enterprise management software to solve this automation challenge. Central policy management software is designed specifically for this purpose. These types of applications create policy rules on a central server. These rules are then sent to the various devices via an agent or agent-less architecture.

Automated policy management tools take security policies and implement them as configuration updates. Once the device is configured, the automated control enforces the policy. The enforcement can be a preventative or detective control. Either way, the control is automated. The control either prevents an event that is outside policy or it detects that an event occurred. Our example of a policy that requires a password to be changed every 30 days is typically a preventative control. The central authentication server forces users to change their password at the end of 30 days.

TIP

Many administrator tools can support policy management. You can use administrator tools as a first step in policy management.

Policy management tools also correlate large amounts of data. They can discover devices on the network. They can track which device has the policies applied. These tools can also monitor for policy violations. The tool can identify devices that do not have the policy applied. These tools identify existing configuration to compare with the desired policy state. Deviation from policies can be automatically corrected. This is a powerful tool. Auditors and regulators often request extracts from the policy management tools. This extract can help them assess the level of policy compliance.

What Manual Security Controls Assist with Enforcement?

Not all controls can or should be automated. Manual controls are appropriate for low volume work. It's also appropriate for work that requires human judgment. Examples of manuals controls are:

- Background checks
- Log reviews
- Access rights reviews
- Attestations

In each of these cases, volumes are low and human judgment is important to the process. It is important that manual processes are clear. This means that both the step is clear and criteria for the judgment are clear.

Let's walk through background checks as a manual control. The process should be clear as to how to collect the information for the background check. The criteria should also be defined. For many jobs, minor traffic violations are acceptable. For other jobs, such as commercial drivers, any traffic violation may be considered unacceptable. A clearly defined security policy ensures everyone is treated equally on background checks. This can avoid legal problems.

A human can review logs for unusual activity that is difficult to automate. For example, when a programmer is granted elevated rights to fix a production problem logs are often reviewed. The logs are reviewed to determine if the programmer performed an activity that exceeded the scope of the fix. For instance, the log review may change if the programmer changed account data in a database. These types of changes to fix an application may be unusual and require management follow-up.

Access rights include a review by the business to ensure adequate separation of duties. This type of review is manual and requires knowledge of how the business operates. Based on this knowledge, a reasonable balance is struck between operational efficiency and reducing risks.

An "attestation" is a formal management verification. Management is attesting that a condition exists. Some regulations require management to attest that security policies and controls are in place. For example, SOX requires this type of attestation from senior management.

When someone makes an attestation, they are personally liable for the accuracy of the statement. This is a way the law holds management accountable to ensure appropriate controls are put in place. Making a false statement is often a crime. However, making a statement you believe is true that later turns out to false may be defendable. How defendable depends on the information on which you based the statement. It's not if you knew but whether you should have known. In other words, simply asking someone if the controls are in place is not sufficient.

Legal Implications of IT Security Policy Enforcement

Technology makes it easy to transact business. Computers provide an effective method of communication and record keeping. Technology offers the ability to automatically keep an audit trail. This ease of use and creation of massive amounts of data has security policy enforcement implications. Data must be preserved and retrievable for a host of legal reasons.

SANS Institute InfoSec Reading Room contributor Brad Rupert reported that the American Management Association survey of 840 businesses indicated that 21 percent had their e-mail and instant messages (IMs) subpoenaed. Failure to properly retain records can lead to significant fines. This is especially true for data related to a lawsuit. Destroying records can jeopardize a company's case. It can also lead to criminal charges. Even an innocent destruction of data can lead to accusations of negligence, withholding or hiding information, and altering or destroying evidence.

It's important to enforce security policies on data retention. This includes the preservation of data. The security policies must ensure that record keeping is accurate and securely maintained. Electronic discovery (e-discovery) is a part of the legal process. It's used to gather computer-generated information for a legal action. This can be far more complicated than the discovery of paper documents. That is because of the massive amount of data an organization holds.

Figure 14-1 illustrates this point. Consider a simple loan document. Notice from the figure that information from the original document is used to generate a monthly statement. The statement now contains personal financial information. That document, in turn, may be used to generate a late notice. The notice may be tied to an e-mail correspondence with the customer. And so on. The personal financial information

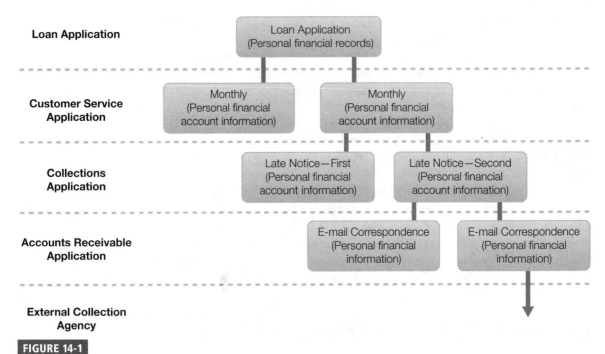

Loan Application

Customer Service Application

Collections Application

Accounts Receivable Application

External Collection Agency

FIGURE 14-1

Illustration of how data quickly expands.

could even be sent to an external collections agency. The data most likely is stored in multiple systems. This is depicted to the far left, noting the information is flowing through loan, customer service, collection, and accounts receivable applications.

Over the years, hundred of documents in a multiple system can be generated. You can quickly see the problem when an organization is required under e-Discovery to produce documents and identify everyone who accessed these documents. The effort to retrieve this information is significant.

The legal implication of policy enforcement is not just about protecting data. There's a host of issues that need to be considered when writing security policies. You may not be able to terminate a user based on a violation of security policy. It depends on how the policy was written, HR policy, and the security awareness training provided.

Even the deployment of security devices can have legal implications. For example, a **honeypot** is a network security device that acts as a decoy. Its sole purpose is to look like a tempting target to a hacker. When a hacker attempts to break into the honeypot it records the hacker's actions. This can be used as evidence of an attack. A honeypot also allows you to analyze the attack methods in great detail. This information can be used to harden other devices. This type of device has legal implications. Other security devices such as a firewall can be used to stop a hacker. Yet, a honeypot by its nature attempts to lure the hacker. Even more legal complications arise when a honeypot is put in the DMZ and publicized. This type of deployment raises the question whether the organization is encouraging an illegal act.

Smartphones not owned by the organization are a challenge, even if the organization has a policy stating they can configure and wipe the device. Who has control when employees use smartphones for company business? It's especially hard to tell when an employee leaves the firm and disconnects the device from the organization's control. How does the organization ensure the device is wiped? There are legal implications for wiping devices not owned by the organization. Policy alone cannot provide sufficient legal authority to access the device unless an employee has granted such rights through some binding agreement.

The key point is that legal implications with security policies come in many forms. It's important that you build a good working relationship with the legal department. It can ensure that security policies can be enforced without causing legal problems.

Who Is Ultimately Liable for Risk, Threats, and Vulnerabilities?

Executive management is ultimately accountable for controlling risks. Executives must explain why major security breaches occurred. They must rebuild trust with the public. They also have to rebuild confidence with shareholders and regulators.

To be accountable means there must be consequences for failure to act. Some organizations find it difficult to apply consequences to top leadership. Worse yet are organizations that identify so many leaders as accountable that, for all practical purposes, no one is accountable.

As a result, not all organizations are capable of holding their leaders accountable. Accountability can come from external forces such as:

* **Public opinion**—Creates bad publicity leading to a loss of trust
* **Shareholders**—Vote and are active at the shareholder level
* **Regulators**—Hold the organization accountable for violation of law
* **Courts**—Hold executives personally accountable

Executive management is ultimately responsible for ensuring that data is protected. That means executives are accountable for selecting key leaders such as the CISO. It also means they need to support the security program. This support includes proper funding, removing barriers, and providing visible support. All levels of management are held accountable to ensure the security program is understood and properly implemented.

This support also means defining clear roles and responsibilities for implementing security policies. Employees are responsible for understanding their roles and the security policies. They are accountable for following those policies.

The organization holds much of the liability. The organization is ultimately in control of the data. There's an obligation on the organization's part to hire competent staff. It's their obligation to give this staff appropriate resources, training, and supervision. Employees can still be held liable for violation of the law. Employees can be prosecuted for illegal acts. But often it's the organization that is ultimately held accountable. It's executive management that is held accountable for allowing such acts to occur.

The information security organization plays a key role on controlling risk. It is accountable to identify risks, threats, and vulnerabilities. Many times it's the IT organization that executes assessments. The IT teams also implement mitigating solutions. The security organization is a **subject matter expert (SME)**. It is often responsible for establishing the policies and procedures to be executive by the IT teams. The teams also review the assessment results.

Where Must IT Security Policy Enforcement Come From?

Multiple layers in the organization enforce security policies. Everyone has a role to play in identifying and managing risks. The following is a sampling of key roles to enforce security policies:

- **General counsel**—Enforces legal binding agreements
- **Executive management**—Implements enterprise risk management
- **Human resources (HR)**—Enforces disciplinary actions
- **Information systems security organization**—Enforces security policies at a program level
- **Front-line manager/supervisor**—Enforces security policies at an employee level

This is not a comprehensive list. For example, the **general counsel** works with law enforcement to prosecute employees who violate the law. The key point is to notice that every layer of the organization enforces security policies. Enforcement is not a single team's responsibility.

The general counsel enforces legal binding agreements. This enforcement takes the form of dealing with opposing legal counsel or filing lawsuits on the organization's behalf to resolve contract disputes. This includes agreements with vendors and outsourcers. The legal department is involved when the contracts are first written. These contracts often define the security policy to be followed. Ideally, any concerns with these contract policies are quickly resolved without involving the legal department. However, when security policy issues cannot be resolved, then the legal department is called. The legal department can either enforce the contract or terminate it. In extreme cases the department can file a lawsuit to recover damages due to the breach of contract. Regardless of the remedy, ultimate enforcement of legal provision falls on the legal department. Beyond this role, general counsel provides legal advice to management on writing and enforcing policies internally.

Executive management often focuses on implementing enterprise risk management. Executive committees (ECs) exist in many organizations. The EC brings multiple lines of business together to resolve strategic business issues. This is also true for enterprise risk management. The approval and enforcement of security policies is an EC responsibility. When two or more executives have differing views on security policies, the CISO tries to facilitate a solution. When the solution cannot be found, often the issue is brought to executive management through the EC. It is this committee's role to enforce security policies at the enterprise and executive level.

HR is a key player in the enforcement of disciplinary actions. The HR area defines the processes to discipline employees. These processes are one tool for enforcing security policies. The discipline could be a simple coaching session or a formal warning. Many HR teams have specific guidelines to be followed. This ensures security violations are handled in a consistent and fair manner. The visibility of a fair process is important in encouraging appropriate behavior.

The information systems security organization enforces security policies at a program level. The team is accountable for identifying violations of policies. It also needs to bring violations to the attention of management. Keep in mind that employees do not report to the security staff. Employees receive direction from their own management. The security staff is not a corporate policeman enforcing policies as corporate law. This perception is exactly what a security team should avoid. Security teams report risks. They also report facts on incidents. It is the employee's management that takes appropriate action.

The front-line manager/supervisor enforces security policies at an employee level. These individuals represent the employee's chain of command. It is these individuals that are responsible for the employee's day-to-day work. This includes ensuring that employees follow policy.

Best Practices for IT Security Policy Enforcement

The information security team should develop a close relationship with the legal team. They need to understand each other's processes and priorities. Teams should communicate their roles and responsibilities to one another. This helps them understand the various ways they can help enforce policies.

The information security team should review the current legislation that governs their business. This helps them understand what the law requires and what their legal team recommends.

The legal department should review all new or major changes to policies. The legal department needs to be briefed on how the policies will be enforced. This includes a discussion of both automated and manual controls.

Enforcement of policies is based on a risk assessment. All policies should be followed. However, those that mitigate the greatest risk to the business should be targeted first. Excessive enforcement of policies with little or no effect on the business damages credibility.

It's important to ensure that consequence and enforcement is properly socialized throughout organization. This can be accomplished through both awareness and executive messaging. Information security policy enforcement is primarily a risk management function.

Wherever possible, use automated controls to enforce policies. If the organization is concerned about social networking sites, then block them. If the organization is concerned about personal e-mail, then block those sites. When sites are blocked, an employee must overtly disable or bypass a control to gain access. The overt act of disabling or bypassing the control would be a significant violation of policy. There should be zero tolerance for such acts.

As much as possible, make a clear distinction between home and work life. Be sure that policies are clear about the use of company equipment. This includes clearly stating that there's no expectation of privacy. Also state that all company equipment can be monitored. Personal devices connected to the network should be prohibited.

Security policies should not be solely based on enforcing laws. Developments in computer technology occur daily. With every new product or upgrade, new vulnerabilities are discovered. Often we are not aware of the vulnerability until it is exploited. When enough exploits occur, laws are sometimes created. Because the legal system is reactionary in nature, it does not have the ability to keep up with exploits. Laws take time to be formulated and approved and then they must be interpreted and regulated.

The CISO position continues to evolve from a technical management position to one that combines both technical and executive functions. In many organizations, the CISO role reports directly to one or more top leadership roles. The CISO must rely on the organization to enforce policy. The role needs to build a relationships and consensus. The enforcement of security policies is about influencing behavior and changing culture.

Case Studies and Examples of Successful IT Security Policy Enforcement

The following case studies discuss various enforcement problems with IT security policies. The first two illustrate a lack of enforcement. This lack of enforcement allowed data security breaches to occur. The third talks about how a policy was effectively enforced. Although data was inappropriately downloaded in the third case study, the study shows how policy changed the culture. This culture change prevented a more serious breach.

Private Sector Case Study

The Cornell *Daily Sun* reported in June 2009 that Cornell University had had a security breach. The article stated that 45,000 personal records of students were potentially compromised. An employee had downloaded the highly sensitive data onto an unsecure computer. That computer was later stolen. The article stated that an employee had "violated existing security policies." The article did not state how the breach was discovered.

This is a classic example of an employee ignoring security policies. The article did mention that Cornell had good security policies. If that was the case, then it's a good assumption they also had good security awareness training.

This employee clearly violated policy by copying the data to an unsecure computer. The employee most likely knew it was a violation of policy. This is speculation but a good assumption. Willful disregard of policies would be a significant security breach. Such a breach is an opportunity for management to visibly show a zero tolerance for willful violation of policies.

Public Sector Case Study

The U.S. Department of Education discovered on March 23, 2010, that 3.3 million records were stolen from one of its vendors. The vendor was Educational Credit Management Corporation (ECMC), which processed $11 billion in student loans. The records that were stolen included personal data on individuals who received student loans. This included names, addresses, Social Security numbers, and dates of birth.

The information was downloaded to a removable media device, which was later stolen. The report indicated that the event was a "very clear violation of our company policies." The report indicated neither whether the data was encrypted nor the type of device used. The report indicated that the data could have dated back as far as 15 years.

Although it's speculation, we can assume the data was not encrypted. Typically, when an incident occurs and the stolen data is encrypted, an organization highlights that fact. If data is properly encrypted there is no data breach. The device can be stolen but no data can be accessed. That doesn't appear to be the case here because the report assumes the data was compromised.

This leaves the issue of enforcement. It appears the enforcement of the policy was manual. The report did not indicate the type of removable media. Portable media devices can be locked down or encrypted. That would be an example of an automated control. That type of control was apparently not in place in this case.

Critical Infrastructure Case Study

A report in March 2010 indicated that the Veterans Affairs (VA) department had a security breach. The breach involved a physician assistant who was accused of copying two sets of recorded patient data onto a personal laptop. The assistant was doing research. One set included three years of patient data and another held 18 years of medical information.

There was an incident with the VA in 2006 in which 26.5 million patient records were downloaded to an unsecured computer. Later that computer was stolen. Because of the incident in 2006, the VA instituted new policies that all patient data stored on department computers must be encrypted.

The assistant was discovered and stopped by a nurse-scientist visiting the medical center. The nurse-scientist discovered that the physician assistant was part of an unapproved project. On February 8, 2010, the nurse-scientist reported the incident to the compliance officer. On February 26, the physician assistant resigned.

This case study is an example of an effective enforcement of security policies. Although there was an original violation of policy by the physician assistant, the breach was quickly stopped by a coworker. It's a clear indication that security awareness was at the top of the nurse-scientist's mind. The quick action of that person prevented data loss. In this case all the data was recovered.

CHAPTER SUMMARY

It's everyone responsibility to enforce security policies. This is accomplished by the collective action of many leaders. The enforcement starts with executive support. This support goes beyond receiving permission to implement security policies. Executive support also means personal commitment by the managers to use their position and skills to influence the direction of their teams.

The organization also enforces policies through committees. These committees act as a gateway to check that security policies are being followed. This may mean monitoring employee use of the computer. When behavior does not conform to policies, it is the role of front-line managers and supervisors to act.

This chapter examined the relationship between laws, regulations, and policies. We defined what is law and policy. We examined different methods of enforcing policies. We examined the strengths and weaknesses of automated and manual controls. Finally, the chapter examined the legal implication of enforcing security policies.

KEY CONCEPTS AND TERMS

Architecture review committee	Honeypot	Security compliance committee
Data leakage	Laws	Subject matter expert (SME)
External connection committee	Pervasive control	Vendor governance committee
Gateway committees	Project committee	
General counsel	Regulations	

CHAPTER 14 ASSESSMENT

1. Which of the following is *not* an organizational gateway committee?

A. Architecture review committee
B. Internal connection committee
C. Vendor governance committee
D. Security compliance committee

2. _____ often focuses on enterprise risk management across multiple lines of business to resolve strategic business issues.

3. The security compliance committee has one role, which is to identify when violations of policies occur.

A. True
B. False

4. Which of the following is *not* an access control?

A. Authentication
B. Authorization
C. Decryption
D. Logging

5. In which of the following areas might a company monitor its employees' actions?

A. Internet
B. E-mail
C. Computers
D. A and B
E. All of the above

6. _____ establish how the organization achieves regulatory requirements.

7. Laws define the specific internal IT processes needed to be compliant.

A. True
B. False

8. What is *not* required in modern-day CISO positions?

A. Must rely on the organization to enforce policy
B. Needs to have strong law enforcement background
C. Needs to build relationships and consensus
D. Must influence behavior and change culture to enforce policy

9. What is an example of a manual control?

A. Background checks
B. Authentication
C. Access rights reviews
D. A and C
E. All of the above

10. Which of the following is *not* a reason to monitor employee computer activity?

A. Maintaining a productive workforce
B. Detecting when security policies are not being followed
C. Finding out whom the employee knows
D. Ensuring quality and protecting organization's reputation

11. Connecting a personal device to the company network can create legal implications.

A. True
B. False

12. Line management does which of the following to make policies operational?

A. Acts as go-to people for addressing questions
B. Applies policies consistently
C. Gathers metrics on the policies' effectiveness
D. A and C
E. All of the above

13. The major challenge in implementing automated security controls is in the deployment of the control.

A. True
B. False

14. Which of the following is *not* reviewed when monitoring a user's e-mail and Internet activity?

A. Data leakage
B. Viruses and malware
C. Unauthorized access to sites
D. Network performance

IT Policy Compliance Systems and Emerging Technologies

I T COMPLIANCE IS EXTREMELY IMPORTANT to organizations today. A lot of time and energy goes into ensuring that security policies cover what is important to an organization. These policies help an organization comply with laws, standards, and guidelines. Implemented properly, they also reduce outages and increase the organization's mission capability.

Baselines are often used to deploy security policy settings. The baseline ensures that all affected systems have the same security settings. Imaging technologies allow a single system to be used as the baseline for newer systems. All new systems receive the image created on this source system. Imaging reduces the time required to configure the systems and ensures security is deployed identically. It doesn't matter if the image is deployed to five systems or 5,000. They will all start in a known secure state in compliance with the security policy.

Many automated tools are available to audit these systems on a regular basis. They ensure the settings haven't changed from the baseline. Additionally, automated tools are available to deploy approved changes. For example, patches and hotfixes resolve known software vulnerabilities. These tools can audit systems to determine if the change is applied. If not, they can deploy the patches. The Security Content Automation Protocol (SCAP) may be the most important emerging technology for security today. This chapter covers all of these topics.

Chapter 15 Topics

This chapter covers the following topics and concepts:

- What a baseline definition for information systems security is
- How to track, monitor, and report IT security baseline definitions and policy compliance
- What automating IT security policy compliance involves
- What some emerging technologies and solutions are
- What best practices for IT security policy compliance monitoring are
- What some case studies and examples of successful IT security policy compliance monitoring are

Chapter 15 Goals

When you complete this chapter, you will be able to:

- Explain a baseline definition for information systems security
- Define the vulnerability window and information security gap
- Discuss the importance of tracking, monitoring, and reporting IT security baseline definitions and policy compliance
- Compare and contrast automated and manual systems used to track, monitor, and report security baselines and policy compliance
- Describe the requirements to automate policy distribution
- Describe configuration management and change control management
- Discuss the importance of collaboration and policy compliance across business areas
- Define and contrast Security Content Automation Protocol (SCAP), Simple Network Management Protocol (SNMP), Web-Based Enterprise Management (WBEM), and Windows Management Instrumentation (WMI)
- Describe digital signing
- List best practices for IT security policy compliance monitoring

Defining a Baseline Definition for Information Systems Security

A baseline is a starting point or a standard. Within IT, a baseline provides a standard focused on a specific technology used within an organization. When applied to security policies, the baseline represents the minimum security settings that must be applied.

For example, imagine that an organization has determined every system needs to be hardened. The security policy defines specifically what to do to harden the systems. For example, the security policy could provide the following information:

- **Protocols**—Only specific protocols listed within the security policy are allowed. Other protocols must be removed.
- **Services**—Only specific services listed within the security policy are allowed. All other services are disabled.
- **Accounts**—The administrator account must be renamed. The actual name of the new administrator may be listed in the security policy, or this information could be treated as a company secret.

The security policy would have much more information but these few items give you an idea of what is included. Many security policies are 40 pages or more.

Baselines have many uses in IT. Anomaly-based intrusion detection systems (IDSs) use baselines to determine changes in network behavior. Server monitoring tools also use baselines to detect changes in system performance. This chapter focuses on the use of baselines as a security starting point.

An anomaly-based IDS detects changes in the network's behavior. You start by measuring normal activity on the network, which becomes your baseline. The IDS then monitors activity and compares it against the baseline. As long as the comparisons are similar, activity is normal. When the network activity changes so that it is outside a predefined threshold, activity is abnormal. For example, if a worm infected a network, it would increase network activity. The IDS recognizes the change as an anomaly and sends an alert. The anomaly-based IDS can't work without first creating the baseline. You can also think of an anomaly-based IDS as a behavior-based IDS because it is monitoring the network behavior.

Administrators commonly measure server performance by measuring four core resources. These resources are the processor, the memory, the disk, and the network interface. When these are first measured and recorded, it provides a performance baseline. Sometime later, the administrator measures the resources again. As long as the measurements are similar, the server is still performing as expected. However, if there are significant differences that are not explainable, the change indicates a potential problem. For example, a denial of service (DoS) attack on the server may cause the processor and memory resource usage to increase.

A security baseline is also a starting point. For example, a security baseline definition for Windows 7 identifies a secure configuration for the operating system in an organization. As long as all Windows 7 systems use the same security baseline, they all start in a known secure state. Later, you can compare the security baseline against the current configuration of any system. If they are different, something has changed. The change indicates the system no longer has the same security settings. If a security policy mandated the original security settings, the comparison shows the system is not compliant.

Policy-Defining Overall IT Infrastructure Security Definition

Many organizations use **imaging** techniques to provide baselines. An image can include the full operating system, applications, and system settings. This includes all the desired security and configuration settings required for the system.

Figure 15-1 shows an example of how imaging is accomplished. You start with a clean system referred to as a source computer. You install the operating system and any desired applications on the source computer. Next, you configure specific settings needed by users. Then you configure the security settings to comply with the security policy. For example, you could remove unneeded protocols, disable unused services, and rename the administrator account. You can lock this system down with as much security as you need or desire.

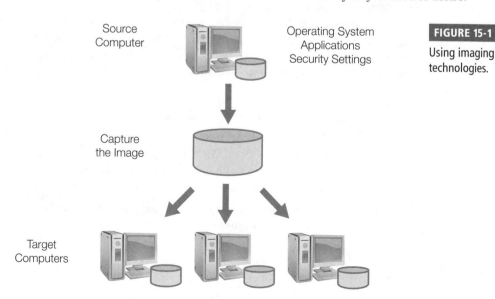

Source Computer

Operating System
Applications
Security Settings

Capture the Image

Target Computers

FIGURE 15-1

Using imaging technologies.

NOTE

Before capturing the image, you may need to run programs to remove unique information. For example, you may deploy this image to 50 computers. If the source computer name is Computer1, the 50 imaged computers would also be named Computer1, which represents 50 conflicts on the network. Microsoft includes a tool called Sysprep. Sysprep removes unique information from systems before the image is captured.

Next, you capture an image of the system. You can think of this like taking a snapshot. Imaging captures the entire software contents of the system at that moment. Symantec Ghost is a popular imaging program used to capture images of any operating system. Microsoft Windows Server 2008 includes Windows Deployment Services (WDS). WDS is free and can capture and deploy images of Microsoft systems only.

Once you've captured the image, you can deploy it to other systems. Each system that receives the image will have the same operating system and applications. It will also have the same security and configuration settings.

This baseline improves security for systems. It also reduces the total cost of ownership. Imagine that the security policy required changing 50 different security settings. Without the baseline, these settings would have to be configured separately. The time involved to configure them separately may be substantial. Additionally, there's no guarantee that all the settings would be configured exactly the same on each system when done manually.

If all the systems are configured the same, help desk personnel can troubleshoot them more quickly. This improves availability. Imagine if 50 different systems were configured 50 different ways. Help desk personnel would first need to determine the normal configuration when troubleshooting problems. Once they determined normal operation, they would then determine what's abnormal in order to fix it. Each time they worked on a new system, they'd repeat the process.

However, if all the systems are the same, help desk personnel need to learn only one system. This knowledge transfers to all the other systems. Troubleshooting and down time is reduced. Availability is increased.

It is possible to use a standard for all systems without imaging. You would start by installing the operating system and any desired applications. Next, you'd apply all the configuration and security settings. You would use a checklist to ensure that all the settings were configured the same. However, this manual method presents several challenges:

- Personnel must know about the checklist and be able to find it.
- Completing the checklist could take a long time. Depending on how long a single checklist takes, and the number of systems to configure, it could be cost prohibitive. For example, if a single system takes one hour to complete and there are 50 systems, it would take 50 labor hours to complete—more than a full work week.
- Typos and mistakes are possible. The technician could easily make mistakes. These mistakes may be difficult to detect.

Vulnerability Window and Information Security Gap Definition

The vulnerability window is the gap between when a new vulnerability is discovered and when software developers start writing a patch. Attacks during this time are referred to as zero-day attacks. You don't know when the vulnerability window opens, since you don't know when an attacker will find the vulnerability. However, most vendors will start writing patches as soon as they learn about the vulnerability.

Similarly, there's a delay between the time a patch is released and an organization patches their systems. Even if you start with a baseline, there is no way that it will always be up to date or will meet the needs for all your systems. The difference between the baseline and the actual security needs represents a security gap. For example, you may create an image on June 1. One month later, you may deploy the image to a new system. Most of the configuration and security settings will be the same. However, there may have been some changes or updates that occurred during the past month. These changes present attackers with a vulnerability window and must be plugged.

 TIP

Patch management is an important security practice. Software vulnerabilities are routinely discovered in operating systems and applications. Vendors release patches or updates to plug the vulnerability holes. However, if the patches aren't applied, the system remains vulnerable. Keeping systems patched helps an organization avoid significant attacks and outages.

If your organization uses change management procedures, you can easily identify any changes that should be applied to the system. If you have automated methods to get updates to systems, you can use those to update it. If not, the system will need to be updated manually.

Within a Microsoft domain, **Group Policy** deploys many settings. Group Policy allows an administrator to configure a setting once and it will automatically apply to multiple systems or users. If Group Policy is used to change settings, the changes will automatically apply to the computer when it authenticates on the domain. Additional steps are not required.

Tracking, Monitoring, and Reporting IT Security Baseline Definition and Policy Compliance

A baseline is a good place to start. It ensures that the systems are in compliance with security requirements when they are deployed. However, it's still important to verify that the systems stay in compliance. An obvious question is how the systems may have been changed so they aren't in compliance. It's a good question. Administrators or technicians may change a setting to resolve a problem. For example, an application may not work unless security is relaxed. These changes may weaken security so that the application works. Malicious software (malware) such as a virus may also change a security setting.

It doesn't matter how or why the setting was changed. The important point is that if it was an unauthorized change, you want to know about it. You can verify compliance using one or more of several different methods. These methods simply check the settings on the systems to verify they haven't been changed. Methods include:

- Automated systems
- Manual tracking and reporting
- Random audits and departmental compliance
- Overall organizational report card for policy compliance

Automated Systems

Automated systems can regularly query systems to verify compliance. For example, the security policy may dictate that specific protocols must be removed or specific services must be disabled. It may require password-protected screen savers. An automated system can query the systems to determine if these settings are still the same.

Many automated tools include scheduling abilities. You can schedule the tool to run on a regular basis. Advanced tools can also reconfigure systems that aren't in compliance. All you have to do is review the resulting report to verify systems are in compliance. For example, assume your company has 100 computers. You could schedule the tool to run every Saturday night. It would query each of the systems to determine their configuration and verify compliance. When the scans are complete, the tool would provide a report showing all of the systems that are out of compliance including the specific issues. If your organization is very large, you could configure the scans to run on different computers every night.

Microsoft provides several automated tools you can use to manage Microsoft products. Although Microsoft isn't the only tool developer to choose from, it does have the largest installed base of computers in organizations. It's worthwhile knowing which tools are available. These include:

- **Microsoft Baseline Security Analyzer (MBSA)**—MBSA is a free download that can query systems for common vulnerabilities. It starts by downloading an up-to-date Extensible Markup Language (XML) file. This file includes information on known vulnerabilities and released patches. MBSA can scan one or more systems in a network for these vulnerabilities. It keeps a history of reports showing all previous scans.

- **Windows Server Update Services (WSUS)**—WSUS is a free server product used to manage client patches and updates. Administrators download and test updates for clients in their network. WSUS then deploys approved updates to the clients. WSUS can also scan and audit systems to ensure that approved patches are applied.

- **Systems Management Server (SMS)**—This is an older server product but is still used in many organizations. It combines and improves the capabilities of several other products. It can query systems for vulnerabilities using the same methods used by MBSA. It can deploy updates just as WSUS can. It adds capabilities to these tasks, such as the ability to schedule the deployment of updates and the ability to push out software applications.

- **System Center Configuration Manager (SCCM)**—SCCM is an upgrade to SMS. It can do everything that SMS can do and provides several enhancements. SCCM can deploy entire operating system images to clients.

In addition to the Microsoft products, there is a wide assortment of other automated tools. These can run on other operating systems and scan both Microsoft and other operating systems such as UNIX and UNIX derivatives.

- **Nessus**—Nessus is considered by many to be the best UNIX vulnerability scanner. It is listed as No. 1 on Fyodor's Top 10 Vulnerability Scanners list. Renai LeMay reported in CNET News in 2005 that Nessus was being used by more than 75,000 organizations worldwide before it switched from a free product to one you had to purchase.

- **Nmap**—A network scanner that can identify hosts on a network and determine services running on the hosts. It uses a ping scanner to identify active hosts. It uses a port scanner to identify open ports, and likely protocols running on these ports. It is also able to determine the operating system.

> **TIP**
>
> Gordon "Fyodor" Lyon wrote and maintains the Nmap Security Scanner tool and maintains Insecure.org. He goes by the name Fyodor on the Internet.

- **eEye Digital Security Retina**—Retina is a suite of vulnerability management tools. It can assess multiple operating systems such as Microsoft, Linux, and other UNIX distributions. It also includes patch deployment and verification capabilities.

- **SAINT (Security Administrators Integrated Network Tool)**—SAINT provides vulnerability assessments by scanning systems for known vulnerabilities. It can perform penetration testing which attempts to exploit vulnerabilities. SAINT runs on a UNIX/Linux platform but it can test any system that has an Internet Protocol (IP) address. It also provides reports indicating how to resolve the detected problems.

- **Symantec Altiris**—Altiris includes a full suite of products. It can manage and monitor multiple operating systems. This includes monitoring systems for security issues and deployed patches.

It's also possible to use logon scripts to check for a few key settings. For example, a script can check to see if anti-malware software is installed and up to date, or if the system has current patches. The script runs each time a user logs on.

Some organizations quarantine systems that are out of compliance. In other words, if a scan or a script shows the system is not in compliance, a script modifies settings to restrict the computer's access on the network. The user must contact an administrator to return the system to normal.

15

Compliance Systems and
Emerging Technologies

SCAP Compliance Tools

The Security Content Automation Protocol (SCAP) is presented later in this chapter. SCAP is one of the programs of the National Institute of Standards and Technology (NIST). SCAP defines protocols and standards used to create a wide variety of automated scanners and compliance tools.

NIST accredits independent laboratories. These independent laboratories validate SCAP-compliant tools for the following automated capabilities:

- **Authenticated configuration scanner**—The scanner uses a privileged account to authenticate on the target system. It then scans the system to determine compliance with a defined set of configuration requirements.

- **Authenticated vulnerability and patch scanner**—The scanner uses a privileged account to authenticate on the target system. It then scans the system for known vulnerabilities. It can also determine if the system is patched, based on a defined patch policy.

- **Unauthenticated vulnerability scanner**—The scanner doesn't use a system account to scan the system. This is similar to how an attacker may scan the system. It scans the system over the network to determine the presence of known vulnerabilities.

- **Patch remediation**—This tool installs patches on target systems. These tools include a scan or auditing component. The patch scanner determines a patch is missing and the patch remediation tool applies the missing patch.

- **Misconfiguration remediation**—This tool reconfigures systems to bring them into compliance. It starts by scanning the system to determine if a defined set of configuration settings are accurate. It then reconfigures any settings that are out of compliance.

You can read more about the SCAP validation program on NIST's site here: *http://scap.nist.gov/validation/index.html.*

Manual Tracking and Reporting

It's also possible to do manual tracking and reporting of IT security policy issues. This is much more tedious and time consuming if you're checking multiple systems and multiple settings. However, if you only have a few systems, the cost of an automated tool may not be affordable. For example, imagine you had three Linux systems in a network. You may choose to manually check and verify these systems on a regular basis.

The biggest challenge is ensuring that these manual checks don't fall through the cracks. Administrators have multiple challenges and multiple tasks at any given time. The crisis of a system that is down is more important than a system that is operational. It becomes easier and easier to postpone and forget manual checks. However, automated checks will continue to run no matter how busy the administrator is.

Chapter 3 presented the Payment Card Industry Data Security Standard (PCI DSS) standard. PCI DSS has six control objectives that an organization needs to follow to be in compliance. These rules protect credit cardholder data. An organization can implement these rules within their network. Administrators or security professionals could then create a checklist identifying the different steps and settings they've configured. On a regular basis such as monthly, or quarterly, the organization can recheck the systems.

For example, the organization could be using Advanced Encryption Standard (AES) to encrypt data stored on a server. It could use Internet Protocol Security (IPSec) to encrypt transmitted data. A few checks can easily verify these encryption standards are still in place. Similarly, the systems can be checked manually to determine if they are up to date. Some systems may need patches applied manually. In other words, an administrator will need to log onto each individual system, check for needed patches, and apply them.

Random Audits and Departmental Compliance

You can also perform random audits to determine compliance. This is often useful when IT tasks have been delegated to different elements in the organization. For example, a large organization could have a decentralized IT model. A central IT department manages some core services such as network access and e-mail, and individual departments manage their own IT services. The organization still has an overall security policy. However, the individual departments are responsible for implementing them. In this case, the central IT department could randomly audit the departments to ensure compliance. Some larger organizations employ specialized security teams. These teams have a wide variety of responsibilities in the organization such as incident response and boundary protection. They could also regularly scan systems in the network and randomly target specific department resources.

It's important to realize the goal of these scans. It isn't to point fingers at individual departments for noncompliance. Instead, it's to help the organization raise its overall security posture. Of course, when departments realize their systems could be scanned at any time, this provides increased motivation to ensure the systems are in compliance.

▶TIP

Seven days within their release may sound like a short period. However, organizations often have close relationships with vendors that ensure they are aware of patches prior to their actual release. For example, many organizations have agreements with Microsoft that gives them advance notice of patches before their public release.

Overall Organizational Report Card for Policy Compliance

Many organizations use a report card format to evaluate policy compliance. Organizations can create their own grading criteria. However, just as in school, a grade of A is excellent while a grade of F is failing. The included criteria depend on the organization's requirements. For example, the following elements can be included in the calculation of the grade:

- **Patch compliance**—This compares the number of patches that should be applied versus the number of patches that are applied. A time period should be considered. For example, the organization could state a goal of having 100 percent of the patches deployed within seven days of their release. The only exception would be if testing of any patch verified that the patch caused problems.

- **Security settings**—The baseline sets multiple security settings. These should all stay in place. However, if an audit or scan shows that the settings are different, it represents a conflict. Each security setting that is not in compliance is assigned a value. For example, every setting that is different from the baseline could represent a score of 5 percent. If scans detect three differences, the score could be 85 percent (100 percent minus 15 percent).

- **Number of unauthorized changes**—Most organizations have formal change control processes. When these are not followed, or they do not exist, changes frequently cause problems. These problems may be minor problems affecting a single system or major problems affecting multiple systems or the entire network. Every unauthorized change would represent something less than 100 percent. For example, 15 unauthorized changes within a month could represent a score of 85 percent, or a grade of B in this category.

Once you identify the rules or standards, you could use a spreadsheet to calculate the grades. An administrator could pull the numbers from the scans and enter them into the spreadsheet monthly. You could use individual grade reports for each department that manages IT resources, and combine them into a single grade report for the entire organization.

Automating IT Security Policy Compliance

The one thing that computers are good at is repetition. They can do the same task repeatedly and always give the same result. Conversely, people aren't so good at repetitious tasks. Ask an administrator to change the same setting on 100 different computers and it's very possible that one or more of the computers will not be configured correctly.

Additionally, automated tasks take less labor and ultimately cost less money. For example, a task that takes 15 minutes to complete will take 25 labor hours ($15 \times 100 / 60$). If an administrator took 2 hours to write and schedule a script, it results in a savings of 23 labor hours. Depending on how much your administrators are paid, the savings can be significant.

Many security tasks can also be accomplished with dedicated tools. For example, the "Automated Systems" section earlier in this chapter listed several different tools with a short description of some of their capabilities. However, if you plan to automate any tasks related to IT security policy compliance, you should address some basic concerns. These include:

- Automated policy distribution
- Configuration and change management

Automated Policy Distribution

Earlier, in this chapter, imaging was described as a method to start all computers with a known baseline. This is certainly an effective way to create baselines. However, after the deployment of the baseline, how do you ensure that systems stay up to date? For example, you could deploy an image to a system on July 1. On July 15, the organization approves a change. You can modify the image for new systems, but how do you implement the change on the system that received the image on July 1, as well as on the other existing systems? Additionally, if you didn't start with an image as a baseline, how do you apply these security settings to all the systems on the network?

The automated methods you use are dependent on the operating systems in the organization. If the organization uses Microsoft products, you have several technologies you can use. Some such as SMS and SCCM were mentioned previously. Another tool is Group Policy.

Group Policy is available in Microsoft domains. It can increase security for certain users or departments in your organization. You could first apply a baseline to all the systems with an image. You would then use Group Policy to close any security gaps, or increase security settings for some users or computers.

---

technical TIP

Microsoft isn't the only operating system out there. However, the company has the most market share. With this in mind, it's useful to know which tools are available for the majority of computers used in networks today. Preston Gralla reported in his ComputerWorld blog in January 2010 that more than 92 percent of computers were running Microsoft Windows. About 5 percent ran Mac OS X, and about 1 percent ran Linux. Other operating systems took up the other 2 percent. This actually represented a decline for Microsoft, but the popularity of Windows 7 may increase Microsoft's market share as time moves forward.

15

Compliance Systems and
Emerging Technologies

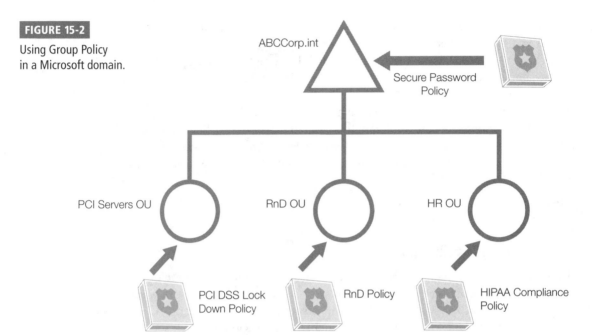

FIGURE 15-2

Using Group Policy
in a Microsoft domain.

Consider Figure 15-2 as an example. The organization name
is ABC Corp and the domain name is ABCCorp.int. The Secure
Password Policy is linked to the domain level to require secure
passwords for all users in the domain. The organization could
define a password policy requiring all users to have strong
passwords of at least six characters. If the organization later
decides it wants to change this to a more secure eight-character
policy, an administrator could change the Secure Password Policy
once and then it would apply to all users in the domain. It doesn't
matter if there are 50 or 50,000 users—a single change applies
to all equally.

All the PCI DSS server objects are placed in the PCI Servers
organizational unit (OU). A policy named PCI DSS Lock Down
Policy is linked to this OU. It configures specific settings to ensure
these servers are in compliance with PCI DSS requirements.

Human resources (HR) personnel handle health data covered by the Health Insurance
Portability and Accountability Act (HIPAA). These users and computers can be placed
in the HR OU. The HIPAA Compliance Policy includes Group Policy settings to enforce
HIPAA requirements. For example, it could include a script that includes a logon screen
reminding users of HIPAA compliance requirements and penalties.

The figure also shows a research and development OU, named RnD OU, for that area.
Users and computers in the research and development department would be placed in
the RnD OU. The RnD policy could include extra security settings to protect data created
by the RnD department.

Group Policy not only configures the changes when systems power on, but also provides automatic auditing and updating. Systems query the domain every 90 to 120 minutes by default. Any Group Policy changes are applied to affected systems within two hours. Additionally, systems will retrieve and apply security settings from Group Policy every 16 hours even if there are no changes.

Training Administrators and Users

These tools and technologies aren't always easy to understand. They include a rich set of capabilities that require a deep understanding before they can be used effectively. It takes time and money to train administrators and users how to get the most out of these tools.

Almost all the companies that sell these tools also sell training. You can send administrators to train at a vendor location. If you have enough employees who require training, you can conduct it on-site.

The important point to remember is that even the most "valuable" tool is of no value if it's not used. Training should be considered when evaluating tools. Determine if training is available and its cost.

Organizational Acceptance

Organizational acceptance is also an important consideration. Resistance to change can be a powerful block in many organizations. If the method you're using represents a significant change, it may be difficult for some personnel to accept. As an example, using a baseline of security settings can cause problems. Applications that worked previously may no longer work. Web sites that were accessible may no longer be. There are usually work-around steps that will resolve the problem, but it will take additional time and effort.

To illustrate, assume that a baseline is being tested for deployment. Administrators in one department determine that the baseline settings prevent an application from working. There are three methods for resolving the problem. First, the administrators could weaken security by not using the baseline settings. However, weakening security is not a good option. Second, the department may decide it can no longer use the application. If the application is critical to its mission, this may not be a good option. Third, a work-around method can be identified that doesn't bypass the original baseline settings, but also allows the application to work. The third option will require digging in to resolve the problem. If the administrators are already overburdened, or don't have the knowledge or ability to resolve the problem, they may push back. This requires a climate of collaboration to address the problem.

 NOTE

Some problems may not be resolvable. Senior management may be forced to make a decision between security and usability. In other words, management may decide to weaken security so that an application runs. Managers decide to accept a certain level of risk.

Testing for Effectiveness

Not all automated tools work the same. Before investing too much time and energy into any single tool, it's worthwhile testing them to determine their effectiveness. Some of the common things to look for in a tool include:

NOTE

Both IIS and Apache are Web servers. They run Hypertext Transfer Protocol (HTTP) on port 80. If the tool checks only for port 80, it may inaccurately identify an IIS server as an Apache server. Because they both have different vulnerabilities, the results cannot be accurate.

- **Accurate identification**—Can the tool accurately identify systems? Does it know the difference between a Microsoft server running Internet Information Services (IIS) and a Linux system running Apache, for example?

- **Assessment capabilities**—Does it scan for common known vulnerabilities? For example, can it detect weak or blank passwords for accounts?

- **Discovery**—Can the system accurately discover systems on the network? Can it discover both wired and wireless systems?

- **False positives**—Does it report problems that aren't there? For example, does it report that a patch has not been applied when it has?

- **False negatives**—Does it miss problems that exist? In other words, if a system is missing a patch, can the tool detect it?

- **Resolution capabilities**—Can the tool resolve the problem, or at least identify how it can be resolved? Some tools can automatically correct the vulnerability. Other tools provide directions or links to point you in the right direction.

- **Performance**—The speed of the scans is important, especially in large organizations. How long does the scan of a single system take? How long will it take to scan your entire network?

Audit Trails

If a tool makes any changes on the network, it's important that these changes are recorded. Changes are recorded in change management logs that create an audit trail. The tool making the change can record changes it makes on any systems. However, it's common for logs to be maintained for individual systems being changed, separate from the change management log.

Logs can be maintained on the system, or off-system. The value in having off-system logs is that if the system is attacked or fails, the logs are still available. Additionally, some legal and regulatory requirements dictate that logs be maintained off-system.

Audit trails are especially useful for identifying unauthorized changes. Auditing logs the details of different events. This includes who, what, where, when, and how. If a user made a change, for example, the audit log would record who the user was, what the user changed, when the change occurred, and how it was done.

TIP

Some auditing is enabled by default on systems. However, you may need to enable additional auditing to determine details on specific events.

Imagine a security baseline is deployed in the organization. You discover that one system is regularly being reconfigured. The security tool fixes it, but the next scan shows it's been changed again. You may want to know who is making this change. If auditing is enabled, it will record the details. You only need to view the audit trail to determine what is going on.

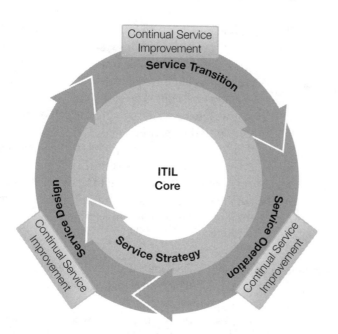

FIGURE 15-3

The ITIL life cycle.

Configuration Management and Change Control Management

Chapter 3 presented the Information Technology Infrastructure Library (ITIL). As a reminder, it includes five books that represent the ITIL life cycle, as shown in Figure 15-3. A central part of ITIL is Service Transition. This relates to the transition of services into production. It includes configuration management and change management.

ITIL isn't an all or nothing approach. Organizations often adopt portions of ITIL practices without adopting others. Configuration management and change management are two elements within the Service Transition stage that many organizations do adopt.

Configuration management (CM) establishes and maintains configuration information on systems throughout their life cycle. This includes the initial configuration established in the baseline. It also includes recording changes. The initial public draft of NIST SP 800-128 defines CM as a collection of activities. These activities focus on establishing the integrity of the systems by controlling the processes that affect their configurations. It starts with the baseline configuration. CM then controls the process of changing and monitoring configuration throughout the system's lifetime.

Change management is a formal process that controls changes to systems. One of the common problems with changes in many organizations is that they cause outages. When an unauthorized change is completed on one system, it can negatively affect another system. These changes aren't done to cause problems. Instead, well-meaning technicians make a change to solve a smaller problem and unintentionally create bigger problems. Successful change management ensures changes have minimal impact on operations. In other words, change management ensures that a change to one system does not take down another system.

> **NOTE**
>
> Two case studies at the end of this chapter provide examples of what can occur when change management isn't used.

TIP

NIST SP 800-128, "Guide for Security Configuration Management of Information Systems," covers configuration management in much more depth. At this writing, it is in the initial public draft stage and NIST is requesting comments until June 2010.

Change management is also important to use with basic security activities such as patching systems. Consider for a moment what the worst possible result of a patch might be. Although patches are intended to solve problems, they occasionally cause problems. The worst-case scenario is when a patch breaks a system. After applying the patch, the system no longer boots into the operating system.

If a patch broke your home computer, it'd be inconvenient. However, if a patch broke 500 systems in an organization, it could be catastrophic. Patches need to be tested and approved before they are applied. Many organizations use a change management process before patching systems.

Configuration Management Database

A configuration management database (CMDB) holds the configuration information for systems throughout a system's life cycle. The goal is to identify the accurate configuration of any system at any moment.

The CMDB holds all the configuration settings, not just the security settings. However, this still applies to security. The security triad includes confidentiality, integrity, and availability. Many of the configuration settings ensure the system operates correctly. A wrongly configured system may fail, resulting in loss of availability.

Change Control Work Order Database

Many organizations document change requests in a database. This is the change control work order database. Changes are tracked from the initial request to the implementation of the change in this database.

The change management process manages this database. This process often uses some type of application. In other words, users would be able to submit changes using an application. This application then records the change requests in the database. As different experts evaluate the change, comments are recorded in the database. When a change is completed, it is recorded in the change control work order database. It is also recorded in the CMDB.

Tracking, Monitoring, and Reporting Configuration Changes

Many organizations use a formal process for change requests. It's not just a technician asking a supervisor if he or she can make a change. For example, a Web application could be used to submit changes. Administrators or technicians submit the request via an internal Web page. The Web page would collect all the details of the change and record them in the change control work order database. Details may include the system, the actual change, justification, and the submitter.

Key players in the organization review the change requests and provide input using the same intranet Web application. These key players may include senior IT experts, security experts, management personnel, and disaster recovery experts. Each will examine the change as it relates to his or her area of expertise and determine if it will result in a negative impact. If all the experts agree to the change, it's approved.

Some changes may negatively affect the computing environment and require additional discussion. Change management review boards examine these change requests closely before approving them.

Collaboration and Policy Compliance across Business Areas

It's always important for different elements of a business to get along. One element of the business should not make changes without any thought to how it may affect other areas. Collaboration is also important within IT and security policy compliance.

Some security policies must apply to all business areas equally. However, other policies can be targeted to specific departments. If you look back to Figure 15-2, this shows an excellent example of how different requirements are addressed within a Microsoft domain. Group Policy applies some settings to all business areas equally. Additionally, it can configure different settings for different departments or business areas if needed.

In Figure 15-2, different policies were required for PCI DSS servers, HR personnel, and research and development personnel. Each of these business areas has its own settings that don't interfere with the other units.

Version Control for Policy Implementation Guidelines and Compliance

Another consideration related to automating IT security policy compliance is version control. First, it's important to use version control for the security policy itself. In other words, if the security policy is changed, the document should record the change. A reader should be able to determine if changes have occurred since the policy was originally released, with an idea of what those changes were.

Version control requirements for a document can be as simple as including a version control page. The page identifies all the changes made to the original in a table format. It would often include the date and other details of the change. It may also include who made the change.

It's also important to record the actual changes to systems. However, these changes are also recorded in the change control work order database and the CMDB discussed in the previous section.

Emerging Technologies and Solutions

More and more tools are becoming available to ensure IT policy compliance. Many of these tools are appearing as a direct result of standards in the security industry. These standards provide common frameworks that any organization can use to build security tools.

This section presents some of the notable technologies. They are:

- Security Content Automation Protocol (SCAP)
- Simple Network Management Protocol (SNMP)
- Web-Based Enterprise Management (WBEM)
- Windows Management Instrumentation (WMI)
- Digital signatures

SCAP

The **Security Content Automation Protocol (SCAP)**, pronounced "S-cap," is a newer technology used to measure systems and networks. It's actually a suite of six specifications. Together these specifications standardize how security software products identify and report security issues. SCAP is a trademark of NIST.

NIST created SCAP as part of its responsibilities under the Federal Information Security Management ACT (FISMA). The goal is to establish standards, guidelines, and minimum requirements for tools used to scan systems. Although SCAP is designed for the creation of tools to be used by the U.S. government, private entities can use the same tools.

The six specifications are:

- **eXtensible Configuration Checklist Description Format (XCCDF)**—This is a language used for writing security checklists and benchmarks. It can also report results of any checklist evaluations.

- **Open Vulnerability and Assessment Language (OVAL)**—This is a language used to represent system configuration information. It can assess the state of systems and report the assessment results.

- **Common Platform Enumeration (CPE)**—This provides specific names for hardware, operation systems, and applications. CPE provides a standard system-naming convention for consistent use among different products.

- **Common Configuration Enumeration (CCE)**—This provides specific names for security software configurations. CCE is a dictionary of names for these settings. It provides a standard naming convention used by different SCAP products.

- **Common Vulnerabilities and Exposures (CVE)**—This provides specific names for security related software flaws. CVE is a dictionary of publicly known software flaws. The MITRE Corporation manages the CVE.

FYI

The MITRE Corporation is a private company that performs a lot of work for U.S. government agencies. For example, MITRE maintains the CVE for the National Cyber Security Division of the U.S. Department of Homeland Security. Many of the original employees came from MIT and they work on research and engineering (RE). However, MITRE is not an acronym. Additionally, MITRE is not part of Massachusetts Institute of Technology (MIT).

- **Common Vulnerability Score Systems (CVSS)**—This provides an open specification to measure the relative severity of software flaw vulnerabilities. It provides formulas using standard measurements. The resulting score is from zero to 10 with 10 being the most severe.

SCAP isn't a tool itself. Instead, it's the protocol used to build the tools. Compare this to HTTP, the protocol that transmits traffic over the Internet so that applications can display data in user applications. Web browsers can display pages written in Hypertext Markup Language (HTML) and Extensible Markup Language (XML). However, HTTP can't display the traffic itself. Instead, Web browsers such as Internet Explorer are the tools that use HTTP to transmit and receive HTTP traffic and display the HTML-formatted pages. Similarly, SCAP-compliant tools use the underlying specifications of SCAP to scan systems and report the results. There are a wide variety of tool purposes. These include the ability to audit and assess systems for compliance of specific requirements. They can scan systems for vulnerabilities. They can detect systems that don't have proper patches or are misconfigured.

Some of the tools currently available are:

- BigFix Security Configuration and Vulnerability Management Suite (SCVM) by BigFix
- Retina by eEye Digital Security
- HP SCAP Scanner by HP
- SAINT vulnerability scanner by SAINT
- Control Compliance Suite—Federal Toolkit by Symantec
- Tripwire Enterprise by Tripwire

> **NOTE**
>
> NIST has established a formal validation program for NIST products. You can view a full list of SCAP validated products at *http://nvd.nist.gov/ scapproducts.cfm.*

If you want to read more about SCAP, read NIST SP 800-126. This is the technical specification for SCAP version 1.0. At this writing, NIST SP 800-126 rev 1 is in draft. It is the technical specification for SCAP version 1.1. You can access NIST SP 800-126 and other NIST 800-series special publications at *http://csrc.nist.gov/publications/PubsSPs.html.*

SNMP

The **Simple Network Management Protocol (SNMP)** is used to manage and query network devices. SNMP commonly manages routers, switches, and other intelligent devices on the network with IP addresses. SNMP is a part of the TCP/IP suite of protocols, so it's a bit of a stretch to call it an emerging technology. However, SNMP has improved over the years. The first version of SNMP was SNMP v1. It had a significant vulnerability. Devices used community strings for authentication. The default community string was "Public" and SNMP sent it over the network in clear text. Attackers using a sniffer such as Wireshark could capture the community string even if it was changed from the default. They could then use it to reconfigure devices.

SNMP was improved with versions 2 and 3. Version 3 provides three primary improvements:

- **Confidentiality**—Packets are encrypted. Attackers can still capture the packets with a sniffer. However, they are in a ciphered form, which prevents attackers from reading them.

- **Integrity**—A message authentication code (MAC) (not to be confused with Media Access Control) is used to ensure that data has not been modified. The MAC uses an abbreviated hash. The hash is calculated at the source and included in the packet. The hash is recalculated at the destination. As long as the data has not changed, the hash will always provide the same result. If the hash is the same, the message has not lost integrity.

- **Authentication**—This provides verification that the SNMP messages are from a known source. It prevents attackers from reconfiguring the devices without being able to prove who they are.

WBEM

> **NOTE**
>
> WBEM uses HTTP, which is commonly used on the Internet. However, WBEM can operate on internal networks using HTTP.

Web-Based Enterprise Management (WBEM) is a set of management and Internet standard technologies. They standardize the language used to exchange data among different platforms for management of systems and applications. Just as SCAP provides the standards used to create tools, WBEM also provides standards used in different management tools. The tools can be graphical user interface (GUI)-based tools. Some tools are command line tools that don't use a GUI.

WBEM is based on different standards from the Internet and from the Distributed Management Task Force (DMTF), Inc. DMTF is a not-for-profit association. Members promote enterprise and systems management and interoperability. These standards include:

- **CIM-XML**—The Common Information Model (CIM) over XML protocol. This protocol allows XML-formatted data to be transmitted over HTTP. CIM defines IT resources as related objects in a rich object-oriented model. Just about any hardware or software element can be referenced with the CIM. Applications use the CIM to query and configure systems.

- **WS-Management**—The Web Services for Management protocol. This protocol provides a common way for systems to exchange information. Web services are commonly used for a wide assortment of purposes on the Internet. For example, Web services are used to retrieve weather data or shipping data on the Internet. Clients send Web service queries and receive Web service responses. The WS-Management protocol specifies how these queries and responses retrieve data from devices. It can also be used to send commands to devices.

- **CIM Query Language (CQL)**—This language is based on the Structured Query Language (SQL) used for databases, and the W3C XML Query language. The CQL defines the specific syntax rules used to query systems with CIM-XML and WS-Management.

WMI

The **Windows Management Instrumentation (WMI)** specification is Microsoft's implementation of WBEM. It has been included in Microsoft products since Windows 2000. It is also available as a free download for older Microsoft products.

NOTE

WMI is sometimes referenced as Windows Management Interface.

Scripting languages such as VBScript and Windows PowerShell support WMI commands. Scripts embed WMI queries using the same CIM standards that are within WBEM. You can query and manage both local and remote systems with WMI. Additionally, you can use the WMI Command-line (WMIC) interface to execute WMI commands at the command line.

Microsoft uses WMI in many of its management products. The following tools were mentioned previously in this chapter and include WMI capabilities to scan the systems:

- Microsoft Baseline Security Analyzer (MBSA)
- Windows Server Update Services (WSUS)
- Systems Management Server (SMS)
- System Center Configuration Manager (SCCM)

SCCM is also a SCAP-validated product.

Digital Signing

A digital signature is simply a string of data that is associated with a file. Digital signing technologies provide added security for files. A file signed with a digital signature provides authentication and integrity assurances. It also provides nonrepudiation. In other words, it provides assurances that a specific sender sent the file. It also provides assurances that the file has not been modified.

A public key infrastructure (PKI) is needed to support digital signatures. A PKI includes certificate authorities (CAs) that issue certificates. The certificate includes a public key matched to a private key. Anything encrypted with the private key can be decrypted with the public key. Additionally, anything encrypted with the public key can be decrypted with the private key.

Digital signatures provide added security for many different types of policy compliance files. For example, consider patches and other update files. You would download these files and use them to patch vulnerabilities. If an attacker somehow modified the patch, instead of plugging vulnerability, you would be installing malware. Similarly, many definition updates for security tools are digitally signed.

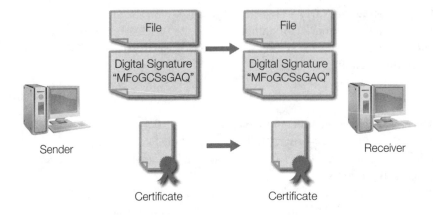

FIGURE 15-4
Using a digital signature.

Creating Digital Signature
- File hashed (123456)
- Hash encrypted with company's private key to get MFoGCSsGAQ
- Digital signature included with file

Validating Digital Signature
- Hash decrypted with company's public key (from certificate)
- Received file hashed
- If received hash is same as decrypted hash, file has not changed
- If decryption successful, it must have been encrypted with private key

If a file is digitally signed, you know it has not been modified. The following steps show one way that a digital signature is used for a company named Acme Security. The company first obtains a certificate from a CA with the following steps:

1. Acme Security creates a public and private key pair.

2. Acme Security includes the public key that is part of its key pair to the CA with the company's request. It keeps the private key private and protected.

3. The CA verifies Acme Security is a valid company and is who it says it is. The CA then creates a digital certificate for Acme Security. The certificate includes the public key provided by Acme Security.

At this point, the company is able to digitally sign files. Consider Figure 15-4 as you follow the steps for creating and using a digital signature.

4. Acme Security creates the file.

5. Acme Security hashes the file. The hash is a number normally expressed in hexadecimal. The hash in this example is 123456.

> **NOTE**
>
> No matter how many times you calculate a hash, it will always be the same as long as the source is the same. This is similar to counting the number of apples in a bowl. As long as the number of apples stays the same, you'll always come up with the same number. If someone takes an apple away, or adds an apple, the resulting number will change.

6. Acme Security encrypts the hash with its private key. The result is "MFoGCSsGAQ". Remember, something encrypted with a private key can only be decrypted with the matching public key. Said another way, if you can decrypt data with a public key, you know it was encrypted with the matching private key.

7. Acme Security packages the file and the digital signature together. It sends them to the receiving client. The digital certificate could be sent at the same time or separately.

8. The receiving client uses the certificate to verify that Acme Security sent the file. Additionally, the client checks with the CA to verify the certificate is valid and hasn't been revoked.

9. The client decrypts the encrypted hash (MFoGCSsGAQ) with the public key from the certificate. The decrypted hash is 123456.

10. The received file is hashed giving a hash of 123456. This hash is compared to the decrypted hash. If they are both the same, the file is the same. In other words, it has not been modified. Additionally, it provides verification that the digital signature was provided by Acme Security because only the matching public key can decrypt data encrypted with the private key.

Digital signatures aren't a new technology. However, their use with security tools and downloads has significantly increased over the years. A digital signature provides you with an additional tool to verify authentication and integrity for downloaded files.

Best Practices for IT Security Policy Compliance Monitoring

When implementing a plan for IT security policy compliance monitoring, you can use several different best practices. The following list shows some of these:

- **Start with a security policy**—The security policy acts as the road map. This is a written document, not just some ideas in someone's head. Without the written document, the actual security policy becomes a moving target and monitoring for compliance is challenging if not impossible.

- **Create a baseline based on the security policy**—Use images whenever possible to deploy new operating systems. These images will ensure that systems start in a secure state. They also accelerate deployments, save money, and increase availability.

- **Audit systems regularly**—After the baseline is deployed, regularly check the systems. Ensure that the security settings that have been configured stay configured. Well-meaning administrators can change settings. Malware can also modify settings. However, auditing will catch the modifications.

- **Automate checks as much as possible**—Use tools and scripts to check systems. Some tools are free. Other tools cost some money but all are better than doing everything manually. They reduce the amount of time necessary and increase the accuracy.
- **Manage changes**—Ensure that a change management process is used. This allows experts to review the changes before they are implemented and reduces the possibility that the change will cause problems. It also provides built-in documentation for changes.

Case Studies and Examples of Successful IT Security Policy Compliance Monitoring

The following sections show different case studies and examples related to IT security policies and compliance monitoring. Private sector, public sector, and critical infrastructure case studies and examples are included.

Private Sector Case Studies

The following case studies show how things can go wrong when change management policies are not used or followed. The first example is with a small training company. The second concerns a larger sales organization. Both companies suffered outages due to a lack of change management policies.

Small Training Company

A small training organization with about 50 employees provides a good example of how things can go wrong without a change management policy. This company didn't have a full-time IT staff. Instead, IT trainers managed the network when necessary. They were running a network of primarily Microsoft desktop and server computers. The e-mail server was running Microsoft Exchange.

One day, two trainers decided to upgrade the Exchange server. They had talked about it before. Even though they didn't have a formal plan nor did they have formal approval, they were confident they could pull it off. Once they were done, employees in the organization would be happy with the change.

They waited until the end of the day after other employees had left. They charged into action. By about midnight, they were exhausted. However, due to unforeseen problems, they weren't anywhere near completion. They ultimately called one of the company vice presidents and explained their situation.

After getting an earful about modifying a production system without authorization, they were ultimately told to return the system to normal. They were told to undo all of the work they had done, and to return the system to how it was working earlier in the day. Of course, if they had asked for approval, someone would have reminded them to ensure they had a back-out plan. If things went sour, the back-out plan would allow them to return to normal. Unfortunately, they didn't have a back-out plan.

Ultimately, they were able to return the system to normal but it took another day. The organization was without e-mail capabilities for a full day. This could have been much worse. However, it could have been much better with a change management process in place.

Large Sales Organization

Small organizations without dedicated IT staff aren't the only organizations vulnerable to outages from unauthorized changes. A large sales organization with a dedicated IT staff suffered a major outage due to a minor change to a printer.

The organization has a subnet hosting multiple servers and a printer. Routers connect this subnet to other subnets on the network. All systems were working until a new server was added to the network with the same IP address as the printer. This IP address conflict prevented the printer from printing, and prevented the new server from communicating on the network. This problem is like having two identical street addresses in the same zip code. At best, each address will get some mail, but not all of it. Similarly, on a network, each IP address will receive some traffic, but not all traffic that is expected. At best, you will see inconsistent performance.

The problem with the new server wasn't discovered right away. However, a technician began troubleshooting a problem with the printer on the same subnet. While troubleshooting, the technician suspected a problem with the IP address. The technician changed the IP address for the printer to 10.1.1.1, as shown in Figure 15-1. This change didn't solve the problem, but the technician forgot to change the IP address back to normal. As you can see in the figure, the change caused a conflict between the printer and the default gateway. The printer and the near side of the router both had the same IP address and neither was working.

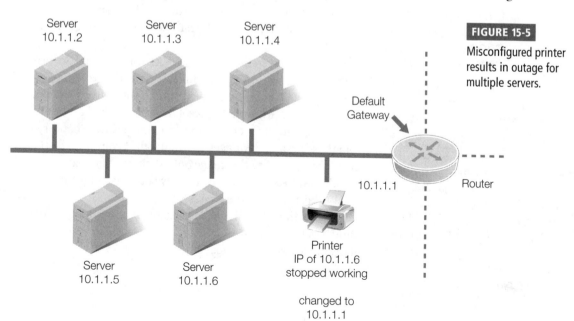

FIGURE 15-5

Misconfigured printer results in outage for multiple servers.

Server 10.1.1.2

Server 10.1.1.3

Server 10.1.1.4

Default Gateway

10.1.1.1

Router

Server 10.1.1.5

Server 10.1.1.6

Printer IP of 10.1.1.6 stopped working

changed to 10.1.1.1

15

Compliance Systems and Emerging Technologies

The default gateway is the path for all server communications out of the subnet. Because there was a conflict with the default gateway, none of the servers on the subnet were able to get traffic out of the subnet. They were all operating, but clients outside of the subnet couldn't use them. With several servers no longer working, the problem was quickly escalated. Senior administrators were called in and discovered the problems. They corrected the IP address on the printer and provided some on-the-job training to the original technician.

Notice how this problem started with a small error. The new server was added using an IP address that was already used by the printer. After the printer IP address change, all the servers on the subnet lost network access. Change management and configuration management processes would have ensured this new server was added using a configuration that didn't interfere with other systems. Additionally, change management would have prevented the change to the printer's IP address.

As it turns out, this was the turning point for this company. It was one of a long string of problems caused by unauthorized changes. Management finally decided to implement a formal change management process and hired an outside consultant to help them.

Public Sector Example

One of the problems the U.S. government has is ensuring that basic errors are not repeated by different agencies. Security experts know that certain settings should be set. They know how systems are hacked. They know how to protect the systems. However, communicating this information so that every system in the government is protected isn't so easy.

Indeed, many attacks on government systems have been the result of common errors. If these systems were configured correctly, many attacks wouldn't have succeeded. Security experts knew they needed a solution. The **Federal Desktop Core Configuration (FDCC)** was the solution.

Experts from the Defense Information Systems Agency (DISA), the National Security Agency (NSA), and NIST contributed to the FDCC. It includes a wide assortment of security settings. These settings reduce the vulnerabilities of the systems from attacks.

It's not perfect. However, it is a solid baseline. The baseline was loaded onto target computers and images were captured from these systems. For agencies that didn't want to redo their machines by casting the image onto their systems, extensive checklists were available. The agency could manually follow the checklist to apply the changes to the systems.

In 2007, the U.S. Office of Management and Budget (OMB) mandated the use of the FDCC for all systems used within all federal agencies. The deadline was February 2008.

> **NOTE**
>
> At this writing, there are two FDCC images available. One is for Windows XP and one is for Windows Vista. However, other images are in various stages of development. A frequently asked questions (FAQ) list on the FDCC is available at *http://nvd.nist.gov/fdcc/fdcc_faq.cfm*.

There was some pushback with the mandate. However, the OMB stressed that compliance was required. Organizations were mandated to report their compliance. If they didn't reach full compliance, they were required to identify their progress. NIST and the OMB work with individual agencies to identify solutions for applications or systems not working with the FDCC. For example, if an agency can't comply, the security experts at NIST may be able to identify what needs to be done. This becomes a much better solution than an agency simply accepting that security needs to be weakened. Even worse, many agencies weren't aware that their security was weakened.

Several SCAP tools include an FDCC scanner. These scanners audit systems in the agency's network and report compliance. These reports can be used to verify to the OMB that the agency is in compliance. You can view a list of SCAP tools that include an FDCC scanner here: *http://nvd.nist.gov/scapproducts.cfm.*

At this stage, the FDCC is deployed in all federal agencies. Even though the FDCC presented some technical challenges for some organizations, it significantly raised the security posture of all systems in the U.S. government. No one will say that it has eliminated all the security issues. Far from it. However, it has helped computers throughout the entire U.S. government raise the security baseline.

Critical Infrastructure Case Study

Compass Group North America provides catering and dining services to large clients throughout North America. It's a $9 billion organization with tens of thousands of employees scattered among corporate headquarters and field offices.

Although their primary IT infrastructure was sound, they had problems reaching some clients in remote locations. Many of these clients had low-bandwidth connections to the network. They connected to the corporate network for critical business applications, including processing credit cards. However, they had to share the bandwidth for updates and monitoring. Many of the updates failed due to a lack of bandwidth. Security settings were set with an initial baseline but couldn't be easily monitored while deployed in the field. During a deployment of a routine security update in 2008, a critical business function failed, since the update was hogging the bandwidth. Additionally, these remote systems were often in hacker-prone locations such as college campuses and entertainment venues. These systems needed a higher level of monitoring to ensure security was maintained. However, there wasn't an easy solution to accomplish this.

Later that year, Compass deployed Microsoft System Center Configuration Manager (SCCM) in its network. The company placed one distribution server in a perimeter network dedicated to servicing these remote clients over the Internet. The result was several benefits including:

- Security updates were deployed to Internet clients using less bandwidth.
- Total bandwidth needs for these remote clients were cut in half.
- Security-update deployment work was reduced by 80 percent.
- The Compass Group estimates it saved $100,000 using SCCM instead of other options it evaluated.

CHAPTER SUMMARY

This chapter covered some of the technologies used to ensure IT policy compliance. Imaging technologies can deploy identical baseline images for new systems. However, the baseline is up to date only for a short period of time. As patches are released or other changes are approved, the baseline becomes out of date. The difference between the baseline and the required changes represents a vulnerability or a security gap. This gap must be closed to ensure systems stay secure.

Many automated tools are available to IT administrators today. These tools can examine systems to ensure the baseline security settings have not changed. They can also scan systems for vulnerabilities such as ensuring the computers have current patches. Many tools include the ability to scan for issues, and deploy changes to correct the issues. NIST published standards for SCAP in SP 800-126. These standards are resulting in a wealth of available tools to increase security for networks today.

KEY CONCEPTS AND TERMS

Change management
Configuration management (CM)
Federal Desktop Core Configuration (FDCC)

Group Policy
Imaging
Security Content Automation Protocol (SCAP)
Simple Network Management Protocol (SNMP)

Web-Based Enterprise Management (WBEM)
Windows Management Instrumentation (WMI)

CHAPTER 15 ASSESSMENT

1. A _____ is a starting point or standard. Within IT, it provides a standard focused on a specific technology used within an organization.

2. An operating system and different applications are installed on a system. The system is then locked down with various settings. You want the same operating system, applications, and settings deployed to 50 other computers. What's the easiest way?

A. Scripting
B. Imaging
C. Manually
D. Spread the work among different departments

3. After a set of security settings has been applied to a system, there is no need to recheck these settings on the system.

A. True
B. False

4. The time between when a new vulnerability is discovered and when software developers start writing a patch is known as a _____.

5. Your organization wants to automate the distribution of security policy settings. What should be considered?

A. Training of administrators
B. Organizational acceptance
C. Testing for effectiveness
D. All of the above

6. Several tools are available to automate the deployment of security policy settings. Some tools can deploy baseline settings. Other tools can deploy changes in security policy settings.

A. True
B. False

7. An organization uses a decentralized IT model with a central IT department for core services and security. The organization wants to ensure that each department is complying with primary security requirements. What can be used to verify compliance?

A. Group Policy
B. Centralized change management policies
C. Centralized configuration management policies
D. Random audits

8. Change requests are tracked in a control work order database. Approved changes are also recorded in a CMDB.

A. True
B. False

9. An organization wants to maintain a database of system settings. The database should include the original system settings and any changes. What should be implemented within the organization?

A. Change management
B. Configuration management
C. Full ITIL life cycle support
D. Security Content Automation Protocol

10. An organization wants to reduce the possibility of outages when changes are implemented on the network. What should the organization use?

A. Change management
B. Configuration management
C. Configuration management database
D. Simple Network Management Protocol

11. Which NIST standard was developed for different scanning and vulnerability assessment tools, and comprises six specifications including XCCDF?

A. SNMP
B. WBEM
C. SCAP
D. WMI

12. Microsoft created the Web-Based Enterprise Management (WBEM) technologies for Microsoft products.

A. True
B. False

13. Which of the following specifications is used exclusively in Microsoft products to query and configure systems in the network?

A. WMI
B. WBEM
C. SNMP
D. SCAP

14. Which of the following is used to manage and query network devices such as routers and switches?

A. WMI
B. WBEM
C. SNMP
D. SCAP

15. A _____ can be used with a downloaded file. It offers verification that the file was provided by a specific entity. It also verifies the file has not been modified.

Answer Key

CHAPTER 1 Information Systems Security Policy Management

1. C   2. Standards   3. A   4. D and E   5. Procedure   6. D   7. B
8. Human   9. E   10. B

CHAPTER 2 Business Drivers for Information Security Policies

1. C   2. A   3. A   4. Preventive   5. C   6. B   7. D   8. B
9. D   10. A   11. A   12. B   13. B   14. D   15. D

CHAPTER 3 U.S. Compliance Laws and Information Security Policy Requirements

1. B   2. E   3. E   4. D   5. Control environment   6. B   7. CIPA
8. A   9. B   10. B   11. D

CHAPTER 4 Business Challenges Within the Seven Domains of IT Responsibility

1. B   2. A   3. C   4. C   5. LAN-to-WAN Domain   6. D
7. Segmented network   8. A   9. B   10. B   11. D   12. B
13. C   14. B   15. C

CHAPTER 5 Information Security Policy Implementation Issues

1. E   2. B   3. Be in the background; precisely what is asked of them
4. The cost of business   5. B   6. A   7. C   8. This avoids language that could
be interpreted as an employment contract or unintended promise. Also, the use
of vague terms such as "generally," "typically," or "usually" give managers
and attorneys the flexibility to interpret and apply policies broadly.   9. A
10. A   11. Security policy   12. A   13. D   14. B   15. C

CHAPTER 6 IT Security Policy Frameworks

1. F   2. A   3. A, B, and C   4. A   5. Policies   6. B   7. C   8. A
9. Confidentiality, integrity, availability, authorization, and nonrepudiation
10. Unauthorized persons or processes   11. G

CHAPTER 7 How to Design, Organize, Implement, and Maintain IT Security Policies

1. A   2. B   3. A   4. D   5. C   6. A, B, C, and E   7. B   8. C
9. Answers may include devices and processes used to control physical access;
examples include fences, security guards, locked doors, motion detectors, and
alarms   10. Procedures   11. Policy   12. Defense in depth   13. A
14. B   15. A and D

CHAPTER 8 IT Security Policy Framework Approaches

1. A   2. C   3. D   4. E   5. A   6. B   7. B   8. A   9. B
10. Priorities or specialties   11. A   12. Expensive or burdensome
13. C   14. B

CHAPTER 9 User Domain Policies

1. B   2. D   3. Firecall-ID   4. A   5. Auditor   6. B   7. B   8. Insider
9. B   10. B   11. Escalate

CHAPTER 10 IT Infrastructure Security Policies

1. D   2. B   3. D   4. A   5. D   6. E   7. B   8. B   9. LAN-to-WAN
10. Cohesive, coherent   11. A   12. B

CHAPTER 11 Data Classification and Handling Policies and Risk Management Policies

1. C   2. B   3. E   4. E   5. A   6. B   7. Confidential   8. B   9. D
10. B   11. D   12. B   13. C   14. B

CHAPTER 12 Incident Response Team (IRT) Policies

1. B   2. C   3. D   4. D   5. Severity   6. B   7. Incident is declared
8. A   9. B   10. D   11. B   12. D   13. Public relations   14. A   15. B

CHAPTER 13 IT Security Policy Implementations

1. D   2. A   3. Committee meeting minutes   4. B   5. B   6. D   7. D
8. A   9. B   10. D   11. B   12. Motivations or needs   13. B   14. B
15. Executive support

CHAPTER 14 IT Security Policy Enforcement

1. B   2. Executive management   3. B   4. C   5. E   6. Security policies
7. B   8. B   9. D   10. C   11. A   12. E   13. A   14. D

CHAPTER 15 IT Policy Compliance Systems and Emerging Technologies

1. Baseline   2. B   3. B   4. Vulnerability window or security gap
5. D   6. A   7. D   8. A   9. B   10. A   11. C   12. B   13. A
14. C   15. Digital signature

Standard Acronyms

3DES	triple data encryption standard	**DMZ**	demilitarized zone
ACD	automatic call distributor	**DoS**	denial of service
AES	Advanced Encryption Standard	**DPI**	deep packet inspection
ANSI	American National Standards Institute	**DRP**	disaster recovery plan
AP	access point	**DSL**	digital subscriber line
API	application programming interface	**DSS**	Digital Signature Standard
B2B	business to business	**DSU**	data service unit
B2C	business to consumer	**EDI**	Electronic Data Interchange
BBB	Better Business Bureau	**EIDE**	Enhanced IDE
BCP	business continuity planning	**FACTA**	Fair and Accurate Credit Transactions Act
C2C	consumer to consumer	**FAR**	false acceptance rate
CA	certificate authority	**FBI**	Federal Bureau of Investigation
CAP	Certification and Accreditation Professional	**FDIC**	Federal Deposit Insurance Corporation
		FEP	front-end processor
CAUCE	Coalition Against Unsolicited Commercial Email	**FRCP**	Federal Rules of Civil Procedure
		FRR	false rejection rate
CCC	CERT Coordination Center	**FTC**	Federal Trade Commission
CCNA	Cisco Certified Network Associate	**FTP**	file transfer protocol
CERT	Computer Emergency Response Team	**GIAC**	Global Information Assurance Certification
CFE	Certified Fraud Examiner		
CISA	Certified Information Systems Auditor	**GLBA**	Gramm-Leach-Bliley Act
CISM	Certified Information Security Manager	**HIDS**	host-based intrusion detection system
CISSP	Certified Information System Security Professional	**HIPAA**	Health Insurance Portability and Accountability Act
CMIP	common management information protocol	**HIPS**	host-based intrusion prevention system
		HTTP	hypertext transfer protocol
COPPA	Children's Online Privacy Protection	**HTTPS**	HTTP over Secure Socket Layer
CRC	cyclic redundancy check	**HTML**	hypertext markup language
CSI	Computer Security Institute	**IAB**	Internet Activities Board
CTI	Computer Telephony Integration	**IDEA**	International Data Encryption Algorithm
DBMS	database management system	**IDPS**	intrusion detection and prevention
DDoS	distributed denial of service	**IDS**	intrusion detection system
DES	Data Encryption Standard		

IEEE	Institute of Electrical and Electronics Engineers	**SAN**	storage area network
IETF	Internet Engineering Task Force	**SANCP**	Security Analyst Network Connection Profiler
InfoSec	information security	**SANS**	SysAdmin, Audit, Network, Security
IPS	intrusion prevention system	**SAP**	service access point
IPSec	IP Security	**SCSI**	small computer system interface
IPv4	Internet protocol version 4	**SET**	Secure electronic transaction
IPv6	Internet protocol version 6	**SGC**	server-gated cryptography
IRS	Internal Revenue Service	**SHA**	Secure Hash Algorithm
(ISC)^2	International Information System Security Certification Consortium	**S-HTTP**	secure HTTP
ISO	International Organization for Standardization	**SLA**	service level agreement
		SMFA	specific management functional area
ISP	Internet service provider	**SNMP**	simple network management protocol
ISS	Internet security systems	**SOX**	Sarbanes-Oxley Act of 2002 (also Sarbox)
ITRC	Identity Theft Resource Center	**SSA**	Social Security Administration
IVR	interactive voice response	**SSCP**	Systems Security Certified Practitioner
LAN	local area network	**SSL**	Secure Socket Layer
MAN	metropolitan area network	**SSO**	single system sign-on
MD5	Message Digest 5	**STP**	shielded twisted cable
modem	modulator demodulator	**TCP/IP**	Transmission Control Protocol/Internet Protocol
NFIC	National Fraud Information Center	**TCSEC**	Trusted Computer System Evaluation Criteria
NIDS	network intrusion detection system		
NIPS	network intrusion prevention system	**TFTP**	Trivial File Transfer Protocol
NIST	National Institute of Standards and Technology	**TNI**	Trusted Network Interpretation
		UDP	User Datagram Protocol
NMS	network management system	**UPS**	uninterruptible power supply
OS	operating system	**UTP**	unshielded twisted cable
OSI	open system interconnection	**VLAN**	virtual local area network
PBX	private branch exchange	**VOIP**	Voice over Internet Protocol
PCI	Payment Card Industry	**VPN**	virtual private network
PGP	Pretty Good Privacy	**WAN**	wide area network
PKI	public-key infrastructure	**WLAN**	wireless local area network
RAID	redundant array of independent disks	**WNIC**	wireless network interface card
RFC	Request for Comments	**W3C**	World Wide Web Consortium
RSA	Rivest, Shamir, and Adleman (algorithm)	**WWW**	World Wide Web

Glossary of Key Terms

Business impact analysis (BIA) | A formal analysis to determine the impact on an organization in the event that key processes and technology are not available.

Business process reengineering (BPR) | A management technique used to improve the efficiency and effectiveness of a process within an organization.

C

Chain of custody | A legal term referring to how evidence is documented and protected. Evidence must be documented and protected from the time it's obtained to the time it's presented in court.

Change management | A formal process that controls changes to systems. Successful change management ensures changes have minimal impact on operations.

Chief privacy officer (CPO) | Most senior leader responsible for managing risks related to data privacy.

Classification | The process of labeling information so that only authorized personal may access it.

Committee of Sponsoring Organizations (COSO) | An organization that developed a framework for validating internal controls and managing enterprise risks; focuses on financial operations and risk management.

Communications plan | Outlines what information is to be shared and how the information will be disseminated.

Compliance | The ability to reasonably ensure conformity and adherence to organization policies, standards, procedures, laws, and regulations.

Compliance officer | An individual accountable for monitoring adherence to laws and regulations.

Compliance risk | Relates to the impact on the business for failing to comply with legal obligations.

Computer-based training (CBT) | Training done partly or fully on computer-based channels of communication, such as the Internet or through training software.

Confidential | A level of government classification that refers to data in which unauthorized disclosure would reasonably be expected to cause some damage to the national security.

Confidentiality agreement (CA) | Legally binding agreements on the handling and disclosure of company material.

Confidentiality | Limiting access to information/data to authorized users only.

Configuration management (CM) | A collection of activities that track system configuration. It starts with a baseline configuration. It continues through a system's life cycle including changing and monitoring configurations.

Consumer rights | Established rules on how consumers and their information should be handled during an e-commerce transaction.

Continuity of operation plan (COOP) | A plan that provides the detail procedures and processes needed to coordinate operations during a disaster.

Continuous improvement | An ad hoc, ongoing effort to improve business products, services, or processes.

Contractors | Temporary workers who can be assigned to any role.

Control Objectives for Information and related Technology (COBIT) | A widely accepted framework that brings together business and control requirements with technical issues.

Corrective control | A security control that restores a system or process.

Critical infrastructure | Assets that are essential for the society and economy to function.

D

Data administrator | Implements policies and procedures such as backup, versioning, uploading, downloading, and database administration.

Data at rest | The state of data stored on any type of media.

Data classification | Level of protection based on data type.

Data custodian | An individual responsible for the day-to-day maintenance of data and the quality of that data. May perform backups and recover data as needed. A data custodian also grants access based on approval from the data owner.

Data encryption | When data is encrypted, the actual information can be viewed only when the data is decrypted with a key.

Data in transit | The state of data when traveling over or through a network.

Data leakage | Unauthorized sharing of sensitive company information, whether intentional or accidental.

Data Leakage Protection (DLP) | A formal program that reduces the likelihood of accidental or malicious loss of data. May also stand for "Data Loss Protection."

Data Loss Protection (DLP) | A formal program that reduces the likelihood of accidental or malicious loss of data. May also stand for "Data Leakage Protection."

Data manager | An individual who establishes procedures on how data should be handled.

Data owner | An individual who approves user access rights to information that is needed to perform day-to-day operations.

Data privacy | The laws that set expectations on how your personal information should be protected and limits place on how the data should be shared.

Data security administrator | Grants access rights and assesses information security threats to organization.

Data steward | Owner of data and approver of access rights; responsible for data quality.

Data user | The end user of an application. A data user is accountable for handling data appropriately by understanding security policies and following approved processes and procedures.

Declassification | The process of changing the status of classified data to unclassified data.

Defense in depth | The approach of using multiple layers of security to protect against a single point of failure.

Demilitarized zone (DMZ) | Taken from the military, a buffer between two opposing forces. With regards to networks, it is the segment that sits between the public Internet and a private local area network (LAN). A DMZ is built to protect private LANs from the Internet. It uses a series of firewalls, routers, IDSs, and/or IPSs. The DMZ is where public Web servers, e-mail servers, and public DNS servers are located.

Detective control | A manual security control that identifies a behavior after it has happened.

Digital assets | Any digital material owned by an organization including text, graphics, audio, video, and animations.

Disaster recovery plan (DRP) | A plan to recover an organization's IT assets during a disaster, including software, data, and hardware.

Discovery management | In the context of workstation central management systems, refers to processes that determine what is installed on a workstation. It could also refer to knowing what information sits on a workstation.

Division of labor | How various tasks are grouped into specialties to enhance the depth and quality of work product.

Domain | A logical piece of our technology infrastructure with similar risks and business requirements.

Due care | A legal term that refers to effort made to avoid harm to another party. It essentially refers to the care that a person would reasonably be expected to see under particular circumstances.

E

E-mail policy | A policy that discusses what's acceptable when using the company e-mail system.

Enterprise risk management (ERM) | A framework that aligns strategic goals, operations effectiveness, reporting, and compliance objectives; not technology specific.

Escalation | In the context of information security, refers to a process by which senior leaders through a chain of command are apprised of a risk. An escalation continues one level of organizational structure at a time until the issue is addressed or the escalation reaches the highest level of the organization.

Evangelist | A person with enthusiasm for a cause or project. An evangelist often gains acceptance for a project from a wide audience.

Evidence | *1.* Information that supports a conclusion. *2.* Material presented to a regulator to show compliance.

Exception | A deviation from a centrally supported and approved IT security standard. Exceptions can come about because of a lack of preparedness by the organization to comply with a standard or due to the use of a technology that has not been sanctioned by the standards.

Executive | A senior business leader accountable for approving security policy implementation, driving the security message within an organization, and ensuring that policies are given appropriate priority.

Executive committee | A committee that helps align the security committee to organization goals and objectives.

Executive management sponsorship | Getting senior management to participate in training to improve the effectiveness of security policies.

External connection committee | A gateway committee that approves external data connections.

F

Federal Desktop Core Configuration (FDCC) | A standard image mandated for use on all systems running Windows XP or Vista in any federal agency. This image locks down the operating system with specific security settings.

File Transfer Protocol (FTP) | A protocol used to exchange files over a local area network (LAN) or wide area network (WAN).

Financial risk | Events that could potentially impact the business when it fails to provide adequate liquidity to meet its obligations.

Firecall-ID process | Granting elevated rights temporarily to enable a person to resolve a problem quickly. Provides emergency access to unprivileged users.

Firewall | A device that filters the traffic in and out of a local area network (LAN). Many firewalls can do deep packet inspection, in which they examine the content, as well as the type, of the traffic. A firewall can be used internally on the network to further protect segments. Firewalls are most commonly used to filter traffic between the public Internet and an internal private LAN.

Flat network | A network with little or no controls that limit network traffic.

Flat organizational structure | An organization with few layers separating the leaders from the bottom ranks of workers.

Full disclosure | The concept that an individual should know what information about them is being collected. An individual should also be told how that information is being used.

G

Gateway committees | Committees that review technology activity and provide approvals before the project or activity can proceed to the next stage.

General counsel | The highest ranking lawyer in an organization, who usually reports to the president or chief executive officer. He or she is asked to give legal opinions on various organization issues, participate in contract negotiations, and to act as a liaison with outside law firms retained by the organization.

Governance | The act of managing implementation and compliance with organizational policies.

Governance, risk management, and compliance (GRC) | A set of tools that bring together the capabilities to systematically manage risk and policy compliance.

Group Policy | An automated management tool used in Microsoft domains. Administrators can configure a setting one time in Group Policy and it will apply to multiple users and computers.

Guideline | The parameters within which a policy, standard, or procedure recommended when possible but are optional.

H

Harden | To eliminate as many security risks as possible by reducing access rights to the minimum needed to perform any task, ensuring access is authenticated to unique individuals, removing all nonessential software, and other configuration steps that eliminate opportunities for unauthorized access.

Head of information management | A role that deals with all aspects of information such as security, quality, definition, and availability; responsible for data quality.

Help desk management | In the context of workstation central management systems, provides support to the end user. This includes allowing the help desk technician to remotely access the workstation to diagnose problems, reconfigure software, and reset IDs.

Hierarchical organizational structure | An organization with multiple layers of reporting, which separates leaders from the bottom ranks of workers.

Highly sensitive classification | A classification level used to protect highly regulated data or strategic information.

Honeypot | A network security device that acts as a decoy to analyze hacker activity.

Host hardening | The process of removing unnecessary software on a server or workstation, turning off unneeded network ports and services, and preventing users from changing a machine's configuration.

Hub | Used to connect multiple devices within a local area network (LAN). It has ports and as the traffic flows through the device, the traffic is duplicated so all ports can see the traffic. You use a hub to connect computers or segments. Often switches are preferred over hubs for added security.

Human resources representative | An individual who is an expert on HR policies and disciplinary proceedings or employee counseling.

I

Imaging | A technology used to create baselines of systems. An image is captured from a source computer. This image can then be deployed to other systems. Images include the operating system, applications, configuration settings, and security settings.

Incident | An event that violates an organization's security policies.

Incident response team (IRT) | A specialized group of people whose purpose is to respond to major incidents.

Information assurance | The implementation of controls designed to ensure confidentiality, integrity, availability, and non-repudiation.

Information security | The act of protecting information or data from unauthorized use, access, disruption, or destruction.

Information security officer (ISO) | An individual accountable for identifying, developing, and implementing security policies and corresponding security controls.

Information security program charter | A capstone document that establishes the reporting lines and delegation of responsibilities for Information Security to management below the organization's chief information officer (CEO) or other executive leader.

Information security representative | In the context of an IRT team, an information security representative provides risk management and analytical skills. A representative may also have specialized forensic skills for collecting and analyzing evidence.

Information security risk assessment | A formal process to identify threats, potential attacks, and impacts to an organization.

Information systems security (ISS) | The act of protecting information systems or IT infrastructures from unauthorized use, access, disruption, or destruction.

Information systems security management life cycle | The five-phase management process of controlling the planning, implementation, evaluation, and maintenance of information systems security.

Information Technology and Infrastructure Library (ITIL) | A framework that contains a comprehensive list of concepts, practices, and processes for managing IT services.

Information technology subject matter expert | An individual who has intimate knowledge of the systems and configurations of an organization. This individual is typically a developer, system administrator or network administrators. He or she has the needed technical skills to make critical recommendations on how to top an attack.

Insider | An employee, consultant, contractor, or vendor. The insider may even be the IT technical people who designed the system, application, or security that is being hacked. The insider knows the organization and the applications.

Integrated audit | An audit in which two or more audit disciplines are combined to conduct a single audit.

Integrity | The act of ensuring that information has not been improperly changed.

Intellectual property (IP) | Any product of human intellect that is unique and not obvious with some value in the marketplace.

Internal classification | A classification level for data that would cause disruption to daily operations and some financial loss to the business if leaked.

International Organization for Standardization (ISO) | An organization that creates widely accepted international standards on information security and IT risks.

Internet filters | Software that blocks access to specific sites on the Internet.

Intrusion detection system (IDS) | A series of software agents, appliances, and servers that monitor for network activity that is deemed a threat, alerts administrators, and logs the information. IDSs operate by matching signatures of known possible network attack traffic or by building over time a baseline of normal behavior then alerting on traffic that is anomalous to that normal pattern of behavior.

Intrusion prevention system (IPS) | A system that intercepts potentially hostile activity prior to it being processed.

Inventory management | In the context of workstation central management systems, refers to tracking what workstation and related network devices exist. This usually takes place whenever a workstation connects to the local area network (LAN).

IRT coordinator | The person who keeps track of all the activity if the IRT during an incident. He or she acts as the official scribe of the team. All activity flows through this person. The person records who's doing what.

IRT manager | The IRT manager is the team lead. This individual makes all the final calls on how to respond to an incident. He or she is the interface with management.

ISO/IEC 27000 series | Information security standards published by the ISO and by the International Electrotechnical Commission (IEC). ISO/IEC 27002, for example, provides best practice recommendations on information security management for those who are responsible for initiating, implementing, or maintaining an information security management system.

Issue-specific standard | A standard that focuses on areas of current relevance and concern to an organization. Such standards are used to express security control requirements, typically for non-technical processes and are used to guide human behavior.

IT policy framework | A logical structure that is established to organize policy documentation into groupings and categories that make it easier for employees to find and understand the contents of various policy documents. Policy frameworks can also be used to help in the planning and development of the policies for an organization.

Keylogger software | Captures the keystrokes of a user.

Label | A mark or comment placed inside the document itself indicating a level of protection.

LAN Domain | This domain refers to the organization's local area network (LAN) infrastructure. A LAN allows two or more computers to be connected within a small area. The small area could be a home, office, or group of buildings.

LAN-to-WAN Domain | This domain refers to the technical infrastructure that connects the organization's local area network (LAN) to a wide area network (WAN), such as the Internet. This allows end users to surf the Internet.

Laws | Any rules prescribed under the authority of a government entity. Establishes legal thresholds.

Layered security approach | Having two or more layers of independent controls to reduce risk.

Legal representative | An individual who has an understanding of laws and regulatory compliance.

Log management | In the context of workstation central management systems, refers to extracting logs from the workstation. Typically, moving the logs to a central repository. Later these logs are scanned to look for security weakness or patterns of problems.

Log server | Is a separate platform used to collect logs from platforms throughout the network.

M

Malicious code attack | An attack using viruses, worms, Trojan horses, and scripts. Such an attack is launched to gain access to systems, applications, and data.

Mandatory declassification | A process of reviewing specific records when requested and declassifying them if warranted.

Manual control | A security control that does not stop behavior immediately and relies on human decisions.

N

National Institute of Standards and Technology (NIST) | An organization that creates security guidelines on security controls for federal information systems.

Need to know | A principle that restricts information access to only those users with an approved and valid requirement.

Network reconnaissance probe | A software tools that runs a series of network commands to determine security weaknesses.

NIST SP 800-53 | A publication for the U.S. National Institute of Standards and Technology (NIST), titled "Recommended Security Controls for Federal Information Systems and Organizations."

Non-disclosure agreement (NDA) | Legally binding agreement on the handling and disclosure of company material. This is also known as a confidentiality agreement.

Nonrepudiation | The concept of applying technology in way that an individual cannot deny or dispute they were part of a transaction.

O

OCTAVE | An acronym for Operationally Critical Threat, Asset, and Vulnerability Evaluation. OCTAVE is a framework for information security assessment and planning consisting of tools, techniques, and methods.

Operational deviation | The difference between what policies and procedure state should be done and what is actually performed.

Operational risk | An event that disrupts the daily activities of an organization.

Operational risk committee | A committee that provides important information on the risk appetite of the organization and various businesses.

Opt-in | The practice of agreeing to use of personal information beyond its original purpose. An example of opt-in is asking a consumer who just sold his or her home if the real-estate company can share the consumer's information with a moving company.

Opt-out | The practice of declining permission to use personal information beyond its original purpose. For example, a consumer who just sold his or her home may decline permission for the real estate company to share his or her information with a moving company.

P

Patch management | Refers to making sure that devices on the network, such as workstations and servers, have current patches from the vendor. It's particularly important to apply security patches in a timely way to address known vulnerabilities.

Payment Card Industry Data Security Standard (PCI DSS) | A worldwide information security standard that describes how to protect credit card information. If you accept Visa, MasterCard, or American Express, you are required to follow PCI DSS.

Personal privacy | In e-commerce, broadly deals with how personal information is handled and what it used for.

Personally identifiable information (PII) | Sensitive information used to uniquely identify an individual in a way that could potentially be exploited.

Pervasive control | A common control, such as the same ID and password, which is used across a significant population of systems, applications, and operations.

Policy | A document that states how the organization is to perform and conduct business functions and transactions with a desired outcome.

Policy framework | A structure for organizing policies, standards, procedures, and guidelines.

Pretexting | When a hacker outlines a story in which the employee is asked to reveal information that weakens the security.

Preventive control | An automated security control that stops a behavior immediately.

Privacy policy | Places importance on privacy in the business and discusses the regulatory landscape and government mandates. This policy often talks about physical security and the importance of "locking up" sensitive information.

Privileged-level access agreement (PAA) | Designed to heighten the awareness and accountability of those users with administrator rights.

Procedure | A written statement describing the steps required to implement a process.

Project committee | A gateway committee that approves project funding, phases, and base requirements.

Public classification | A classification level for data that has no negative impact on the business if released to the public.

Public record | Any record required by law to be made available to the public. These types of records are made or filed by a governmental entity.

Public relations representative | In the context of an IRT team, it is an individual who can advise on how to communicate to the public and customers that might be impacted by the incident. This person is valuable in ensuring that accurate information gets out and damaging misconceptions are prevented.

R

Recovery point objective (RPO) | The maximum acceptable level of data loss after a disaster.

Recovery time objective (RTO) | A measure of how quickly a business process should be recovered after a disaster. The RTO identifies the maximum allowed downtime for a given business process.

Regulations | Established rules of what an organization has to do to meet legal requirements.

Remote Access Domain | This domain refers to the technology that controls how end users connect to organization's local area network (LAN). A typical example is someone needing to connect to the office from his or her home.

Remote authentication | Enhanced authentication over what's typically found in the office. Usually it requires more than an ID and password, such as a security token or smartcard.

Residual risk | The risk that remains after all the controls have been applied.

Risk appetite | Understanding risks and determining how much potential risk and related problems the business is willing accept.

Risk assessment | *See* information security risk assessment.

Risk Evaluation | A domain in the ISACA Risk IT framework that calls for analyzing risk and determining impact on the business.

Risk Governance | A domain in the ISACA Risk IT framework that ensures that risk management activity aligns with the business goals, objectives, and tolerances.

Risk Response | A domain in the ISACA Risk IT framework that specifies the ability to react so that risks are reduced and remedied in a cost-effective manner.

Router | Connects local area networks (LANs) or a LAN and a wide area network (WAN).

S

Secret | A level of government classification that refers to data, the unauthorized disclosure of which would reasonably be expected to cause serious damage to the national security.

Security awareness program | Training about security policies, threats, and handling of digital assets.

Security committee | A committee that acts as a steering committee for the information security program.

Security compliance committee | A gateway committee that approves uses of specific controls for compliance.

Security Content Automation Protocol (SCAP) | A group of specifications that standardize how security software products measure, evaluate, and report compliance. NIST created SCAP and several private companies created SCAP-compliant tools.

Security control mapping | When related to compliance, it's the mapping of regulatory requirements to policies and controls.

Security management | Refers to managing security in an organization, usually IT security. This can include making sure end users have limited rights and access controls are in place, among many other techniques and processes.

Security personnel | Individuals responsible for designing and implementing a security program within an organization.

Security policy compliance | Adherence to the organization's set of rules with regard to security policies.

Security policies | A set of policies that establish how an organization secures its facilities and IT infrastructure. Can also address how the organization meets regulatory requirements.

Security token | A hardware device or software code that generates a token (usually represented as a series of numbers) at logon. A security token is extremely difficult and some say impossible to replicate. When assigned to an individual as part his or her required logon, it provides assurance of who is accessing the network.

Segmented network | A network that limits how computers are able to talk to each other.

Sensitive but unclassified | A level of government classification that refers to data that is confidential and not subject to release under the Freedom of Information Act.

Sensitive classification | A classification level for data that would mean significant financial loss if leaked.

Separation of duties (SOD) | Underlying principle states that no individual should be able to execute a high-risk transaction or conceal errors or fraud in the normal course of their duties.

Service level agreement (SLA) | The portion of a service contract that formally defines the level of service. These agreements are typical in telecommunications contracts for voice and data transmission circuits.

Shareholder | A person who buys stock in a company (investor).

Simple Network Management Protocol (SNMP) | A protocol used to query and manage network devices. SNMP v1 had known vulnerabilities such as transmitting the community name in clear text. SNMP v2 and v3 improved security and performance of SNMP.

Sniffer | A network device that can read communications traffic on a local area network (LAN).

Social engineering | Manipulating or tricking a person into weakening the security of an organization.

Span of control | Relates to the number of areas of control achieved through the number of direct reports found in an organization.

Standard | An established and proven norm or method. This can be a procedural standard or a technical standard implemented organization-wide.

Statement on Auditing Standard 70 (SAS 70) | A widely accepted auditing standard created by the American Institute of Certified Public Accountants (AICPA). A SAS 70 audit examines an organization's control environment. This usually includes an audit of the information security controls.

Strategic risk | An event that may change how the entire organization operates.

Structured Query Language (SQL) injection | A type of attack in which the hacker adds SQL code to a Web or application input box to gain access to or alter data in the database.

Structured Query Language (SQL) | A standardized language used to access a database.

Subject Matter Expert (SME) | An individual who has extensive knowledge in a particular field.

Supervisory Control and Data Acquisition (SCADA) system | Hardware and software that collects critical information to keep a facility operating.

Switch | A piece of equipment similar to a hub but can filter traffic. You can set up rules that control what traffic can flow where. Unlike hubs that duplicate the traffic to all ports, a switch typically routes traffic only to the port where the system is connected. This reduces network traffic, thus reducing the chance of someone intercepting the traffic.

System access policy | Rules of conduct on how and when access to systems is permitted. This policy covers end user credentials like IDs and passwords. The policy may also be specific to the business or application, such as the use of role based access control (RBAC).

System software | Software that supports the running of the applications.

System/Application Domain | This domain refers to the technology needed to collect, process, and store the information. It includes controls related to hardware and software.

Systematic declassification | A process of reviewing records exempted from automatic declassification and then removing the data from classification.

Systems administrator | An IT individual who provides administrative support to the systems and databases.

System-specific standard | A standard that focuses on specific technology or systems being used within an organization. These are used to express the security control implementation requirements for some specific technology.

T

Taxonomy | The practice and science of classification. A hierarchical taxonomy is a tree structure of classifications for a given set of objects or documents.

Top Secret | A level of government classification that refers to data, the unauthorized disclosure of which would reasonably be expected to cause grave damage to the national security.

Town hall meeting | A gathering of teams to make announcements and discuss topics.

Trouble ticket | A complete record of what access was granted and the business reason behind it in order to resolve a problem.

Two-factor authentication | Requires end users to authenticate their identity using at least two of three different types of credentials. The three most commonly accepted types of credentials are something you know, something you have, and something you are.

U

Unclassified | A level of government classification that refers to data available to the public.

User Domain | This domain refers to any user accessing information. This includes customers, employees, consultants, contractors, or any other third party. These users are often referred to as an "end user."

User proxy | An application firewall that is used to control the flow of traffic to and from the Internet to user workstations attached to a local area network (LAN). The proxy intercepts the user's request for an Internet resource, initiates a new connection, and proxies the result back to the requestor.

V

Value delivery | Focusing resources to deliver the greatest benefits.

Vendor governance committee | A gateway committee that approves new vendors and has oversight of existing vendors. This includes making sure new vendors meet minimum security policy requirements such as having a formal contract in place and adequate proof of security controls like a SAS 70.

Virtual Private Network (VPN) | A VPN is set up between two devices to create an encrypted tunnel. All communications are protected from eavesdropping and considered highly secure.

W

WAN Domain | This domain includes wide area networks (WANs), which are networks that cover large geographical areas. The Internet is an example of a WAN. A private WAN can be built for a specific company to link offices across the country or globally.

Web graffiti | Alterations to a Web page that result from a Web site defacement attack. Web site graffiti can contain abusive language or even pornographic images.

Web services | Automated information services over the Internet using standardized technologies and formats/protocols that simplify the exchange and integration of data. Web services help organizations to inter-operate regardless of the types of operating systems, programming languages, and databases being used.

Web site defacement | An attack on a Web site in which the site's content is altered, usually in a way that embarrasses the Web site owner.

Web-Based Enterprise Management (WBEM) | A set of standards and technologies used to query and manage systems and applications in a network. It is used on the Internet and internal networks. WBEM capabilities are built into GUI-based applications and command line applications.

Windows Management Instrumentation (WMI) | Microsoft's implementation of WBEM. WMI is a specification defining how to query and manage Microsoft clients and servers. WMI queries are embedded in graphical user interface-based applications. WMIC is the command-line equivalent and is used in scripts.

Workstation Domain | This domain refers to any computing device used by end users. This usually means a desktop or laptop that is the main computer for the end user.

References

"501(b) Examination Guidance," FIL-68-2001 (Federal Deposit Insurance Corporation, Financial Guidance Letters, August 24, 2001). http://www.fdic.gov/news/news/financial/2001/fil0168.html (accessed May 20, 2010).

Barrett, Jim. "Electronic Discovery Employment Roundtable" (AterWynne LLP, October 19, 2006). http://www.aterwynne.com/files/ERT_%20Electronic%20discovery.PDF (accessed March 26, 2010).

"Boston Attorney General Investigates E-Mail Destruction" (Allbusiness, January 1, 2010). http://www.allbusiness.com/government/government-bodies-offices-public/13829522-1.html (accessed May 14, 2010).

"Building a Security Program Using ISO 27001" (Halock Security Labs, n.d.). http://www.halock.com/Downloads/Case_Study/AIM%20Case%20Study.pdf (accessed March 17, 2010).

"Call Anywhere in the U.S. with No Monthly Fee" (OOMA.com, 2010). http://www.ooma.com/ (accessed March 27, 2010).

Caputo, Kim. *CMM Implementation Guide: Choreographing Software Process Improvement*. New York, NY: Addison-Wesley Professional, 1998.

"Case Study: Fast Food Franchise Security Breach (Multiple Locations)" (VendorSafe Technologies, October 2008). http://www.vendorsafe.com/images/pdfs/CaseStudy_FastFood.pdf (accessed April 30, 2010).

"A Case Study in Security Incident Forensics and Response" (eSecurity Planet, March 5, 2001). http://www.esecurityplanet.com/trends/article.php/10751_688797/article.htm (accessed May 2, 2010).

"Case Study: Using Security Awareness to Combat the Advanced Persistent Threat" (13th Colloquium for Information Systems Security Education, June 2009). http://www.cisse2009.com/colloquia/cisse13/proceedings/PDFs/Papers/S03P02.pdf (accessed May 20, 2010).

"COBIT 4.1" (ISACA, 2007). http://www.isaca.org/Knowledge-Center/COBIT/Pages/Overview.aspx (accessed February 13 and March 24, 2010).

"COBIT 5 Design Paper Exposure Draft" (ISACA, 2010). http://www.isaca.org/ContentManagement/ContentDisplay.cfm?ContentID=56448 (accessed April 30, 2010).

"Compass Group North America Case Study" (Microsoft Corporation, 2010). http://www.microsoft.com/casestudies/Case_Study_Detail.aspx?CaseStudyID=4000006677 (accessed May 16, 2010).

"Compliance E-mail Retention System Crucial under SEC17a-4" (SEC17a-4Compliance.com, n.d.). http://www.sec17a-4compliance.com/ediscovery (accessed May 9, 2010).

"Computer Security Incident Response Planning" (Internet Security Systems, n.d.). http://documents.iss.net/whitepapers/csirplanning.pdf (accessed May 1, 2010).

"Contingency Planning Guide for Information Technology Systems," NIST Special Publication 800-34 (National Institute of Standards and Technology [NIST], June 2002). http://csrc .nist.gov/publications/nistpubs/800-34/sp800-34.pdf (accessed March 26, 2010).

"Creating a Financial Institution CSIRT: A Case Study" (CERT, n.d.). http://www.cert.org/csirts/ AFI_case-study.html (accessed May 2, 2010).

"CyberLaw 101: A Primer on US Laws Related to Honeypot Deployments" (SANS Institute Reading Room, 2007). http://www.sans.org/reading_room/whitepapers/honors/cyberlaw -101-primer-laws-related-honeypot-deployments_1746 (accessed May 14, 2010).

"Data Classification Standard" (University of Texas, September 14, 2007). http://www.utexas .edu/its/policies/opsmanual/dataclassification.php (accessed March 28, 2010).

"Database Credentials Coding Policy," Information Security Policy Templates (SANS Institute, 2010). http://www.sans.org/security-resources/policies/DB_Credentials_Policy.pdf (accessed April 15, 2010).

"Developing a Security-Awareness Culture—Improving Security Decision Making" (SANS, July 2004). http://www.sans.org/reading_room/whitepapers/awareness/developing-security -awareness-culture-improving-security-decision-making_1526 (accessed May 1, 2010).

"Diagnosing Cornell's Security Breach" (Cornell Daily Sun, June 24, 2009). http://cornellsun.com/node/37476 (accessed May 14, 2010).

"Disk and Data Sanitization Policy and Guidelines" (Stanford University, July 2005). http:// www.stanford.edu/group/security/securecomputing/data_destruction_guidelines.html (accessed March 17, 2010).

"E-commerce Quick Facts" (MachroTech, 2002). http://www.machrotech.com/services/ ecommerce-marketsize-statistics.asp (accessed April 30, 2010).

"EMA's 2008 Survey of IT Governance, Risk and Compliance Management in the Real World" (EMA, 2008). http://eval.symantec.com/mktginfo/enterprise/other_resources/b-whitepaper _ema_symantec-it-grc_an_06-2008.en-us.pdf (accessed April 30, 2010).

"Employee Internet Use Monitoring and Filtering Policy" (SANS Technology Institute Student Projects, November 2007). www.sans.edu/resources/student_projects/200711_004.pdf (accessed April 15, 2010).

"Enterprise Information Security Policies" (State of Tennessee, Department of Finance and Administration, Office for Information Resources, Information Security Program, April 4, 2008). http://www.tennessee.gov/finance/oir/security/PUBLIC-Enterprise -Information-Security-Policies-v1-6.pdf (accessed March 8, 2010).

"European Programme for Critical Infrastructure Protection" (Europa.eu, October 30, 2008). http://europa.eu/legislation_summaries/justice_freedom_security/fight_against_terrorism/ l33260_en.htm (accessed March 17, 2010).

"Federal Desktop Core Configuration (FDCC)" (National Institute of Standards and Technology [NIST], 2010). http://nvd.nist.gov/fdcc/index.cfm (accessed May 12, 2010).

"A Few Facts on Information Security and Accountability" (ArticleInput.com, 2009). http:// www.articleinput.com/e/a/title/A-few-facts-on-information-security-and-accountability/ (accessed March 10, 2010).

"Financial Industry Standards" (Accredited Standards Committee X9 Incorporated, 2010). http://www.x9.org (accessed March 8, 2010).

"Financial Roundup: Total Bank Losses to $3.6 Trillion, Mortgage Lender Breaks, Half of CDOs in Default" (Industry.bnet.com, February 13, 2009). http://industry.bnet.com/financial -services/1000403/financial-roundup-total-bank-losses-to-36-trillion-mortgage-lender -breaks-half-of-cdos-in-default/ (accessed March 6, 2010).

Gorman, Siobhan, August Cole, and Yochi Dreazen. "Computer Spies Breach Fighter-Jet Project." *Wall Street Journal*, April 21, 2009. http://online.wsj.com/article/SB124027491029837401 .html (accessed April 11, 2010).

"Governor O'Malley's 15 Strategic Policy Goals" (State of Maryland StateStat, n.d.). http://www.gov.state.md.us/statestat/gdu.asp (accessed March 14, 2010). "Guidelines for Appropriate Use of External Communication Systems" (University of Montana, June 29, 2009). http://www.umt.edu/it/policies/externalwebsystems.aspx (accessed March 15, 2010).

Gralla, Preston. "Windows Market Share Dips Again; World and Microsoft Survive" (ComputerWorld Blogs, January 4, 2010). http://blogs.computerworld.com/15344/ windows_market_share_dips_again_world_and_microsoft_survive (accessed April 2010).

"How To Set Social Networking Policies for Employees" (eSecurity Planet, April 20, 2010). http://www.esecurityplanet.com/views/article.php/3877481/How-To-Set-Social -Networking-Policies-for-Employees.htm (accessed May 14, 2010).

IBM Security Solutions. "IBM Security Solutions X-Force(r) 2009 Trend and Risk Report: Annual Review of 2009" (IBM, 2010). http://www-935.ibm.com/services/us/iss/xforce/ trendreports/ (accessed April 10, 2010).

"Incident Response: Lessons Learned from Georgia Tech, the University of Montana, and the University of Texas Austin" (ECAR, July 2003). http://net.educause.edu/ir/library/ pdf/ers0305/cs/ecs0307.pdf (accessed May 2, 2010).

"Information Resources Management Administration" (State of Maryland, Department of Health and Mental Hygiene, n.d.). http://dhmh.maryland.gov/irma/ (accessed March 8, 2010).

"Information Security Oversight Report 2009" (ISOO, March 10, 2010). http://www.archives.gov/isoo/reports/2009-annual-report.pdf (accessed March 27, 2010).

"Information Security Policy—A Development Guide for Large and Small Companies" (SANS Institute Reading Room, 2007). http://www.sans.org/reading_room/whitepapers/ policyissues/information_security_policy_a_development_guide_for_large_and_small _companies_1331?show=1331.php&cat=policyissues (accessed March 7, 2010).

"Information Sharing and the Private Sector" (Ise.gov, n.d.). http://www.ise.gov/pages/ partner-private.aspx (accessed March 10, 2010).

"Information Technology Security Policy Framework" (University of Guelph, January 27, 2010). http://www.uoguelph.ca/cio/sites/uoguelph.ca.cio/files/ CIO-ITSecurity-00-PolicyFramework-2009Approved.pdf (accessed April 30, 2010).

"Innovation Implementation: The Role of Technology Diffusion Agencies," J. *Technol. Manag. Innov.* 3, no. 3 (2008): 1-10. http://www.scielo.cl/scielo.php?pid=S0718 -27242008000100001&script=sci_arttext (accessed March 6, 2010).

"ISACA Releases the Risk IT Framework Draft" (IT Manager's Inbox, n.d.). http://itmanagersinbox.com/1007/isaca-releases-the-risk-it-framework-draft/ (accessed April 30, 2010).

"ISO/IEC 27002:2005 Information Technology—Security Techniques—Code of Practice for Information Security Management" (InsecT Ltd., 2010). http://www.iso27001security.com/html/27002.html (accessed March 8, 2010).

Jansen, Wayne, and Karen Scarfone. "Guidelines on Cell Phone and PDA Security," NIST SP 800-124. (NIST Computer Security Division, October 2008). http://csrc.nist.gov/publications/nistpubs/800-124/SP800-124.pdf (accessed March 8, 2010).

Jarmom, David. "A Preparation Guide to Information Security Policies" (SANS Institute, 2002). http://www.sans.org/reading_room/whitepapers/policyissues/preparation-guide-information-security-policies_503 (accessed March 7, 2010).

Job Street. "Salary Report," Position Title: Call Center Agent, Country: Philippines. (JobStreet.com, 2010). http://myjobstreet.jobstreet.com/career-enhancer/basic-salary-report.php?param=Call%20Center%20Agent%7C000%7Cph%7C%7Cph (accessed March 24, 2010).

Johnson, Arnold, Kelley Dempsey, Ron Ross, Sarbari Gupta, and Dennis Bailey. "Guide for Security Configuration Management of Information Systems," National Institute of Standards and Technology Special Publication 800-128 initial public draft (NIST SP 800-128). Gaithersburg, MD, United States Department of Commerce, 2010.

Kaplan, Dan. "U.S. House to Toughen Internal Cybersecurity Policy" (*SC Magazine*, December 16, 2009). http://www.scmagazineus.com/us-house-to-toughen-internal-cybersecurity-policy/article/159785/ (accessed May 2, 2010).

"Kerviel's New Lawyers Will Focus on SocGen Conduct" (Bloomberg.com, July 30, 2008). http://www.bloomberg.com/apps/news?pid=20601085&sid=aWbERdIeyYO4&refer=europe (accessed April 12, 2010).

LeMay, Renai. "Nessus Security Tool Closes Its Source" (CNET News, October 6, 2005). http://news.cnet.com/Nessus-security-tool-closes-its-source/2100-7344_3-5890093.html (accessed May 15, 2010).

Leyden, John. "The Enemy Within" (The Register, December 2005). http://www.theregister.co.uk/2005/12/15/mcafee_internal_security_survey/ (accessed May 1, 2010).

"Microsoft Responds: WMF Vulnerability" (eWeek, February 2, 2006). http://www.eweek.com/c/a/Windows/Microsoft-Responds-WMF-Vulnerability/ (accessed March 28, 2010).

Milford, Kim, Tracy Mitrano, and Steve Shuster. "Educause" electronic presentation, n.d.. net.educause.edu/ir/library/powerpoint/SPC0662.pps (accessed March 17, 2010).

"Monitoring Employees' Use of Company Computers and the Internet" (TexasWorkForce, n.d.). http://www.twc.state.tx.us/news/efte/monitoring_computers_internet.html (accessed May 14, 2010).

Nash, Troy. An Undirected Attack Against Critical Infrastructures: A Case Study for Improving Your Control System Security. US-CERT Control Systems Security Center, Lawrence Livermore National Laboratory, September 2005. http://www.us-cert.gov/control_systems/pdf/undirected_attack0905.pdf (accessed April 11, 2010).

"National Institute of Standards and Technology Special Publications (800 Series)" (NIST Computer Security Division, 2010). http://csrc.nist.gov/publications/PubsSPs.html (accessed March 8, 2010).

"National Security Information EO 12356" (President EO, April 2, 1982). http://www.fas.org/irp/offdocs/eo12356.htm (accessed March 27, 2010).

"Nevada Mandates PCI DSS" (NACS Online, June 24, 2009). http://www.nacsonline.com/NACS/News/Daily/Pages/ND0624094.aspx (accessed March 26, 2010).

Nichols, Russell. "California Issues Telework Policy to Curb Cyber-Security Risks." *Government Technology*, March 3, 2010. http://www.govtech.com/gt/748172 (accessed March 17, 2010).

"Organized Security" (Health Management Technology, 2010).

http://www.healthmgttech.com/index.php/solutions/hospitals/organized-security.html (accessed March 8, 2010).

Prince, Brian. "Stolen Credit Card Data Goes for Cheap on Cyber-Black Market." *eWeek*, August 20, 2009. http://www.eweek.com/c/a/Security/Stolen-Credit-Card-Data-Goes-for-Cheap-on-Cyber-Black-Market-891275/ (accessed March 24, 2010).

Purcell, James. "Security Control Types and Operational Security" (GIAC.org, February 12, 2007). http://www.giac.org/resources/whitepaper/operations/207.php (accessed March 15, 2010).

Quinn, Stephen, David Waltermire, Christopher Johnson, Karen Scarfone, and John Banghart. "The Technical Specification for the Security Content Automation Protocol (SCAP)," National Institute of Standards and Technology Special Publication 800-126 NIST SP 800-126. Gaithersburg, MD, United States Department of Commerce, 2009.

Ranum, Marcus J. *The Myth of Homeland Security*. Indianapolis: Wiley Publications, 2004.

"Re: Privacy" (*New York Post*, April 12, 2010). http://www.nypost.com/f/print/news/business/jobs/re_privacy_zUsPRscheD905WKCSVv2qM (accessed May 12, 2010).

"Recommended Practice: Developing an Industrial Control Systems Cybersecurity Incident Response Capability" (Homeland Security, October 2009). http://csrp.inl.gov/Documents/final-RP_ics_cybersecurity_incident_response_100609.pdf (accessed May 2, 2010).

"Remote Access Standard" (Montgomery College, August 12, 2008). http://cms.montgomerycollege.edu/WorkArea/linkit.aspx?LinkIdentifier=id&ItemID=846 (accessed April 14, 2010).

"Report to the Congress on Review of Regulations Affecting Online Delivery of Financial Products and Services" (U.S. Department of the Treasury, Comptroller of the Currency, November 2001). http://www.occ.treas.gov/netbank/729jrptnov1601.doc (accessed May 20, 2010).

"Rising Numbers and Costs of Data Breaches" (Healthitlawblog.com, January 28, 2010). http://www.healthitlawblog.com/tags/data-breach/ (accessed March 4, 2010).

Rupert, Brad. "IT Guidance to the Legal Team" (SANS Institute Reading Room, April 15, 2009). http://www.sans.org/reading_room/whitepapers/legal/guidance-legal-team_33308 (accessed May 14, 2010).

"Security Incident Response Procedure (Visa, 2007). http://www.visa-asia.com/ap/sea/merchants/riskmgmt/includes/uploads/SecurityIncidentRespProcd.pdf (accessed May 3, 2010).

Silvers, Robert. "Rethinking FISMA and Federal Information Security Policy" (*New York University Law Review*, October 11, 2006). http://www1.law.nyu.edu/journals/lawreview/issues/vol81/no5/NYU507.pdf (accessed April 30, 2010).

"Social Security Administration Electronic Service Provision A STRATEGIC ASSESSMENT" (National Academic Press, n.d.). http://www.nap.edu/openbook.php?record_id=11920&page=5450254 (accessed May 2, 2010).

"Standards for Security Categorization of Federal Information and Information Systems," Publication 199. U.S. Dept. of Commerce, National Institute of Standards and Technology, February 2004.

"Standards for Security Categorization of Federal Information and Information Systems," NIST Special Publication 199 (National Institute of Standards and Technology [NIST], February 2004). http://csrc.nist.gov/publications/fips/fips199/FIPS-PUB-199-final.pdf (accessed March 26, 2010).

"TechEncyclopedia." Definition of system software (Techweb.com, 2010). http://www.techweb .com/encyclopedia/defineterm.jhtml?term=systemsoftware (accessed March 25, 2010).

Telecommunications Industry Association. http://www.tiaonline.org/index.cfm (accessed March 8, 2010).

Teschner, Charles, Dr. Peter Golder, and Thorsten Liebert. "Bringing Back Best Practices in Risk Management: Banks' Three Lines Of Defense," Booz & Company, October 17, 2008. http://www.booz.com/global/home/what_we_think/reports_and_white_papers/ ic-display/42753543 (accessed April 30, 2010).

"The Eight Classic Types of Workplace Behavior" (*HR Magazine*, September 2000). http:// findarticles.com/p/articles/mi_m3495/is_9_45/ai_65578688/ (accessed March 7, 2010).

"The Risk of At-Work Surfers" (E-CommerceAleter.com, November 23, 2004). http://www.e-commercealert.com/article645.shtml (accessed April 24, 2010).

"TJX Data Security Breach Saga Continues: Financial Institution Class Action against TJX Survives on Based on Unfair Competition Claim Predicated on Statements in FTC Complaint against T.J. Maxx / Marshalls' Parent Company" (Disigalmedialawyerblog.com, August 10, 2009). http://www.digitalmedialawyerblog.com/2009/08/tjx_data_security _breach_saga.html (accessed March 4, 2010).

"Top 10 Information Security Threats for 2010" (Help Net Security, January 14, 2010). http://www.net-security.org/secworld.php?id=8709 (accessed April 10, 2010).

"Top 10 Vulnerability Scanners" (SecTools.org, n.d.). http://sectools.org/vuln-scanners.html (accessed May 15, 2010).

"Unlearnt Lessons from Barings" (Karvy.com, n.d.). http://www.karvy.com/articles/ baringsdebacle.htm (accessed April 11, 2010).

U.S. Department of Energy. "DNS Policies & Procedures" (U.S. Department of Energy, n.d.). http://cio.energy.gov/policy-guidance/952.htm (accessed April 15, 2010).

U.S. Secret Service and Carnegie Mellon University. "Insider Threat Study: Computer Sabotage in Critical Infrastructure Sectors" (U.S. Secret Service and Carnegie Mellon University CERT Program, May 2005). http://www.cert.org/insider_threat/insidercross.html (accessed April 12, 2010).

"VA Investigating Security Breach of Veterans' Medical Data" (Nextgov.com, March 9, 2010) http://www.nextgov.com/nextgov/ng_20100309_9888.php (accessed May 14, 2010).

Verizon Business RISK team. "2009 Data Breach Investigations Report" (Verizonbusiness.com, 2009). http://www.verizonbusiness.com/resources/security/reports/2009_databreach _rp.pdf (Accessed on April 11, 2010).

Verizon Business RISK team. "2009 Data Breach Investigations Supplemental Report" (Verizonbusiness.com, 2010). http://www.bankinfosecurity.com/external/rp_2009 -data-breach-investigations-supplemental-report_en_xg.pdf (accessed April 11, 2010).

Vijayan, Jaikumar. "Computer Theft May Have Exposed Patient Data Across Five States" (Computerworld.com, January 4, 2007). http://www.computerworld.com/s/article/9007199/Computer_theft_may_have_exposed_patient_data_across_five_states?intsrc=hm_list (accessed March 25, 2010).

"Violation of Sensitive Data Storage Policy Led to Exposure of Info on 3.3 Million Student Loan Recipients" (Dark Reading, March 29, 2010). http://www.darkreading.com/insiderthreat/security/privacy/showArticle.jhtml?articleID=224200648 (accessed May 14, 2010).

"Virtual Private Network Policy," Information Security Policy Templates Web site (SANS Institute, 2010). http://www.sans.org/security-resources/policies/Virtual_Private_Network.pdf (accessed April 15, 2010).

"Voice Over Internet Protocol (VoIP) Security Policy" (U.S. Department of Transportation, Federal Aviation Administration, September 21, 2009). http://www.faa.gov/documentLibrary/media/Order/1370.108.pdf (accessed April 15, 2010).

Wack, John, Ken Cutler, and Jamie Pole. "Guidelines on Firewalls and Firewall Policy," NIST SP 800-41, U.S. Department of Commerce, January 2002. http:// www.ffiec.gov/.../nis-guide_on_firewall_and_firewall_pol_800_41.pdf (accessed April 15, 2010).

"Wide Area Network Security Policy" (Government of Nova Scotia, Corporate Policy Manuals, 2010) http://www.gov.ns.ca/treasuryboard/manuals/PDF/300/30408-04.pdf (accessed April 15, 2010).

Index